SPERRY
SYMPOSIUM
CLASSICS

SPERRY SYMPOSIUM CLASSICS

The DOCTRINE *and* COVENANTS

EDITED BY

CRAIG K. MANSCILL

B Y U

DESERET
BOOK

SALT LAKE CITY, UTAH

Copublished by the Religious Studies Center, Brigham Young University, Provo, Utah, and Deseret Book Company, Salt Lake City, Utah.

Library of Congress Cataloging-in-Publication Data

Sperry Symposium (Brigham Young University)
    Sperry Symposium classics : the Doctrine and Covenants / edited by Craig K. Manscill.
        p.   cm.
    Includes bibliographical references and indexes.
    ISBN 1-59038-388-5 (hardcover : alk. paper)
    1. Doctrine and Covenants—Congresses. I. Manscill, Craig K. II. Title.
    BX8628.S72 2004
    289.3'2—dc22

                                                                      2004017723

Printed in the United States of America   18961
R. R. Donnelley and Sons, Crawfordsville, IN

10   9   8   7   6   5   4   3   2

CONTENTS

FOREWORD

Over the past three decades, the annual Sidney B. Sperry Symposium on the scriptures has been sponsored by Religious Education and the Religious Studies Center at Brigham Young University. These symposia honored Dr. Sperry for his forty years of faithful service and thoughtful scholarship.

Of the thirty-two Sperry symposia, five were devoted to the study of the Doctrine and Covenants: 1979, 1984, 1989, 1992, and 1996. From these symposia, outstanding papers and presentations were published, offering valuable and delightful information to those seeking understanding of the Doctrine and Covenants and the events of the Restoration.

Unfortunately, most of these excellent Sperry publications of the Doctrine and Covenants are no longer readily available for public use. This has left a void. In addition, an important objective of the Religious Studies Center is to promote sound scholarship that will enhance understanding of the scriptures and the history of the Church. To advance this objective and to fill this void, we have compiled a treasury of significant articles from past Sperry symposia on the Doctrine and Covenants, including a few new chapters that fill in historical gaps. Much like the preceding volume on the Book of Mormon, this compilation provides valuable information to Church members in their study of the Doctrine and Covenants. It is hoped that this collection of articles will motivate learning toward, increase understanding of, and strengthen testimonies of this powerful book of scripture often referred to as the "capstone"—the Doctrine and Covenants.

The articles in this volume are, for the most part, arranged in the order that the revelations came forth. These articles are selected with the intended purposes of helping the reader gain a better understanding of the historical context of the discussed revelation and of deepening the reader's general understanding of doctrine, gospel principles, and application. All articles reflect sound scholarship and faith.

Three of the first five articles in this volume are keynote addresses given by General Authorities at the Sperry symposia. The other two pieces originally appeared in other settings; Elder Dallin H. Oaks gave his address on revelation at a Brigham Young University devotional, and Elder John K. Carmack first published his piece on Fayette in the *Ensign* magazine.

Within the context of this compilation, it is important to understand that it is not practicable or possible to provide a comprehensive study of all doctrines, gospel insights, historical backgrounds, and applications for each revelation. However, it is hoped that these classic addresses and articles will bring the reader to a greater understanding of the precious truths in the Doctrine and Covenants.

Readers will note that a scripture index is provided, linking verse and section numbers to the page numbers in the book. The use of such an aid allows readers to review multiple entries of a scripture reference throughout the book.

We are pleased to help make these timeless articles accessible to all who are interested, realizing as we do that the Doctrine and Covenants carries with it the message to "teach one another the doctrine of the kingdom. Teach ye diligently and my grace shall attend you, that you may be instructed more perfectly in theory, in principle, in doctrine, in the law of the gospel, in all things that pertain unto the kingdom of God, that are expedient for you to understand" (D&C 88:77–78).

Historical Context for Each Section

"These sacred revelations were received in answer to prayer, in times of need, and came out of real-life situations involving real people" (Explanatory Introduction).

Section	Situation that brought forth the section*
1	A committee was appointed to draft a preface for a collection of revelations to be published as the Book of Commandments. When the committee made their report to the elders, who had gathered for a conference in Hiram, they asked the Prophet to inquire of the Lord about their work. The brethren united in prayer, and Joseph Smith was the voice. When he concluded, the Prophet then dictated the words of this revelation by the Spirit, and Sidney Rigdon wrote it down.
2	Confident of obtaining a divine manifestation, young Joseph Smith prayed for forgiveness of his sins and a knowledge of his standing before God.
3	Following the loss of 116 pages of Book of Mormon manuscript, Joseph Smith had the plates taken from him in consequence of repeatedly asking the Lord for the privilege of letting Martin Harris take the writings. Joseph inquired through the Urim and Thummim as to his standing with the Lord.
4	Joseph Smith Sr. asked his son to inquire of the Lord on his behalf concerning how he could help in the Lord's work.

---

*See section headings for historical references.

Section	Situation that brought forth the section
5	A repentant Martin Harris asked Joseph Smith if he possessed the plates and wanted him to inquire of the Lord whether he would be privileged to see the plates in the future.
6	Joseph Smith's scribe, Oliver Cowdery, desired an additional divine witness that the work of translation was true. The Prophet inquired of the Lord for him through the Urim and Thummim.
7	While translating the plates, a difference of opinion arose between Oliver Cowdery and Joseph Smith concerning what had happened to John the Beloved. They inquired of the Lord through the Urim and Thummim.
8	Having been promised an opportunity to translate (see section 6), Oliver Cowdery desired to assist in translating.
9	When Oliver Cowdery failed in his attempt to translate, the Prophet inquired of the Lord so that he could understand his part in the translation.
10	Once the plates and the Urim and Thummim were returned by Moroni, Joseph inquired of the Lord as to how he should proceed with the work of translation.
11	Hyrum Smith asked his brother Joseph to inquire concerning the Lord's will for him.
12	Joseph Knight Sr. was anxious to know his duty and part in the work of the Restoration.
13	While translating the Book of Mormon, Joseph Smith and Oliver Cowdery desired to know more about baptism for the remission of sins. They walked to the banks of the Susquehanna River and prayed.
14, 15, 16	David, John, and Peter Whitmer were anxious to know their duties concerning the work of the Lord. The Prophet inquired of the Lord through the Urim and Thummim on their behalf.
17	Oliver Cowdery, David Whitmer, and Martin Harris wanted to know if they might be the three witnesses spoken of in the Book of Mormon (see *History of the Church*, 1:52–53).
18	In preparation for the organization of the Church, the Prophet Joseph Smith directed Oliver Cowdery to write a foundational document outlining the history, basic beliefs, and procedures of the Church. Frustrated in his efforts, Oliver asked Joseph to inquire of the Lord for direction.

Section	Situation that brought forth the section
19	Martin Harris had mortgaged his farm for the printing of the Book of Mormon. Fearing he would lose his farm if the Book of Mormon did not sell and wanting to know if he was in good standing with the Lord, Martin Harris asked the Prophet for reassurance and direction from the Lord.
20	Known as the "Articles and Covenants" of the Church, this section was a combination of several inspired writings written sometime in 1829 and not completed until after April 6, 1830, by Joseph Smith and Oliver Cowdery (see section 18).
21	Oliver Cowdery recorded the words of this revelation as the Prophet Joseph Smith dictated them by the Spirit during the meeting to officially organize the Church.
22	People who had been baptized by immersion in other churches wanted to know whether they needed to be rebaptized in order to join the Church.
23	Oliver Cowdery, Hyrum Smith, Samuel H. Smith, Joseph Smith Sr., and Joseph Knight were anxious to know their duties in the Lord's newly organized Church.
24	After ministering to the branches of the Church in New York during a time of intense persecution, the Prophet and Oliver Cowdery arrived home in Harmony, Pennsylvania, in need of encouragement and instruction from the Lord.
25	Emma Hale Smith had suffered much persecution, humiliation, and harassment from others over the past several months. The Prophet received this revelation on her behalf to encourage, instruct, and strengthen her.
26	The Prophet Joseph, Oliver Cowdery, and the Whitmers became involved in a disagreement over the wording of section 20, verse 37. These instructions proved helpful in resolving the matter.
27	Earlier Emma Smith and Sally Knight had been baptized but had not been confirmed members of the Church. Joseph Smith desired all to partake of the sacrament prior to these confirmations. Joseph left home to buy wine for the service when a heavenly messenger appeared and gave him instructions.
28	The Prophet was distressed over Hiram Page's claim to divine revelations through a seer stone. Oliver Cowdery and some of the Whitmers were also deceived. Joseph was uneasy about

Section	Situation that brought forth the section
	commencing the second conference of the Church until he had settled this incident, so he inquired of the Lord for instruction.
29	Given for the benefit of the six elders about to depart on a mission to the Lamanites, this revelation came at a time when many were interested in the doctrine of Zion, or the New Jerusalem.
30	The Prophet received three separate revelations for David, Peter, and John Whitmer based on their actions during the Hiram Page incident.
31	Thomas B. Marsh desired to know the will of the Lord concerning him.
32	Oliver Cowdery and Peter Whitmer Jr. wondered if the number of missionaries assigned to go to teach the gospel to the Lamanites could be increased.
33	Ezra Thayre and Northrop Sweet, as newly ordained elders, desired to know the will of the Lord concerning them.
34	Orson Pratt, who had traveled two hundred miles to see Joseph Smith, wanted to learn the Lord's will concerning him.
35	Sidney Rigdon, who had been baptized by the missionaries to the Lamanites, asked the Prophet to reveal the Lord's will concerning him.
36	Edward Partridge, who had not yet been baptized, asked the Prophet Joseph Smith to inquire of the Lord on his behalf.
37	The Church in New York had been under constant harassment, and the lives of the leaders of the Church were in danger. As the Prophet and Sidney Rigdon worked on the inspired translation of the Bible, the Lord gave this commandment.
38	Many of the Saints were poor and expressed a desire to know more about how and why they should move to Ohio.
39	James Covill, a Baptist minister for about forty years, promised to obey any command the Lord gave him through Joseph Smith. The Prophet inquired of the Lord on his behalf.
40	When James Covill rejected the command of the Lord, the Prophet and Sidney Rigdon wondered why.
41	The Prophet found some strange notions and false spirits among the Saints in Ohio. He inquired of the Lord to know how best to govern the Church.

Section	Situation that brought forth the section
42	Groups of elders united in prayer on two separate occasions with the desire to receive the law of the Lord, as promised in D&C 38:32 and 41:2–3. They also wanted to know how to organize missionary work and how to proceed in cases of adultery or other serious transgressions (see D&C 42:70–93).
43	A self-proclaimed prophetess named Hubble deceived some Saints with her revelations and commandments. The Prophet knew she was an imposter and inquired of the Lord concerning the matter.
44	The Prophet Joseph Smith inquired of the Lord for instructions concerning the next general meeting of the Church.
45	At a special conference for elders leaving on missions, the Prophet sought clarification of the meaning of prophecies concerning the Second Coming of Christ (see Matthew 24).
46	Following a discussion of whether only Church members should be admitted to sacrament and confirmation meetings, the Prophet inquired of the Lord.
47	John Whitmer was reluctant to accept the responsibility for keeping a history of the Church. He said he would do it, however, if it was the will of the Lord. The Prophet inquired of the Lord on John's behalf.
48	Church leaders were concerned about purchasing land in Ohio on which the New York Saints could settle. The Prophet inquired of the Lord.
49	Leman Copley was eager to share his newfound faith with his friends in a religious order called the Shakers. He asked the Prophet Joseph to inquire of the Lord concerning some of the teachings of his former religion.
50	Several elders asked the Prophet to inquire of the Lord concerning the many strange and extreme spiritual manifestations among the Saints. After joining them in prayer, Joseph dictated the Lord's answer.
51	Bishop Edward Partridge sought further direction on how to implement the law of consecration on behalf of the New York Saints arriving in Ohio. The Prophet's countenance shone as he dictated the revelation.
52	Following a three-day priesthood conference, the Prophet inquired of the Lord what the elders should do until the convening of the next conference in Independence, Missouri.

Section	Situation that brought forth the section
53	Having just been ordained an elder, Sidney Gilbert asked the Prophet to inquire of the Lord concerning his part in the Lord's work.
54	When selfishness caused confusion over consecrated land in Thompson, Ohio, Newel Knight and others asked the Prophet what they should do.
55	When William W. Phelps, a former newspaper editor and recent convert, arrived in Ohio, he asked the Prophet to inquire of the Lord on his behalf.
56	When Ezra Thayer refused to go to Missouri, Thomas Marsh, his appointed traveling companion, asked the Prophet what he should do.
57	Upon his arrival in Independence, Missouri, the Prophet greeted the Saints and viewed the countryside and its people. He diligently sought the Lord for answers to questions concerning the establishment of Zion in the last days.
58	Many Saints in Jackson County, Missouri, were anxious to know the will of the Lord concerning where they would live, how they should be organized, and what they should do.
59	Following the funeral of the faithful Polly Knight, the Prophet sought assurance from the Lord concerning the future prosperity of the Saints in Missouri.
60	As missionaries prepared to return home to Ohio, they inquired of the Prophet about the return trip to Kirtland.
61	A serious canoe accident on the Missouri River caused the Prophet and ten elders to stop and make camp. William W. Phelps saw the destroyer riding in power upon the waters. The next morning, the Prophet sought the Lord in prayer.
62	The Prophet met by chance a group of Saints headed to Missouri. Wanting to know whether they should continue their journey to Missouri, the Prophet inquired of the Lord.
63	The Saints in Ohio desired to know more about the land of Zion. The Prophet inquired of the Lord concerning the gathering of the Saints, the purchasing of land, and other matters.
64	Influenced by the apostasy of Ezra Booth and others, some Saints began to question the character of the Prophet. On behalf of several elders, Joseph Smith sought the Lord's guidance.

Section	Situation that brought forth the section
65	This section was given during the period that the Prophet was preparing to recommence translation of the Bible.
66	William McLellin, a recent convert, had asked the Lord to reveal the answers to five questions. All his questions were answered in this revelation.
67	At the November 1831 conference Joseph Smith had promised the brethren a manifestation from God as to the truthfulness of the compiled revelations. The Lord explained in this revelation why that manifestation did not occur.
68	Elders Orson Hyde, Luke Johnson, Lyman E. Johnson, and William E. McLellin were desirous to know the mind of the Lord concerning themselves.
69	Oliver Cowdery had been appointed to carry the manuscripts for the Book of Commandments and Church monies through the often hazardous wilderness to Independence.
70	At the conclusion of the November 1831 conference the Lord gave stewardship of all official Church literature and its publication to Joseph Smith Jr., Oliver Cowdery, Sidney Rigdon, John Whitmer, and Martin Harris. These men in their stewardship were known as the Literary Firm.
71	Ezra Booth had apostatized and printed nine scandalous letters in the *Ohio Star.* These letters had inflamed the public against the Church, and Joseph and Sidney were commanded to stem the tide of lies.
72	Several of the Church members and leadership gathered for instruction and edification, and the discussion turned to the temporal and spiritual welfare of the Church and its members.
73	The elders of the Church were desirous to know what they should do while waiting for the January 1832 conference in Amherst, Ohio.
74	This revelation was received during the period of the translation of the Bible as an explanation of 1 Corinthians 7:14.
75	At the January 1832 conference in Amherst, the elders were anxious to know how they were to bring people to a knowledge of their fallen condition.
76	Joseph and Sidney were deep in translation of the Bible. When they came to John 5:29, the heavens were opened and the revelation known as the Vision was given.

Section	Situation that brought forth the section
77	During translation of the book of Revelation, the brethren had many questions about the meaning of the writings of John.
78	The following four revelations comprising sections 78–81 were received by the Prophet in March 1832. This revelation outlines the Lord's will in organizing and establishing a storehouse for the poor.
79	Jared Carter had come to Hiram, Ohio, to inquire of the Lord through the Prophet about where he should labor as a missionary.
80	Stephen Burnett and Eden Smith were admonished to preach the gospel in whatever place they chose.
81	This section was given in preparation for the formal organization of the First Presidency. Originally it was addressed to Jesse Gause, who, due to apostasy, was replaced by Fredrick G. Williams.
82	Joseph had been commanded in section 78 to go to Zion and establish the United Order. At the same meeting he was also sustained in Zion as the president of the High Priesthood just as he had been in Ohio.
83	During the brief visit to Zion in April 1832, the Prophet sought to organize the Saints in the law of consecration. This revelation came at the end of his visit.
84	Elders had been returning and reporting on their missions in the East.
85	William W. Phelps had been appointed to assist the bishop in administering the law of consecration and had many concerns over the great responsibility that was laid on him. Section 85 is an extract from the letter that the Prophet wrote addressing his concerns.
86	This revelation was given to the Prophet Joseph as an explanation of the parable of the wheat and tares while translating and editing the Bible.
87	Troubles among the nations and within the United States itself were foremost on the minds of the Saints. During this time Joseph received this revelation.
88	At a meeting of high priests two days after section 87 had been received, Joseph gave instructions on how to receive revelation and the blessing of heaven. Each of the brethren present in turn offered prayer to the Lord that they might be of one heart and

Section	Situation that brought forth the section

mind and receive the will of the Lord. This revelation, known as the Olive Leaf, followed.

89 Widespread use of tobacco amongst the brethren attending the School of the Prophets and the filthy conditions that resulted led the Prophet to inquire of the Lord concerning the matter.

90 This revelation was given as an answer to the petitions of the Prophet and the brethren through prayer.

91 The Bible used for the inspired translation by the Prophet contained the Apocrypha. Upon inquiry the Lord revealed that it was not necessary to translate them.

92 Fredrick G. Williams had been ordained a member of the First Presidency. He was to be equal in all rights and keys to Joseph Smith, and the Lord directed that Brother Williams should be made a part of the United Order, which at the time governed the business affairs of the Church.

93 No historical records give any indication as to what precipitated this revelation.

94 In a meeting a committee was appointed for raising funds to build a place for the School of the Prophets to meet. Shortly after, this revelation was given.

95 Hyrum Smith, Jared Carter, and Reynolds Cahoon were the committee that had been appointed to gather funds for the Church's building projects. They issued a circular encouraging the Saints to fulfill the divine command given six months previous to build the house of the Lord. Section 95 was given the same day the circular was issued.

96 In a meeting of high priests, the brethren were not able to decide who should be in charge of the lands that had been acquired by the Church. They decided to ask the Lord what to do.

97 This revelation was an answer to letters from Oliver Cowdery and other brethren in Zion.

98 The Saints in Missouri had been experiencing severe persecutions. This revelation was given in answer to their prayers.

99 Revelation for John Murdock.

100 While on a mission in the company of Sidney Rigdon and Freeman Nickerson, the Prophet was worried about the welfare of his family.

Section	Situation that brought forth the section
101	The Prophet had received news of the expulsion of the Saints from Jackson County, Missouri, just six days before.
102	Minutes of the organization of the first high council. The Prophet set forth the ancient pattern for Church councils revealed to him in vision.
103	The Saints in Missouri sent Parley P. Pratt and Lyman Wight to find out by what means they would be restored to their inheritances in Zion.
104	In order to stabilize the financial situation of the Church before the members of Zion's Camp departed, the United Order was divided into individual stewardships. The Lord confirmed the action in this revelation.
105	After the arrival of Zion's Camp in Clay County, Missouri, the aid promised by the governor was rescinded, and the efforts of the brethren to restore the Saints to their inheritances were frustrated.
106	This revelation was given while Joseph Smith was preparing for the beginning of another session of the School of the Prophets.
107	In preparation for their mission to the eastern states, the Twelve Apostles requested a written revelation from the Lord to guide and comfort them in their labors.
108	Under the influence of the Spirit, Lyman Sherman, one of the seven Presidents of the Seventy, came to the Prophet to express his feelings and desires and to receive a revelation teaching him his duty.
109	This dedicatory prayer of the Kirtland Temple was composed and copied under the direction of the Spirit by Joseph Smith, Sidney Rigdon, Oliver Cowdery, Warren Cowdery, and Warren Parrish.
110	One week after the Kirtland Temple was dedicated, a general meeting was held. In that meeting Joseph Smith and Oliver Cowdery, separated from the congregation by a veil, offered a silent prayer at the pulpit. When they had finished, this glorious vision was given to them.
111	Having heard of available monies in Salem, Joseph Smith, Sidney Rigdon, Hyrum Smith, and Oliver Cowdery went hoping to alleviate the heavy debt that hung over the Church. Shortly thereafter this revelation was given.

Section	Situation that brought forth the section
112	This section was given to help delineate the roles of the First Presidency and the Quorum of the Twelve and their relationship to one another.
113	Soon after the arrival of the Prophet Joseph Smith to Far West, Missouri, Elias Higbee and other Church members inquired about particular passages of scripture from the book of Isaiah.
114	David Patten, a member of the first Quorum of Twelve Apostles and a leader in the Church at Far West, was given council to prepare for his mission with other members of the Twelve to Great Britain.
115	The Prophet Joseph Smith identified this revelation as a "Revelation given at Far West making known the will of God concerning the building up of that place."
116	This section was an extract from the journal of the Prophet Joseph Smith regarding his visit to various sites for settlement.
117	William Marks and Newel K. Whitney had been negligent in their duties and needed instruction.
118	Revelation given through Joseph Smith the Prophet, at Far West, Missouri, July 8, 1838, in response to the supplication, "Show us thy will, O Lord, concerning the Twelve" (*History of the Church,* 3:46–47).
119	The financial troubles of the Church, its leaders, and the failure of the Saints to keep the law of consecration led to this revelation and extension of the law of tithing to all members of the Church.
120	The brethren wished to know how to dispense the properties given through tithing.
121, 122, 123	The persecutions against and sufferings of the Saints led Joseph Smith to plead with the Lord in their behalf while he was in Liberty Jail.
124	This revelation was preceded by numerous events that allowed for the establishment of the Saints to gather to Nauvoo, Illinois. Once the Saints had established themselves in Nauvoo, they sought direction from the Lord.
125	After plans for a temple in Nauvoo were declared, the question arose whether the Saints in the settlement across the Mississippi should move into Nauvoo.

Section	Situation that brought forth the section
126	This section was given because the Lord wanted Brigham Young near the Prophet to prepare to succeed him.
127, 128	Performance of ordinances for the dead without any organization or record keeping led to instructions concerning baptism for the dead.
129	Satan's continued efforts to deceive the Saints necessitated instructions on how to perceive if an angel was from God or the devil.
130	This revelation corrected statements presented in a talk by Orson Hyde.
131	Verses 1–4 came up when the Prophet was giving instruction on the priesthood.
132	This section came at the request of Hyrum Smith for the convincing of Emma Smith of the truthfulness of the principles of eternal marriage and plural wives.
133	When the Book of Commandments was brought before the Lord for acceptance, He gave this revelation to be an appendix to it.
134	This section was a declaration to be included in the first publication of the Doctrine and Covenants on earthly government and laws in order that the Church would not be misinterpreted or misunderstood.
135	The Saints wished to know the circumstances surrounding the Prophet's martyrdom.
136	President Brigham Young needed to know how to organize the Saints in the trek westward.
137	In preparation for the future dedication of the Kirtland Temple, two meetings were held wherein the endowment was administered to leaders of the Church. In the first meeting this revelation was received.
138	President Joseph F. Smith was studying the scriptures in order to understand our postmortal existence.
OD—1	President Wilford Woodruff sought for a solution to the problems resulting from persecution of those practicing polygamy.
OD—2	President Spencer W. Kimball desired to know the will of the Lord concerning extending the blessings of the priesthood to all Saints, regardless of race or color.

CHAPTER ONE

THE DOCTRINE AND COVENANTS AND MODERN REVELATION

PRESIDENT JAMES E. FAUST

My dear brothers and sisters, I am humbled to be participating with so many distinguished scholars as they address various dimensions of the Doctrine and Covenants. My feelings are fueled in part by the fact that I have never been quite comfortable being considered a scholar. I should like to enlarge upon a theme today from the Doctrine and Covenants: "You shall declare the things which have been revealed to my servant, Joseph Smith, Jun." (D&C 31:4). To that I would add "and his successors in interest."

The dean of the law school that I attended constantly impressed upon us that his primary mission was not to teach us the law, for the law would change; rather, his primary mission was to teach us to think straight, based upon sound principles.

Comparing that to our task today, we find that the body of modern scripture has changed only in the sense that it is not closed and static but being constantly added to. My desire today is to give some orientation, keeping one's thinking straight regarding the process and importance of modern revelation as well as its content.

In an attempt to provide a background to this orientation with respect to the Doctrine and Covenants, I think it well to begin with the statement of the Prophet Joseph Smith, "I told the brethren that the Book of Mormon was the most correct of any book on earth, and

President James E. Faust is the Second Counselor in the First Presidency.

the keystone of our religion, and a man would get nearer to God by abiding by its precepts, than by any other book."[1] This statement takes nothing away from the other scriptures. The Book of Mormon is a key to understanding the Bible. We also know that the Doctrine and Covenants stands in a class by itself.

Perhaps beyond that statement of Joseph concerning the Book of Mormon as the keystone of our religion, I do not feel comfortable in going further in classifying our standard works in terms of their importance. Each is unique. Each is the word of God. Each is special. Each is vital for understanding the principles of the gospel. Each is essential to our salvation. Since revelations continue to come to this divine institution all of the time, I would suggest that some priority should be given to the declarations of the modern prophets as against those received many, many centuries ago and that were intended for a different people at a different time. For instance, I feel that the counsel of our current prophet should receive far greater attention than the pronouncements of Ezekiel.

Of all the scripture, however, the Doctrine and Covenants is unique for many reasons. It is unique because, unlike the book of Revelation, it is not closed. The Lord has made contemporaneous declarations to the generations of our great-grandparents, our grandparents, and our parents, and to us and our children. Also for those of us who read English, it has gone through no language translations. It is a first impression from the Lord in English. All other scripture is, of course, pretty much from a translation of a language now archaic.

In an effort to try to understand the nature of how revelation comes, it is essential to understand that the right and function of inspiration comes through keys. Perhaps it would be worthwhile to make some personal observations with respect to the most recent revelation added to the Doctrine and Covenants, known as Official Declaration—2. Some of us are still living who had a glorious worm's-eye view at close range of this great revelation. Perhaps it would be worthwhile for me to comment on some of the background. Declaration number 2, of course, refers to the granting of the priesthood to all worthy male members of the Church. This is significant for many reasons, including the fact that with the coming of this revelation the whole world was literally opened up for the spreading of the work of God in all the world. Keys, blessings, and endowments, including those of the ancient patriarchs, now became possible for everyone. Of this President Spencer W. Kimball said:

"As you know, on the ninth of June a policy was changed that affects great numbers of people throughout the world. Millions and millions of people will be affected by the revelation which came. I remember very vividly that day after day I walked to the temple and ascended to the fourth floor where we have our solemn assemblies and where we have our meetings of the Twelve and the First Presidency. After everybody had gone out of the temple, I knelt and prayed. I prayed with much fervency. I knew that something was before us that was extremely important to many of the children of God. I knew that we could receive the revelations of the Lord only by being worthy and ready for them and ready to accept them and put them into place. Day after day I went alone and with great solemnity and seriousness in the upper rooms of the temple, and there I offered my soul and offered my efforts to go forward with the program. I wanted to do what He wanted. I talked about it to Him and said: 'Lord, I want only what is right. We are not making any plans to be spectacularly moving. We want only the thing that thou dost want, and we want it when you want it and not until.'

"We met with the Council of the Twelve Apostles, time after time, in the holy room where there is a picture of the Savior in many different moods and also pictures of all the Presidents of the church. Finally we had the feeling and the impression from the Lord, who made it very clear to us, that this was the thing to do to make the gospel universal to all worthy people."[2]

Of this experience, Elder Bruce R. McConkie states: "It was on a glorious June day in 1978. All of us were together in an upper room in the Salt Lake Temple. We were engaged in fervent prayer, pleading with the Lord to manifest his mind and will concerning those who are entitled to receive his holy priesthood. President Kimball himself was mouth, offering the desires of his heart and of our hearts to that God whose servants we are." Previously in the same meeting, President Kimball had discussed the possible conferral of the priesthood upon all races. Elder McConkie continues: "The President restated the problem involved, reminded us of our prior discussions, and said he had spent many days alone in this upper room pleading with the Lord for an answer to our prayers. He said that if the answer was to continue our present course of denying the priesthood to the seed of Cain, as the Lord had theretofore directed, he was prepared to defend that decision to the death. But, he said, if the long-sought day had come in which the curse of the past was to be removed, he thought we might prevail upon the Lord to so indicate. He expressed the hope that we might receive a clear answer one way or the other so the matter might be laid to rest."[3]

A week following the meeting referred to by Elder McConkie, all of the General Authorities were summoned to the upper room of the temple for a special meeting. President Kimball announced the revelation, which was received by all of the Brethren with great joy. On the way over to the meeting, I was walking with one of my fellow Presidents of the First Quorum of the Seventy (at that time I was not a member of the Twelve). My beloved associate asked me if I thought the meeting pertained to a particular current problem, and I indicated that I thought not, without making any further explanation. In my heart, however, I had the hope that such a revelation as did come might be announced. No one had indicated that such might be forthcoming; my feelings came only from the broodings of the Spirit.

President Kimball's own words describe this best of all: "We had the glorious experience of having the Lord indicate clearly that the time had come when all worthy men and women everywhere can be fellow heirs and partakers of the full blessings of the gospel. I want you to know, as a special witness of the Savior, how close I have felt to him and to our Heavenly Father as I have made numerous visits to the upper rooms in the temple, going on some days several times by myself. The Lord made it very clear to me what was to be done. We do not expect the people of the world to understand such things, for they will always be quick to assign their own reasons or to discount the divine process of revelation."[4]

President Kimball further said of the process of revelation:

"For many it seems difficult to accept as revelation those numerous messages . . . which come to prophets as deep, unassailable impressions settling down on the prophet's mind and heart as dew from heaven or as the dawn displaces the darkness of night. Many men seem to have no ear for spiritual messages nor comprehension of them when they come in common dress. . . . Expecting the spectacular, one may not be fully alerted to the constant flow of revealed communication.

"When in a Thursday temple meeting, after prayer and fasting, important decisions are made, new missions and new stakes are created, new patterns and policies initiated, the news is taken for granted and possibly thought of as mere human calculations. But to those who sit in the intimate circles and hear the prayers of the prophet and the testimony of the man of God; to those who see the astuteness of his deliberations and the sagacity of his decisions and pronouncements, to them he is verily a prophet. To hear him conclude important new developments with such solemn expressions as 'the Lord is pleased'; 'that move is right'; 'our Heavenly Father has spoken,' is to know positively."[5]

There is so much continuous, ongoing revelation that comes to this people that the extent of it cannot be fully appreciated. It does not ever, however, become commonplace. As one who is involved in the calling of stake presidents, patriarchs, and other Church officers, from my own experience, I think perhaps Enos said it well: "And while I was thus struggling in the spirit, behold, the voice of the Lord came into my mind" (Enos 1:10).

The process explained by President Kimball and others who were present may be something like other revelations contained in the Doctrine and Covenants, which may have involved deep impressions. President Kimball quoted a paragraph by Parley P. Pratt that showed how those revelations came to the Prophet Joseph Smith: "Each sentence was uttered slowly and very distinctly and with a pause between each, sufficiently long for it to be recorded by an ordinary writer in long hand. This was the manner in which all his written revelations were dictated and written. There was never any hesitation, reviewing or reading back, in order to keep the run of the subject; neither did any of these communications undergo revisions, interlinings or corrections. As he dictated them, so they stood, so far as I have witnessed; and I was present to witness the dictation of several communications of several pages each."[6]

Of the majesty and grandeur of the Doctrine and Covenants in general, President Joseph F. Smith said, "I say to my brethren that the book of Doctrine and Covenants contains some of the most glorious principles ever revealed to the world, some that have been revealed in greater fulness than they were ever revealed before to the world; and this, in fulfilment of the promise of the ancient prophets that in the latter times the Lord would reveal things to the world that had been kept hidden from the foundation thereof; and the Lord has revealed them through the Prophet Joseph Smith."[7]

As to the larger importance of these divine declarations, let us keep our thinking straight. After they are received, the Lord expects something to change in our lives.

President Heber J. Grant felt, however, that the marvelous utterances were of little value unless they became a part of our practical religion. Said he: "The Doctrine and Covenants is full of splendid things with which we ought to be familiar. But you can read this book through and through, and learn it off by heart, and it won't do you a particle of good unless you put into practice the teachings. To read a book through without carrying out any of the things that are taught in the book is of no value. It is the things that we read and learn and then put into practice that count."[8]

President Wilford Woodruff had a great testimony of the Doctrine and Covenants: "I consider that the Doctrine and Covenants, our Testament, contains a code of the most solemn, the most Godlike proclamations ever made to the human family."[9]

There is a great responsibility resting upon the individual student of the scriptures to live so as to qualify himself to have the spiritual maturity to have some understanding of the pronouncements of God and then the strength to make something happen. On this subject, Brigham Young stated: "It is your privilege and duty to live so as to be able to understand the things of God. There are the Old and New Testaments, the Book of Mormon, and the book of Doctrine and Covenants, which Joseph has given us, and they are of great worth to a person wandering in darkness. They are like a lighthouse in the ocean, or a finger-post which points out the road we should travel. Where do they point? To the Fountain of light."[10]

In conclusion, I should like to share one or two of the profound concepts in the Doctrine and Covenants that have impressed themselves upon my mind. One of the greatest doctrines ever pronounced is the concept of universal salvation. Because of the Atonement, all mankind will rise from the dead. The Doctrine and Covenants explains the doctrine of universal salvation clearly:

"That as many as would believe and be baptized in his holy name, and endure in faith to the end, should be saved—

"Not only those who believed after he came in the meridian of time, in the flesh, but all those from the beginning, even as many as were before he came, who believed in the words of the holy prophets, who spake as they were inspired by the gift of the Holy Ghost, who truly testified of him in all things, should have eternal life, 'As well as those who should come after, who should believe in the gifts and callings of God by the Holy Ghost, which beareth record of the Father and of the Son'" (D&C 20:25–27).

This concept is one of fairness; a companion doctrine to it is the great vicarious labor in our temple for those who are dead, whereby it may be brought into being uniformly. Temple work is required for implementing the doctrine of universal salvation. The instruction given through Thomas B. Marsh is profoundly enlightening in terms of our responsibility to receive and teach the word of God:

"Let thy heart be of good cheer before my face; and thou shalt bear record of my name, not only unto the Gentiles, but also unto the Jews; and thou shalt send forth my word unto the ends of the earth.

"Contend thou, therefore, morning by morning; and day after day let thy warning voice go forth; and when the night cometh let not the inhabitants of the earth slumber, because of thy speech. . . .

"Thy voice shall be a rebuke unto the transgressor; and at thy rebuke let the tongue of the slanderer cease its perverseness. . . .

"Now, I say unto you, and what I say unto you, I say unto all the Twelve: Arise and gird up your loins, take up your cross, follow me, and feed my sheep" (D&C 112:4–5, 9, 14).

A chilling warning comes to us through section 87, wherein the Civil War between the Southern and Northern States was foretold. Verse 6 tells of the bloodshed, famine, plague, earthquake, and wrath to come under the chastening hand of Almighty God. That verse concludes that the calamities would continue "until the consumption decreed hath made a full end of all nations" (D&C 87:6).

I rejoice that in our time the heavens have been opened and the ears of our great prophet have been opened to receive further light and knowledge. I am satisfied that it is not much dissimilar from the process that the Prophet Joseph enjoyed in bringing forth the majority of the Doctrine and Covenants. Of course, you know of the other revelations that have been added to it in our recent lifetime, testifying to the fact that the heavens are opened and the scriptures are not closed. I am grateful and add my testimony to the correctness of the doctrine and the inspiration that came in Official Declaration—2, of which, as I indicated earlier, I personally had a worm's-eye view and, along with my brethren, some involvement. I am satisfied that Official Declaration—2 is as great a pronouncement as we have otherwise in the Book of Mormon, and it came in our time; now, the gospel can roll forth in the many countries of the world.

And so I counsel and testify "ye shall declare the things which have been received to my servant, Joseph Smith, Jun., and his successors in interest." I ask the Lord to bless this body of scholars that they will have the spiritual enlightenment and understanding to comprehend the subtle, great, and spiritual messages that are contained not only in the Doctrine and Covenants but in the other scriptures as well, and then, having received them and having come to some understanding of what the Lord had intended in them, that we then have the strength and the courage and the wisdom to implement them into our lives.

I ask the blessings of heaven to be upon each and every one of you and upon the great department of this marvelous university that has sponsored this symposium, Religious Education. This department is something of the eye of the storm of this great university and something of the fulcrum around which it all centers in this university for the promulgation of truth. And the center of all truth is, of course, from our Heavenly Father.

I leave you the witness of my soul that God has revealed and does constantly reveal through His servants throughout all the Church, from the levels of the Relief Society presidents, the Primary presidents, the bishops, the stake presidents, the mission presidents, and the General Authorities, a flow of constant revelation, which, if our spiritual ears are attuned, we shall be able to receive and interpret.

I personally testify of having had the Lord speak to my mind on frequent and regular occasions and declare this witness and leave you this blessing and testimony.

NOTES

1. Joseph Smith, *History of the Church of Jesus Christ of Latter-day Saints,* ed. B. H. Roberts, 2nd ed., rev. (Salt Lake City: Deseret Book, 1957), 4:461.

2. Spencer W. Kimball, *The Teachings of Spencer W. Kimball,* ed. Edward L. Kimball (Salt Lake City: Bookcraft, 1982), 450–51.
3. Bruce R. McConkie, "The New Revelation on Priesthood," in *Priesthood* (Salt Lake City: Deseret Book, 1981), 126–27.
4. Kimball, *Teachings,* 452.
5. Kimball, *Teachings,* 457–58.
6. Kimball, *Teachings,* 456.
7. Joseph F. Smith, *Gospel Doctrine* (Salt Lake City: Deseret Book, 1986), 45.
8. Heber J. Grant, *Gospel Standards,* comp. G. Homer Durham (Salt Lake City: Improvement Era, 1941), 39.
9. Wilford Woodruff, in *Journal of Discourses* (London: Latter-day Saints' Book Depot, 1854–86), 22:146.
10. Brigham Young, *Discourses of Brigham Young,* comp. John A. Widtsoe (Salt Lake City: Deseret Book, 1954), 127.

CHAPTER TWO

REVELATION

ELDER DALLIN H. OAKS

Revelation is communication from God to man. It can occur in many different ways. Some prophets, like Moses and Joseph Smith, have talked with God face to face. Some persons have had personal communication with angels. Other revelations have come, as Elder James E. Talmage described it, "through the dreams of sleep or in waking visions of the mind."[1]

In its more familiar forms, revelation or inspiration comes by means of words or thoughts communicated to the mind (see D&C 8:2–3; Enos 1:10), by sudden enlightenment (see D&C 6:14–15), by positive or negative feelings about proposed courses of action, or even by inspiring performances, as in the performing arts. As President Boyd K. Packer has stated, "Inspiration comes more as a feeling than as a sound."[2]

Assuming you are familiar with these different forms of revelation or inspiration, I have chosen to discuss this subject in terms of a different classification—the purpose of the communication. I can identify eight different purposes served by communication from God: (1) to testify, (2) to prophesy, (3) to comfort, (4) to uplift, (5) to inform, (6) to restrain, (7) to confirm, and (8) to impel. I will describe each of these in that order, giving examples.

My purpose in suggesting this classification and in giving these examples is to persuade each of you to search your own experience and to conclude that you have already received revelations and that you can receive more revelations, because communication from God

Elder Dallin H. Oaks is a member of the Quorum of the Twelve Apostles. This address was given at a Brigham Young University devotional assembly on September 29, 1981.

10

to men and women is a reality. President Lorenzo Snow declared that it is "the grand privilege of every Latter-day Saint . . . to have the manifestations of the spirit every day of our lives."[3]

President Harold B. Lee taught that "every man has the privilege to exercise these gifts and these privileges in the conduct of his own affairs; in bringing up his children in the way they should go; in the management of his business, or whatever he does. It is his right to enjoy the spirit of revelation and of inspiration to do the right thing, to be wise and prudent, just and good, in everything that he does."[4]

As I review the following eight purposes of revelation, I hope you will recognize the extent to which you have already received revelation or inspiration and resolve to cultivate this spiritual gift for more frequent use in the future.

1. The Holy Ghost *testifies* or reveals that Jesus is the Christ and that the gospel is true.

When the Apostle Peter affirmed that Jesus Christ was the Son of the living God, the Savior called him blessed, "for flesh and blood hath not revealed it unto thee, but my Father which is in heaven" (Matthew 16:17). This precious revelation can be part of the personal experience of every seeker after truth and, once received, becomes a polestar to guide in all the activities of life.

2. *Prophecy* is another purpose or function of revelation.

Speaking under the influence of the Holy Ghost and within the limits of his or her responsibility, a person may be inspired to predict what will come to pass in the future.

The one who holds the office of the prophet, seer, and revelator prophesies for the Church, as when Joseph Smith prophesied concerning the Civil War (see D&C 87) and foretold that the Saints would become a mighty people in the Rocky Mountains. Prophecy is part of the calling of a patriarch. Each of us is also privileged occasionally to receive prophetic revelation illuminating future events in our lives, like a Church calling we are to receive. To cite another example, after our fifth child was born, my wife and I did not have any more children. After more than ten years, we concluded that our family would not be any larger, which grieved us. Then one day, while my wife was in the temple, the Spirit whispered to her that she would have another child. That prophetic revelation was fulfilled about a year and a half later with the birth of our sixth child, for whom we had waited thirteen years.

3. A third purpose of revelation is to give *comfort*.

Such a revelation came to the Prophet Joseph Smith in Liberty Jail. After many months in deplorable conditions, he cried out in agony and loneliness, pleading for the Lord to remember him and the persecuted Saints. The comforting answer came:

"My son, peace be unto thy soul; thine adversity and thine afflictions shall be but a small moment; and then, if thou endure it well, God shall exalt thee on high; thou shalt triumph over all thy foes" (D&C 121:7–8).

In that same revelation the Lord declared that no matter what tragedies or injustices should befall the Prophet, "Know thou, my son, that all these things shall give thee experience, and shall be for thy good" (D&C 122:7).

Each of us knows of other examples of revelations of comfort. Some have been comforted by visions of departed loved ones or by feeling their presence. The widow of a good friend told me that she had felt the presence of her departed husband, giving her assurance of his love and concern for her. Others have been comforted in adjusting to the loss of a job or a business advantage or even a marriage. A revelation of comfort can also come in connection with a blessing of the priesthood, either from the words spoken or simply from the feeling communicated in connection with the blessing.

Another type of comforting revelation is the assurance received that a sin has been forgiven. After praying fervently for an entire day and night, a Book of Mormon prophet recorded that he heard a voice, which said, "Thy sins are forgiven thee, and thou shalt be blessed.

"Wherefore," Enos wrote, "my guilt was swept away" (Enos 1:5–6; see also D&C 61:2). This assurance, which comes when a person has completed all the steps of repentance, gives assurance that the price has been paid, that God has heard the repentant sinner, and that his or her sins are forgiven. Alma described that moment as a time when he was no longer "harrowed up by the memory" of his sins. "And oh, what joy, and what marvelous light I did behold; yea, my soul was filled with joy. . . . There can be nothing so exquisite and sweet as was my joy" (Alma 36:19–21).

4. Closely related to the feeling of comfort is the fourth purpose or function of revelation, to *uplift*.

At some time in our lives each of us needs to be lifted up from a depression, from a sense of foreboding or inadequacy, or just from a plateau of spiritual mediocrity. Because it raises our spirits and helps us resist evil and seek good, I believe that the feeling of uplift that is communicated by reading the scriptures or by enjoying wholesome music, art, or literature is a distinct purpose of revelation.

5. The fifth purpose of revelation is to *inform*.

This may consist of inspiration giving a person the words to speak on a particular occasion, such as in the blessings pronounced by a patriarch or in sermons or other words spoken under the influence of the Holy Ghost. The Lord commanded Joseph Smith and Sidney Rigdon to lift up their voices and speak the thoughts that would be put into their hearts, "for it shall be given you in the very hour, yea, in the very moment, what ye shall say" (D&C 100:5–6; see also D&C 84:85; 124:97).

On some sacred occasions, information has been given by face-to-face conversations with heavenly personages, such as in the visions related in ancient and modern scripture. In other circumstances, needed information is communicated by the quiet whisperings of the Spirit. A child loses a treasured possession, prays for help, and is inspired to find it; an adult has a problem at work, at home, or in genealogical research, prays, and is led to the information necessary to resolve it; a Church leader prays to know who the Lord would have him call to fill a position, and the Spirit whispers a name. In all of these examples—familiar to each of us—the Holy Ghost acts in His office as a teacher and revelator, communicating information and truths for the edification and guidance of the recipient.

Revelation from God serves all five of these purposes: testimony, prophecy, comfort, uplift, and information. I have spoken of these only briefly, giving examples principally from the scriptures. I will speak at greater length about the remaining three purposes of revelation, giving examples from my personal experience.

6. The sixth type or purpose of revelation is to *restrain* us from doing something.

Thus, in the midst of a great sermon explaining the power of the Holy Ghost, Nephi suddenly declares, "And now I . . . cannot say more; the Spirit stoppeth mine utterance" (2 Nephi 32:7). The revelation that restrains is one of the most common forms of revelation. It often comes by surprise, when we have not asked for revelation or guidance on a particular subject. But if we are keeping the commandments of God and living in tune with His Spirit, a restraining force will steer us away from things we should not do.

One of my first experiences in being restrained by the Spirit came soon after I was called as a counselor in a stake presidency in Chicago. In one of our first stake presidency meetings, our stake president made a proposal that our new stake center be built in a particular location. I immediately saw four or five good reasons why that was the wrong location. When asked for my counsel, I opposed the proposal, giving each of those reasons. The stake president wisely proposed that each of us consider the matter prayerfully for a week and discuss it further in our next meeting. Almost perfunctorily I prayed about the subject and immediately received a strong impression that I was wrong, that I was standing in the way of the Lord's will, and that I should remove myself from opposition to it. Needless to say, I was restrained and promptly gave my approval to the proposed construction. Incidentally, the wisdom of constructing the stake center at that location was soon evident, even to me. My reasons to the contrary turned out to be short-sighted, and I was soon grateful to have been restrained from relying on them.

Several years ago I picked up the desk pen in my office at Brigham Young University (BYU) to sign a paper that had been prepared for my signature, something I did at least a dozen times each day. That document committed the university to a particular course of action we had decided to follow. All the staff work had been done, and all appeared to be in order. But as I went to sign the document, I was filled with such negative thoughts and forebodings that I put it to one side and asked for the entire matter to be reviewed again. It was, and within a few days additional facts came to light which showed that the proposed course of action would have caused the university serious problems in the future.

On another occasion the Spirit came to my assistance as I was editing a casebook on a legal subject. A casebook consists of several hundred court opinions, together with explanatory material and text written by the editor. My assistant and I had finished almost all of the work on the book, including the necessary research to assure that these court opinions had not been reversed or overruled. Just before sending it to the publisher, I was leafing through the manuscript and a particular court opinion caught my attention. As I looked at it, I had a profoundly uneasy feeling. I asked my assistant to check that opinion again to see if everything was in order. He reported that it was. In a subsequent check of the completed manuscript, I was again stopped at that case, again with great feelings of uneasiness. This time I went to the law library myself. There, in some newly received publications, I discovered that this case had just been reversed on appeal. If that opinion had been published in my casebook, it would have been a serious professional embarrassment. I was saved by the restraining power of revelation.

7. A common way to seek revelation is to propose a particular course of action and then to pray for inspiration to *confirm* it.

The Lord explained the confirming type of revelation when Oliver Cowdery failed in his efforts to translate the Book of Mormon: "Behold, you have not understood; you have supposed that I would give it unto you, when you took no thought save it was to ask me.

"But, behold, I say unto you, that you must study it out in your mind; then you must ask me if it be right, and if it is right I will cause that your bosom shall burn within you; therefore, you shall feel that it is right" (D&C 9:7–8).

Similarly, the prophet Alma likens the word of God to a seed and tells persons studying the gospel that if they will give place for the seed to be planted in their heart, the seed will enlarge their souls and enlighten their understanding and begin to be delicious to them (see Alma 32). That feeling is the Holy Ghost's confirming revelation of the truth of the word.

When he spoke on the BYU campus some years ago on the subject "Agency or Inspiration," Elder Bruce R. McConkie stressed our responsibility to do all that we can before we seek a revelation. He gave a very personal example. When he set out to choose a companion for eternity, he did not go to the Lord and ask whom he ought to marry. "I went out and found the girl I wanted," he said. "She suited me; . . . it just seemed . . . as though this ought to be. . . . [Then] all I did was pray to the Lord and ask for some guidance and direction in connection with the decision that I'd reached."[5]

Elder McConkie summarized his counsel on the balance between agency and inspiration as follows: "We're expected to use the gifts and talents and abilities, the sense and judgment and agency with which we are endowed. . . . Implicit in asking in faith is the precedent requirement that we do everything in our power to accomplish the goal that we seek. . . . We're expected to do everything in our power that we can, and then to seek an answer from the Lord, a confirming seal that we've reached the right conclusion."[6]

As a regional representative I was privileged to work with four different members of the Quorum of the Twelve and with other General Authorities as they sought revelation in the calling of stake presidents. All proceeded in the same manner. They interviewed persons residing in the stake—counselors in the stake presidency, members of the high council, bishops, and others who had gained special experience in Church administration—asking them questions and hearing their counsel. As these interviews were conducted, the servants of the Lord gave prayerful consideration to each person interviewed and mentioned. Finally, they reached a tentative decision on the new stake president. This proposal was then prayerfully submitted to the Lord. If confirmed, the call was issued. If not confirmed, or if restrained, that proposal was tabled and the process continued until a new proposal was formed and the confirming revelation was received.

Sometimes confirming and restraining revelations are combined. For example, during my service at BYU I was invited to give a speech before a national association of attorneys. Because it would require many days to prepare, this was the kind of speaking invitation I had routinely declined. But as I began to dictate a letter declining this particular invitation, I felt restrained. I paused and reconsidered my action. I then considered how I might accept the invitation, and as I came to consider it in that light, I felt the confirming assurance of the Spirit and knew that this was what I must do.

The speech that resulted, "A Private University Looks at Government Regulation," opened the door to a host of important opportunities. I was invited to repeat that same speech before several other nationally prominent groups. It was published in *Vital Speeches,* in a professional journal, and in several other periodicals and books, from which it was used as a leading statement of the private university's interest in freedom from government regulation. This speech led to BYU's being consulted by various church groups on the proper relationship between government and a church-related college. These consultations in turn contributed to the formation of a national organization of church-related colleges and universities that has provided a significant coalition to oppose unlawful or unwise government regulation in the future. I have no doubt, as I look back on the event, that this speaking invitation I almost declined was one of those occasions when a seemingly insignificant act made a great deal of difference.

Those are the times when it is vital for us to receive the guidance of the Lord, and those are the times when revelation will come to aid us if we will hear and heed it.

8. The eighth purpose or type of revelation consists of those instances where the Spirit *impels* a person to action.

This is not a case where a person proposes to take a particular action and the Spirit either confirms or restrains. This is a case where revelation comes when it is not being sought and impels some action not proposed. This type of revelation is obviously less common than other types, but its rarity makes it all the more significant.

A scriptural example is recorded in the first book of Nephi. After Nephi obtained the precious records from the treasury in Jerusalem, the Spirit of the Lord directed him to kill Laban as he lay drunk in the street. This act was so far from Nephi's heart that he recoiled and wrestled with the Spirit, but he was again directed to slay Laban, and he finally followed that revelation (see 1 Nephi 4).

Students of Church history will recall Wilford Woodruff's account of an impression that came to him in the night telling him to move his carriage and mules away from a large tree. He did so, and his family and livestock were saved when the tree crashed to the ground in a tornado that struck thirty minutes later.[7]

As a young girl, my grandmother Chasty Olsen Harris had a similar experience. She was tending some children who were playing in a dry riverbed near their home in Castle Dale, Utah. Suddenly she heard a voice that called her by name and directed her to get the children out of the riverbed and up on the bank. It was a clear day, and there was no sign of rain. She saw no reason to heed the voice and continued to play. The voice spoke to her again, urgently. This time she heeded the warning. Quickly gathering the children, she made a run for the bank. Just as they reached it, an enormous wall of water, originating with a cloudburst in the mountains many miles away, swept down the canyon and roared across where the children had played. Except for this impelling revelation, she and the children would have been lost.

For nine years Professor Marvin Hill and I had worked on the book *Carthage Conspiracy,* which concerns the 1845 court trial of the murderers of Joseph Smith. We had several different sources of minutes on the trial, some bearing their author's name and others unsigned. The fullest set of minutes was unsigned, but because we had located them in the Church Historian's Office, we were sure they were the minutes kept by George Watt, the Church's official scribe who was sent to record the proceedings of the trial. We so stated in seven drafts of our manuscript and analyzed all of our sources on that assumption.

Finally, the book was completed, and within a few weeks the final manuscript would be sent to the publisher. As I sat in my office at BYU one Saturday afternoon, I felt impelled to go through the pile of unexamined books and pamphlets accumulated on the table behind my desk. At the very bottom of a pile of fifty or sixty publications, I found a printed catalog of the contents of the Wilford C. Wood Museum, which Professor LaMar Berrett, the author, had sent to me a year and a half earlier. As I quickly flipped through the pages of this catalog of Church history manuscripts, my eyes fell on a page describing the manuscript of the trial minutes we had attributed to George Watt. This catalog page told how Wilford Wood had purchased the original of that set of minutes in Illinois and had given the Church the typewritten version we had obtained from the Church historian.

We immediately visited the Wilford Wood Museum in Woods Cross, Utah, and obtained additional information which enabled us to determine that the minutes we had thought were the official Church source had been prepared by one of the lawyers for the defense. With this knowledge we returned to the Church Historian's Office and were able to locate for the first time George Watt's official and highly authentic set of minutes on the trial. This discovery saved us from a grievous error in the identification of one of our major sources and also permitted us to enrich the contents of our book significantly. The impression I received that day in my office is a cherished example of the way the Lord will help us in our righteous professional pursuits when we qualify for the impressions of His Spirit.

I had another choice experience with impelling revelation a few months after I began my service at BYU. As a new and inexperienced president, I had many problems to analyze and many decisions to reach. I was very dependent on the Lord. One day in October I drove up Provo Canyon to ponder a particular problem. Although alone and without any interruption, I found myself unable to think of the problem at hand. Another pending issue I was not yet ready to consider kept thrusting itself into my mind: should we modify BYU's academic calendar to complete the fall semester before Christmas?

After ten or fifteen minutes of unsuccessful efforts to exclude thoughts of this subject, I realized what was happening. The issue of the calendar did not seem timely to me, and I was certainly not seeking any guidance on it, but the Spirit was trying to communicate on that subject. I immediately turned my full attention to that question and began to record my thoughts on a piece of paper. Within a few minutes I had recorded the details of a three-semester calendar, with all of its powerful advantages.

Hurrying back to the campus, I reviewed this with my colleagues and found them enthusiastic. A few days later the Board of Trustees approved our proposed new calendar, and we published its dates, barely in time to make them effective in the fall of 1972. Since that time I have reread these words of the Prophet Joseph Smith and realized that I had had the experience he described: "A person may profit by noticing the first intimation of the spirit of revelation; for instance, when you feel pure intelligence flowing into you, it may give you sudden strokes of ideas . . . and thus by learning the Spirit of God and understanding it, you may grow into the principle of revelation."[8]

I have now described eight different purposes or types of revelation: (1) testifying, (2) prophesying, (3) comforting, (4) uplifting, (5) informing, (6) restraining, (7) confirming, and (8) impelling. Each of these refers to revelations that are received. Before concluding, I will suggest a few ideas about revelations that are not received.

First, we should understand what can be called the principle of "responsibility in revelation." Our Heavenly Father's house is a house of order, where His servants are commanded to "act in the office in which [they are] appointed" (D&C 107:99). This principle applies to revelation. Only the President of the Church receives revelation to guide the entire Church. Only the stake president receives revelation for the special guidance of the stake. The person who receives revelation for the ward is the bishop. For a family, it is the priesthood leadership of the family. Leaders receive revelation for their own areas of responsibility. Individuals can receive revelation to guide their own lives.

But when one person purports to receive revelation for another person outside his or her own area of responsibility—such as a Church member who claims to have revelation to guide the entire Church or a person who claims to have a revelation to guide another person over whom he or she has no presiding authority according to the order of the Church—you can be sure that such revelations are not from the Lord. "There are counterfeit signals."[9] Satan is a great deceiver, and he is the source of some of these spurious revelations. Others are imagined.

If a revelation is outside the limits of your specific responsibility, you know it is not from the Lord and you are not bound by it. I have heard of cases where a young man told a young woman she should marry him because he had received a revelation that she was to be his eternal companion. If this is a true revelation, it will be confirmed directly to the woman if she seeks to know. In the meantime, she is under no obligation to heed it. She should seek her own guidance and make up her own mind. The man can receive revelation to guide his own actions, but he cannot properly receive revelation to direct hers. She is outside his jurisdiction.

What about those times when we seek revelation and do not receive it? We do not always receive inspiration or revelation when we request it. Sometimes we are delayed in the receipt of revelation, and sometimes we are left to our own judgment. We cannot force spiritual things. It must be so. Our life's purpose to obtain experience and to develop faith would be frustrated if our Heavenly Father directed us in every act, even in every important act. We must make decisions and experience the consequences in order to develop self-reliance and faith.

Even in decisions we think very important, we sometimes receive no answer to our prayers. This does not mean that our prayers have not been heard. It only means that we have prayed about a decision which, for one reason or another, we should make without guidance by revelation. Perhaps we have asked for guidance in choosing between alternatives that are equally acceptable or equally unacceptable. I suggest that there is *not* a right and wrong to *every* question. To many questions, there are only two wrong answers or two right answers. Thus, a person who seeks guidance on which of two different ways he should pursue to get even with a person who has wronged him is not likely to receive a revelation. Neither is a person who seeks guidance on a choice he will never have to make because some future event will intervene, such as a third alternative that is clearly preferable. On one occasion, my wife and I prayed earnestly for guidance on a decision that seemed very important. No answer came. We were left to proceed on our own best judgment. We could not imagine why the Lord had not aided us with a confirming or restraining impression. But it was not long before we learned that we did not have to make a decision on that question because something else happened that made a decision unnecessary. The Lord would not guide us in a selection that made no difference.

No answer is likely to come to a person who seeks guidance in choosing between two alternatives that are equally acceptable to the Lord. Thus, there are times when we can serve productively in two different fields of labor. Either answer is right. Similarly, the Spirit of the Lord is not likely to give us revelations on matters that are trivial. I once heard a young woman in testimony meeting praise the spirituality of her husband, indicating that he submitted every question to the Lord. She told how he accompanied her shopping and would not even choose between different brands of canned vegetables without making his selection a matter of prayer. That strikes me as improper. I believe the Lord expects us to use the intelligence and experience He has given us to make these kinds of choices. When a member asked the Prophet Joseph Smith for advice on a particular matter, the Prophet stated: "It is a great thing to inquire at the hands of God, or to come into His presence: and we feel fearful to approach Him on subjects that are of little or no consequence."[10]

Of course, we are not always able to judge what is trivial. If a matter appears of little or no consequence, we should proceed on the basis of our own judgment. If the choice is important for reasons unknown to us, such as the speaking invitation I mentioned earlier or a choice between two cans of vegetables when one contains a hidden poison, the Lord will intervene and give us guidance. Where a choice will make a real difference in our lives—obvious or not—and where we are living in tune with the Spirit and seeking its guidance, we can be sure that we will receive the guidance we need to attain our goal. The Lord will not leave us unassisted when a choice is important to our eternal welfare.

NOTES

1. James E. Talmage, *Articles of Faith*, 12th ed. (Salt Lake City: The Church of Jesus Christ of Latter-day Saints, 1924), 229.
2. Boyd K. Packer, "Prayers and Answers," *Ensign*, November 1979, 19–20.
3. Lorenzo Snow, in Conference Report, April 1899, 52.
4. Harold B. Lee, *Stand Ye in Holy Places* (Salt Lake City: Deseret Book, 1974), 141–42.
5. Bruce R. McConkie, "Agency or Inspiration—Which?" in *Speeches of the Year: BYU Devotional Addresses 1972–1973* (Provo, Utah: Brigham Young University Press, 1973), 107, 111.
6. See McConkie, "Agency or Inspiration—Which?" 108, 110, 113.
7. See Matthias F. Cowley, *Wilford Woodruff, History of His Life and Labors* (Salt Lake City: Bookcraft, 1964), 31–32.
8. Joseph Smith, *Teachings of the Prophet Joseph Smith*, comp. Joseph Fielding Smith (Salt Lake City: Deseret Book, 1976), 151.
9. Packer, "Prayers and Answers," *Ensign*, November 1979, 19–20.
10. Joseph Smith, *History of the Church of Jesus Christ of Latter-day Saints*, ed. B. H. Roberts, 2nd ed., rev. (Salt Lake City: Deseret Book, 1957), 1:339.

CHAPTER THREE

THE LORD'S PREFACE
(D&C 1)

ELDER JEFFREY R. HOLLAND

"The births of all things are weak and tender," said Michel de Montaigne, "and therefore we should have our eyes intent on beginnings."[1] In this chapter I wish to draw our attention to the beginning of the Doctrine and Covenants—section 1 specifically—revealed by the Lord as the "preface unto the book of . . . commandments" (D&C 1:6).

In looking at section 1, it is as obvious as it is important to note that this was not the first of the Prophet Joseph's revelations, nor the twentieth, nor the fiftieth. As you well know, it was received at Hiram, Ohio, on November 1, 1831, after more than sixty of the revelations now comprising sections of the Doctrine and Covenants had been received. In sequence it was received *after* what we now call section 66 and *before* section 67.

What was there in this divine instruction that set it apart, that justified its removal from the midsection of the compiled revelations and suggested its insertion as "the beginning" or "the preface" of the modern revelations? Perhaps the answers are obvious, but suffice it to say here that this is, by every standard, a remarkable introduction to a remarkable book, and we enthusiastically endorse Elder John A. Widtsoe's appraisal: "A good preface should prepare the reader for the contents of the book. It should help him understand the book. It should display in a concentrated manner the full contents of the

---

Elder Jeffrey R. Holland is a member of the Quorum of the Twelve Apostles.

book. Section 1 of the Doctrine and Covenants is one of the great prefaces in the possession of mankind."[2]

It is not known just when the Prophet began writing down the major revelations he received, but his personal history indicates that early in 1829 he was regularly doing so and that on April 6, 1830, while in the process of organizing the Church, he received a revelation commanding the Church to keep a record of its activities. Because that counsel is important to what later developed in the Hiram Conference, let me quote:

"Behold, there shall be a record kept among you; and in it thou [Joseph Smith] shalt be called a seer, a translator, a prophet, an Apostle of Jesus Christ, an elder of the church through the will of God the Father, and the grace of your Lord Jesus Christ. . . .

"Wherefore, meaning the church, thou shalt give heed unto all his words and commandments which he shall give unto you as he receiveth them, walking in all holiness before me;

"For his word ye shall receive, as if from mine own mouth, in all patience and faith.

"For by doing these things the gates of hell shall not prevail against you; yea, and the Lord God will disperse the powers of darkness from before you, and cause the heavens to shake for your good, and his name's glory" (D&C 21:1, 4–6).

The language and direction is repeated nearly twenty months later when there was more tension in the air and less inclination to fully accept Joseph's prophesied role. We will refer to this later.

CRITICISM OF THE PROPHET

During 1830 and 1831 the Prophet continued to receive revelations, putting the most important of them into writing. By the fall of 1831 he felt that these, together with earlier recorded revelations, were of sufficient importance to justify publication in book form. With that purpose in mind, Joseph invited the priesthood members to gather at Hiram during the first and second days of November 1831. To that body he then proposed that these sixty or more revelations be accepted as scripture and published under the title Book of Commandments. As a result there was some study of these collected writings made by the group. And, although our information is not fully adequate, the minutes indicate there was some criticism of the language of the revelations by certain members present.

As a revealed preface to the proposed compilation, section 1 was received during the course of these deliberations, and forbearance in the matter of language was encouraged there: "Behold, I am God and have spoken it; these commandments are of me, and were given unto my servants in their weakness, after the manner of their language, that they might come to understanding" (D&C 1:24).

But William E. McLellin was still not satisfied and finally challenged the Prophet openly, charging that Joseph had fabricated some elements of the revelations entirely out of his own mind. In response to that challenge, section 67 was then received:

"And now I, the Lord, give you a testimony of the truth of these commandments which are lying before you.

"Your eyes have been upon my servant Joseph Smith, Jun., and his language you have known, and his imperfections you have known; and you have sought in your hearts knowledge that you might express beyond his language; this you also know.

"Now, seek ye out of the Book of Commandments, even the least that is among them, and appoint him that is the most wise among you;

"Or, if there be any among you that shall make one like unto it, then ye are justified in saying that ye do not know that they are true;

"But if you cannot make one like unto it, ye are under condemnation if ye do not bear record that they are true.

"For ye know that there is no unrighteousness in them, and that which is righteous cometh down from above, from the Father of lights" (D&C 67:4–9).

Here I ask you to remember the commandments and cautions of section 21, given nearly twenty months earlier: light being promised those who support Joseph and the revelations, darkness promised in any denial of them.

Of course, McLellin felt he was equal to the challenge. Only a schoolteacher would have thought himself so well prepared, a sobering reminder to those of us in the Church Educational System. In seclusion, he attempted to write what he thought sounded like a revelation. But he proved to have, in the Prophet Joseph's language, "more learning than sense."[3] After a long night he appeared before the conference participants on November 2 and, with tears in his eyes, begged the forgiveness of the Prophet, of his brethren, and of the Lord. He had been devastatingly unsuccessful, virtually unable to write a word. Such abject failure by one so respected had a profound effect upon the conference. Each priesthood bearer, in his turn, arose and bore testimony concerning God's dealings with the Prophet Joseph and the revelations which had been given. Following these testimonies the conference authorized the publication of the revelations of the Book of Commandments and appointed Oliver Cowdery to go to Independence, Missouri, to supervise their publication.

So the crucial testimony of section 1—regarding the prophetic role and the divinity of the revelatory process—lies not only in its contents, which we will examine, but also in the historical context in which it was received. In that sense what it *is* is as important to the Restoration as what it *says*. In a very real way, the faith of the early brethren and their commitment to these revelations hung in the balance as these sections were being compiled. They simply had to know—or had to come to know—that issues of grammar and usage and phrasing notwithstanding, these revelations were not simply manufactured from a vivid and fruitful imagination. The new church's future was on the line. Or more precisely, the salvation of individual souls was on the line. To them and to us, the Lord's command is simple and unambiguous: "Search these commandments, for they are true and faithful, and the prophecies and promises which are in them shall all be fulfilled. What I the Lord have spoken, I have spoken, and I excuse not myself; and though the heavens and the earth pass away, my word shall not pass away, but shall all be fulfilled, whether by mine own voice or by the voice of my servants, it is the same" (D&C 1:37–38).

This may seem a minor thing to fourth- and fifth-generation Latter-day Saints, but I suspect it was no minor thing to the Prophet Joseph and no minor thing to either the faithful or the skeptical who had to muscle through it and make peace with their own conscience and with the Lord. Indeed we sense a painful poignancy in the Prophet Joseph's phrase written on that day, "It was an awful responsibility to write in the name of the Lord."[4] Surely it was, and now William E. McLellin and the others understood it also. Perhaps here once again we see the Lord's wisdom in choosing virtually an unlettered lad to be the vessel through which He would speak. In light of the educated McLellin's failure, it seemed compellingly clear that neither the Prophet Joseph nor any other man was capable, on his own, of revealing prophecies that come true or of writing revelations that bear the familiar spirit of divinity. Elder Orson F. Whitney once noted that a vain boaster, ridiculing the proverbs of Solomon, had said, "Anybody can make a few proverbs." The reply was simply, "Try a few."

So both in terms of its internal message and the brief but dramatic confrontation out of which it came, section 1 establishes for the rest of the book and the rest of our reading the prophetic role, the divine process, the reality of revelation from the Almighty, and the virtual impossibility of pretense and posing and chicanery. Any man who is only man will be found out soon enough in this business.

THE JOURNEY MOTIF

Now about the revelation itself. Ever since Homer first sent Odysseus off to war and then tried to get him back home again, the suggestion of a journey or a quest or an odyssey is one of the great motifs in the world's literature. But even without that general review, it is perhaps even more obviously true in the world's great religious literature.

One of the great religious poems is Dante's *Divine Comedy,* and those of you who know that poem—and all of us should—know that it is not only a journey but it is in a sense an autobiography of a soul.

The decline and rise of the *Divine Comedy,* intentionally biblical, points toward the Fall and Atonement, death and resurrection, and underscores the familiar doctrine of Christ's "journey." Dante, accompanied by Virgil, begins his descent into hell on the evening of Good Friday. They descend rung by rung into the deepest circles of hell, then emerge on Easter Sunday morning, ready to ascend. Up the steep mountainside, Dante drags himself. On the ledges are other repentant souls preparing themselves by discipline for a heavenly life. As Dante and Virgil are approaching the summit, they are joined by Statius, who has just completed his penitence, and the three mount together to the top, where they find paradise.

Some two and a half centuries later, John Bunyan would use

aspects of this same journey to write the most influential Christian allegory ever penned in the English language, his *Pilgrim's Progress.*

I allude to these nonprophetic, unscriptural writings so that I might focus on what I consider to be a similar but far more literal kind of experience in section 1, received by divine revelation to a living prophet of God. These opening passages are in a very real way, both in themselves and as a symbol for the rest of the Doctrine and Covenants, a *divine comedy.* That does not mean the section is comical. Comedy, after descending, ascends, leading to happiness and peace and fulfillment. Tragedy, on the other hand, after ascending, descends, leading to pain, impediment, and frequently death.

AN OMINOUS BEGINNING

Section 1 is, understandably, more like Deuteronomy than Dante, but the movement of God's people is there, whether in poetry or in the sands of Sinai or on the ragged edge of the Ohio reserve. Israel—and for our purposes, modern Israel—is always on the move. Note the ominous tone of the passages, quite literally the hell into which we are allowed to look and against which we must warn. The section is very grim at the outset and quickly gets grimmer.

"Hearken, O ye people of my church, saith the voice of him who dwells on high, and whose eyes are upon all men; yea, verily I say: Hearken ye people from afar; and ye that are upon the islands of the sea, listen together.

"For verily the voice of the Lord is unto all men, and there is none to escape; and there is no eye that shall not see, neither ear that shall not hear, neither heart that shall not be penetrated.

"And the rebellious shall be pierced with much sorrow; for their iniquities shall be spoken upon the housetops, and their secret acts shall be revealed.

"And the voice of warning shall be unto all people, by the mouths of my disciples, whom I have chosen in these last days.

"And they shall go forth and none shall stay them, for I the Lord have commanded them.

"Behold, this is mine authority, and the authority of my servants, and my preface unto the book of my commandments, which I have given them to publish unto you, O inhabitants of the earth.

"Wherefore, fear and tremble, O ye people, for what I the Lord have decreed in them shall be fulfilled.

"And verily I say unto you, that they who go forth, bearing these tidings unto the inhabitants of the earth, to them is power given to seal both on earth and in heaven, the unbelieving and rebellious;

"Yea, verily, to seal them up unto the day when the wrath of God shall be poured out upon the wicked without measure—

"Unto the day when the Lord shall come to recompense unto every man according to his work, and measure to every man according to the measure which he has measured to his fellow man.

"Wherefore the voice of the Lord is unto the ends of the earth, that all that will hear may hear:

"Prepare ye, prepare ye for that which is to come, for the Lord is nigh;

"And the anger of the Lord is kindled, and his sword is bathed in heaven, and it shall fall upon the inhabitants of the earth.

"And the arm of the Lord shall be revealed; and the day cometh that they who will not hear the voice of the Lord, neither the voice of his servants, neither give heed to the words of the prophets and apostles, shall be cut off from among the people" (D&C 1:1–14).

It is obvious after these first fourteen verses that we are in *big* trouble. We have descended, as it were, to a frightful moment in time where the arm of the Lord is revealed, His anger kindled, His sword bathed in heaven with an imminent fall upon the inhabitants of the earth. It will fall *at least* (William E. McLellin, take note) upon those "who will not hear the voice of the Lord, neither the voice of his servants, neither give heed to the words of the prophets and apostles." *These* shall be "cut off from among [my] people" (D&C 1:14). Obviously the sword of heaven was hanging not only over the world but also over the little gathering at the Hiram conference. Remember the opening of section 1, "O ye people of my church."

DESCENT INTO IDOLATRY

But back to the hellish descent. It is here we see the ultimate transgression of our times, the sin of our dispensation, indeed the cardinal sin of every dispensation. In verses 15 and 16 we come to bedrock, to the final circle where people, including those in the Church, can descend if they are not faithful in every way to the revelations of

God. The Lord says, "They have strayed from mine ordinances, and have broken mine everlasting covenant; they seek not the Lord to establish his righteousness, but every man walketh in his own way, and after the image of his own God, whose image is in the likeness of the world, and whose substance is that of an idol, which waxeth old and shall perish in Babylon, even Babylon the great, which shall fall" (D&C 1:15–16). Babylon is, of course, the figurative symbol of decadent life in the scriptures, all that is unworthy in this world. And it is Babylon to which we have descended in verse 16. Amidst great sin and sinners, we find the greatest sin of all: unfaithfulness and disobedience in its most flagrant form—idolatry.

Of the ten great commandments given on Sinai, the first, the foremost, the ever abiding one, is "Thou shalt have no other gods before me"; and, in case we did not understand, "Thou shalt not make unto thee any graven image" (Exodus 20:3, 4). With only ten laws to get on twin tablets, Jehovah consumes two-tenths, one-fifth, 20 percent of that precious space by establishing two commandments which if not understood and obeyed will render every other commandment in time or eternity useless. As important as honoring our parents and keeping the Sabbath day holy and being honest and remaining chaste and preserving life are, none will have the saving, sanctifying power they must have if we do not first understand that God is our Father, that we are His children, that there must be no other loyalty in this world great enough to turn us away from Him.

And yet that was the disloyalty of a world entering the nineteenth century. Furthermore, the world seems clearly more unfaithful today. As a people we have strayed from the ordinances and broken the covenants and are *not* seeking the Lord to establish His righteousness. We are indeed walking in our own way, after the image of our own gods, whose images are in the likeness of the world and whose substance *is* that of an idol. The flame and the finger of Sinai point accusingly at our time. You will remember this editorial from President Spencer W. Kimball:

"The Brethren constantly cry out against that which is intolerable in the sight of the Lord: against pollution of mind, body, and our surroundings; against vulgarity, stealing, lying, pride, and blasphemy; against fornication, adultery, homosexuality, and all other abuses of the sacred power to create; against murder and all that is like unto it; against all manner of desecration.

"That such a cry should be necessary among a people so blessed is amazing to me. And that such things should be found even among the Saints to some degree is scarcely believable, for these are a people who are in possession of many gifts of the Spirit, who have knowledge that puts the eternities into perspective, who have been shown the way to eternal life.

"Sadly, however, we find that to be shown the way is not necessarily to walk in it, and many have not been able to continue in faith. These have submitted themselves in one degree or another to the enticings of Satan and his servants and joined with those of 'the world' in lives of ever-deepening idolatry.

"I use the word *idolatry* intentionally. As I study ancient scripture, I am more and more convinced that there is significance in the fact that the commandment 'Thou shalt have no other gods before me' is the first of the Ten Commandments.

"Few men have ever knowingly and deliberately chosen to reject God and his blessings. Rather, we learn from the scriptures that because the exercise of faith has always appeared to be more difficult than relying on things more immediately at hand, carnal man has tended to transfer his trust in God to material things. Therefore, in all ages when men have fallen under the power of Satan and lost the faith, they have put in its place a hope in the 'arm of flesh' and in 'gods of silver, and gold, of brass, iron, wood, and stone, which see not, nor hear, nor know' (Dan. 5:23)—that is, in idols. This I find to be a dominant theme in the Old Testament. Whatever thing a man sets his heart and his trust in most is his god; and if his god doesn't also happen to be the true and living God of Israel, that man is laboring in idolatry. . . .

"In spite of our delight in defining ourselves as modern, and our tendency to think we possess a sophistication that no people in the past ever had—in spite of these things, we are, on the whole, an idolatrous people—a condition most repugnant to the Lord."[5]

Men are, as Oliver Wendell Holmes once said, idolaters at heart, and if we are not conscious of and do not guard against the tendency towards this most grievous sin, as this great preface to the Doctrine and Covenants indicates, then we will not benefit from any of the counsel that follows in any other section or any other book. There simply will not be ordinances or revelations or teachings enough to save our souls if we have failed to abide by that first and great commandment: "Thou shalt love the Lord thy God with all thy heart, and with all thy soul, and with all thy might" (Deuteronomy 6:5). This unyielding fact seems central to the message of the Lord's preface.

These verses (D&C 1:15–16), this rock-bottom confrontation with our sins in a world facing the flames of hell and fearing a sword bathed in heaven, are the turning point of the revelation. They are also a turning point for everyone who takes the journey. If we wish to respond, if we wish to do something about our lives and the future of the world and the meaning of this dispensation, then verse 17 surely comes as water to the tongue of the tormented. I quote: "Wherefore, I the Lord, knowing the calamity which should come upon the inhabitants of the earth, called upon my servant Joseph Smith, Jun., and spake unto him from heaven, and gave him commandments" (D&C 1:17).

Ascension from Babylon

There is the moment of truth for an entire dispensation. Was Joseph what he said he was? Are these revelations what they claim to be? Is this the way of the Master? This verse marks the moment in this "story" where, if we will, we may begin to ascend out of the circles of hell, out of the bonds of Babylon. Our Father, the God of heaven and earth, knowing the calamities in which this world has so consistently entangled itself, once again spoke to a prophet and gave him commandments. There and there only—in those revelations regarding the principles and ordinances of the gospel of Jesus Christ—lies our safety. That is the Latter-day Saint message to a sinful and idolatrous world.

Once again it is noted that such a prophetic voice may be human and immediate and living just next door or on the neighboring farm. He may even use less-than-perfect language, but that is because "the weak things of the world shall come forth and break down the mighty and strong ones" (D&C 1:19). And so the Prophet Joseph and his successors have proceeded to do, "that every man might speak in the name of God . . . ; that faith also might increase in the earth; that mine everlasting covenant might be established; that the fulness of my gospel might be proclaimed by the *weak* and the *simple* unto the ends of the world, and before kings and rulers" (D&C 1:20–23; emphasis added). With that kind of accelerated step, we see the ascension up the mountain toward the "promised land," and that is indeed the object and promise of the gospel of Jesus Christ. Section 1 reassures us that these revelations will correct those who have been in error. They will instruct those who have honestly sought wisdom. They will chasten the sinful onto the redeeming road of repentance. And all along the way those who are humble will be made strong and receive knowledge from time to time from on high. Thus with this increasing progress, up out of the long night of apostasy and error in which this world had lived, power comes forward to lay the foundation of the Church, and to bring it out of obscurity and out of darkness.

In all of this the Lord cannot look upon sin with the least degree of allowance, but as the Prophet Joseph said, "When men have sinned there must be allowance made for them,"[6] if not necessarily for their transgression. The promises are to all: "I the Lord am willing to make these things known unto all flesh; for I am no respecter of persons, and will that all men shall know that the day speedily cometh . . . when . . . the Lord shall have power over his saints, and shall reign in their midst, and shall come down in judgment upon Idumea, or the world" (D&C 1:34–36). And then, closing the circle where we began: "Search these commandments, for they are true and faithful, and the prophecies and promises which are in them shall all be fulfilled. What I the Lord have spoken, I have spoken, and I excuse not myself; and though the heavens and the earth pass away, my word shall not pass away, but shall all be fulfilled, whether by mine own voice or by the voice of my servants, it is the same. For behold, and lo, the Lord is God, and the Spirit beareth record, and the record is true, and the truth abideth forever and ever" (D&C 1:37–39).

Whatever else it is, the book of Doctrine and Covenants is a revelatory document, revelations abounding, a promise of prophetic utterance. These communications are delivered through the Urim and Thummim, by open vision, through the still, small voice, by audible voice, through translated scripture, by angels, through dedicatory prayers, by letters, by items of instruction, by declarations of belief through historical items, by priesthood ordinations, by answers to scriptural questions, by prophecies, in minutes of meetings, and on, and on, and on to impress in bold relief that undergirding and inevitable and absolutely essential principle of revelation to the gospel of Jesus Christ in its fullest dispensation. And why are these revelations given? To tear down the graven images of our time, to reenthrone God as Father to His children, to reestablish those covenants linking heaven and earth which the prince of darkness beneath the earth would have us mutilate. In the language of the Doctrine and Covenants itself, the revelations are given so "that you may understand and know how to worship, and know what you worship, that you may come unto the Father in my name, and in due time receive of his fulness" (D&C 93:19), *to know how to worship and what we worship so that we might come unto Him and receive of His fulness.* To that end the dispensation and its doctrines and these compilations are dedicated. To that end the preface, the first section, is committed. Surely it is one of the great prefaces in the possession of mankind. This is my prayer: that such a successful journey through the rest of the revelations might be our happy lot, that we might individually and collectively turn ourselves and our world away from Babylon and ascend the mountain of the Most High, and that we might enjoy His presence in righteous living.

NOTES

1. Montaigne, "Of Managing the Will," *Essays*, trans. Charles Cotton, ed. William Carew Hazlitt (London: Reeves & Turner, 1877).
2. John A. Widtsoe, *The Message of the Doctrine and Covenants*, ed. G. Homer Durham (Salt Lake City: Bookcraft, 1969), 11–12.
3. Joseph Smith, *History of the Church of Jesus Christ of Latter-day Saints*, ed. B. H. Roberts, 2nd ed., rev. (London: Latter-day Saints' Book Depot, 1957), 1:226.
4. Smith, *History of the Church*, 1:226.
5. Spencer W. Kimball, "The False Gods We Worship," *Ensign*, June 1976, 4, 6.
6. Smith, *History of the Church*, 5:24.

CHAPTER FOUR

"THIS GENERATION SHALL HAVE MY WORD THROUGH YOU"

ELDER BRUCE R. McCONKIE

In 1829 the Lord gave information of unsurpassed importance to the people of our time when He said to Joseph Smith, His latter-day seer, "This generation shall have my word through you" (D&C 5:10).

It is my desire to show that this statement truly describes conditions as they are. It is also my desire to describe these conditions in a manner that bears testimony of the great work of the Prophet Joseph Smith in restoring the gospel of our Savior and Master, the Lord Jesus Christ.

"This generation shall have my word through you." The word is the gospel of salvation; the word is the plan of salvation; the word is the mind and will and purposes of the Lord as pertaining to His children on earth; the word is all the truths and rights and powers and doctrines and principles that are needed by men so they can take the souls they possess and transform them into the kind of souls that can go where God and Christ are.

And the generation of which we speak is this era or period of time. It is the dispensation in which we live; it is the time from the opening of our dispensation down to the second coming of the Son of Man; and for that allotted period of the earth's history, the word of the Lord, the word of salvation, the word of light and truth are going

---

Elder Bruce R. McConkie (1915–85) was a member of the Quorum of the Twelve Apostles.

to the world through Joseph Smith, and in no other way and through no one else.

THE WORD AND THE DISPENSATION

Some background is essential to our understanding of what is involved. We all know that salvation is in Christ. He is the Firstborn of the Father. He was like unto God in the premortal life, and He became, under the Father, the Creator of all things. We look to Him; our faith centers in Him, and in the Father through Him.

Second to Christ stands that great spirit person Michael, who led the armies and hosts of heaven when there was war and rebellion in heaven, and who, being foreordained so to do, came here as the first man of all men and became the presiding high priest over the earth. The next person in this hierarchy is Gabriel, who came into this life as Noah. After that, we do not know the order of priority, except that singled out from among the hosts of heaven were certain men who were foreordained to be the heads of dispensations.

Dispensations are those periods of time when the plan of salvation, the word—the eternal word—is dispensed to men on earth. How many there have been we do not know. I suppose there have been ten; maybe there have been twenty; there could have been more. I am speaking now not of what sometimes are called dispensations in the sense that John the Baptist and Paul and some of the other prophets had special appointments. I am speaking of those great eras or periods, of those designated portions of the earth's history, when the Lord, through one man, gives His word to the whole world and makes all the prophets, and all the seers, and all the administrators, and all the Apostles of that period subject to, and exponents of, what came through that individual. What this means is that the head of a gospel dispensation stands as one of the ten or twenty greatest spirits who have so far been born on earth.

We know very little about the caliber of men who will be born during the Millennium. Many great spirits will come then. It seems reasonable to suppose, however, that the Lord has singled out certain ones who had special spiritual talents and capabilities to come to earth in periods of turmoil and wickedness and rebellion and evil, to be lights and guides to the world. This gives us a little perspective of what is involved in the life and in the status and position of Joseph Smith.

You start out with the Lord Jesus, and then you have Adam and Noah. Thereafter come the dispensation heads. Then you come to the prophets, to Apostles, to the elders of Israel, and to wise and good and sagacious men who have the spirit of light and understanding. Every dispensation head is a revealer of Christ for his day; every prophet is a witness of Christ; and every other prophet or Apostle who comes is a reflection and an echo and an exponent of the dispensation head. All such come to echo to the world and to expound and unfold what God has revealed through the man who was appointed to give His eternal word to the world for that era. Such is the dispensation concept.

THE WORD COMING THROUGH JOSEPH SMITH

We come now to our dispensation. We shall not deal in minutia. We are not concerned with small or insignificant things. We need to get under this head an overall concept of what is involved in giving the word to the world through a particular prophet.

Joseph Smith gave three great truths to the world. These truths override all others; they take precedence over all things; they have more of an influence on the salvation of men than any others, and without the knowledge of them, men cannot be saved. The first great truth is that God, our Heavenly Father, is the Creator, Upholder, and Preserver of all things and that He ordained and established the plan of salvation. It is His gospel, "the gospel of God, . . . concerning his Son Jesus Christ our Lord, which was made of the seed of David according to the flesh," as Paul expressed it (Romans 1:1, 3).

As we look for the word, both in the Doctrine and Covenants and elsewhere, the first thing we look for is the knowledge of God as it was revealed through Joseph Smith. Knowledge of God is the greatest truth in all eternity. But there must needs be an opposition in all things, and the opposite of the knowledge of God that has come through Joseph Smith is the greatest heresy in the sectarian world. That heresy is that God is a spirit nothingness that fills the immensity of space, and that creation came through evolutionary processes. In truth and in fact, Joseph Smith came to reveal God, in a day of almost total spiritual darkness, in a day when men no longer knew the nature and kind of Being whom they should worship.

The second great truth is that Jesus Christ is the Savior and Redeemer of the world, that salvation comes through His atoning sacrifice, and that the Atonement is the foundation whereon we can build so that by obedience to the laws and ordinances of the everlasting gospel we can be saved. That is the number-two truth in all eternity. There is nothing more important to us—having first discovered who God our Father is—than to know about Christ and the salvation that is in Him. The heresy and perversion of this truth is the common sectarian concept that people are saved by grace alone, without works.

The third most important thing in all eternity is a knowledge of God the Testator, who is the Holy Ghost. The Holy Spirit of God is a revealer who reveals truth; He is a sanctifier who cleanses and perfects human souls; and it is through Him that the gifts of the Spirit are available to the faithful, so that they can have in their lives what Apostles and prophets and great men of all ages have had in theirs. The heresy that exists in the sectarian world in this field is that the heavens are sealed, that there is no revelation, that there are no miracles, and that there are no gifts of the Spirit. These three great truths are what we look for with reference to the word coming through the Prophet Joseph Smith.

Now, just a word or two from our revelations relative to Joseph Smith's prophetic position: "I the Lord, knowing the calamity which should come upon the inhabitants of the earth, called upon my servant Joseph Smith, Jun., and spake unto him from heaven, and gave him commandments" (D&C 1:17). Such is the revealed statement in the Lord's preface to His book of commandments.

In section 21 we read this: "Behold, there shall be a record kept among you; and in it thou shalt be called a seer, a translator, a prophet, an apostle of Jesus Christ, an elder of the church through the will of God the Father, and the grace of your Lord Jesus Christ, being inspired of the Holy Ghost to lay the foundation thereof, and to build it up unto the most holy faith. . . . Wherefore, meaning the church, thou shalt give heed unto all his words and commandments which he shall give unto you as he receiveth them, walking in all holiness before me" (D&C 21:1–2, 4).

Then comes this proclamation, which in the full sense of the word applies more completely to a dispensation head: "For his word ye shall receive, as if from mine own mouth, in all patience and faith" (D&C 21:5). When Joseph Smith spoke by the power of the Holy Ghost, it was as though the Lord Jesus Himself was saying the words. The Prophet's voice was the voice of the Lord; he was not perfect; only Christ was free from sin and evil. But the Prophet was as near perfection as mortals can get without being translated. He was a man of such spiritual stature that he reflected the image of the Lord Jesus to the people. His voice was the voice of the Lord.

"For by doing these things"—that is, by giving heed to the words of Joseph Smith as though Jesus Himself had spoken them—"the gates of hell shall not prevail against you; yea, and the Lord God will disperse the powers of darkness from before you, and cause the heavens to shake for your good, and his name's glory" (D&C 21:6). In some measure, we have seen a fulfillment of this in the explosive, dynamic, progressive enlargement of the Church in our day. "For thus saith the Lord God: Him have I inspired to move the cause of Zion in mighty power for good, and his diligence I know, and his prayers I have heard. Yea, his weeping for Zion I have seen, and I will cause that he shall mourn for her no longer; for his days of rejoicing are come unto the remission of his sins, and the manifestations of my blessings upon his works" (D&C 21:7–8).

There is one more verse we should note particularly; we can take it as a test to measure personal discipleship: "For, behold, I will bless all those who labor in my vineyard with a mighty blessing"—this applies to all of us—"and they shall believe on his words [those of Joseph Smith], which are given him through me by the Comforter, which manifesteth that Jesus was crucified by sinful men for the sins of the word, yea, for the remission of sins unto the contrite heart" (D&C 21:9). The test of discipleship is how totally and completely and fully we believe the word that was revealed through Joseph Smith, and how effectively we echo or proclaim that word to the world.

WHERE THE WORD IS FOUND

The word is found in the visions and revelations and inspired utterances of Joseph Smith. Many of these are recorded in the *History*

of the Church. The account of the First Vision is also in the Pearl of
Great Price. The Wentworth letter is the equal and equivalent of what
is already in the Pearl of Great Price; it is scripture, except that we
have not presented it to the Church and bound ourselves to accept
it and proclaim it to the world. There are many things of equal validity, truth, and literary excellence to those that have formally been
placed in our scriptural accounts.

This is the statement the Prophet made when he and his associates formally adopted what we now call the Doctrine and Covenants:
"After deliberate consideration, in consequence of the book of revelations, now to be printed, being the foundation of the Church in
these last days, and a benefit to the world, showing that the keys of
the mysteries of the kingdom of our Savior are again entrusted to
man; and the riches of eternity within the compass of those who are
willing to live by every word that proceedeth out of the mouth of
God—therefore the conference voted that they prize the revelations
to be worth to the Church the riches of the whole earth, speaking
temporally."[1] Such is our vision and view of the Doctrine and
Covenants.

The word given through Joseph Smith is also found in the records
he translated. The chief of these is the Book of Mormon. This book
is a new witness for Christ; it is comparable to the Holy Bible; it is a
record of God's dealings with people in the Old World. Of the Book
of Mormon, Joseph Smith said, "I told the brethren," referring to a
discussion with the Quorum of the Twelve, "that the Book of
Mormon was the most correct of any book on earth, and the keystone of our religion, and a man would get nearer to God by abiding
by its precepts, than by any other book."[2] The Book of Mormon contains that portion of the Lord's word which is needed to prove the
divinity of His great latter-day work, and which is needed to teach
the basic doctrines of salvation to mankind generally. It is the basic,
fundamental, standard work of the latter days.

Some of the other translations made by the Prophet are found in
the Pearl of Great Price. He translated the book of Abraham and what
is called the Joseph Smith Translation of the Bible. This latter is a mar-
velously inspired work; it is one of the great evidences of the divine
mission of the Prophet. By pure revelation, he inserted many new
concepts and views, such as the material in the fourteenth chapter of

Genesis about Melchizedek. Some chapters he rewrote and realigned so that the things said in them take on a new perspective and meaning, such as the twenty-fourth chapter of Matthew and the first chapter in the gospel of John.

Another source of the Prophet's material is his sermons and his teachings. We have what is in the standard works, but there is something more—that which he spoke and which was then recorded. When the Lord revealed what we should teach, He said in that revelation known as the law of the Church (D&C 42): "The elders, priests and teachers of this church," and all other officers, "shall teach the principles of my gospel, which are in the Bible and the Book of Mormon, in the which is the fulness of the gospel" (D&C 42:12). They did not then have our other scriptures. "And they shall observe the covenants and church articles to do them, and these shall be their teachings, as they shall be directed by the Spirit" (D&C 42:13). So our obligation is to teach out of the standard works by the power of the Holy Ghost. "And the Spirit shall be given unto you by the prayer of faith; and if ye receive not the Spirit ye shall not teach. And all this ye shall observe to do as I have commanded concerning your teaching, until the fulness of my scriptures is given" (D&C 42:14–15).

We have more now, though we do not have that fulness which one day shall be ours. "And as ye shall lift up your voices by the Comforter, ye shall speak and prophesy as seemeth me good; for, behold, the Comforter knoweth all things, and beareth record of the Father and of the Son" (D&C 42:16–17).

Now, as I said, we are to do more than teach out of the standard works. The Lord's servants are to go forth "preaching the word, . . . saying none other things than that which the prophets and apostles have written, *and that which is taught them by the Comforter through the prayer of faith*" (D&C 52:9; emphasis added).

Joseph Smith had, as no other man in our dispensation, the ability to be in tune with the Comforter and to speak forth things that were the mind and voice of the Lord, including things that are not in the standard works. I suppose that most notable of all that he did in this respect was the King Follett sermon, said to be the greatest sermon of his entire ministry. I suppose there is not anything that surpasses the sermon he gave on the Second Comforter. It was as though God spoke when the Prophet spoke.

Those things that have come through the revelations and sermons of others of the brethren who have lived since Joseph Smith, as, for instance, the vision of the redemption of the dead that President Joseph F. Smith received, or what any inspired person in the Church says, these things are a reflection, an explanation, an amplification of what originated with the Prophet Joseph Smith.

THE WORD AND THE DOCTRINE AND COVENANTS

The Doctrine and Covenants presents the word in a variety of ways. There are appearances of holy beings. The Lord Himself came, as is recorded in section 110. The first part of section 27 was recited by an angel who met the Prophet and gave the instructions to him. The word came by the voice of God, as in the revelation that is now section 137 in the Doctrine and Covenants (the vision of Alvin in the celestial kingdom). The word came by visions, as in section 76. The word came by the power of the Holy Ghost, primarily. Most of the revelations came in that way.

If the Holy Ghost rests upon a person, that person speaks what the Lord would speak and that person's voice becomes the voice of the Lord. Notice this verse of scripture: "In that day the Holy Ghost fell upon Adam, which beareth record of the Father and the Son, saying"—now notice who is speaking and notice the message given by the Holy Ghost—"I am the Only Begotten of the Father from the beginning, henceforth and forever, that as thou hast fallen thou mayest be redeemed, and all mankind, even as many as will" (Moses 5:9). The Holy Ghost speaks in the first person as though He were the Son of God, dramatizing the fact that when we speak by the power of the Holy Ghost, the words spoken are the words of Christ. We are familiar with Nephi's expression that angels speak by the power of the Holy Ghost, and hence they speak the words of Christ (see 2 Nephi 32:3). Prophets who speak by the power of the Holy Ghost speak the word of Christ. Every elder in the Church, as he is moved upon by the Holy Ghost, gives forth words that are scripture and they are just as true and just as binding in their central truthful import as any words ever uttered by any prophet. We may not segregate them out, and vote on them, and decide that we, formally and officially, will be bound by them in our conduct. But they are scripture, and they are the voice and word of the Lord. This is what is involved in the sermons of the Prophet. The Father and the Son and the Holy Ghost are one; no matter which one of them says something, it is always the same word. If a man says by inspiration what they would have said, it is scripture.

Some of the revelations came by spiritual confirmation, meaning that the Prophet worked out the problem in his mind, using his agency as he was obligated to do, and then took the matter to the Lord and got a spiritual confirmation that his conclusions were right. He then wrote them down, in the name of the Lord, and we publish them as revelation.

There are also some epistles, such as sections 127 and 128; there are some inspired writings, such as sections 121, 122, and 123; and there are some items of instruction, such as section 131.

HOW TO KNOW IT IS THE WORD OF GOD

This statement is taken from the testimony of the Twelve, given on the occasion of the formal adoption of the revelations: "We, therefore, feel willing to bear testimony to all the world of mankind, to every creature upon the face of all the earth, that the Lord has borne record to our souls, through the Holy Ghost shed forth upon us, that these commandments were given by inspiration of God, and are profitable for all men and are verily true" (Introduction to the Doctrine and Covenants).

Now, there is not any way in heaven or on earth for anyone to know of the truth and validity of a revelation except to have the same Spirit rest upon him that rested upon the revelator who received it. We are dealing with the things of the Spirit. We cannot weigh and evaluate and judge and handle them in a laboratory, unless we are speaking of a spiritual laboratory. There is no private interpretation to scripture. The scripture "came not in old time by the will of man: but holy men of God spake as they were moved by the Holy Ghost" (2 Peter 1:21). And so when the Twelve bear record, as here we read, that the revelations in the Doctrine and Covenants are true, that means that the Holy Spirit of God had spoken to the spirit within each individual, and to all of them collectively, and certified that the revelations received by Joseph Smith were true. There is no other way to know of the truth and divinity of a spiritual thing than by receiving a spiritual revelation.

The Word Yet to Come

We have not received, by any means, all of the word of the Lord. I think we have received most of the word of the Lord that is required until the Second Coming. The Lord has given all that people in the world have the spiritual capacity to receive at this time. There is going to be another great dispensation—that is, another great period of enlightenment—when He comes. At that time He will reveal all things, such as the sealed portion of the Book of Mormon. But He will not reveal the sealed portion of the Book of Mormon now, or let us publish it to the world because what it contains is so far beyond the spiritual capacity of men that it would drive people away from the truth rather than lead them to the truth. Actually, it is an act of mercy for the Lord to limit, to a particular people, the amount of revelation they receive.

We are now in a glorious dispensation in which we have received substantially all of the revelations we are able to bear; it is true, however, that if we were able to unite and have faith, we would get more. That is one of the things that was involved in 1978 when President Kimball received the revelation that the gospel and all of its blessings (the priesthood and the ordinances of the house of the Lord) were now to go to those of every race and kindred and tongue without any reservation except that people live in righteousness and be worthy to receive what is offered to them. That new revelation came in large measure because the prophet of God and those associated with him united in faith and in prayer and in desire, and sought for an answer from the Lord. There are added revelations we could receive, and I hope we will receive, as we manage to get in tune with the Spirit. But the great reservoir of revelation for our dispensation—meaning the things that we need to know to govern our conduct in order to gain an eternal life—these things have already been given. And there will not be great added reservoirs of substantive revelation that will come before the Second Coming because of the wickedness of the world. Some of that wickedness spills over and prevails among the Latter-day Saints. But eventually, there will be a day of great added revelation.

The Reaffirmation of the Word in Our Hearts

This reaffirmation is what brings this subject down to us as individuals. Every man is supposed to be a prophet for himself. Every head of a house should be the revelator for his family. Joseph Smith said these glorious words as he talked about the Second Comforter: "God hath not revealed anything to Joseph, but what He will make known unto the Twelve, and even the least Saint may know all things as fast as he is able to bear them."³ The initial verses in section 76 announce this glorious concept: "Thus saith the Lord—I, the Lord, am merciful and gracious unto those who fear me, and delight to honor those who serve me in righteousness and in truth unto the end" (D&C 76:5).

We are not talking now about Apostles and prophets alone; we are talking about the whole body of faithful members: "Great shall be their reward and eternal shall be their glory.

"And to them will I reveal all mysteries, yea, all the hidden mysteries of my kingdom from days of old, and for ages to come, will I make known unto them the good pleasure of my will concerning all things pertaining to my kingdom.

"Yea, even the wonders of eternity shall they know, and things to come will I show them, even the things of many generations.

"And their wisdom shall be great, and their understanding reach to heaven; and before them the wisdom of the wise shall perish, and the understanding of the prudent shall come to naught.

"For by my Spirit will I enlighten them, and by my power will I make known unto them the secrets of my will—yea, even those things which eye has not seen, nor ear heard, nor yet entered into the heart of man" (D&C 76:6–10).

Those words introduce the vision that the Prophet and Sidney Rigdon received of three degrees of glory. When the vision had been duly recorded, and while the Spirit still rested upon them, by way of conclusion and summary the Prophet wrote: "But great and marvelous are the works of the Lord, and the mysteries of his kingdom which he showed unto us, which surpass all understanding in glory, and in might, and in dominion" (D&C 76:114).

Such things could not be written. They cannot be written because they can only be understood and felt. They do not come through the intellect. They come through the power of the Spirit. They are things "which he commanded us we should not write while we were yet in the Spirit, and are not lawful for man to utter;

"Neither is man capable to make them known, for they are only to be seen and understood by the power of the Holy Spirit, which God bestows on those who love him, and purify themselves before him;

"To whom he grants this privilege of seeing and knowing for themselves;

"That through the power and manifestation of the Spirit, while in the flesh, they may be able to bear his presence in the world of glory.

"And to God and the Lamb be glory, and honor, and dominion forever and ever" (D&C 76:115–19).

The reaffirmation of the word through us is such a glorious thing that we do not have words to express it. We cannot explain the wonder and the marvel of living in a day when God has sent a revealer to speak His word to the whole world, and when He sent supplemental prophets to echo the message and proclaim the truth and get as much into the hearts of men as they are able to receive.

"This generation shall have my word through you" (D&C 5:10). Joseph Smith has given the word, and we echo the message, and a great part of the message is that every one of us—equally precious—has power to get in tune with the Holy Spirit and learn personally what the prophet receives. There is going to be a day—it is millennial, the ancient prophets (Jeremiah, for one) foretold it—"when no man need say to his neighbor, Know ye the Lord; for all shall know Him . . . from the least to the greatest."[4] The Prophet Joseph Smith said that this promise has reference to personal revelation, to a visitation of the Lord to an individual.[5] It is within our capability, if we adhere as we ought to the standards of righteousness that we have received, to have a total, complete reaffirmation of the word to us, the word the Lord gave first through Joseph Smith. We begin to get that reaffirmation when we get in our hearts the spirit of testimony, and the Holy Spirit of God tells us the work is true.

What I am saying is that the ultimate end of spiritual progression is not only to know that the revelations are true, but also to see visions and feel the Spirit and get the added light and knowledge which it is not lawful to utter and which was not recorded in the revealed record. What a glorious dispensation we live in. We live in a day when the Lord desires to confirm His word in the hearts of all who will heed His voice, and it is our privilege so to obtain.

The most glorious thing about this whole system of revealed religion that we have received is that the word is true. You cannot think of anything in connection with our whole system of revealed religion that in any way compares in importance to the simple fact that it is true. And because it is true, it works. Because it is true, we will triumph. Because it is true, if we do what we already know we ought to do, we shall have peace and joy and happiness in this life and be inheritors of eternal life in our Father's kingdom hereafter. God grant that it may be so for all of us.

NOTES

1. Joseph Smith, *History of the Church of Jesus Christ of Latter-day Saints*, ed., B. H. Roberts, 2nd ed., rev. (Salt Lake City: Deseret Book, 1957), 1:235.
2. Joseph Smith, *Teachings of the Prophet Joseph Smith*, comp. Joseph Fielding Smith (Salt Lake City: Deseret Book, 1976), 194.
3. Smith, *History of the Church*, 3:380.
4. Smith, *History of the Church*, 3:380.
5. See Smith, *History of the Church*, 3:381.

CHAPTER FIVE

FAYETTE: THE PLACE THE CHURCH WAS ORGANIZED

ELDER JOHN K. CARMACK

The first verse of Doctrine and Covenants 20 announces "the rise of the Church of Christ in these last days, being one thousand eight hundred and thirty years since the coming of our Lord and Savior Jesus Christ in the flesh, *it being regularly organized and established agreeable to the laws of our country* . . . in the fourth month, and on the sixth day of the month which is called April" (emphasis added).[1]

The headnote to the next section, Doctrine and Covenants 21, declares that the Church was in fact organized on April 6, 1830, at Fayette, New York, "in the home of Peter Whitmer, Sen." (D&C 21).

It is clear that the Prophet Joseph Smith felt that the event was highly significant, that he and his brethren were complying with directives given by the Lord. It is also clear that the Prophet Joseph felt he was complying with laws decreed by government for organizing a church. At the time, however, some members did not fully appreciate the significance of the occasion. Even one of Joseph's colleagues in the organizational event, David Whitmer, downplayed the events of April 6, 1830. Writing many years later in his booklet, *An Address to All Believers in Christ,* he commented, "It is all a mistake about the church being organized on April 6, 1830, as I will show. We were as fully organized—spiritually—before April 6th as we were on that day. The reason why we met on that day was this; the world had been telling us that we were not a regularly organized church, and we had no right to officiate in the ordinance of marriage, hold

---

Elder John K. Carmack is an emeritus member of the First Quorum of the Seventy.

church property, etc., and that we should organize according to the laws of the land."[2]

David Whitmer was not alone in missing the significance of that meeting in Fayette. Others even became confused about the place the Church was organized. *The Evening and the Morning Star*[3] and Orson Pratt's pamphlet *Interesting Account of Several Remarkable Visions, and of the Late Discovery of Ancient American Records*[4] both suggest Manchester, New York, as the place the Church was organized.

Because of these and similarly confusing statements, I have examined the pertinent historical documents in their context in an effort to confirm the time and place of the Church's legal organization. I have firmly concluded that there is no reason to doubt that the Church was organized in Fayette, New York, on April 6, 1830, in accordance with divine directive and existing governmental laws.

RELATED NEW YORK STATUTES

We return, then, to the statement in Doctrine and Covenants 20 that the Church was "regularly organized and established agreeable to the laws of our country" (D&C 20:1).

To what laws does the statement refer? By 1830, the United States Constitution had been ratified and its first amendment was in force, protecting the freedom of religion. The specific laws under which the Church was incorporated, however, seem to have been the laws of New York State. By 1784 the state of New York had enacted a procedure for incorporating religious societies. This statute was updated in 1813[5] and was in effect on April 6, 1830.

Although the law did not require a group of worshipers to incorporate to exist as a church, certain legal privileges, such as the right to acquire and hold property and perform marriages, would flow from the act of incorporation. In summary, the statute required a church or congregation to elect from three to nine trustees to take charge of church property and transact business affairs. Two elders of the congregation were to be selected to preside over the election. Fifteen days' notice, given for two successive Sabbaths, was required. A certificate establishing a name for the church and evidencing completion of the organizational events was to be recorded in the county or counties where the church was located.[6]

What Steps Were Taken to Comply?

Joseph Smith, Oliver Cowdery, and their fellow disciples kept no known records that detail how they complied with the New York law. But the documents we do have make it clear that the Prophet and his colleagues did take steps to comply with the law.

The first known recorded instructions from the Lord to Joseph Smith to organize the Church came as early as June of 1829.[7] Less than a year later, on a date set by revelation, the Church was incorporated. In *History of the Church,* the Prophet Joseph Smith wrote, "Whilst the Book of Mormon was in the hands of the printer, we . . . made known to our brethren that we had received a commandment to organize the church; and accordingly we met together for that purpose, at the house of Mr. Peter Whitmer, Sen., (being six in number,) on Tuesday, the sixth day of April, A.D., one thousand eight hundred and thirty."[8]

From what we read, the number of organizers was clearly within the statutory requirement of three to nine persons. Another requirement was met during the meeting when Joseph asked for a vote to name himself and Oliver as the presiding elders of the Church. This would have satisfied the requirement in the New York statute requiring two presiding elders at the incorporation proceedings.

The Prophet next asked for a vote on the central proposition that a church be organized. The vote was unanimous. Then he ordained Oliver to be an elder of the Church, and Oliver in turn ordained Joseph.

There was a rich outpouring of the Holy Ghost on the occasion, and new revelation was received. During the day, other brethren were called and ordained to offices of the priesthood. The account concludes: "We dismissed with the pleasing knowledge that we were now individually members of, and acknowledged of God, 'The Church of Jesus Christ,' organized in accordance with commandments and revelations given by Him to ourselves in these last days, as well as according to the order of the Church as recorded in the New Testament."[9]

That day several persons, including Joseph's mother and father, were baptized members of the Church.

WHERE IS THE CERTIFICATE OF INCORPORATION?

Although these events make it clear that at least two of the legal requirements for church incorporation were followed, the documents we currently have do not mention the other requirements. One important requirement, of course, was the filing of a certificate of incorporation. We do know that leaders of the Church took the necessary steps to qualify the Church as a legal entity under Illinois law, and actually filed the required certificate.[10] Did they do the same in New York?

In August 1879, President John Taylor sent a letter to William C. Staines asking him to search for a New York incorporation certificate.[11] William Staines hurried to the area and sent a detailed report to President Taylor that evidenced a careful but fruitless search in several local government offices for the certificate.[12]

I too have searched for the certificate. On March 28, 1988, thinking that the certificate may have been transferred to Albany, New York's state capital, I searched the state archives and the office where corporation papers are filed. I found no trace of the certificate. I was advised that if the papers still existed, they would be in Waterloo, New York, the county seat of Seneca County, near Fayette. There, on April 29, 1988, President Richard Christensen of the New York Rochester Mission and I searched unsuccessfully for the certificate. We then conferred with the Seneca County historian, Betty Auten, who confirmed that her ongoing search for references to the Church had revealed no such certificate.

Because of the confusion in some early records about whether Manchester or Fayette was the place of organization, we next went to Canandaigua, New York, the county seat of Ontario County, in which Manchester is located, to continue our search. So far as we could determine, the certificate was not on file there either.

Other searches have been made for the Church's original certificate of incorporation, but to date nothing has been located. The Church Historical Department has instituted a further search of old New York state and county files through Columbia University.

FAYETTE WAS THE PLACE

One may ask what difference it makes where the Church was organized and why the issue needs to be raised. It is true that the gospel remains true whether or not the Church's original certificate of incorporation is found. But it is natural to want to know the place of important events. Places such as Bethlehem, Sharon, and Mount Vernon take on significance because of events that occurred there.

Likewise, Fayette, New York, has become important as the birthplace of the Church. As part of April general conference in 1980, for example, President Spencer W. Kimball presided at Fayette over a sesquicentennial celebration of the organization of the Church.

Since the Doctrine and Covenants, the official history of the Church, and careful scholarship *all* establish that the Peter Whitmer farm near Fayette was where the official organization took place, how does one view the several references that suggest otherwise? For example, in the Book of Commandments, published in 1833, several revelations received by Joseph Smith carry introductory headnotes by the publisher, W. W. Phelps, describing them as having been received in Manchester, New York, on April 6, 1830.[13] The perceptive student will ask, "If Joseph was in Fayette participating in the organization of the Church, could he also have been thirty miles away in Manchester receiving revelations?"

Significantly, the matter was resolved when the reference to Manchester and the date—"six"—were deleted in the introductory material for these revelations when the Doctrine and Covenants was published in 1835. These early corrections have been followed in all subsequent editions. The 1835 correction was probably made when Joseph Smith or other eyewitnesses, noticing the mistakes, corrected them to conform to the events as they occurred.

Another confusing statement is found in a published copy of a letter Joseph Smith sent in 1842 to John Wentworth, editor and owner of the *Chicago Democrat.* Wentworth had requested a "sketch of the rise, progress, persecution and faith of the Latter-day Saints."[14] The Prophet's published response refers to the Church as having been organized in Manchester.

Did the Prophet actually write that the Church "was organized, in the town of Manchester, Ontario County, state of New York"?[15] We cannot know for sure. Neither the original nor a copy of Joseph's letter has survived, except as published in the *Times and Seasons.*

For purposes of discussion, let us assume that the original letter contained the reference to Manchester. There are several possible explanations for the statement. One is simply that Joseph Smith made a mistake in citing Manchester as the place of organization in the Wentworth letter. So many of the significant events of the Restoration did happen near Manchester that the name could easily slip into his discussion of those events twelve years later.

Another explanation may be that meetings in Manchester played an important, though informal, role in the organizational process. Manchester was one of three places, including Fayette, where meetings were being held by April 1830. The reference to Manchester as a place of birth for the Church may have merely been a recognition that Manchester played a key role as a meeting place where details for the formal Church organization were worked out. In this light, it is interesting that in the official history of the state of New York, the author states that "at Manchester, in 1830, the new sect was *founded*, and at Fayette was *formally organized* a few weeks later."[16]

Still another explanation for the reference to Manchester is that the statement may have been influenced by Orson Pratt. There are two reasons for believing that Orson Pratt may have been involved. First, as Latter-day Saint scholar David Whittaker has detailed, Orson Pratt seems to have had a hand in drafting the portion of the letter that later became the Articles of Faith.[17] Perhaps, then, Elder Pratt is the source of the Manchester reference in the Wentworth letter, because in his pamphlet cited earlier he had already mistakenly referred to Manchester as the place of organization. Still, it should be clearly noted that Elder Pratt's pamphlet was changed in 1848, during his lifetime, to designate Fayette as the place of organization.

The simplest and most plausible explanation for the ambiguous statements concerning the place of organization is that, in publishing the Book of Commandments and *The Evening and the Morning Star*, W. W. Phelps was not as careful as he might have been and mistakenly designated Manchester as the site of events that took place on April 6, 1830. Formal minutes were probably not available to Brother Phelps, who may have relied on memory and made an understandable error, or perhaps he intended to designate Manchester as the place of some of the organizational planning but not the formal organizational meeting. Others, such as Orson Pratt, may simply have misunderstood and perpetuated that imprecise designation by using the Book of Commandments for data on the Church's place of origin.

Later, in some manner and without recording the reasons or even the fact that it was being done, the ambiguities in the Book of Commandments were clarified in the 1835 edition of the Doctrine and Covenants, which included revelations from the Book of Commandments. If the Prophet Joseph Smith did not make the clarification himself, whoever did it had ready access to those who were present at the organization. The lack of explanation for the change, and the subsequent designation of Fayette as the place of organization, is mute evidence that the correction was perceived as a simple and natural act requiring no elaboration.

CONCLUSION

All official sources, including the *History of the Church* and nearly every author writing in the last century or more, designate Fayette as the location of the first meeting.

Furthermore, contemporary eyewitnesses designate Fayette as the site. All agree that David Whitmer was a participant in, and thus an eyewitness to, the organizing event. In his 1887 document entitled *An Address to All Believers in Christ,* he states specifically: "We met at my father's house in Fayette, N.Y., on April 6, 1830, to attend to this matter of organizing according to the Laws of the land. . . . The church was organized on April 6th 'agreeable to the laws of our country.'"[18]

The beginning of The Church of Jesus Christ of Latter-day Saints as a legal organization in the farm home of Peter Whitmer Sr. is securely established by the evidence. Though research may yet shed additional light on this fascinating and important event, the Church, 174 years later with some 11.9 million members, continues to grow, and the Lord's gospel plans continue to patiently and thoughtfully unfold.

NOTES

The author expresses gratitude to Ronald O. Barney of the Family and Church History Department for his help in gathering the information used to write this article.

1. Doctrine and Covenants 20 includes a number of concepts, some prepared by Oliver Cowdery earlier than April 1830 to provide a statement of procedure and doctrine for governing the Church, which was soon to be organized.
2. David Whitmer, *An Address to All Believers in Christ* (Richmond, Missouri: David Whitmer, 1887), 33.

3. See *The Evening and the Morning Star,* March 1833, 76; and April 1833, 167. But minutes of a conference, reported on page 160 of the May 1834 issue, identify Fayette as the place where the Church was organized.

4. See Orson Pratt, *An Interesting Account of Several Remarkable Visions, and of the Late Discovery of Ancient American Records* (Edinburgh, Scotland: Ballantyne and Hughes, 1840).

5. See chapter LX of the *Laws of the State of New-York, Revised and Passed at the Thirty-sixth Session of the Legislature* (Albany, New York: H. C. Southwick & Co., 1813), 212–19.

6. See *Laws of the State of New-York,* 214.

7. See Dean Jessee, "Joseph Knight's Recollection of Early Mormon History," *BYU Studies* 17, no. 1 (Autumn 1976): 36–37.

8. Joseph Smith, *History of the Church of Jesus Christ of Latter-day Saints,* ed. B. H. Roberts, 2nd ed., rev. (Salt Lake City: Deseret Book, 1957), 1:74–77.

9. Smith, *History of the Church,* 1:79.

10. See Dallin H. Oaks and Joseph I. Bentley, "Joseph Smith and Legal Process: In the Wake of the Steamboat *Nauvoo,*" *Brigham Young University Law Review* 3 (1976): 746.

11. See John Taylor to Elder W. C. Staines, correspondence, August 23, 1879, *First Presidency Letterbooks,* Historical Department, The Church of Jesus Christ of Latter-day Saints, Salt Lake City.

12. See W. C. Staines to President John Taylor, correspondence, September 4, 1879, Church Historical Department.

13. See W. W. Phelps, *A Book of Commandments for the Government of the Church of Christ* (1833), chapters XVII–XXII.

14. *Times and Seasons,* March 1, 1842, 706.

15. Orson Pratt, *An Interesting Account,* 22.

16. Alexander C. Flick, *History of the State of New York* (New York: New York State Historical Association, 1934), 5:171; emphasis added.

17. See David J. Whittaker, "The 'Articles of Faith' in Early Mormon Literature and Thought," in *New Views of Mormon History, A Collection of Essays in Honor of Leonard J. Arrington,* ed. Davis Bitton and Maureen Ursenbach Beecher (Salt Lake City: University of Utah Press, 1987), 63–93, for a thoughtful review of the Articles of Faith as found in the Pearl of Great Price. This scholarly article indicates that these statements of belief may have been borrowed by Joseph Smith from other writings, particularly Orson Pratt's, in composing his letter to John Wentworth.

18. Whitmer, *An Address to All Believers in Christ,* 33.

CHAPTER SIX

THE EXPLANATORY INTRODUCTION: A GUIDE TO THE DOCTRINE AND COVENANTS

CRAIG K. MANSCILL

Following the title page of the Doctrine and Covenants and preceding the text of the revelations are three pages of helpful text called the Explanatory Introduction.[1] Unfortunately, many members of the Church overlook this important study aid, perhaps because section 1 of the Doctrine and Covenants is named by the Lord as His "preface." However, serious students of the Doctrine and Covenants will find that in addition to the Lord's preface, the Explanatory Introduction acts as an excellent guide to a thoughtful and prayerful study of the Doctrine and Covenants.

The idea of an explanatory introduction is not unique to the Doctrine and Covenants. The Bible, the Book of Mormon, and the Pearl of Great Price all offer such explanatory pages. In these books, this front material sets the necessary stage for an in-depth study of the gospel. Primarily, these introductions provide a contextual history that is necessary to an understanding of the settings and circumstances from which these books of scripture originate.

Previous editions of the Doctrine and Covenants called the explanatory pages the "preface," such as in the earliest edition in 1835. Over the years this seeming discrepancy of two prefaces led to

---

Craig K. Manscill is an associate professor of Church history and doctrine at Brigham Young University.

some confusion. To resolve the confusion, in the 1921 edition the preface was renamed the Explanatory Introduction.

Compared with its previous 1921 version, our current version of the Explanatory Introduction is quite different. The 1921 edition of the scriptures was under the supervision of Elder George F. Richards of the Quorum of the Twelve Apostles. On December 17, 1921, the First Presidency, while making an official announcement concerning the new 1921 edition, stated that the Explanatory Introduction comprised "in concise form the essential facts relating to the history of this sacred volume of Latter-day revelation."[2] In other words, the content of the 1921 edition briefly told the history of the coming forth of the Doctrine and Covenants. On the other hand, the 1981 edition not only gives a brief history of the editions of the Doctrine and Covenants but also provides more information about the nature and purpose of the Doctrine and Covenants.

The 1981 edition was completed under the direction of President Spencer W. Kimball, with Elders Thomas S. Monson (acting as chair), Bruce R. McConkie, and Boyd K. Packer supervising the work of Ellis T. Rasmussen and Robert J. Matthews.[3] It is noteworthy that the Explanatory Introduction was authored by General Authorities of the Church who sought the spirit of revelation as they wrote it.

Unlike the previous versions, the Explanatory Introduction of the 1981 edition offers its readers several guiding themes on which they may base their study of the Doctrine and Covenants.[4] Of these, we have chosen to highlight and enlarge seven of the major themes. These seven are some of the most prominent and overarching themes in the Doctrine and Covenants.[5] They include the following: the revelations were given in times of real need to real people, the events of the Restoration unfolded under the Lord's direction, the administrative structure of the Church gradually unfolded, the doctrines of the plan of salvation were revealed, the Joseph Smith Translation of the Bible was inspired by God, the westward movement of the Church was guided by God, and these revelations bring people to Jesus Christ. (Each of the following themes begins by quoting directly from the Explanatory Introduction. These words are italicized.)

REVELATIONS GIVEN IN TIMES OF REAL NEED TO REAL PEOPLE

These sacred revelations were received in answer to prayer, in times of need, and came out of real-life situations involving real people. The prophet and his associates sought for divine guidance, and these revelations certify that they received it.

A number of the revelations are directed to specific individuals. There are 136 individuals mentioned by name in the Doctrine and Covenants.[6] For this reason it would be a mistake to overlook these revelations. Though these revelations and instructions are to specific individuals, they hold great importance in that many of them are expressions of gospel principles from which all can benefit. For example, personal instructions to Joseph Smith and Newel K. Whitney (see D&C 93:47–50) remind us that anyone who has not kept the commandments must stand rebuked before the Lord. All have need to be chastened, set their families in order, and see that they are more diligent and concerned to pray always, or they may "be removed out of their place" (D&C 93:48). As the Lord said, "What I say unto one I say unto all" (D&C 93:49). Readers should each apply the principles included in the Lord's instructions to themselves.

The fact that so many people are referred to by name in the Doctrine and Covenants emphasizes the words of the Lord: "Remember the worth of souls is great in the sight of God" (D&C 18:10). This manifestation of God's great love and concern for His children evidences that He knows and loves His children and cares what they do with the time He has given them in mortality.

From these revelations, a number of personal instructions, warnings, commands, and counsels emerge. The revelations warn against murder, theft, dishonesty, adultery, pride, and idleness—to name only a few. Also included is needed counsel on the observance of the Sabbath day, loving the Lord and one's neighbor, treating others as equals, supporting one's family, seeking an education, and teaching one's children.

These revelations were given in times of real need. Often these revelations came as the answer to a question or a real-life circumstance that had arisen. As the Church gradually grew and developed, problems arose that caused the Prophet to approach the Lord for answers or solutions to the matters at hand. This pattern represents the method the Lord uses in dealing with His children—He asks that we reach out to obtain His blessings: "Ask, and ye shall receive; knock, and it shall be opened unto you" (D&C 4:7). Then, as answers come to a question or problem, the Lord often explicates an existing condition. This explains why the revelations of the Doctrine and Covenants may seem somewhat disjointed in nature. Taking the time to become familiar with the people of the Doctrine and Covenants and the history of the Church enveloping each revelation will greatly enhance one's comprehension of this sacred book.[7]

THE UNFOLDING OF THE EVENTS OF THE RESTORATION

In the revelations one sees the restoration and unfolding of the gospel of Jesus Christ and the ushering in of the dispensation of the fulness of times.

The unfolding of the Restoration began with the visitation of the Father and the Son to the boy Joseph Smith Jr.—the First Vision in the spring of 1820. The Doctrine and Covenants refers to this event: "Wherefore, I the Lord, . . . called upon my servant Joseph Smith, Jun., and spake unto him from heaven, and gave him command-ments. . . . And also those to whom these commandments were given, might have power to lay the foundation of this church, and to bring it forth out of obscurity and out of darkness, the only true and living church upon the face of the whole earth" (D&C 1:17, 30).

This marvelous book also testifies of the events of the coming forth of the Book of Mormon, the reestablishment of the order of the priesthood, and the organization of the kingdom of God on earth. Most of the initial revelations given to Joseph Smith focused on these events. The Lord announced in 1831 that "the keys of the kingdom of God are committed unto man on the earth" (D&C 65:2). This started with the Aaronic Priesthood on May 15, 1829 (see D&C 13), was followed shortly thereafter with the Melchizedek Priesthood (see D&C 128:20), and was later enlarged with the restored keys of the gospel of Abraham, gathering, and temple work (see D&C 110). These events had been foreseen and reported to Joseph Smith by the angel Moroni in 1823 in the earliest revelation of the Doctrine and Covenants: "Behold, I will reveal unto you the Priesthood, by the hand of Elijah the prophet, before the coming of the great and dreadful day of the Lord" (D&C 2:1). Most recently, the priesthood has been extended to all worthy males (see Official

Declaration—2). This declaration attests to the doctrine of continued revelation that is given in times of need and in real-life situations, which the Church faced at the time.

In addition to the calling of the Book of Mormon witnesses (see D&C 5, 17), the incidents involving the translation and printing of the Book of Mormon are reported (see D&C 3, 6, 8, 9, 10). Furthermore, after centuries of apostasy, the kingdom of God was organized on earth and recorded in a revelation on April 6, 1830, in Fayette, New York (see D&C 21). Indeed, the return of the Church of Jesus Christ, for the last time, is committed to the dispensation of the fulness of times. "Unto whom I have committed the keys of my kingdom, and a dispensation of the gospel for the last times; and for the fulness of times, in the which I will gather together in one all things, both which are in heaven, and which are on earth" (D&C 27:13).

ESTABLISHMENT OF THE ADMINISTRATIVE STRUCTURE OF THE CHURCH

Likewise the gradual unfolding of the administrative structure of the Church is shown with the calling of bishops, the First Presidency, the Council of the Twelve, and the Seventy, and the establishment of other presiding offices and quorums.

Holding the power of the priesthood of God, the Saints are authorized to act as the body in Christ. The Doctrine and Covenants instructs this body how to act in the administrative affairs in the kingdom. No other book of scripture lays out the administrative structure of the Church as does the Doctrine and Covenants. The revelations report the nature, offices, and ordinances of the priesthood of God. Taken together, these passages constitute the essential order of the priesthood. Chiefly at the Amhurst, Ohio, conference, Joseph Smith was sustained and ordained the president of the High Priesthood. Later the Lord stated, "Verily I say unto you, I now give unto you the officers belonging to my Priesthood, that ye may hold the keys thereof, even the Priesthood which is after the order of Melchizedek, which is after the order of mine Only Begotten Son. . . . I give unto you my servant Joseph to be a presiding elder over all my church, to be a translator, a revelator, a seer, and prophet" (D&C 124:123, 125).

The Doctrine and Covenants goes further as it details the manner in which priesthood offices should discharge their duties and how they would perform the ordinances of the priesthood. In March of 1839, an unparalleled revelation (see D&C 121) addressed the power and rights of the use of any priesthood office or authority. Other revelations contain instructions on the blessings of children (see D&C 20:70), healing the sick (see D&C 42:43–52), baptism (see D&C 20:37, 71–74; 22:1–4; 128:12–14), the sacrament (see D&C 20:68–79), endowment (see D&C 105), baptism for the dead (see D&C 127; 128), the dedicatory prayer for the Kirtland Temple (see D&C 109), and the reception of members into the School of the Prophets (see D&C 88:127–41).

In addition, the revelations give essential principles of Church administration such as the necessity of membership records (see D&C 20:64), the keeping of a history of the Church (see D&C 47:1–4), and the conduct of meetings (see D&C 41:1–8, 12).

In essence, these revelations constitute the first handbook of instructions for Church leaders. These inspired instructions are prescriptive, concise, perceptive, demanding, and rewarding. When seen with all they embrace, they inspire nothing less than the highest degree of devotion, sacrifice, and obedience.

THE DOCTRINES OF THE PLAN OF SALVATION REVEALED

In the revelations the doctrines of the gospel are set forth with explanations about such fundamental matters as the nature of the Godhead, the origin of man, the reality of Satan, the purpose of mortality, the necessity for obedience, the need for repentance, the workings of the Holy Spirit, the ordinances and performances that pertain to salvation, the destiny of the earth, the future conditions of man after the resurrection and the judgment, the eternity of the marriage relationship, and the eternal nature of the family.

Most do not approach the reading of the Doctrine and Covenants as they might a novel—reading it from cover to cover in several sittings. However, if this approach were taken with the Doctrine and Covenants, a significant outcome would be realized—that is, how well the book teaches the doctrines of salvation. Actually, the doctrinal content of the Doctrine and Covenants is encyclopedic in nature. This is seen in part in the 416-page index to the Doctrine and

Covenants and the Book of Mormon. In fact, every doctrine taught by the Church is found or referred to in the Doctrine and Covenants. Specifically, the Doctrine and Covenants is often the sole source of clear knowledge about some of the doctrines of the gospel which are not found in other books of scripture (see D&C 27:7; 84:27–28; 35:4; 77:14). From that point of view, the book naturally becomes the most important doctrinal book we have in the Church. No other book of scripture can lay the same claim to having a full survey of all the doctrines of the Church. This is the dispensation of the fulness of times, and the fulness of the gospel has been revealed in the Doctrine and Covenants. Since we know that our Father in Heaven makes covenants with His children in order to bring about their salvation and eternal life, it should not be surprising that the Doctrine and Covenants contains a great deal of revelation about God's eternal plan of salvation. The prevalence of these revelations may be seen even in a brief survey of the Doctrine and Covenants.

For example, if you wanted to learn about the nature of God, the Doctrine and Covenants teaches about His personality (see D&C 130:1–3, 22–23; 50:10–12); the reason He is God (see D&C 132:20); His attributes (see D&C 20:17; 35:1; 3:10; 39:16; 6:20; 84:102; 87:6); His power (see D&C 61:1; 100:1; 88:13, 47; 121:36); His home (see D&C 88:13; 130:7, 8); His messengers (see D&C 129:1, 4; 130:4–7; 43:25); His omniscience (see D&C 130:7–11; 88:5–13); and His fatherhood (see D&C 27:14; 76:13; 76:24; 88:41). Lest we forget, the voice of the Doctrine and Covenants is that of Jesus Christ. Appropriately so, who could teach us better about God than His Son, a member of the Godhead?

Contributions of the Inspired Translation of the Bible

Some later sections reflect the work of the Prophet Joseph Smith in making an inspired translation of the Bible, during which many of the great doctrinal sections were received (see, for example, Sections 37, 45, 73, 76, 77, 86, 91, and 132, each of which has some direct relationship to the Bible translation).

The Joseph Smith Translation of the Bible had a substantial influence on the content of the Doctrine and Covenants, particularly on these revelations received during the years 1830–33. Joseph's translation of the Bible was a primary source for many of the doctrinal statements in the Doctrine and Covenants. For example, Doctrine and Covenants 29 was received by the Prophet Joseph Smith in September 1830 at Fayette, New York. The immediate circumstances that prompted this revelation are not fully known, yet its contents are highly doctrinal. Verses 31–42 clarify the spiritual and temporal aspects of the Creation as well as the cause and consequences of the Fall of Adam. It is instructive to know that as Genesis 1–3 was being translated in the Bible by Joseph Smith, Doctrine and Covenants 29 was received at the same time in correlation with his study of the Creation and the Fall. Other revelations to consider include parts of sections 6, 8, 9, 29, 35, 41, 42, 74, 93, 104, and 124.

The Doctrine and Covenants also contains regulatory and instructional information about the Joseph Smith Translation. The revelations give direction on when to begin (see D&C 9:1–2), when to pause (see D&C 37:1–4), when to recommence translation (see D&C 41:7), who the scribe was to be (see D&C 35:20; 47:1), and the time in which the parts of the Bible should be translated (see D&C 45:60–62). These came with the exhortation to move more rapidly (see D&C 73:3–4; 93:53) and to make plans for publication (see D&C 94:10; 124:89). These instructive items are found in various revelations in the Doctrine and Covenants. Knowing that they are there will enhance and deepen one's study of the context of the Joseph Smith Translation.[8]

THE WESTWARD MOVEMENT OF THE CHURCH

The westward movement of the Church from New York and Pennsylvania, to Ohio, to Missouri, to Illinois, and finally to the Great Basin of western America, and the mighty struggles of the saints in attempting to build Zion on the earth in modern times, are also shown forth in these revelations.

The westward movement of the Church from New York to the Rocky Mountains was centered in the doctrine of gathering. As few as five months after the Church was organized in 1830 the Lord announced, "Wherefore the decree hath gone forth from the Father that they shall be gathered in unto one place upon the face of this land, to prepare their hearts and be prepared in all things against the day when tribulation and desolation are sent forth upon the wicked" (D&C 29:8).

The purpose for gathering is also a scriptural injunction: "Wherefore, for this cause I gave unto you the commandment that ye should go to the Ohio; and there I will give unto you my law; and there you shall be endowed with power from on high" (D&C 38:32).

The gathering, as witnessed by the westward movement of the Church, was operational from 1830 to the 1890s from New York to Kirtland, Ohio, to Missouri, followed by Illinois, to Council Bluffs, Iowa (as a stopping place on the way to the Rocky Mountains in the Great Basin). The westward movement is an outward manifestation of a covenant-making people who adhere to God's commands.

THE VOICE OF JESUS

In the revelations one hears the tender but firm voice of the Lord Jesus Christ, speaking anew in the dispensation of the fulness of times; and the work that is initiated herein is preparatory to his second coming, in fulfillment of and in concert with the words of all the holy prophets since the world began.

With few exceptions, the speaker in the revelations is the resurrected Jesus Christ. On occasion, Christ will quote or speak as if He is the Father, yet He does not give attribution to God the Father. The language of the revelations, with the exception of a few words by heavenly angels (see D&C 2; 7; 13), is the language of Joseph Smith. As the inspired ideas and thoughts came into his mind, he composed the revelatory language from his own linguistic background (see D&C 1:24).

Unique to the Doctrine and Covenants are the many passages in which Christ speaks autobiographically. These passages run throughout the entirety of the book. An illustration is found in Doctrine and Covenants 38:1–4. Here Christ speaks about His nature, reminding us that He is the creator of the earth and informing us that it was He who took Enoch unto Himself:

"Thus saith the Lord your God, even Jesus Christ, the Great I Am, Alpha and Omega, the beginning and the end, the same which looked upon the wide expanse of eternity, and all the seraphic hosts of heaven, before the world was made;

"The same which knoweth all things, for all things are present before mine eyes;

"I am the same which spake, and the world was made, and all things came by me.

"I am the same which have taken the Zion of Enoch into mine own bosom; and verily, I say, even as many as have believed in my name, for I am Christ, and in mine own name, by the virtue of the blood which I have spilt, have I pleaded before the Father for them."

Taking collective note of these autobiographical passages of scripture from the Lord provides an amazingly rich and full picture of the nature, role, mission, and life of our Savior.

One important aspect of Christ's voice in this sacred book is that of warning—one which indicates a soon-to-come day of judgment and recompense. This significant theme running through the Doctrine and Covenants[9] warns all the world (see D&C 43:17–29, 34–35): the wicked (see D&C 63:1–6), the righteous (see D&C 88:62–68), and kings and paupers alike (see D&C 124:3–11). None will escape this day of God's judgment (see D&C 29:3–21). God expects us to take these revelations seriously. No one who reads this book of scripture can say they have not been warned. The Lord Himself warns, "And all they who receive the oracles of God, let them beware how they hold them lest they are accounted as a light thing, and are brought under condemnation thereby, and stumble and fall when the storms descend, and the winds blow, and the rains descend, and beat upon their house" (D&C 90:5).

This warning comes as an act of love prompted by the balanced necessity of mercy and justice. Moreover, repeatedly in these revelations the Savior extends a tender hand of mercy (D&C 76:5–10), inviting repentance (D&C 19:4–5) and giving peace. In the end, those who heed this divine voice of warning will reap the promised blessings (D&C 56:14–20).

SUMMARY

It may seem that the Doctrine and Covenants is a challenging book of scripture to comprehend because it reads more like a compilation of random historical accounts and doctrinal dissertations. Unlike the Book of Mormon, there is no story line other than the history of the Church—no author pulling it all together. Nor does it read like the unforgettable parables in the New Testament. Reading the revelations in the Doctrine and Covenants is more like reading the letters of Paul; each one has its own topic containing its own insights and background. Hence, it is all the more important that the thoughtful, prayerful student utilize the inspired study aids of the Doctrine and Covenants—specifically the Explanatory Introduction.

The Explanatory Introduction gives direction to a thoughtful study of the Doctrine and Covenants. It guides the reader to become more familiar with the 136 people mentioned and the situations that brought about each revelation. The reader should take note of the revelations concerning the unfolding of the Restoration and of the administrative structure of the Church, learn about the contributions of the Joseph Smith Translation of the Bible, follow the westward movement of the Church through the revelations, and listen to the Lord's voice and adhere to the counsel, direction, and warnings of Jesus Christ. Following this course of study as outlined in the Explanatory Introduction will help the reader see what makes this book, as it states, *"of great value to the human family and of more worth than the riches of the whole earth."*

NOTES

1. The Explanatory Introduction referenced here is found in the 1981 version of the Doctrine and Covenants published by The Church of Jesus Christ of Latter-day Saints.
2. Robert J. Woodford, "The Historical Development of the Doctrine and Covenants" (PhD diss., Brigham Young University, April 1974), 1:76.
3. Bruce T. Harper, "The Church Publishes a New Triple Combination," *Ensign*, October 1981, 9.
4. For other examples of the Doctrine and Covenants themes see John A. Widtsoe, *The Message of the Doctrine and Covenants*, ed. G. Homer Durham (Salt Lake City: Bookcraft, 1969). For another arrangement of main themes, see the chart compiled by Minnie E. Anderson, "Classified Contents of the Doctrine and Covenants," *Instructor*, July 1968, facing page 292.
5. It should be noted that Robert L. Millet and Kent P. Jackson discuss the Explanatory Introduction in terms of four primary purposes in *Studies in Scripture, Vol. 1: The Doctrine and Covenants* (Salt Lake City: Deseret Book, 1989), 25. While their four points seek to constitute what they feel are the purposes of the Explanatory Introduction as a whole, we have taken a different approach in which we look at the themes of the Doctrine and Covenants as they are introduced in the Explanatory Introduction.

6. Susan Easton Black, *Who's Who in the Doctrine and Covenants* (Salt Lake City: Bookcraft, 1997). This book gives a two- or three-page biographical summary of all 136 individuals in the Doctrine and Covenants.

7. A readily available source of Church history is the Church Educational System student manual, *Church History in the Fulness of Times* (Salt Lake City: The Church of Jesus Christ of Latter-day Saints, 2001).

8. Robert J. Matthews, "The Joseph Smith Translation: A Primary Source for the Doctrine and Covenants," in *Hearken, O Ye People: Discourses of the Doctrine and Covenants* (Sandy, Utah: Randall Book, 1984), 90.

9. Christ's voice of warning in the Doctrine and Covenants was influential in the writing of the popular missionary tract titled *A Voice of Warning* by Parley P. Pratt (Independence, Missouri: Herald Publishing House, 1950).

CHAPTER SEVEN

THE RESTORATION OF ALL THINGS: WHAT THE DOCTRINE AND COVENANTS SAYS

ROBERT J. MATTHEWS

The "restitution of all things, which God hath spoken [of] by the mouth of all his holy prophets since the world began" (Acts 3:21) is a prominent theme of both ancient and latter-day scripture. It is to be accomplished through those who are called of God "as was Aaron" (D&C 132:59), and who have the same holy calling and teach the same doctrines as the ancient prophets. The Restoration will eventually and permanently affect everybody and everything on the earth. That is the only true "new world order" because it is the gospel of Jesus Christ.

We live in the modern world of multiple inventions, labor-saving appliances, space travel, rapid earth-travel, and almost instant communication. It is a world of software, hardware, storage, memory, quick retrieval, and split-second timing. These things are all relatively new, and most have been developed in the past half century.

We also live in the dispensation of the fulness of times, which is the fulness of dispensations leading to a culmination of the Lord's work upon the earth. All previous dispensations were open-ended and will flow into this final dispensation like rivers into the seas. This dispensation is known as the time of "restitution of all things," when

Robert J. Matthews, former dean of Religious Education, is an emeritus professor of ancient scripture at Brigham Young University.

the covenants, promises, knowledge, doctrines, priesthood, and divine governing powers that were had by ancient prophets and seers will be established and organized again upon the earth for the benefit of mankind to bring about the purposes of God for the human family. The modern technological developments of travel, and so forth, are inspired by the Lord to assist in His work in this dispensation, which began with the First Vision to Joseph Smith in 1820 and will not end until the earth becomes celestial.

The Book of Mormon uses the concept of restoration (restore, restoring, restored) at least sixty-seven times, often with reference to the gathering and future glory of the house of Israel and also to the plan of salvation, the resurrection of the body, and the Lord's method of rendering a just verdict on the Day of Judgment. The Book of Mormon states that there is a "plan of restoration" which is "requisite with the justice of God; for it is requisite that all things should be restored to their proper order" (Alma 41:2).

Our subject today is what the revelations in the Doctrine and Covenants tell us about that restoration. We frequently talk about the restored gospel, the restored Church, and the restoration of all things, but what does all that mean? What will the Restoration eventually mean to the world? How much of the Restoration has already occurred? What does the future hold for us both in spiritual and in physical things because of the Restoration? How will libraries, schools, and study courses be changed? The Prophet Joseph Smith said, "I calculate to be one of the instruments of setting up the kingdom of Daniel by the word of the Lord, and I intend to lay a foundation that will revolutionize the whole world."[1]

This is the kingdom of Daniel to which the Prophet Joseph Smith referred: "And in the days of these kings shall the God of heaven set up a kingdom, which shall never be destroyed: and the kingdom shall not be left to other people, but it shall break in pieces and consume all these kingdoms, and it shall stand for ever.

"Forasmuch as thou sawest that the stone was cut out of the mountain without hands, and that it brake in pieces the iron, the brass, the clay, the silver, and the gold; the great God hath made known to the king what shall come to pass hereafter: and the dream is certain, and the interpretation thereof sure" (Daniel 2:44–45).

Since the restoration of all things is going to produce a revolution of worldwide proportions, it should be interesting to find out what is going to happen and what it will mean in our individual lives and activities.

The kingdom of God of which Daniel spoke is much more than a church in the usual sense, for it will replace the political kingdoms of the earth. This kingdom will have political, social, and economic, as well as ecclesiastical, aspects. When the kingdom of God is fully established in the earth, it will have all four of those dimensions. Today we are pleased to speak of The Church of Jesus Christ of Latter-day Saints as the kingdom of God on earth, and so it is, but the Church at this time functions primarily in its ecclesiastical dimension. With the restoration of the Aaronic and Melchizedek priesthoods, the authority was given to carry out all of the dimensions of the kingdom, and the doctrinal foundation was also made known. Each dimension was actually functional for a short time in the early days of the Church, but some aspects have been withdrawn from full, active operation until a more appropriate day. For example, the economic order was instituted in Ohio and Missouri under the principles of stewardship and consecration of property. These principles and the authority to implement them still exist in the Church, but the active organizational order has been temporarily discontinued. Likewise, the social order that focuses on a patriarchal family organization and celestial marriage (including plural marriage for some) has been temporarily modified. The authority to administer all aspects of the social order is still with the Church but is not completely active at present. The same is true of the civic or political dimension, which had a brief history and now is dormant. These things are not lost; they are simply not in active operation until the Lord commands that they be renewed at a more propitious time and circumstance. The power and authority for all of these activities reside in the keys held by the First Presidency and the Quorum of the Twelve Apostles.

What does the Doctrine and Covenants make known to us about the restoration of all things? The word *restoration* means that a previous order and system that was once in operation, but which has been lost to the world, shall be reinstituted and become functional again. The Doctrine and Covenants speaks much of a Restoration, or the reestablishment of the ancient priesthood, ancient councils, ancient ordinances, and ancient doctrines.

THE WORDS OF THE PROPHETS SHALL BE FULFILLED

By reading the Doctrine and Covenants in a short span of time, there comes a growing awareness of the emphasis on ancient prophets, ancient prophecy, and ancient promises. No fewer than thirty-one times is mention made that the words of the "prophets of old" will be fulfilled and that faith such as that possessed by the prophets of old will again be had on the earth (see D&C 17:2; 20:4; 22:3; 27:6; 29:10–21; 33:8; 35:6, 23; 42:39; 43:30; 45:10, 15; 49: 11–14; 52:9, 36; 58:8; 59:22; 61:13; 66:2; 76:7–8; 84:64, 108; 85:11, 12; 86:10; 98:32–33; 101:19; 109:23, 41, 45; 128:19). Likewise, there are several comparisons of the ancient Church with the modern Church, and the Lord explains the way that former prophets built up the Church in their day (see D&C 64:8; 84:64, 108; 95:9). Declarations are made concerning Adam, Eve, Enoch, Noah, Gabriel, Raphael, Job, Melchizedek, Shem, Abraham, Sarah, Hagar, Isaac, Jacob, Joseph, Ephraim, Moses, Aaron, the sons of Levi, Pharaoh, David, Solomon, Nathan, Elijah, Elias, Isaiah, Ezekiel, Malachi, Peter, James, John, Paul, and John the Baptist that implant an ancient character and flavor to the Doctrine and Covenants. These names are not simply mentioned and then forgotten, for in most instances personal, individual, and historical information is given that is relevant to the doctrine and practice of the restored Church.

The Doctrine and Covenants also discusses ancient artifacts, such as the gold plates, the breastplate, sword of Laban, the Urim and Thummim, the ball or director (Liahona), and other such very old items. It also speaks of the passing over of the destroying angel, the parting of the Red Sea, the travels of ancient Israel in the wilderness, the tabernacle, the circumstances of Abraham's offering his son Isaac, the Mount of Olives, the Mount of Transfiguration, the washing of the Apostles' feet by Jesus, baptism, and other ancient practices. These are not stated merely as interesting items of history but are introduced as having relevance to activities to be performed in the latter-day Church. Furthermore, Oliver Cowdery was to have the "gift of Aaron" and also the same Spirit that inspired Moses (see D&C 3:2–7, 11); and Joseph Smith was to receive revelations "even as Moses" (D&C 28:2) and to be "like unto Moses" (D&C 107:91). The calling and the preaching of Peter (see D&C 49:11–14) and of Paul (see D&C 18:9) are specified. The ancient gospel of Jesus Christ that was taught by ancient prophets is to be preached by modern teachers through the instrumentality of the Book of Mormon (see D&C 10:44–63).

The First Vision, Spring 1820

In the First Vision the Father and the Son appeared personally to the boy Joseph Smith, and in response to his questions about which of the churches was right and which he should join, he was told to join none of them, for none, individually or collectively, was the Lord's authorized Church. None was doing what the Lord wanted done in the earth among mankind in the last days. Because of the worldwide apostate condition, there needed to be a restoration of the ancient gospel, the ancient priesthood, the ancient covenants, and the ancient performances.

The Visits of Moroni, 1823–1827

The angel Moroni, himself a resurrected ancient prophet, quoted to Joseph Smith many passages from the Old and New Testaments respecting the work of the Lord in the last days. Moroni cited passages from Isaiah, Joel, Jeremiah, Daniel, Malachi, Psalms, and Acts, which in every case deal with the reestablishment of the kingdom of God on the earth preparatory to the Savior's Second Coming (see Joseph Smith—History 1:36–41).[2]

The Promises Made to the Fathers

The angel Moroni, during a visit to Joseph Smith in September 1823, restated the words of Malachi as follows: "Behold, I will reveal unto you the Priesthood, by the hand of Elijah the prophet, before the coming of the great and dreadful day of the Lord. And he shall plant in the hearts of the children the promises made to the fathers, and the hearts of the children shall turn to their fathers" (D&C 2:1–2).

Malachi had lived about 400 B.C. Elijah had lived about 800 B.C. The fathers to whom the promises were made had lived even earlier, all the way back to Adam, Enoch, Abraham, Isaac, Jacob, and Joseph.

The promises spoken of are the covenants of the gospel of Jesus Christ, which are the promises of priesthood, salvation, and exaltation. All of them are contained in the Lord's covenant with Abraham.

These ancient covenants were to be planted in the hearts of living persons on the earth in the last days—the children of the ancient prophets. These promises, in connection with the coming of Elijah, are mentioned three more times in Doctrine and Covenants 27:9; 110:14–15; and 128:17–18. Because the particular ancient prophets to whom these promises were made are not specifically named in these passages, it is instructive to note Doctrine and Covenants 27:10, in which it is stated in connection with Elijah's ministry that these prophets are "Joseph and Jacob, and Isaac, and Abraham, your fathers, by whom the promises remain."

Among the several provisions of the covenant of Abraham was the specific promise of a land inheritance to call their own, a fruitful land of milk and honey, which would be for an everlasting possession (see Genesis 17:8; Acts 7:5). The restoration of all things has brought the renewal of this promise and will yet see the fulfillment of land inheritance. This promise will be defined more clearly below in my discussion of the role of the bishop.

THE RESTORATION OF ANCIENT RECORDS

The earliest evidence of a restoration of ancient records is the Book of Mormon, which is itself a collection of ancient documents, and it tells of other records that will come to light in the last days. These include the sealed portion of the plates that Joseph Smith obtained from the Hill Cumorah, which contain a revelation of "all things from the foundation of the world unto the end thereof" (2 Nephi 27:10). There will be a record of the ten tribes, including the Savior's visit to them. There will also be a complete record of the writings of John the Apostle (see Ether 4:16). The Doctrine and Covenants begins the restoration of John's writing in section 7, which is a translation of a parchment originally written and hidden up by John himself. Furthermore, the larger and more extensive original records of the Nephites and also the complete record of the Jaredites' twenty-four gold plates are yet to be made known. Likewise, a translation of the brass plates of Laban will eventually go to all nations, kindreds, tongues, and peoples (see 1 Nephi 5:17–19; Alma 37:3–5).

While the translation of the Book of Mormon was still in progress in 1829, the Lord informed Joseph Smith and Oliver Cowdery that when they had finished with it, there were other records to be translated (see D&C 8:11; 9:1–2). These other records included the Joseph Smith Translation of the Bible and also the book of Abraham (see D&C 9:2, note *a*).

Doctrine and Covenants 93 verses 6 and 18 speak of the Church yet receiving the "fulness of the record of John." It is not completely clear whether this is a record of John the Baptist (that was the interpretation by President John Taylor, Elder Orson Pratt, and Elder Bruce R. McConkie)[3] or whether it is the writings of John the Apostle. It may very well mean both. In Doctrine and Covenants 107:57, the record of Enoch is spoken of with the promise that it will be available "in due time." Thus the Doctrine and Covenants gives great expectation for much additional reading of ancient documents in the future. None of these are new documents; they are ancient documents revealed anew.

The Book of Mormon makes clear that the Old Testament record once had more books than at present, and even the books it now contains have been reduced in size in some instances. In the restoration of all things, these Old Testament books will be available in their original purity and correctness. A beginning has already been made with the Joseph Smith Translation of the Bible, which gives us a new glimpse of the writings of Enoch, Joseph, and Moses. We now have thirty-nine books in the Old Testament and twenty-seven in the New, making sixty-six books in all in the King James Version of the Bible. This will no doubt be enlarged in days to come.

In our present four-year cycle of the Church Sunday School curriculum, we take one year each to study the Old Testament, the New Testament, the Book of Mormon, and the Doctrine and Covenants, and then we repeat the process. The Brigham Young University curriculum provides two semesters for Old Testament and two semesters for the New Testament, making a total of four semesters (eight credit hours) for study of the Bible on the undergraduate level. There are also graduate-level courses for another seven credit hours of Old Testament and six credit hours of New Testament.

With the restoration of ancient records, it will someday require a much longer time to study the Bible, both in Sunday School and also in Church schools. I expect that at some future time the Brigham Young University religion curriculum for the Old Testament will contain not only the present courses but Brass Plates 303 (five hours) with an emphasis on the prophecies of Joseph and of Zenos. We now have a course specializing in Isaiah. When the brass plates are restored, we will need Old Testament 305, specializing in Zenock; 306, Zenos; 307, Neum and Ezias—each of these courses being three credit hours each. At this rate, it could take a student four years just to study the beginning courses in the Old Testament alone. Instead of the current twenty-one hours in the Old Testament offering, there could easily be as many as forty hours. An equal enlargement would be necessary in the New Testament with additional courses on the teachings of Jesus, a course on the writings of John the Apostle, and another on the writings of John the Baptist. There would also have to be courses in Lost Tribes 101, 102, and 103, two hours each, using as the text the record yet to be revealed that is spoken of in 2 Nephi 29:7–14 and 3 Nephi 17:4.

The Book of Mormon curriculum will also have to be enlarged when the complete restoration finally descends upon us. In addition to the two beginning courses 121 and 122 now in the curriculum, there will have to be a 123, Readings from the 116 Lost Pages (two credit hours); Book of Mormon 124, The Twenty-four Gold Plates of Ether (four hours); and a special course for advanced students, Theology 500, The Sealed Plates (five hours, with labs and seminars). Advanced courses might also be given about the large plates of Nephi. For example, 501, The Book of Lehi; 502, Mosiah; 503, Alma; 504, Helaman, and so on through the entire collection. Today we offer a total of sixteen credit hours in Book of Mormon. In the time of restoration, there could be forty to fifty credit hours in Book of Mormon alone.

But that is not all. The restoration of ancient records will bring forth a large number of books that will be studied in Doctrine and Covenants and in Pearl of Great Price classes. These will include the Book of Remembrance, with the fulness of the writings of Adam, Enoch, and others. Furthermore, there will be the extended writings of Abraham and of Joseph of Egypt. The Book of Remembrance, which was started by Adam, will present not only historical items of great importance but also doctrinal and theological concepts that will require many scholars to revise their present viewpoints of the early patriarchs and concede that those patriarchs were indeed very knowledgeable and great. Abraham said he had records that contained marvelous things: "But I shall endeavor, hereafter, to delineate the chronology running back from myself to the beginning of the creation, for the records have come into my hands, which I hold unto this present time. . . . [And] the records of the fathers, even the patriarchs, concerning the right of Priesthood, the Lord my God preserved in mine own hands; therefore a knowledge of the beginning of the creation, and also of the planets, and of the stars, as they were made known unto the fathers, have I kept even unto this day" (Abraham 1:28, 31).

There will be other wonderful things, for the Lord has said: "Yea, verily I say unto you, in that day when the Lord shall come, he shall reveal all things—things which have passed, and hidden things which no man knew, things of the earth, by which it was made, and the purpose and the end thereof—things most precious, things that are above, and things that are beneath, things that are in the earth, and upon the earth, and in heaven" (D&C 101:32–34).

The documents containing such information will offer a comprehensive doctrinal perspective that will add a great deal to our understanding. Thus there could be information-packed courses in Revelation 501, Enoch; Revelation 502, Writings of John; and such other things as Book of Remembrance 503; Creation 504, and so forth.

We have so far spoken only of the manner in which the promised restoration of ancient records will affect the Sunday School curriculum and the BYU Religious Education curriculum; however, these additional records will shed light on all facets of life and learning, including mankind's origin and history and significant matters of human culture. These records will demonstrate mankind's high intelligence and civilization from the very beginning. The additional records will confirm what we already know from the scriptures we now have and will also give much more information. Hence, there will be a need for revised courses in ancient history, anthropology, biology, and all courses that deal with the origin of mankind, the origin of language, the origin of writing, and so forth. These subjects will then be looked upon with a new perspective. Present courses that teach that mankind is the product of organic evolution will no doubt be viewed as erroneous. It appears that almost all subject matter areas of the university curriculum will be shaken by the effects of the restoration of ancient records.

RESTORATION OF THE AARONIC PRIESTHOOD

The next topic, in order of sequence in the Doctrine and Covenants, is the restoration of the Aaronic Priesthood on May 15, 1829, as recorded in section 13. The conferral was done by no less than John the Baptist, the greatest example of the powers of the Aaronic Priesthood of which we have record. John was, as we know from the New Testament, a direct descendant of Aaron of the tribe of Levi and thus a legitimate bearer of the Aaronic Priesthood and the requisite keys. When John conferred this priesthood on Joseph and Oliver, he spoke of its future relevance to the sons of Levi (see D&C 13:1). Furthermore, the powers and prerogatives of this Aaronic Priesthood are repeated in subsequent revelations in the Doctrine and Covenants. For example, in Doctrine and Covenants 68:14–21, the Lord explains that the office of bishop is of the Aaronic order and rightly belongs to those who are literal, flesh-and-blood descendants of Aaron. It also indicates that at some future time, the literal seed of Aaron will function in that role in the Church.

A statement concerning the continuation of the Aaronic Priesthood from Aaron to John the Baptist (about thirteen hundred years) is given in Doctrine and Covenants 84:18–28, with an emphasis on the hereditary nature of this priesthood throughout all the generations of the seed of Aaron and also that the specific keys and powers associated with the Aaronic Priesthood are reserved for the firstborn among the sons of Aaron (see D&C 68:14–21; 107:13–20). Aaron is mentioned twenty-four times in the Doctrine and Covenants, with considerable said about the hereditary nature of the priesthood that bears His name as well as that men must be called of God "as was Aaron" (D&C 132:59; see also 27:8; 28:3). The emphasis on the hereditary nature of the Aaronic Priesthood is not idle academic exercise. It will someday have very literal application in the Church and kingdom.

THE WORK OF THE BISHOP

The office of bishop was first made known in this Church, and the first bishop, Edward Partridge, was called in 1831. His duties were given in connection with the consecration of properties and the arranging of land inheritances (see D&C 41:9–10). Of particular note is the declaration in Doctrine and Covenants 58:14, 17: "Yea, for this cause I have sent you hither [to Missouri], and have selected my servant Edward Partridge, and have appointed unto him his mission in this land. . . . And whoso standeth in this mission is appointed to be a judge in Israel, *like as it was in ancient days,* to divide the lands of the heritage of God unto his children" (emphasis added).

By this statement we learn that the bishop has the same responsibilities in the fulness of time as in ancient times. The assignment given to Aaron and his sons was not for their day only or even for the duration of the Old Testament and law of Moses but was a perpetual role that will continue among the seed of Aaron, the sons of Levi, in the restoration of all things.

The Doctrine and Covenants leaves no doubt that the office of bishop belongs to the Aaronic Priesthood, that the bishop presides over the quorum of priests, and that he holds the keys of the Aaronic Priesthood. The Lord explains in some detail that the priests' office rightly belongs to the literal seed of Aaron and that the keys are held by the "firstborn among the sons of Aaron" (D&C 68:16). Because the Lord has not as yet designated to the First Presidency in this dispensation a specific person who is a literal descendant and firstborn of Aaron who should serve as the Presiding Bishop, the Lord has explained that a high priest of the Melchizedek Priesthood can function as a bishop. It is clearly stated, however, that the bishop's office is hereditary and someday will be filled by a literal descendent of Aaron when properly designated by revelation to the First Presidency (see D&C 68:15–21; 107:13–20).[4]

The role of bishop is to be a judge and also to be an administrator of the temporalities of the Church. He receives the sacred tithes and offerings and divides the inheritances of land and properties among families when the principles of consecration and stewardship are functioning. That is the economic dimension of the kingdom we spoke of earlier. When the laws of consecration and stewardship are again formally employed, and the Church is large, there will be need for many bishops engaged in the dividing of the lands of inheritance in Zion. It appears that they, at least the Presiding Bishop, will be literally descended from Aaron.

ETERNAL LAND INHERITANCES

It was noted earlier that the covenant to Abraham included the promise of a land inheritance to Abraham and to his seed for an everlasting possession. The Lord renewed this theme in several of the latter-day revelations as part of the restoration of all things. We read as follows: "And I hold forth and deign to give unto you greater riches, even a land of promise, a land flowing with milk and honey, upon which there shall be no curse when the Lord cometh;

"And I will give it unto you for the land of your inheritance, if you seek it with all your hearts.

"And this shall be my covenant with you, ye shall have it for the land of your inheritance, and for the inheritance of your children forever, while the earth shall stand, and ye shall possess it again in eternity, no more to pass away" (D&C 38:18–20).

And also: "And the earth shall be given unto them for an inheritance; and they shall multiply and wax strong, and their children shall grow up without sin unto salvation" (D&C 45:58).

And finally: "But blessed are the poor who are pure in heart, whose hearts are broken, and whose spirits are contrite, for they shall see the kingdom of God coming in power and great glory unto their deliverance; for the fatness of the earth shall be theirs. . . .

"And their generations shall inherit the earth from generation to generation, forever and ever" (D&C 56:18, 20).

Title and possession of such lands for an everlasting possession are not for sale in the open market or at the real estate office but are obtained only by covenant, by consecration, and by obedience to the gospel of Jesus Christ (see Abraham 2:6). We learn from the Doctrine and Covenants that the arrangement of these inheritances is the work of the bishop.

THE RESTORATION OF THE MELCHIZEDEK PRIESTHOOD

Although the exact date of the restoration of the Melchizedek Priesthood by the ancient Apostles Peter, James, and John is not given in the Doctrine and Covenants nor in Church history, it is known to have occurred within a few weeks after the restoration of the Aaronic Priesthood. With the Melchizedek Priesthood, the Prophet Joseph Smith could move ahead as he was directed and lay the foundation for the entire kingdom, in all of its social, ecclesiastical, economic, and political dimensions. Duties of the various priesthood offices, quorums, and councils are made known in Doctrine and Covenants 84 and 107. As a result of the restoration of the Melchizedek Priesthood, all of the ordinances and covenants that were ever made in ancient times could again be enjoyed on the earth. These are contained within the covenant of Abraham, which includes all of the ordinances and covenants necessary for the living to have full salvation as well as the performance of those same ordinances by proxy for the dead.

The ancient character of the priesthood is demonstrated by the statement that the modern Quorum of the Twelve Apostles and First Presidency hold the keys "in connection with all those who have received a dispensation at any time from the beginning of the creation; for verily I say unto you, the keys . . . have come down from the fathers" (D&C 112:31–32).

It becomes apparent from a chronological study of the Doctrine and Covenants that ofttimes doctrines and ordinances were made known to the Prophet Joseph for a considerable time before he was able to implement them in the Church. And as we have noted, some things are still held in abeyance even now, after more than a century and a half of this dispensation.

THE NEW AND EVERLASTING COVENANT

The new and everlasting covenant is the gospel of Jesus Christ. It is made up of a number of individual covenants such as baptism, priesthood, marriage, and so forth. Soon after the Church was organized in April 1830, some wanted to unite with the Church without a new baptism. The Lord revealed that baptism was "a new and an everlasting covenant, even that which was from the beginning" (D&C 22:1). This language is consistent with the whole concept of restoration. Things are "new" to this dispensation but are everlasting and were in existence from the beginning.

The Lord said that authoritative baptism is required of all who join the Church (see D&C 22:2–4). The Lord further clarified the meaning of the phrase "new and everlasting covenant," saying it was "the fulness of my gospel" (D&C 66:2) and that it has stringent laws, bounds, conditions, and covenants that were worked out, decided upon, and ordained by the Father and the Son before the foundation of the earth (see D&C 132:5–12).

CELESTIAL MARRIAGE

We do not know the exact date on which the doctrine of celestial marriage (including plural marriage) was revealed to the Prophet Joseph Smith. It was sometime in 1831, although the written document, Doctrine and Covenants 132, was not composed until July 12, 1843 (see headnote to D&C 132). The eternal nature of the marriage relation and the sealing of children to parents in an eternal family is part of the social dimension of the kingdom. This family connection includes the nature of the marriage ceremony and the patriarchal order with the husband presiding in the home, the eternal nature of each family unit, and the sealing of generations together like links in a chain from Adam and Eve to the latest generation of their posterity on the earth.

The celestial marriage covenant is part of the covenant of Abraham. It is the type of marriage for eternity that Abraham had. Abraham himself is mentioned no fewer than twenty times in section 132 alone and thirty-five times in the entire Doctrine and Covenants. The keys for instituting this type of marriage and family covenant were given in the Kirtland Temple, as recorded in Doctrine and Covenants 110:12, and are there called the "gospel of Abraham."

The temple endowment, the celestial marriage covenant, and the sealing of families and generations are interwoven in the plan of salvation and are all included within "the restoration of all things," which means that these very ordinances and promises were known and practiced by ancient prophets, beginning with Adam (see Abraham, facsimile 2, fig. 3). We note these particular phrases in the revelations:

"And also with Elias, to whom I have committed the keys of bringing to pass the *restoration of all things* spoken by the mouth of all the holy prophets since the world began, concerning the last days" (D&C 27:6).

"And, if you will receive it, this is Elias which was to come to gather together the tribes of Israel and *restore all things*" (D&C 77:9).

"Therefore your life and the priesthood have remained, and must needs remain through you and your lineage *until the restoration of all things* spoken by the mouths of all the holy prophets since the world began" (D&C 86:10).

"For there is not a place found on earth that he may come to and *restore again* that which was lost unto you . . . even the fulness of the priesthood" (D&C 124:28).

"I am the Lord thy God, and I gave unto thee, my servant Joseph, an appointment, *and restore all things*. Ask what ye will, and it shall be given unto you according to my word. . . . For I have conferred upon you the keys and power of the priesthood, *wherein I restore all things* and make known unto you all things in due time" (D&C 132:40, 45).

The concept of restoration is firmly implanted in the Doctrine and Covenants, and because it states that "all things" will be restored, we must conclude that the Restoration includes every eternal gospel doctrine, practice, ordinance, and facet of the kingdom of God that ever was upon the earth in any former dispensation. This restoration does not include some factors of the law of Moses, which were temporary in nature.[5]

The Prophet was well aware of the difficulty that would arise in implementing the doctrine and practice of plural marriage. The following is from an account by Heber C. Kimball's daughter: "[There was a] sensation caused in Nauvoo, one Sabbath morning [in 1840 or 41] . . . by a sermon of the Prophet's on 'the restoration of all things,' in which it was hinted that the patriarchal or plural order of marriage, as practiced by the ancients, would some day again be established. The excitement created by the bare suggestion was such that Joseph deemed it wisdom, in the afternoon, to modify his statement by saying that possibly the Spirit had made the time seem nearer than it really was, when such things would be restored."[6]

Because this earth will be a celestial kingdom, and Abraham and others, including Joseph Smith, Brigham Young, and Heber C. Kimball, each of whom had plural wives, will live here, plural marriage will exist again on the earth in that kingdom. That does not mean that everyone will be required to live that law. It may not be for everyone.

The Temple Endowment

Concerning the endowment, which was given for the first time in this dispensation in the Red Brick Store in Nauvoo, Illinois, on May

4, 1842, the Prophet Joseph Smith explained: "I spent the day in the upper part of the store, that is in my private office . . . in council with General James Adams, of Springfield, Patriarch Hyrum Smith, Bishops Newel K. Whitney and George Miller, and President Brigham Young and Elders Heber C. Kimball and Willard Richards, instructing them in the principles and order of the Priesthood, attending to washings, anointings, endowments and the communication of keys pertaining to the Aaronic Priesthood, and so on to the highest order of the Melchizedek Priesthood, setting forth the order pertaining to the Ancient of Days, and all those plans and principles by which any one is enabled to secure the fullness of those blessings which have been prepared for the Church of the Firstborn, and come up and abide in the presence of the Eloheim in the eternal worlds. In this council was instituted the ancient order of things for the first time in these last days."[7]

It is to be noted that the Prophet Joseph Smith said that these things, which we recognize as the temple endowment, are the "ancient order of things" and pertain to the "Ancient of Days," who is Adam.

THE ROLE OF PRIESTHOOD QUORUMS AND COUNCILS

In the revelation on priesthood, also known as Doctrine and Covenants 107, priesthood councils or quorums are defined and set forth. This revelation is dated March 28, 1835, but some of it was revealed as early as November 1831 (see headnote to D&C 107).

Specifically mentioned are the Seventy, the Twelve, and the First Presidency. The revelation explains that the unanimous decisions made by each of these councils are binding (see D&C 107:27–30). Of special importance is the statement that the presiding quorums which are established in the latter-day Church and kingdom are patterned after *ancient* Melchizedek Priesthood quorums (see D&C 107:29), not modern inventions but part of the restoration of ancient things. Concerning the order of ancient priesthood councils, the Prophet said:

"I had never set before any council in all the order in which it ought to be conducted, which, perhaps, has deprived the councils of some or many blessings. . . .

"In ancient days councils were conducted with such strict propriety, that no one was allowed to whisper, be weary, leave the room, or get uneasy in the least, until the voice of the Lord, by revelation, or the voice of the council by the Spirit, was obtained, which has not been observed in this Church to the present time. It was understood in ancient days, that if one man could stay in council, another could; and if the president could spend his time, the members could also; but in our councils, generally, one will be uneasy, another asleep; one praying, another not; one's mind on the business of the council, and another thinking on something else."[8]

THE POLITICAL OR CIVIL DIMENSION OF THE KINGDOM

At present the priesthood of the Church functions as an ecclesiastical organization—that is, as a church. Nonetheless, the power is inherent in the priesthood and the keys to function in a political manner when circumstances permit. Such was the case with Adam, Noah, the Nephites, and Moses. Concerning the children of Israel under Moses, the Prophet Joseph Smith said:

"Their government was a theocracy; they had God to make their laws, and men chosen by Him to administer them; He was their God, and they were His people. Moses received the word of the Lord from God Himself; he was the mouth of God to Aaron, and Aaron taught the people, in both civil and ecclesiastical affairs; they were both one, there was no distinction; so will it be when the purposes of God shall be accomplished: when 'the Lord shall be King over the whole earth' and 'Jerusalem His throne.' 'The law shall go forth from Zion, and the word of the Lord from Jerusalem.'

"This is the only thing that can bring about the 'restitution of all things spoken of by all the holy Prophets since the world was'—'the dispensation of the fullness of times, when God shall gather together all things in one.'"[9]

That is the civil or political dimension of the kingdom of God on earth, which is not operative at the present time.

The important distinction or separation that sometimes has to exist between civil and ecclesiastical matters was referred to by the Savior when He was questioned by Pilate about His kingship and His kingdom. Surely no believer can doubt Jesus' right to rule the world and the universe as Lord of lords and King of kings. The Jewish rulers, however, wanted to make trouble for Jesus in the eyes of the Roman

Empire. They wanted Jesus to be charged with treason against Rome because He was the king of the Jews. A dialogue on this topic between the Roman governor Pilate and Jesus is found in John 18:33–38:

"Then Pilate entered into the judgment hall again, and called Jesus, and said unto him, Art thou the King of the Jews?

"Jesus answered him, Sayest thou this thing of thyself, or did others tell it thee of me?" [That is, Jesus asked, Are you speaking as a Roman official or citing what the Jews have said? Are you asking a political question or an ecclesiastical question?]

"Pilate answered, Am I a Jew? Thine own nation and the chief priests have delivered thee unto me: what hast thou done?" [Pilate's response, "Am I a Jew?" means, I am not asking as a Jew; I am asking politically as a Roman official.]

"Jesus answered, My kingdom is not of this world: if my kingdom were of this world, then would my servants fight, that I should not be delivered to the Jews: but now is my kingdom not from hence.

"Pilate therefore said unto him, Art thou a king then? Jesus answered, Thou sayest that I am a king. To this end was I born, and for this cause came I into the world, that I should bear witness unto the truth. Every one that is of the truth heareth my voice.

"Pilate saith unto him, What is truth? And when he had said this, he went out again unto the Jews, and saith unto them, I find in him no fault at all."

What all that means is, Yes, I am a king, and eventually my kingdom shall fill the whole earth, but not now. Therefore, I have not set up a kingdom that will rival or threaten the present Roman Empire.

We know that ultimately Jesus' kingdom *is* "of this world," for He said that the meek shall inherit the earth (see Matthew 5:5; D&C 88:17), and in the Revelation of John the promise is made that the faithful shall become kings and priests unto God and "shall reign on the earth" (Revelation 5:10). The time will come when the kingdom spoken of by Daniel, and by Jesus, and by John, and by Joseph Smith, will fill the whole earth and will replace all the kingdoms of the earth. That is what the Twelve in Jerusalem had in mind when they asked Jesus, "Wilt thou at this time restore again the kingdom to Israel?" (Acts 1:6). Jesus answered, in effect, not at this time—but later (see Acts 1:7). The time is not yet, but it will occur sometime in this dispensation. As expressed in Doctrine and Covenants 65:2, 5–6:

"The keys of the kingdom of God are committed unto man on the earth, and from thence shall the gospel roll forth unto the ends of the earth, as the stone which is cut out of the mountain without hands shall roll forth, until it has filled the whole earth. . . .

"Call upon the Lord, that his kingdom may go forth upon the earth, that the inhabitants thereof may receive it, and be prepared for the days to come, in the which the Son of Man shall come down in heaven, clothed in the brightness of his glory, to meet the kingdom of God which is set up on the earth.

"Wherefore, may the kingdom of God go forth, that the kingdom of heaven may come, that thou, O God, mayest be glorified in heaven so on earth, that thine enemies may be subdued; for thine is the honor, power and glory, forever and ever. Amen."

And Doctrine and Covenants 87:6 indicates that the Lord has decreed eventually "a full end of all nations," to be replaced by the Lord's own kingdom.

THE GATHERING OF ISRAEL

A major accomplishment of the restoration of all things will be the literal gathering of the literal seed of Israel. It will be done because of the promise God made to the fathers that He would look after their posterity. Modern Israel has descended from ancient Israel, and are "lawful heirs, according to the flesh" (D&C 86:9). Special blessings were given to the sons of Jacob that have carried down through the years and will reach a fulfillment in the final gathering and restoration of Israel. Judah was given the scepter and the power to govern. From him came David the king, with a promise that from his seed would come the kings that would reign in Israel (see Jeremiah 33:17; Psalms 89:3–4; 35–36; 132:11–12). The Doctrine and Covenants affirms that Jesus Christ came of that very lineage and is the son of David, the stem of Jesse (see Isaiah 9:6–7; 11:1; Luke 1:30–33; D&C 113:1). It was absolutely necessary that Jesus, as King of kings, come through the lineage of Judah and David, in addition to being the Son of God.

The sons of Levi, especially Aaron and his sons, have had a special role in earlier dispensations and will yet have a major role in the restoration of Israel and the consecration of properties, as we have already discussed. It is just as important that a future bishop be of the lineage of Aaron as it was that Jesus be of the lineage of David. Likewise, the descendants of Joseph have the right to be the first to hear the gospel in the last days. Joseph's lineage has the Joseph-like responsibility to gather the tribes of Latter-day Israel by giving them the "bread of life" similar to the way Joseph preserved his brothers anciently. Therefore Ephraim, who was given the birthright in ancient times, has the richer blessing and the particular responsibility to gather Israel (see D&C 133:26–35). It is no accident or coincidence that Joseph Smith and most of the Latter-day Saints are literal blood descendants of ancient Joseph. That is part of the restoration of all things.

CHANGES IN THE EARTH ITSELF

If the covenant people are to be gathered, the land must become productive enough to sustain them. The Lord, through the prophets of old, spoke of the land becoming fruitful and the desert blossoming "as the rose" (Isaiah 35:1).

Genesis 10:24 states that at a certain time the land was physically divided and no longer remained as one land. Doctrine and Covenants 133:23–24 states that in the last days "the islands shall become one land . . . and the earth shall be like as it was in the days before it was divided."

If we contemplate the plan of God on the earth since the beginning and consider the importance of multiple witnesses, we can view the Bible, the Book of Mormon, and the record of the lost tribes as three major witnesses for the work of the Lord. These three separate testimonies came as the result of these peoples being separated by great distances of land and with the oceans as natural barriers. Who can say but that the division of the land into continents and islands separated by large oceans was done in the wisdom of God to bring about the condition in earlier dispensations whereby there would be separate witnesses, or records, from various branches of the house of Israel? Now, in the fulness of times, when the tribes of Israel are to be gathered and their records are also to be gathered—and since the rapid transportation of the last days makes the oceans no longer such major barriers—the need for separation is past. Therefore, as part of the restoration the land shall come together again, "like as it was before it was divided." The Lord has designed to "gather together in one all things, both which are in heaven, and which are on earth" (D&C 27:13; see also Ephesians 1:10).

Furthermore, the earth when created was paradisiacal, before the Fall of Adam. The promise is that "the earth will be renewed and receive its paradisiacal glory" (Articles of Faith 1:10). The Prophet Joseph Smith said the earth is to be renovated.[10]

This glorification of the earth is spoken of in the Doctrine and Covenants as follows: "And the end shall come, and the heaven and the earth shall be consumed and pass away, and there shall be a new heaven and a new earth. For all old things shall pass away, and all things shall become new, even the heaven and the earth, and all the fulness thereof, both men and beasts, the fowls of the air, and the fishes of the sea; and not one hair, neither mote, shall be lost, for it is the workmanship of mine hand" (D&C 29:23–25; see also 101:23–34).

Also: "Nevertheless, he that endureth in faith and doeth my will, the same shall overcome, and shall receive an inheritance upon the earth when the day of transfiguration shall come; when the earth shall be transfigured, even according to the pattern which was shown unto mine apostles upon the mount; of which account the fulness ye have not yet received" (D&C 63:20–21).

THINGS NEVER BEFORE REVEALED

Not only will the ancient order be reestablished on the earth but the final dispensation will be given things never before revealed. We read in Doctrine and Covenants 121:26–28, 31–32:

"God shall give unto you knowledge by his Holy Spirit, yea, by the unspeakable gift of the Holy Ghost, that has not been revealed since the world was until now;

"Which our forefathers have awaited with anxious expectation to be revealed in the last times, which their minds were pointed to by the angels, as held in reserve for the fulness of their glory;

"A time to come in the which nothing shall be withheld. . . .

"All their glories, laws, and set times, shall be revealed in the days of the dispensation of the fulness of times—

"According to that which was ordained in the midst of the

Council of the Eternal God of all other gods before this world was, that should be reserved unto the finishing and the end thereof."

When speaking of the restoration of all things, we must understand that it is the ancient promises, the ancient priesthood, and the doctrinal teachings that are to be renewed. The Restoration does not mean that clothing styles, building construction, and traveling conveyances must revert to those of earlier times. We are not going to live in Abraham-style tents and travel by camel. The Restoration is of eternal things, the promises of eternal glory and exaltation that were made to Adam and to Abraham, as well as the ordinances and covenants by which such blessings can be secured by individuals living today.

In preparation for the Restoration, the Lord moved among the nations of the earth, causing the Renaissance and the Reformation and establishing the United States of America. All of this preparation and the modern inventions we now enjoy were inspired of God to assist in the restoration of all things. Because of the Restoration there has been as much improvement in doctrinal understanding over what churches believed 150 years ago as there has been in communication and travel over what people had 150 years ago.

God lives in a perfect, celestial society with all the advantages and enjoyments of perfect intelligence, rapid communication, rapid travel, and the very best in building construction and utility. The high state of twenty-first-century technology, which exceeds anything this earth has ever known, is very primitive compared with what is yet to be revealed when the earth becomes a celestial world. Because of both present and future technological development, we in this dispensation will be able to do a great many things not possible in earlier times.

True prophets of every dispensation have been working hand in hand with each other and with the Lord Jesus Christ in the same cause, as explained by the Prophet Joseph Smith:

"The building up of Zion is a cause that has interested the people of God in every age; it is a theme upon which prophets, priests and kings have dwelt with peculiar delight; they have looked forward with joyful anticipation to the day in which we live; and fired with heavenly and joyful anticipations they have sung and written and prophesied of this our day; but they died without the sight; we are the favored people that God has made choice of to bring about the

Latter-day glory; it is left for us to see, participate in and help to roll forward the Latter-day glory, 'the dispensation of the fulness of times, when God will gather together all things that are in heaven, and all things that are upon the earth,' 'even in one,' when the Saints of God will be gathered in one from every nation, and kindred, and people, and tongue, when the Jews will be gathered together into one, the wicked will also be gathered together to be destroyed, as spoken of by the prophets; the Spirit of God will also dwell with His people, and be withdrawn from the rest of the nations, and all things whether in heaven or on earth will be in one, even in Christ. The heavenly Priesthood will unite with the earthly, to bring about those great purposes; and whilst we are thus united in one common cause, to roll forth the kingdom of God, the heavenly Priesthood are not idle spectators, the Spirit of God will be showered down from above, and it will dwell in our midst. . . . [We are laying the foundation of] a work that God and angels have contemplated with delight for generations past; that fired the souls of the ancient patriarchs and prophets; a work that is destined to bring about the destruction of the powers of darkness, the renovation of the earth, the glory of God, and the salvation of the human family."[11]

SUMMARY

The Prophet Joseph Smith said that the work the Lord called him to do would revolutionize the world. The Lord called His work "my act, my strange act" (D&C 101:95; see also 95:4; Isaiah 28:21). He also called it "a marvelous work and a wonder" (2 Nephi 25:17). The Restoration is strange to those not of the Church, and it is marvelous to those who are of the Church. Even so, most of us have perhaps had but peripheral comprehension of the marvelous changes that will yet take place in the earth and in the Church in order to bring about the restoration of all things spoken of by the mouths of all the holy prophets since the world began. Such is the role of this dispensation. The restoration of all things is a reality. It has begun, and much has been revealed. There is still much to be implemented that has already been revealed, and there is more yet to be revealed.

NOTES

1. Joseph Smith, *Teachings of the Prophet Joseph Smith*, comp. Joseph Fielding Smith (Salt Lake City: Deseret Book, 1974), 366.

2. See *Messenger and Advocate* 1 (1835), nos. 5, 7, and 10, containing a letter of Oliver Cowdery; and Daniel H. Ludlow, ed., *Encyclopedia of Mormonism* (New York: Macmillan, 1992), 1:355.

3. See also John Taylor, *The Mediation and Atonement of Our Lord and Savior Jesus Christ* (Salt Lake City: Deseret News Press, 1882); Orson Pratt, in *Journal of Discourses* (London: Latter-day Saints' Book Depot, 1854–86), 16:58 (May 18, 1873); Bruce R. McConkie, *Doctrinal New Testament Commentary* (Salt Lake City: Bookcraft, 1965), 1:70–71. A discussion of this subject is also found in Robert J. Matthews, *A Burning Light* (Provo, Utah: Brigham Young University Press, 1972), 79–81.

4. See also Smith, *Teachings*, 112.

5. See Smith, *Teachings*, 173.

6. Orson F. Whitney, *Life of Heber C. Kimball* (Salt Lake City: Stevens & Wallis, 1945), 328.

7. Smith, *Teachings*, 237.

8. Smith, *Teachings*, 69.

9. Smith, *Teachings*, 252.

10. See Smith, *Teachings*, 232.

11. See Smith, *Teachings*, 231–32.

CHAPTER EIGHT

REDEMPTION FOR THE DEAD (D&C 2)

LELAND GENTRY

Moroni visited Joseph Smith three times on the night and early morning of September 21, 1823. During these encounters he quoted a number of Old Testament passages of scripture to the seventeen-year-old prophet. One of the more significant passages was taken from the writings of the prophet Malachi. Almost every sentence is filled with great significance for us who live today. Moroni quoted from Malachi: "For behold, the day cometh that shall burn as an oven, and all the proud, yea, and all that do wickedly shall burn as stubble; for they that come shall burn them, saith the Lord of Hosts, that it shall leave them neither root nor branch. . . . Behold, I will reveal unto you the Priesthood, by the hand of Elijah the prophet, before the coming of the great and dreadful day of the Lord. . . . And he [Elijah] shall plant in the hearts of the children the promises made to the fathers, and the hearts of the children shall turn to their fathers. If it were not so, the whole earth would be utterly wasted at his [Christ's] coming" (Joseph Smith—History 1:37–39).

The last two verses of this prophecy are also found in section 2 of the Doctrine and Covenants. We will examine and explicate these scriptural passages as they relate to the doctrine of the redemption of the dead. We shall do this by asking and then trying to answer certain questions raised by this passage of scripture.

Leland Gentry is a retired Church Educational System instructor who taught at the Salt Lake University Institute of Religion.

"THE GREAT AND DREADFUL DAY"

First, what is meant by the phrase "the great and dreadful day of the Lord," a day that will burn like an oven and leave the wicked with neither root nor branch? Latter-day Saints recognize this phrase as an allusion to the Second Coming of our Savior, a day that will be great for the righteous and dreadful for the wicked. Every corruptible thing on earth shall be consumed by the brightness of our Savior's coming, and to be left with neither root nor branch means to be bereft of both ancestry (roots) and posterity (branches) inasmuch as the wicked will be unsealed either to their children or to those from whom they descend. It is difficult to think of a more appropriate figure to describe this condition than a tree with neither roots nor branches. The whole earth would be utterly wasted at Christ's Second Coming (see D&C 2:1–3).

"THE PROMISES MADE TO THEIR FATHERS"

Second, what is meant by Moroni's phrase of planting in the hearts of the children the "promises made to their fathers," thus causing the "hearts of the children" to "turn to their fathers"? The fathers are the ancient patriarchs, such as Adam, Enoch, Noah, Abraham, Isaac, Jacob, and Joseph. God made unique promises to these men because of their faithfulness. President Joseph Fielding Smith once said:

"What was the promise made to the fathers that was to be fulfilled in the latter-days by the turning of the hearts of the children to their fathers? It was the promise of the Lord made through Enoch, Isaiah, and the prophets, to the nations of the earth, that the time should come when the dead should be redeemed. And the turning of the hearts of the children is fulfilled in the performing of the vicarious temple work and in the preparation of their genealogies. . . .

"Some of these promises made to the fathers are found in the scriptures. For instance, Isaiah said in reference to our Savior: 'I the Lord have called thee in righteousness, and will hold thine hand, and will keep thee, and give thee for a covenant of the people, for a light of the Gentiles; to open the blind eyes, to bring out the prisoners from the prison, and them that sit in darkness out of the prison house.' [Isaiah 42:6–7.] . . .

"Again, he says: 'The Spirit of the Lord God is upon me; because the Lord hath anointed me to preach good tidings unto the meek; he hath sent me to bind up the brokenhearted, to proclaim liberty to the captives, and the opening of the prison to them that are bound.' [Isaiah 61:1.] This was spoken of as the mission of the Redeemer, both His work for the living and the dead, who were prisoners that were bound."[1]

Thus the promises made to the fathers in ancient times included not only a covenant that their descendants' temple work would be performed in the latter days but also a promise that Christ would come, open the eyes of the spiritually blind, enlighten the Gentiles, preach the gospel to those in the spirit prison, and liberate the righteous dead who were handicapped by lack of opportunity. God also made a special covenant with Father Abraham that He would make of him "a great nation," bless him "above measure," and make him a blessing to his seed by giving them "the blessings of the Gospel, which are the blessings of salvation, even of life eternal" (Abraham 2:9, 11).

Our Father in Heaven is at the head of one vast family. This grand system of things He has organized on earth under the direction of Adam, our first earthly father, and given title to as the patriarchal order in which all of the aforementioned blessings are passed from father to son. Patterned after the heavenly arrangement, Adam, often referred to in scripture and elsewhere as the Ancient of Days,[2] stands at the head of this holy order over which he will yet sit in formal judgment as "ten thousand times ten thousands" pass before to acknowledge him as their grand patriarch, the "father of all." He will preside at the great council at Adam-ondi-Ahman to be held at a future date and eventually "reign over his righteous posterity in the Patriarchal Order to all eternity."[3]

The Earth Utterly Wasted

Third, why would the earth be utterly wasted at our Savior's Second Coming if the work of salvation for the dead were not performed? This question has already been answered in part. Interestingly enough, in his original prophecy Malachi used the word "cursed," whereas the angel Moroni used the phrase "utterly wasted." God created this earth as a home for man to work out his eternal life and salvation. Were all men to be left with neither ancestry nor posterity, there would be no eternal family of God to inherit the earth.

Were those in the spirit prison waiting for their temple work to be done never to realize that great blessing (they too once lived on this mortal earth), that would be one of the greatest catastrophes imaginable. To answer the question succinctly, we must view the eternal family organization from Adam and Eve to the present time as one grand unit and realize that God desires the salvation and even the exaltation of all His children. Hear these words of scripture: "The earth will be smitten with a curse unless there is a welding link of some kind or other between the fathers and the children. . . . For we without them cannot be made perfect; neither can they without us be made perfect. Neither can they nor we be made perfect without those who have died in the gospel also" (D&C 128:18). Were this not the case, each person would exist "separately and singly, without exaltation, in their saved condition [that is, with some degree of glory], to all eternity; and from henceforth are not gods, but are angels of God forever and ever" (D&C 132:17). I love the thought of a welding link—the very thing that holds me to my wife and children for time and all eternity, if we live worthy lives.

THE PRIESTHOOD REVEALED BY ELIJAH

Fourth, and finally, what about the promise to reveal the priesthood by the hand of Elijah the prophet? The Prophet Joseph Smith said: "Elijah was the last Prophet that held the keys of the Priesthood, and who will, before the last dispensation, restore the authority and deliver the keys of the Priesthood, in order that all the ordinances may be attended to in righteousness. It is true that the Savior had authority and power to bestow this blessing; but the sons of Levi were too prejudiced. 'And I will send Elijah the Prophet before the great and terrible day of the Lord,' etc., etc. Why send Elijah? Because he holds the keys of the authority to administer in all the ordinances of the Priesthood; and without the authority is given, the ordinances could not be administered in righteousness."[4]

Elijah did come as promised. Shortly after the Kirtland Temple was dedicated, Moses, Elias, Elijah, and the Savior Himself visited there. Elijah bestowed on Joseph Smith and Oliver Cowdery the sealing keys of the Melchizedek Priesthood (see D&C 110:15–16), the very powers that today in modern temples join couples together and commit to them the powers of eternal increase.

Fortunately for us, Joseph Smith made at least two other interesting observations on the work of Elijah:

"Now comes the point. What is this office and work of Elijah? It is one of the greatest and most important subjects that God has revealed. He should send Elijah to seal the children to the fathers, and the fathers to the children.

"Now was this merely confined to the living, to settle difficulties with families on earth? By no means. It was a far greater work. Elijah! what would you do if you were here? Would you confine your work to the living alone? No: I would refer you to the Scriptures, where the subject is manifest: that is, without us, they could not be made perfect, nor we without them; the fathers without the children, nor the children without the fathers.

"I wish you to understand this subject, for it is important; and if you receive it, this is the spirit of Elijah, that we redeem our dead, and connect ourselves with our fathers which are in heaven, and seal up our dead to come forth in the first resurrection; and here we want the power of Elijah to seal those who dwell on earth to those who dwell in heaven. This is the power of Elijah and the keys of the kingdom of Jehovah."[5]

How appropriate for the great prophet of the latter days to refer to Elijah's work as "one of the greatest and most important subjects that God has revealed." The Prophet also said this: "The spirit, power, and calling of Elijah is, that ye have power to hold the key of the revelations, ordinances, oracles, powers and endowments of the fulness of the Melchizedek Priesthood and of the kingdom of God on the earth; and to receive, obtain, and perform all the ordinances belonging to the kingdom of God, even unto the turning of the hearts of the fathers unto the children, and the hearts of the children unto the fathers, even those who are in heaven."[6]

We could scarcely overemphasize the role of Elijah where redemption for the dead is concerned. But the inquiring student might ask, "What evidence do you have that Elijah ever truly held the sealing powers of the holy priesthood?" For the answer, we have only to examine the life and activities of Elijah as they are recorded in the pages of the Old Testament. A careful reading of 1 Kings 17–18 shows that it was Elijah who, in the days of Ahab, king of Israel, sealed up the heavens so that it did not rain for three years, unsealed those same heavens so that the earth received its needed moisture, sealed up a widow woman's flour barrel and cruse of oil against depletion during the famine, raised her only son from the dead, called down fire upon the priests of Baal to impress them with the true God's power, and finally was taken into heaven in a chariot of fire without tasting death.[7] He, as a translated being, appeared with Moses to Peter, James, and John on the Mount of Transfiguration and, in the presence of the Savior of the world, delivered his sealing keys that they, too might bind on earth what is bound in heaven.[8]

REDEMPTION FOR THE DEAD REVEALED

As with most principles of the gospel, the doctrine of redemption for the dead came to the Church gradually, literally "line upon line, precept upon precept, here a little and there a little" (2 Nephi 28:30). This appears to be the usual process by which our Heavenly Father works. How much of the doctrine the young prophet understood as a result of Moroni's first three visits we are not prepared to say, but it seems safe to assume that it was abundantly clear in Moroni's mind. He knew that temple work would be one of the glorious truths introduced by Joseph Smith in these latter days.

As new revelation was added, Joseph Smith and other prophets grew progressively expansive in their expressions about temple work. The following are some of their comments:

"It is sufficient to know, in this case, that the earth will be smitten with a curse unless there is a welding link of some kind or other between the fathers and the children" (D&C 128:18).

"I will give you a quotation from one of the prophets, who had his eye fixed on the restoration of the priesthood, the glories to be revealed in the last days, and in an especial manner this most glorious of all subjects belonging to the everlasting gospel, namely, the baptism for the dead" (D&C 128:17).

"For we without them cannot be made perfect; neither can they without us be made perfect" (D&C 128:18).

"And now, my dearly beloved brethren and sisters, let me assure you that these are principles in relation to the dead and the living that cannot be lightly passed over, as pertaining to our salvation. For their salvation is necessary and essential to our salvation, as Paul says concerning the fathers—that they without us cannot be made perfect—neither can we without our dead be made perfect" (D&C 128:15).

"The saints have not too much time to save and redeem *their* dead. . . . If the whole Church should go to with all their might to save *their* dead . . . and spend none of their time in behalf of the world, they would hardly get through."[9]

"What kind of characters are those who can be saved although their bodies are decaying in the grave? When his [God's] commandments teach us, it is in view of eternity. The greatest responsibility in this world that God has laid upon us, is to seek after our dead.—The apostle [Paul] says, they without us cannot be made perfect. Now I will speak of them:—I say to you Paul, you cannot be perfect without us: it is necessary that those who are gone before, and those who come after us should have salvation in common with us, and thus hath God made it obligatory to man."[10]

"President Joseph Smith, by request of some of the Twelve, gave instructions on the doctrine of Baptism for the Dead. . . . The speaker presented 'Baptism for the Dead' as the only way that men can appear as saviors on mount Zion. The proclamation of the first principles of the gospel was a means of salvation to men individually, and it was the truth, not men that saved them; but men, by actively engaging in rites of salvation substitutionally, became instrumental in bringing multitudes of their kin into the kingdom of God. . . .

"This doctrine [salvation for the dead] he said, presented in a clear light, the wisdom and mercy of God in preparing an ordinance for the salvation of the dead, being baptised by proxy, their names recorded in heaven, and they judged according to the deeds done in the body. This doctrine was the burden of the scriptures. Those saints who neglect it, in behalf of *their* deceased relatives, do it at the peril of their own salvation."[11]

"In 1894, the Lord re-emphasized in a revelation through his prophet, Wilford Woodruff, that it was necessary, in the completion of temple work, to have children sealed to their parents and the parents in turn to their parents in all generations. The saints were told to trace their genealogies and run this chain of generations back into the past as far as it was possible to do so. 'This,' said Pres. Woodruff, 'is the will of the Lord to His people.'"[12]

TEMPLE WORK INSTITUTED

The first temple completed in this dispensation was built in Kirtland, Ohio. Although a full complement of temple ordinances was never performed therein, small inklings of future events did emerge. Shortly before Elijah restored his keys, the School of the Prophets met in the attic of the printing office and there attended to "the ordinance of washing our bodies in pure water." That same evening, Joseph Smith and others took oil in their hands, blessed it, and "consecrated it in the name of Jesus Christ," and anointed the head of Joseph's father with the holy oil and pronounced upon him "many blessings," and those present blessed him to be their patriarch. Each in his turn then received a blessing and an anointing from the hands of the new patriarch. Joseph then reports that the heavens were opened and he "beheld the celestial kingdom of God, and the glory thereof," the Father and the Son, Adam and Abraham, and Joseph Smith's own mother, father, and brother Alvin. It was this view of Alvin that caused Joseph to marvel, since the older brother had never been baptized. The revelation recorded in section 137 of our Doctrine and Covenants was then given. From this Joseph learned the great doctrinal truth that "all who have died without a knowledge of this Gospel, who would have received it if they had been permitted to tarry shall be heirs of the celestial kingdom of God."[13]

From this point on, the Prophet began to use the term *endowment* with greater and greater frequency, and the word soon became well known throughout the Church.[14] Practically nothing was known about the endowment, however, as we know it today. Not until the fulness of the priesthood was revealed in Nauvoo, Illinois, was the Church to have a clearer understanding of the higher ordinances.

The first real reference to temple work as we know it occurred in a revelation given at Nauvoo on 14 January 1841, while the temple was still under construction. The Lord speaks in section 124 of "your anointings, and your washings, and your baptisms for the dead" and said these were to be attended to in that place. Among much else, the revelation states: "And verily I say unto you, let this house be built unto my name, that I may reveal mine ordinances therein unto my people; for I deign to reveal unto my church things which have been kept hid from before the foundation of the world, things that pertain to the dispensation of the fulness of times. And I will show unto my servant Joseph all things pertaining to this house, and the priesthood thereof, and the place whereon it shall be built" (D&C 124:39–42).

Baptisms for the dead began shortly after Joseph Smith preached about them on August 16, 1840, at the funeral of Seymour Brunson.[15] From that time, although careful records were not always kept, the Saints commenced to think about the necessity for this ordinance and began to attend to it. Jane Nyman appears to have been among the first. After consultation with her husband, she entered the waters of the Mississippi River on September 13, 1840, and was baptized in behalf of her deceased son.[16] One month later, on October 15, residents on the Iowa side of the Mississippi commenced to do the same.[17] One year later, at the October conference, the Prophet brought the baptisms for the dead outside the temple to a halt: "There shall be no more baptisms for the dead, until the ordinance can be attended to in the Lord's House."[18] The first baptisms for the dead performed in the temple took place on November 21, 1841.[19]

Many of the ordinances required for salvation cannot be attended to in person by those in need of the ordinances. Like Joseph's brother Alvin, they died before the fulness of the priesthood was restored, or they never heard the gospel message while in life. Thus, we learn from President Joseph F. Smith's vision of the redemption of the dead that the Savior visited the spirits in prison, organized His missionary forces, and sent them forth to preach the gospel to the dead:

"These were taught faith in God, repentance from sin, vicarious baptism for the remission of sins, the gift of the Holy Ghost by the laying on of hands,

"And all other principles of the gospel that were necessary for them to know in order to qualify themselves that they might be judged according to men in the flesh, but live according to God in the spirit. . . .

"Thus it was made known that our Redeemer spent his time during his sojourn in the world of spirits, instructing and preparing the faithful spirits of the prophets who had testified of him in the flesh;

"That they might carry the message of redemption unto all the dead, unto whom he could not go personally, because of their rebellion and transgression, that they through the ministration of his servants might also hear his words" (D&C 138:33–34, 36–37).

CONCLUSION

Vicarious, or proxy, work is the very heart of the gospel of Jesus Christ. Our Savior's Atonement in our behalf was a vicarious act, the strong doing for the weak that which they cannot do for themselves if they would only comply with His principles and ordinances. It is the same in the spirit world. Water and the laying on of hands are elements of this physical world and are essential features of redemption. They must be complied with here. It is an act of purest love to make it possible for the living to comply with earthly ordinances in behalf of those who never had that opportunity. May I commend all faithful temple workers who unselfishly devote hours of loving service in behalf of the worthy deceased. May I also compliment those untiring servants of the Lord who spend countless hours researching to locate names, dates, places, and relationships that make temple work the blessed work it is. Small wonder that the Prophet Joseph Smith should issue his fervent appeal to those of us who live today, to us whose hearts have turned to our fathers in the world of spirits, who never had the chance to comply with the ordinances of salvation: "Brethren, shall we not go on in so great a cause? Go forward and not backward. Courage, brethren; and on, on to the victory! Let your hearts rejoice, and be exceedingly glad. Let the earth break forth into singing. Let the dead speak forth anthems of eternal praise to the King Immanuel, who hath ordained, before the world was, that which would enable us to redeem them out of their prison; for the prisoners shall go free" (D&C 128:22).

NOTES

1. Joseph Fielding Smith, *Doctrines of Salvation,* comp. Bruce R. McConkie (Salt Lake City: Bookcraft, 1954–56), 2:154–55.

2. See Daniel 7:9–14; see also Joseph Smith, *Teachings of the Prophet Joseph Smith,* comp. Joseph Fielding Smith (Salt Lake City: Deseret Book, 1938), 157–59, 167–69.

3. Bruce R. McConkie, *Mormon Doctrine,* 2nd ed. (Salt Lake City: Bookcraft, 1966), 17–18.

4. Joseph Smith, *History of the Church of Jesus Christ of Latter-day Saints,*

ed. B. H. Roberts, 2nd ed., rev. (Salt Lake City: Deseret Book, 1932–51), 4:211.

5. Smith, *Teachings,* 337–38.

6. Smith, *Teachings,* 337.

7. See 1 Kings 17:1, 14, 21–24; 18:32–39; 2 Kings 2:9–12.

8. See Matthew 17:1–13; see also Smith, *Teachings,* 158.

9. History of Joseph Smith, January 1844, Archives, The Church of Jesus Christ of Latter-day Saints, Salt Lake City, Utah; hereafter Church Archives.

10. Conference minutes for April 1844, *Times and Seasons,* 5:616.

11. Conference minutes for October 1, 1841, *Times and Seasons,* 2:577–78.

12. *Handbook for Genealogy and Temple Work* (Salt Lake City: Genealogical Society of Utah, 1956), 2.

13. Smith, *History of the Church,* 2:379–80.

14. See D&C 32:32, 38; 95:8; 105:11–12; 110:9; 124:39; 132:59.

15. Joseph Smith's Letter Book, November 6, 1838 to February 9, 1843, 191–96, Church Archives.

16. Letter of George A. Smith, n.p., n.d., Church Archives.

17. John Smith Diary, Thursday, October 15, 1840, Church Archives.

18. Smith, *History of the Church,* 4:426.

19. Smith, *History of the Church,* 4:454.

CHAPTER NINE

The Articles and Covenants of the Church of Christ and the Book of Mormon

ROBERT J. WOODFORD

In 1959 Brenda Daily and her brother Bill attended Ravenna High School in Ravenna, Ohio. They had recently moved there with their family from the Canal Zone, where their father, William D. Daily, served in the military. While in the Canal Zone, these two young people had learned conversational Spanish. They were anxious to study the language at their new school. Unfortunately, the school was not large enough for a regular Spanish class; however, the principal, Wayne E. Watters, had experience teaching Spanish. He was willing to teach a class before school if Brenda and Bill could also get some other students to attend. They found several willing classmates, and soon they had an enthusiastic class functioning.

During the year, Mr. Watters found out that Bill and Brenda were Latter-day Saints. Once he knew that, he had several discussions with them about the Church. On one occasion he mentioned that his wife's father had an early document of the LDS Church in his possession. He told them that the family had preserved it through four generations. His wife's maiden name is Virginia Ryder, and she is a great-great-granddaughter of Symonds Ryder. He was an 1831 convert

Robert J. Woodford, now retired, was an instructor at the Salt Lake Institute of Religion.

103

to the Church from Hiram, Ohio.[1] How Symonds Ryder obtained this document is an interesting story itself.[2]

Later in the year, during a serious illness, Wayne and Virginia Watters feared her father would soon die. They thought that he had no more use for the document, and so they gave it to Brenda.[3] They felt it would be of greater value to a member of the Church than it was to them. Brenda took it to her father, and he immediately realized that it was a record of some worth. He conveyed it to the mission president in Ohio, who sent it to Church headquarters with the next missionary returning to Utah.[4] The Church historian placed it in the archives of the Church, where researchers can have access to it today.

This document is in the handwriting of Oliver Cowdery[5] and is three pages in length. It begins, "A commandment from God unto Oliver how he should build up his Church & the manner thereof." It ends, "Written in the year of our Lord & Saviour 1829—A true copy of the Articles of the Church of Christ &c."[6]

The body of the document is composed of scriptures from the Book of Mormon and the Doctrine and Covenants interspersed with inspired commentary by Oliver Cowdery.[7] Through these, Oliver Cowdery established several important doctrinal truths. First, because the world is becoming a more wicked place, there is a great need to repent and be baptized. He then explained the procedures for proper baptism.

Second, he established that men are to be ordained to the priesthood, and he demonstrated the proper method of performing these ordinations. Those who are so ordained are to pray for the Church and teach the members the truths of the gospel.

Third, he explained the doctrine concerning the sacrament. The members are to meet together often to partake of it. He related from the scriptures the form of the ordinance, including the prayers that should be said. He also included the warning from 3 Nephi about partaking of the sacrament unworthily.

Fourth, he taught that the Church members should meet together often to tell each other of their progress toward eternal life, and he explained a standard of moral conduct which every member should live. He also explained that those who will not repent must be cast out of the Church.

Finally, he issued a call for all people to come to Christ and take His name upon them. If they will walk uprightly before the Lord, then His grace is sufficient for them.

There is a close connection between this 1829 manuscript of Oliver Cowdery and section 20 of the Doctrine and Covenants. The title of section 20 in the surviving manuscripts and early published copies is "The Articles and Covenants of the Church of Christ." The title of section 20 as it was published in *The Evening and the Morning Star,* in the June 1832 issue, is the same, and it is similar to the title of Oliver Cowdery's early manuscript, "The Articles of the Church of Christ." Section 20 also contains some of the Book of Mormon scriptures quoted by Oliver Cowdery in his manuscript. Oliver Cowdery's manuscript is an early forerunner to the more comprehensive section 20. The following is an attempt to reconstruct the events leading to the composition of both the 1829 "Articles" and our present Doctrine and Covenants 20.

In section 20 are short statements about the origin of the Church, the basic doctrines, and the ordinances. There are also statements about the duties of members and priesthood bearers. The intent of the articles and covenants was to provide members and investigators with a summary about the Church. In one short reading they could gain a comprehensive overview of the whole Church.[8] The Lord may have inspired the Prophet Joseph Smith to assign Oliver Cowdery to write the early "Articles."

Oliver Cowdery had wanted to know what material to put into the "Articles of the Church" and approached the Prophet for help. Joseph Smith prayed about the matter and received the revelation known as Doctrine and Covenants 18. In verse 1 of section 18 we learn that the Lord gave this revelation because of "the thing" that Oliver Cowdery desired to know. Oliver Cowdery wanted to know what to write.

The Lord told Oliver Cowdery He had manifested to him many times that the things he had written were true (see D&C 18:2). Oliver Cowdery was the principal scribe for the Book of Mormon as the Prophet dictated it.

The Lord told Oliver Cowdery to rely on the things he had written that he already knew were true (see D&C 18:3). That is, he was to get the information he needed for the 1829 "Articles" of the Church from the Book of Mormon.

The Lord said He placed "all things . . . concerning the foundation of [His] church" in the Book of Mormon (D&C 18:4). The Lord had already inspired prophets to put in that book the basic principles Oliver Cowdery needed for the earliest procedural statement of the Church of Christ. The Lord told Oliver to "build up my church, upon the foundation of my gospel" (D&C 18:5). If he did, the gates of hell could not prevail against him. Note that Oliver Cowdery included the phrase "build up my church" in the introduction of the Ryder document. Oliver Cowdery then composed his three-page version of the articles of the Church from Book of Mormon scriptures. This is the same document that Symonds Ryder acquired.

Oliver Cowdery must have submitted his manuscript to Joseph Smith, but the 1829 Articles were superceded in the first half of 1830 by the articles and covenants. Cowdery's document remained with the official papers of the Church until Ryder acquired them in the summer of 1831.[9]

The importance attached to Doctrine and Covenants 20 by early members of the Church is obvious from the many historical accounts of its use. Joseph Smith had the articles and covenants of the Church read aloud at the first conference of the Church in June 1830. The members of the Church then received it as the word of the Lord by the "unanimous voice of the whole congregation."[10] Thus, section 20 became the first revelation of this dispensation canonized by the Church.[11] Since that time, the leaders of the Church have made sure that the basic practices of the Church correspond with this revelation. Possibly the earliest example of this is the issuance of ten priesthood licenses during the June 9, 1830, conference.[12] Joseph Smith and other leaders read the articles and covenants to the congregation at succeeding conferences. Presumably they did that so members and new converts might retain in their minds the truths revealed in it.[13]

Such men as Zebedee Coltrin, Orson Hyde, A. Sidney Gilbert, Orson Pratt, and others had manuscript copies of this revelation. They took their copies with them when they went on short missionary journeys or on preaching assignments to branches of the Church. They read the articles and covenants of the Church aloud in the meetings they conducted for the benefit of those people.[14]

A major division of section 20 is correlated to the priesthood of God. Many priesthood certificates of that time recorded that the bearer had been ordained "according to the Articles and Covenants of the Church."[15]

Several other revelations in the Doctrine and Covenants refer to the articles and covenants of the Church, including 28:12, 14; 33:14; 42:13; 51:4; 68:24; and 107:12, 63. The Lord, in each of these passages, requested the Saints to remember the articles and covenants and to obey the principles revealed there.

The articles and covenants of the Church may have served an additional purpose. Some researchers feel that it may be the certificate of incorporation that the state of New York required of churches. Any group that wanted recognition as a legally organized religious society had to submit such a certificate. Researchers have never found any document submitted by this Church in the government archives in New York. There is even a possibility that no one ever submitted it.[16] The beginning verses of section 20 are certainly reminiscent of a legal document, and some think it may be the missing certificate.

The importance of section 20 has not diminished over the years. For example, President Harold B. Lee emphasized the principles revealed in section 20 during his administration.[17] Also, according to my own statistics, the General Authorities since 1974 cite only sections 84, 88, and 121 from the Doctrine and Covenants more often than they cite section 20.[18]

Doctrine and Covenants 20 contains some passages of scripture quoted directly from the Book of Mormon. Several other passages are paraphrased or summarized. The sacrament prayers are probably the most widely known of these scriptures. Moroni recorded them in Moroni 4:3 and 5:2, and Joseph Smith published them as verses 77 and 79 of section 20. Joseph Smith also included the instruction in Moroni 6:6 to partake of the sacrament frequently as verse 75 in section 20.

Verse 73 of section 20 contains the baptismal prayer from 3 Nephi 11:25. The phrase "having authority given me of Jesus Christ" appears in all sources of section 20 before 1835, including the extant manuscripts of section 20 and the published accounts in the Book of Commandments and *The Evening and the Morning Star.* Joseph Smith altered the phrase to read "having been commissioned of Jesus

Christ" in the 1835 edition of the Doctrine and Covenants. That is the form of the prayer we use today. Joseph Smith also included the additional instructions concerning baptism from 3 Nephi 11:23–26 in verses 73 and 74 of section 20.

Moroni taught, in Moroni 3:4, how men are to be ordained to the priesthood. Joseph Smith included these same instructions in verse 60. He also placed in verse 37 the prerequisites for baptism that are given in Moroni 6:1–3.[19]

The elders are to conduct Church meetings as the Holy Ghost directs them. This teaching comes from Moroni 6:9. Joseph Smith published this same doctrine in verse 45. Moroni recorded his teachings concerning transgressors in Moroni 6:7, and Joseph Smith included this material in verses 80 through 83.

President Ezra Taft Benson said: "In the twentieth section of the Doctrine and Covenants, the Lord devotes several verses to summarizing the vital truths which the Book of Mormon teaches (see D&C 20:17–36). It speaks of God, the creation of man, the Fall, the Atonement, the ascension of Christ into heaven, prophets, faith, repentance, baptism, the Holy Ghost, endurance, prayer, justification and sanctification through grace, and loving and serving God.

"We must know these essential truths. Aaron and Ammon and their brethren in the Book of Mormon taught these same kinds of truths to the Lamanite people (see Alma 18:22–39), who were 'in the darkest abyss' (Alma 26:3). After accepting these eternal truths, the Book of Mormon states, those converted Lamanites never did fall away. (See Alma 23:6.)"[20]

Joseph Smith included a large number of passages from the Book of Mormon in Doctrine and Covenants 20. The placement of these scriptures in the articles and covenants of the Church affirms that present Church leaders are to implement the same doctrines and teachings that the Savior gave anciently to the people of the Book of Mormon. Many of these passages of scripture come from the book of Moroni. We can be eternally grateful that Moroni was granted the time and had the inclination to include this book in the record, because including it was "contrary to that which [he] had supposed" (Moroni 1:4).

Doctrine and Covenants 20 also instructs us about the Book of Mormon. Verses 6–9 include information about the origin of the

Book of Mormon and the mission of Moroni to Joseph Smith. The Lord states in verse 9 that the Book of Mormon contains the fulness of the gospel of Christ. Moroni revealed this truth to Joseph Smith in his first visit to the Prophet in September 1823 (see Joseph Smith—History 1:34). The Lord further stated it in Doctrine and Covenants 27:5 and 42:12. President Benson explained precisely what this phrase means:

"The Lord Himself has stated that the Book of Mormon contains the 'fulness of the gospel of Jesus Christ' (D&C 20:9). That does not mean it contains every teaching, every doctrine ever revealed. Rather, it means that in the Book of Mormon we will find the fulness of those doctrines required for our salvation. And they are taught plainly and simply so that even children can learn the ways of salvation and exaltation. The Book of Mormon offers so much that broadens our understandings of the doctrines of salvation. Without it, much of what is taught in other scriptures would not be nearly so plain and precious."[21]

In Doctrine and Covenants 20:10, the Lord uses the testimony of the Three Witnesses and the Eight Witnesses to declare to mankind that the Book of Mormon is true.[22] Those testimonies are part of every copy of the Book of Mormon, and every reader of the book has access to them. Angels who ministered to the witnesses "confirmed" the testimonies they bear. Elder Sterling W. Sill of the Seventy made an interesting point about the power of the testimony of these witnesses:

"I said to my friend, 'If you were on trial for your life and you had this kind of testimony out against you, you wouldn't have a chance. This kind of testimony where eleven men say they saw and they heard and they know would be accepted in any court of law, either human or divine.' And I patted him on the leg again and said, 'Now my friend, I think you have great abilities, but if you understood this testimony then I don't think you [would] have enough courage to disbelieve in the Book of Mormon. In this case, you have the kind of courage my little granddaughter has. I have a granddaughter two years old and she is very courageous. If you were to put her here on the floor with three rattlesnakes around her she would not have the slightest fear where I would be almost scared to death. The difference being that I know more about the situation than she does.' And I would say about anyone in this assembly who understands this testimony that he would not dare disbelieve the Book of Mormon or disobey its counsel."[23]

Verse 11 of Doctrine and Covenants 20 adds two additional truths concerning the Book of Mormon. First, the Book of Mormon proves to the people of the world that the Bible is true. President Brigham Young taught, "No man can say that this book (laying his hand on the Bible) is true, is the word of the Lord, is the way, is the guideboard in the path, and a charter by which we may learn the will of God; and at the same time say, that the Book of Mormon is untrue; if he has had the privilege of reading it, or of hearing it read, and learning its doctrines. There is not that person on the face of the earth who has had the privilege of learning the Gospel of Jesus Christ from these two books, that can say that one is true, and the other is false. No Latter-day Saint, no man or woman, can say the Book of Mormon is true, and at the same time say that the Bible is untrue. If one be true, both are; and if one be false, both are false."[24]

The Book of Mormon verifies the truths of the Bible in several ways. The Book of Mormon testifies that the Bible is a true record of God's dealings with Israel (see Mormon 7:9, for example). It also states that wicked men have removed many "plain and precious" truths from the record. The Book of Mormon tells of the modern Bible and how early settlers brought it to the Americas. Also, prophets in the Book of Mormon quote many Old and New Testament passages in their writings. Finally, many historic events in the one are corroborated in the other.

The second truth we learn in Doctrine and Covenants 20:11 is that the Book of Mormon establishes the actuality of prophets in our own day. President Benson explained how the Book of Mormon does that:

"We are to use the Book of Mormon in handling objections to the Church. God the Father and his Son Jesus Christ revealed themselves to Joseph Smith in a marvelous vision. After that glorious event, Joseph Smith told a minister about it. Joseph was surprised to hear the minister say that there were no such things as visions or revelations in these days, that all such things had ceased [see Joseph Smith—History 1:21].

"This remark symbolizes practically all of the objections that have ever been made against the Church by nonmembers and dissident members alike. Namely, they do not believe that God reveals his will today to the Church through prophets of God. All objections, whether they be on abortion, plural marriage, seventh-day worship, etc., basically hinge on whether Joseph Smith and his successors were and are prophets of God receiving divine revelation. Here, then, is a procedure to handle most objections through the use of the Book of Mormon.

"First, understand the objection.

"Second, give the answer from revelation.

"Third, show how the correctness of the answer really depends on whether or not we have modern revelation through modern prophets.

"Fourth, explain that whether or not we have modern prophets and revelation really depends on whether the Book of Mormon is true.

"Therefore, the only problem the objector has to resolve for himself is whether the Book of Mormon is true. For if the Book of Mormon is true, then Jesus is the Christ, Joseph Smith was his prophet, The Church of Jesus Christ of Latter-day Saints is true, and it is being led today by a prophet receiving revelation."[25]

In Doctrine and Covenants 20:12, the Lord teaches that God is the same yesterday, today, and forever. This conclusion can be drawn because the Book of Mormon establishes the truth of the Bible and because there are living prophets on the earth. Living prophets and additional scripture are features of all past dispensations. This dispensation is no different from past ones, and so God is the same today.

The Lord reveals in Doctrine and Covenants 20:13 that He will judge those who "come to a knowledge" of the Book of Mormon. Those who accept the Book of Mormon and who obey the commandments in it will "receive a crown of eternal life" (D&C 20:14). Those who reject the Book of Mormon will find that that decision "shall turn to their own condemnation" (D&C 20:15).[26]

One important truth that the Lord revealed in section 20 is that He will hold all those who "come to a knowledge" of the Book of Mormon accountable for what they know (D&C 20:13). Moroni said he will meet every person who has had knowledge of the Book of

Mormon at the judgment bar of God. In Ether 12:38–39, Moroni says they will then know that his garments are not spotted with their blood. He taught them all God commanded him to teach them, and they are now accountable for their own actions.

In Moroni 10:27–29, Moroni says the Lord will ask every one of them if they had the words "written by this man." God will then declare that He revealed His word to Moroni. He will also declare that Moroni wrote the truth. Moroni then urges those who have the Book of Mormon to come to Christ and forsake all evil so they won't be condemned.

Moroni made a third statement to the readers of the Book of Mormon in Moroni 10:34. This is the last verse of scripture in the Book of Mormon. Moroni promises he will meet them at the "pleasing bar of the great Jehovah, the Eternal Judge of both quick and dead." Judgment will be a pleasant experience for those who have made their lives conform to the standards taught in the Book of Mormon. They will stand with Moroni at the judgment bar of God and receive a crown of eternal life (see D&C 20:14).

Nephi also promised that he would meet the readers of the Book of Mormon at the time of judgment. In 2 Nephi 33:11–15, Nephi attests that the Lord will then declare that Nephi wrote the truth. Nephi urges the readers to abide by the principles he taught. If they will not, he bids them an everlasting farewell. Nephi knew that he would have eternal life. He knew that those who read his record would not have the same reward unless they would also obey the truth.

Jacob, who was Nephi's brother, also promised to meet the readers of the Book of Mormon at the time of judgment. In his account, Jacob 6:13, he speaks of the pleasing bar of God. The bar is pleasing to those who have not wasted their probation; however, this bar "striketh the wicked with awful dread and fear." They are fearful because they are facing the condemnation the Lord promised in Doctrine and Covenants 20:15.

All the Book of Mormon scriptures found in Doctrine and Covenants 20 teach that the Book of Mormon is a significant component of the work of the Lord in this dispensation.

Until the revelations were put in chronological order in the 1876 edition of the Doctrine and Covenants, section 20 was always the second revelation in the book, immediately following the Lord's preface to this book of scripture. Section 20 of the Doctrine and Covenants integrates the teachings of the Book of Mormon into the Church of this dispensation. It emphasizes the eternal covenants and commitments required by the Lord of the Nephites and also of us. It sets the same standard of conduct for us that the Savior set during His ministry to the Book of Mormon people. It is, in reality, a constitution to guide us in these latter days.

NOTES

I wish to thank Scott H. Faulring, research historian at the Joseph Fielding Smith Institute for Latter-day Saint History, for his helpful review of this article.

1. The Lord called Symonds Ryder on a mission. Unfortunately, Joseph Smith's scribe who wrote the letter notifying him of the call misspelled his name. Symonds Ryder complained about the Spirit that called him on a mission. If it could not spell his name correctly, then perhaps it erred in calling him on a mission. And so he refused to go. His name is still not spelled correctly in the Doctrine and Covenants and other Church publications. His tombstone and his signature give the spelling as *Symonds Ryder*, not *Symonds Rider* or *Simonds Ryder*.

2. In 1868, just two years before he died, Symonds Ryder told an acquaintance that when Joseph Smith and the other Church authorities visited Zion (Jackson County, Missouri) in the summer of 1831, they "left their papers behind." While not specifically identifying himself as one of the "new converts," Symonds described how the "new converts [took] an opportunity to become acquainted with the internal arrangement of their church" (Symonds Ryder to A. S. Hayden, February 1, 1868, published in A. S. Hayden, *Early History of the Disciples in the Western Reserve, Ohio* [Cincinnati: Chase & Hall Publishers, 1876], 221). In addition to Oliver Cowdery's 1829 articles, Symonds Ryder had in his possession manuscript copies of the following revelations: Doctrine and Covenants 20, 35, 36, 42, 52, and 56. This listing was noted by then LDS Church archivist Earl Olson in his May 27, 1964, typewritten notation on William D. Daily's September 27, 1960 statement, in the Archives of The Church of Jesus Christ of Latter-day Saints (hereafter cited as Church Archives), that accompanied the documents to Salt Lake City. It seems that Ryder was concerned about the recent revelation on the law of consecration (D&C 42:30–39) and that his farm in Hiram might be taken from him for Church use. It is interesting to note that Ryder ended up with

manuscript copies of Cowdery's 1829 articles, the 1830 articles and covenants (D&C 20), and the law of the Church (D&C 42).

3. Virginia Ryder Watters's father recovered, however, and was upset that they had given the documents away. The Church Archives did supply him with a set of photocopies.

4. As mentioned in the note above, William D. Daily's September 27, 1960, statement accompanied the documents to the Church Archives in Salt Lake City.

5. Dean C. Jessee, then of the LDS Church's History Division, verified that the handwriting was that of Oliver Cowdery.

6. This is a *corrected* reading. It was originally misread as "O.C." (Oliver Cowdery's initials) at the time of my dissertation when, upon closer examination, the document actually reads "&c."—the archaic abbreviation for "etc." (see Scott H. Faulring, "An Examination of the 1829 'Articles of the Church of Christ' in Relation to Section 20 of the Doctrine and Covenants," *BYU Studies* [forthcoming]).

7. For the complete text of this document, see Faulring's upcoming article in *BYU Studies*.

8. Many other churches have formulated similar confessions of their faith. Some have designated these confessions as their creed, others as their platform, and still others as their articles of faith. In these confessions they intended to give a brief statement about their basic beliefs and doctrine. They also would include something about requirements for church membership and other information that would be useful to church members and investigators. These confessions have many parallels to Doctrine and Covenants 20. See an example in Milton V. Backman Jr., *American Religions and the Rise of Mormonism* (Salt Lake City: Deseret Book, 1965), 446–56. See also Williston Walker, ed., *Creeds and Platforms of Congregationalism* (New York, 1969), 367–402; and The Confession of Faith and Covenant, of the Baptists Church of Christ in Middleborough, Bridgewater and Rayniam (prepared by the Rev. Isaac Backus, and adopted by the First Baptist Church in Middleboro, at its organization, January 16, 1756). This document is subtitled Articles of Faith.

9. It is supposed that Ryder somehow gained access to these official papers at the second-floor office of the Prophet Joseph Smith in the Newel K. Whitney store in Kirtland, Ohio.

10. The Conference Minutes, and Record Book of Christ's Church of the Latter Day Saints (commonly called the "Far West Record"), Church Archives, 1. The Far West Record has been published in Donald Q. Cannon and Lyndon W. Cook, eds., *Far West Record: Minutes of the Church of Jesus Christ of Latter-day Saints, 1830–1844* (Salt Lake City: Deseret Book, 1983), 1.

11. The members of the Church first voted on the other revelations

when the Doctrine and Covenants was presented for a sustaining vote in 1835. They voted on the revelations again in 1880 after Brigham Young had Orson Pratt add twenty-six additional sections to the book. In 1890 Lorenzo Snow presented Official Declaration—1 in general conference, and the members sustained it. In 1976 N. Eldon Tanner presented sections 137 and 138 in conference, and the members sustained them. He also presented Official Declaration—2 in 1978, and they sustained it.

12. Of the ten licenses written out by Oliver Cowdery that day, three have survived. All three refer to the authority of the articles and covenants (see Joseph Smith Sr. priest license, June 9, 1830, Joseph Smith Papers, Church Archives; John Whitmer elder license, June 9, 1830, Western Americana Collection, Beinecke Rare Book and Manuscript Library, Yale University; and Christian Whitmer teacher license, June 9, 1830, Western Americana Collection, Beinecke Rare Book and Manuscript Library).

13. Far West Record, 1, 2, 11, 22; published in Cannon and Cook, eds., *Far West Record*, 1, 3, 20, 39.

14. See, for example, the following documents in the Church Archives: Evan Melbourne Green Journal (1833–35), 4, 15; Orson Pratt Journal, March 27, 1834; Wilford Woodruff Journal, February 26, 1836.

15. Cook, *Revelations of the Prophet Joseph Smith*, 125. See also note 12 above.

16. Larry C. Porter, "A Study of the Origins of the Church of Jesus Christ of Latter-day Saints in the States of New York and Pennsylvania" (PhD diss., Brigham Young University, 1971), 374–86.

17. While I was doing research on the Doctrine and Covenants during the spring of 1973, Lauritz G. Petersen of the Historical Department of the Church requested a copy of anything I might find concerning Doctrine and Covenants 20. When I asked him why he wanted it, he said that President Lee had requested copies of any document historically connected with section 20. He wanted to administer the affairs of the Church using principles revealed in that section.

18. Database of scriptural quotations by General Authorities kept by the author.

19. The Prophet Joseph Smith added to these prerequisites that persons must also "truly manifest by their works that they have received of the Spirit of Christ unto a remission of their sins." During the summer of 1830, Oliver Cowdery wrote to the Prophet and commanded Joseph to delete this addition (see *History of the Church*, 1:104–5). Eventually Joseph was able to convince Oliver Cowdery and the Whitmer family (who agreed with Oliver that it should be

removed) that the phrase was doctrinal and should be retained. Even though Oliver Cowdery was presumptuous in commanding the Prophet to remove this phrase, we can appreciate his forceful approach when we remember that he wrote the earliest set of the articles of the Church and, as second elder, had a definite interest in the 1830 articles and covenants.

20. Ezra Taft Benson, "A New Witness for Christ," *Ensign*, November 1984, 7.

21. Ezra Taft Benson, "The Book of Mormon—Keystone of Our Religion," *Ensign*, November 1986, 6.

22. The Savior's own testimony concerning the Book of Mormon is in Doctrine and Covenants 17:6. Elder Bruce R. McConkie said of that testimony:

    "One of the most solemn oaths ever given to man is found in these words of the Lord relative to Joseph Smith and the Book of Mormon. 'He [meaning Joseph Smith] has translated the book, even that part which I have commanded him,' saith the Lord, 'and as your Lord and your God liveth it is true.' (D&C 17:6.)

    "This is God's testimony of the Book of Mormon. In it Deity himself has laid his godhood on the line. Either the book is true or God ceases to be God. There neither is nor can be any more formal or powerful language known to men or gods" ("The Doctrine of the Priesthood," *Ensign*, May 1982, 33).

23. Sterling W. Sill, "Mormon and Moroni," address delivered at Salt Lake Institute of Religion devotional assembly, October 26, 1973, 8–9.

24. Brigham Young, in *Journal of Discourses* (London: Latter-day Saints' Book Depot, 1855–86), 1:38.

25. Ezra Taft Benson, "The Book of Mormon Is the Word of God," *Ensign*, May 1975, 64–65.

26. This same doctrine is also taught in Doctrine and Covenants 5:15–19, and to a lesser extent in Doctrine and Covenants 10:23 and D&C 93:32.

CHAPTER TEN

THE "ELECT LADY" REVELATION (D&C 25): ITS HISTORICAL AND DOCTRINAL CONTEXT

CAROL CORNWALL MADSEN

In the last anxious hours before the Prophet Joseph Smith left for Carthage in June 1844, his wife Emma asked for a blessing. Unable to grant her wish at the time, Joseph instructed her to write out "the desires of her heart" and he would confirm the blessing by his signature upon his return. Among the desires she expressed in her short, self-inscribed blessing was her fervent wish "to honor and respect my husband as my head, ever to live in his confidence and by acting in unison with him retain the place which God has given me by his side."[1]

What unspoken thoughts moved Emma Smith to write those words? Could she have been affirming her belief that God had called her to be the wife and companion of a latter-day prophet? Might she have been thinking of the ordinances she had received with him in 1843, which promised her exaltation and a place by his side eternally? Or, after more than a year of anguishing over the principle of plural marriage, was Emma finally acknowledging that only by acting in concert with Joseph, even on this divisive issue, could she fulfill the revelation given to her fourteen years earlier through her prophet-husband?

Carol Cornwall Madsen is a senior research fellow at the Joseph Fielding Smith Institute.

Emma's self-written 1844 blessing, of which the quoted passage is only a part, in many ways is a companion piece to the revelation she received in 1830, which was codified as Doctrine and Covenants 25. Each of these two spiritual documents is better understood in relation to the other. The enduring influence of the 1830 revelation to Emma is evident in the 1844 blessing, which carries strong echoes of the Lord's words to her fourteen years earlier. The later blessing illuminates not only the importance and reality of the 1830 revelation in Emma's life but also the timeless and universal quality of its content.

Doctrine and Covenants 25 has long been read primarily as a revelation commissioning a hymnbook for the newly organized Church. In recent years more attention has been given to the revelation's injunction to Emma "to expound doctrine and exhort the church" and to define Emma's role as an "elect lady."[2] Less examined have been its points of universal application and its correlation with the 1844 blessing, which this paper will address.

This sacred, personal communication embodies elements of a long tradition of women's personal theophanies. Dating back to the eleventh century, their spiritual autobiographies record these sacred moments. Some of them recount striking religious awakenings or a newly quickened sense of God's overarching love emerging from a variety of spiritual manifestations. These include visions of light in which God's presence is unmistakably felt and spiritual doubts are resolved.[3] Some recount long periods of spiritual struggle and study leading to "a divine change" and a discernment "of the fullness of God" and His divine power in all things.[4] One woman, after living a life of pleasure and luxury, felt her heart unaccountably pierced "by a sudden and immense love of God" which drew her away from her former life and set her on a path of total religious devotion manifest by her service to the sick.[5] An eighteenth-century American woman, Sarah Pierrepont, left no account of a miraculous vision or sudden revelation, but she wrote of occasions when the Spirit seemed to engulf her and she basked in "a glow of divine love" which came from "the heart of Christ into [her] heart in a constant stream, or pencil of light."[6]

Similar experiences, recorded by early Latter-day Saint women in their diaries and journals, also fall within this tradition, the pattern of spiritual enlightenment often the same. For instance, after weeks of fervent prayer to be led to the truth, Elizabeth Ann Whitney one night felt herself enveloped in the midst of a cloud from which a voice spoke, saying, "Prepare to receive the word of the Lord, for it is coming." Shortly thereafter Parley P. Pratt brought her the gospel message and she was baptized, becoming one of the earliest and most faithful members of the Church.[7] In a light that illuminated her mind as she received a healing blessing, Jane Snyder Richards "saw as plainly as if a book was opened before me with it written in it, my need of baptism, if Christ who was sinless needed to be baptized should I hold myself as better than He."[8] Eliza R. Snow, on the night following her baptism, as she later recorded, felt an "indescribable, tangible sensation" that filled her with an "inexpressible happiness" as she saw in a vision a brilliant light from a candle blazing over her feet at the foot of her bed, which signified, she learned in the vision, that "the lamp of intelligence shall be lighted over your path."[9] And Mary Gibbs Bigelow, another early convert, sick and bedridden, thinking she was soon to die, received a vision in which the Savior promised her peace, health, and life long enough to complete the work she was still to do.[10] Such heavenly manifestations moved their recipients to conversion or confirmation of their faith and to lives of service and devotion to Christ.[11] Emma's revelation similarly confirmed her acceptance by God and showed her the way to service in His kingdom.

But the 1830 revelation for Emma was different from these other women's personal communications from the heavens. Preceding the introduction of patriarchal blessings in the Church by three years, its form and content were very much their prototype. It was received through an intermediary, it declared to Emma that she was one of the elect, or of the Abrahamic covenant and lineage,[12] and its promises and foretellings were conditional on her faith and obedience. Why, then, we might ask, was this individual spiritual guide included in a book of scripture for all Latter-day Saints?

The answer might possibly lie in its distinctiveness from the patriarchal blessings it prefigured. First, Emma was the Prophet's wife, and any blessing given to her was therefore distinctive. More specifically, like the other revelations that make up the Doctrine and Covenants, the revelation to Emma came directly from God through His prophet, not through a patriarch, bishop, or other ecclesiastical leader. Moreover, unlike personal revelations, patriarchal blessings, or even some of the other personally directed revelations in the Doctrine and Covenants,[13] it concludes with these significant words, which Joseph Smith repeated years later to the Relief Society in reference to the revelation: "And this is my word unto all."[14] Thus, in significant ways, it transcends the merely personal, fitting the parameters of scripture and thereby acquiring permanence, authority, and universality. While its specifics are addressed to Emma, its principles are applicable to all.

And what was God's message to Emma and, by implication, to the Church? The revelation's sixteen verses address four essential aspects of Emma's life: her actions and desires, her relationship to her prophet-husband, her responsibilities to the Church, and her relationship with the Lord.

ACTIONS AND DESIRES

In His consistent pattern of promise for performance, the Lord tells Emma in the revelation precisely what He expects of her as a Latter-day Saint and in return promises her aid in fulfilling those expectations. Though verses 4 and 10 appear to be mild rebukes, they could also be read as appeals for trust and faith in His divine will: "Murmur not because of the things which thou hast not seen, for they are withheld from thee and from the world, which is wisdom in me in a time to come" the Lord tells Emma in Doctrine and Covenants 25:4. He may have been referring only to Emma's regret at not having seen the gold plates, though she had held them, protected them, and acted as scribe in their translation, but He may also have been alluding to the tumultuous experiences Emma had endured since her marriage to Joseph three years earlier. The attempts by gold seekers to wrest the plates from Joseph, the harassment during their translation, the mobs who interfered with Emma's baptism, the unwarranted arrest of Joseph the same night, as well as the alienation of her parents, the loss of home and roots, and the death of her first child all gave Emma a harsh introduction to the life of a prophet's wife. An early lesson from these experiences was that only patience and trust in God's wisdom and often inscrutable purposes would sustain her through the difficult times.

Then in verse 10 the Lord counsels Emma, in what certainly must be one of the most oft-repeated commands in Christian literature, to "lay aside the things of this world, and seek for the things of a better," surely a call to keep perspective on the uncertainties her life offered. But her compliance to these two admonitions would not go unaided. "Lift up thy heart and rejoice," He encourages her in verse 13, "and cleave unto the covenants which thou hast made." Only a month earlier Emma had entered into the covenant of baptism, which promised her that if she would "serve [the Lord] and keep his commandments," He would in turn "pour out his Spirit more abundantly upon [her]" (Mosiah 18:10). Furthermore, before another month passed, at her long-delayed confirmation she would receive the gift of the Holy Ghost, an additional source of solace and guidance.

MARRIAGE RELATIONSHIP

At the time of the revelation Emma had just turned twenty-six and Joseph was not yet twenty-five. They were relatively inexperienced and unsophisticated young people who had been given momentous responsibilities. A supportive and trusting relationship would be crucial to the fulfillment of their respective callings. Its reciprocal nature is explained in verses 5 and 9 of the revelation. Emma was counseled to comfort and console her prophet-husband in his times of affliction and to continue to assist him when needed in his ecclesiastical duties as scribe (verse 5). In turn, she was promised Joseph's support in the Church, presumably to enable her to fulfill the mission to which the Lord had called her (verse 9). The import of this counsel became clear as circumstances challenged Joseph and Emma's efforts to fulfill their obligations to each other. While Joseph's support gave legitimacy and significance to Emma's assignments in the Church, her support of Joseph eased the burden of his calling. But the merging of their marital and ecclesiastical relationships often created an emotional kaleidoscope alternating joy with sorrow, peace with anxiety, trust with suspicion, and unity with doubt. For equilibrium, the Lord urged Emma to maintain her spirit of meekness and let her soul "delight in [her] husband, and the glory which [would] come upon him" (verse 14). To enjoy these blessings, He warned, she must "beware of pride" (verse 14).

The binding force of that counsel united Joseph and Emma in a supportive and truly complementary relationship for most of their seventeen years together. Joseph's letters to her express affection and confidence. Though few of Emma's letters to Joseph remain, the anxiety and urgency evident in her published letters to Illinois governor Thomas Carlin, pleading against Joseph's extradition to Missouri, along with her boldness in daring to interfere with the processes of law, certainly testify of her willingness to be more than a comfort and consolation. One can only wonder why the strength of their union was not sufficient for Emma to accept plural marriage, a principle accepted in faith by so many other devoted couples. Perhaps for Emma it was *because* of that unity, the oneness that had so characterized their relationship, that she was unable to open it to others. Could Emma's reluctance to share her prophet-husband be a manifestation of the pride she had been warned against? Did her faith falter only in this final test when the sacrifice claimed too much of her own identity? The answers remain elusive.

Duties to the Church

But the revelation called for Emma to do more than support and assist Joseph. There were specific tasks for her to perform that would benefit the Church, in preparation for which her time was to "be given to writing, and to learning much" (verse 8). One assignment was "to make a selection of sacred hymns" (verse 11). By this mandate the Lord sanctioned music as an appropriate form of religious worship. Hymn texts have long been a medium to express religious thought and emotion, and the birth of Mormonism evoked a wide range of both, from the millennialist fervor of the poems of Parley P. Pratt and the doctrinal assertions of Eliza R. Snow to the joyous affirmations of W. W. Phelps. Now these and other poetic testimonies would become part of Latter-day Saint worship.

It took two years for Emma to complete the hymn selection, and another three passed before the hymns were printed in a single volume. From July 1830 to April 1832, when the selection process was completed and W. W. Phelps was instructed to correct and publish the hymns, Emma worked despite a growing antagonism toward the Church in Kirtland and a series of personal tragedies. Through them all, she persisted in fulfilling this assignment of the Lord. Her mother-in-law observed that during this time "her whole heart was in the work of the Lord and she felt no interest except for the church and the cause of truth."[15]

Finally, in June 1832, *The Evening and the Morning Star* began printing Emma's selection of hymn texts described as "Hymns, selected and prepared for the Church of Christ, in the last days." The destruction of Phelps's press in 1833 suspended the printing of hymns and other Church publications. Until then, thirty-eight hymn texts had appeared in either the *Star* or its successor, the *Latter Day Saints' Messenger and Advocate*.[16] But in 1835 the Church council instructed Phelps to continue his work with Emma, and early in 1836 the first Latter-day Saint hymnal finally came off the press, entitled *A Collection of Hymns for the Church of the Latter Day Saints*. The 127-page hymnal contained ninety hymns, approximately forty of them written by Latter-day Saint authors, primarily Phelps himself. Emma's preface drew on the words of the 1830 revelation, affirming that "the song of the righteous" was "a prayer unto God" and suggesting that the hymnal was only a beginning effort "till more are composed or we are blessed with a copious variety of the songs of Zion."[17]

The idea that Emma Smith should be the sole compiler of the Church's hymnal emerged in 1839 when the high council authorized an expanded hymnbook. David Rogers, a New York convert, had previously published for the New York Saints a hymnal that had drawn heavily on Emma's 1835 selection, and Brigham Young had taken a collection of hymns to England with the intent of publishing a hymnal there. But the Nauvoo high council voted to destroy all copies of Rogers's hymnbook and to forbid Brigham Young to publish a British edition.[18] The prohibition evidently did not reach Young in time to prevent the publication of three thousand Latter-day Saint hymnals in Manchester, England, in 1840. When he decided to revise the hymnal the next year, Brigham Young wrote to Joseph Smith for permission. Apparently the needs of the growing Church prompted Joseph to permit a second edition in England and a new, enlarged edition, under Emma's direction, in Nauvoo. Emma's exclusive stewardship over the church hymnal had been modified to allow the publication of a volume of hymns appropriate to the British Saints under Brigham Young's direction.[19]

A second, more problematic commission of the Lord to Emma in the revelation was "to expound scriptures, and to exhort the church, according as it shall be given thee by my Spirit" (verse 7). With only a few exceptions, no religious denominations at that time gave public platforms in mixed congregations to women. Tradition and contemporary ideals of feminine propriety were powerful agents in defining a woman's appropriate public behavior, and preaching in public was not a feminine occupation in the nineteenth century.[20] These social strictures, however, did not affect the small, informal Church meetings, characteristic of Latter-day Saint worship from its beginnings. In Nauvoo, women regularly addressed the mixed Church gatherings in one another's homes for a Sunday or weeknight prayer, blessing, or cottage meeting. Along with the men, they bore testimony, expounded doctrine, and read scriptures to the assembled members. They prophesied, spoke in tongues, and blessed one another.[21] Emma often accompanied Joseph to such meetings.[22] Few could have been more conversant with Mormon doctrine than Emma Smith or had more incentive to expound its truths.

The patriarchal blessings of other women during this period admonished them, also, to instruct one another, mentor the young in gospel principles, and "encourage and strengthen" others in the faith.[23] One so blessed was Phoebe Woodruff before she left on a mission to England with her husband, Wilford. Brigham Young promised her that she would be "looked up to as A mother in Israel for council and for Instruction." He granted her "power & wisdom to teach the truth to thy friends and thy se[x]," and guaranteed that she would "not be at a loss for Ideas & words in [her] teaching."[24]

The organization of the Relief Society in 1842 provided Emma Smith with the public setting most conducive to the fulfillment of her own commission. At its initial meeting, Joseph Smith proposed that the sisters should "elect a president to preside over them." After Elizabeth Ann Whitney nominated Emma, she was elected by the nineteen other women present. Joseph then read the 1830 revelation, explaining that at the time it had been given, Emma had been "ordained to expound the scriptures to all and to teach the female part of the community."[25] Though she met with the Relief Society only from March to October in 1842, when it adjourned for the winter months, briefly in 1843, and again for just four meetings in March 1844, Emma was clearly its head and moving spirit.[26]

She took her calling to exhort the sisters seriously and immediately set about instructing them to purify their own lives and help in creating a virtuous community. She urged them to extend their compassionate service to all distressed Saints and to draw around them empowering bands of unity. The Relief Society was to save souls as well as relieve the poor, Joseph counseled, and Emma advised the sisters in this important obligation. "Each member should be ambitious to do good," she urged, "deal frankly with each other, watch over the morals, and be very careful of the character and reputation of the members of the Institution etc."[27] To this end, Emma zealously acceded to Joseph's charge to assist in "correcting the morals and strengthening the virtues of the community" and "to reform persons . . . and by kindness sanctify and cleanse [them] from all unrighteousness."[28] Ferreting out iniquity was a delicate task, but Emma, with the help of her counselors, endeavored to fulfill Joseph's charge. Like that of hundreds of female moral reform associations throughout the country, all bent on exposing sin, one of the Relief Society's aims was to cleanse the Church of any wrongdoing. Noting their reluctance to be moral caretakers, Emma lamented that "the sisters are not *careful enough* to expose iniquity; the time had been when charity had covered a multitude of sins," she said, "but now it is necessary that sin should be exposed."[29] Her commitment to "uphold virtue" and "put down transgression" dominated the final meetings of the Relief Society in March 1844, in which she used her authority as president to denounce the false doctrine of "spiritual wifery," a counterfeit of the revealed doctrine of plural marriage, and warn the sisters to guard against it and "any other improper practice."[30] It is generally conceded that Emma used her position as Relief Society president and her commission to exhort the sisters as a license also to thwart the establishment of plural marriage.[31] The evidence shows that she did indeed attempt to mobilize overt action against the practice through the Relief Society, which numbered more than thirteen hundred by 1844. Moreover, the minutes of the final meetings of the Relief Society clearly indicate that she never questioned her right or her authority to instruct the sisters of the Church in their duties as she saw them.

In contrast to the controversial nature of the Relief Society's moral purity campaign was Emma's equally emphatic desire that the sisters clothe themselves in Christian service, "Seek out and relieve the distressed," she urged, and she counseled them to give help and material aid to one another, invoking the Spirit by blessing one another when needed for healing, for comfort, for childbirth, and for spiritual support and guidance.[32] If the sisters needed a model of selfless service, Emma could provide it. In this benevolent charge, Emma's actions far outweighed her words. From the Kirtland days, when she and Elizabeth Ann Whitney prepared a "love feast" for the poor, Emma, so often a beneficiary of the compassion of friends, was the first to extend it to others. Her compassion and hospitality in Nauvoo were legendary. Her home was often a sanctuary for the homeless, the orphaned, and the sick. Lucy Walker and her siblings were only a few of the dozens of individuals who came under her protective care. Virtually orphaned at their mother's death because their father was abroad on a mission, the Walker children were offered a home with the Prophet and Emma. "Our own father and mother could scarcely have done more," Lucy noted when her younger sister died. "The Prophet and his wife introduced us as their sons and daughters. Every privilege was accorded us in the home. Every pleasure within reach was ours."[33]

Emma's counselors were also exemplars to the sisters. Elizabeth Ann Whitney, then a stranger to Emma, opened her home to Emma and Joseph when they arrived in Kirtland almost destitute, and Sarah Cleveland, also a stranger at the time, gave Emma and her children refuge in Quincy when Emma fled from the Missouri persecutions, leaving her husband still imprisoned in Liberty Jail. It is little wonder that Emma turned to these women for her closest associates and advisers in the new organization.

Another persistent theme in Emma's exhortations to the Relief Society was her appeal for unity. "Measures to promote union in this society must be carefully attended to," she urged the members at the outset.[34] As membership dramatically increased, Emma was even more urgent in her plea for unity. "We shall have sufficient difficulty from abroad," she presciently warned in August 1842, "without stirring up strife among ourselves and hardness and evil feelings, one towards another etc."[35] This call to "circle the wagons," she was saying, was to guard themselves against an encroaching disloyalty to

Joseph and disunion within the Church more than against threats from the outside.

But, as is often the case, the principle of unity was easier for Emma to preach than to practice. Even as she pleaded for a united sisterhood, she was herself becoming a symbol of disunion. Both the 1830 revelation and her 1844 blessing centered on her unity with Joseph as the key to the success of her own calling. But in the end unity gave way to doubt, and doubt invoked disloyalty. Her exhortations to the Relief Society in its final four meetings in March 1844 seemed frantic but futile. Immediately thereafter both the Relief Society and Emma's place as its "elect lady" abruptly ended. Emma's commitment to the 1830 revelation seriously faltered, and the consequences were monumental.

RELATIONSHIP WITH THE LORD

Finally, how did the 1830 revelation define Emma's relationship with the Lord? Was it unique, or can principles be extrapolated to all believers? The first three verses of the revelation set forth the primary elements of that relationship. First, the Lord claims Emma as a daughter because of her willingness to accept the gospel, a condition applicable to all who desire to be sons and daughters of God.[36] Second, He covenants with her, promising her eternal blessings in return for obedience and faith, another universal principle. Finally, He forgives Emma her sins, personally validating the efficacy of her recent baptism, and receives her into the circle of the "elect," who are those, He explains elsewhere, who "hear my voice and harden not their hearts" (D&C 29:7).

Emma, like others of the elect, had proven her faithfulness even before mortality and through the "covenant of grace" was permitted to enter this life at a time and place that would bring her into contact with the gospel.[37] But being of the elect also carried responsibilities, foreordained missions that varied with each individual according to God's purposes. A passage in Joseph Smith's private journal for March 17, 1842, affirms that definition: "*Elect* meant to be *Elected* to a *certain work*," a broad definition of the term. The Prophet then noted that Emma fulfilled this part of the 1830 revelation when she was elected president of the Relief Society, the specific work to which she had been "previously ordained."[38] In the Relief Society minutes of that date, however, he seemed to narrow the meaning, indicating that "elect lady" specifically meant "elected to preside," a term presumably applicable to any woman who presided. Certainly that was how the term was applied in later years. In that same meeting, John Taylor confirmed Emma's earlier blessing from Joseph, also declaring her to be "a mother in Israel" who was "to look to the wants of the needy, and be a pattern of virtue." In referring to the 1830 revelation, he said he "rejoiced to see this Institution organized according to the law of Heaven . . . according to the revelation" previously given to Emma "appointing her to this important calling."[39] His words suggest that the organization of the Relief Society facilitated the fulfillment of Emma's call as an elect lady.

One might wonder why it took twelve years for this part of the revelation to be realized. Perhaps Emma's service to the Church before 1842 was merely preparatory, although certainly falling within the range of Emma's special calling. The Lord evidently directed the proceedings of that organizational meeting, for there was a possibility for other women to be elected president, particularly Sarah M. Kimball, a logical choice, when Joseph opened the meeting for nominations. Elizabeth Ann Whitney, however, gave the nomination to Emma, and her election by the women present ratified her call as the "elect lady."[40] From that time on, the title "elect lady" in reference to Emma Smith developed a mystique that curtailed its use for others until after her death, despite her dissociation with the Relief Society and the Church. Though Brigham Young authorized Eliza R. Snow to organize Relief Societies throughout the Church and direct its activities in 1868, she was not officially set apart "to preside" as the new "elect lady" until 1880, the year after Emma's death.[41]

The final element that defined Emma's relationship with the Lord is the fifteenth verse of the revelation. "Keep my commandments continually," He told her, "and a crown of righteousness thou shalt receive. And except thou do this," He cautioned, "where I am you cannot come" (D&C 25:15). In that passage Emma was taught a fundamental principle of the gospel—that God's blessings are obtained only by obedience to the laws upon which they are predicated (see also D&C 130:20–21). This principle underlies every command and blessing the Lord expressed to Emma in the revelation, which was as complete and certain a personal guide to Emma

Smith, the Latter-day Saint, as it was a special calling to Emma Smith, the wife of the Prophet.

CONCLUSION

Despite the years between the two, the 1844 blessing reads like a reprise of the 1830 revelation on several points. It repeats, expands, and develops several of the themes introduced in the earlier document, reflecting the seasoning of fourteen years. Perhaps more than her words and actions in those final mercurial years before the Prophet's death, the 1844 blessing is the best index to Emma's mind and spirit at that time and the enduring effect of the 1830 revelation upon her.

Besides her "deepest desire to act in unison with Joseph and retain her place by his side," a remarkable statement in view of the events of the preceding months, Emma made several other self-revelatory requests of the Lord in that 1844 blessing. She expressed a "craving for wisdom" that she would not do or say anything she would regret; she desired the Spirit of God and a fruitful mind that she would be able "to comprehend the designs of God, when revealed through his servants without doubting"; she sought wisdom to rear her children to be "useful ornaments in the Kingdom of God" and prudence to care for her body that she would live to perform "all the work that [she] covenanted to perform in the spirit world"; and finally, she asked for "humility . . . that she might rejoice in the blessings which God has in store for all who are willing to be obedient to his requirements."

Were these the words of a prophet's wife hoping only to retain her place with him, or could they have been a penitent's recovenant with God? Perhaps they were both. As a glimpse into the heart of Emma Smith on the eve of her husband's death, this final blessing, I believe, expresses an intense desire to reconnect with the 1830 revelation that gave her a blueprint for her life. If the words of the blessing can be taken as a measure of her soul at that moment, they testify of Emma's longing to feel the approbation of the Lord and spiritual union once again with Joseph.

What she was *then* willing to sacrifice to fulfill those longings, however, will remain forever moot. The tragedy that followed closed that chapter in Emma's life, even as it opened a new one in the life of the Church.

Though documenting the spiritual journey of just one woman, the 1830 revelation and its companion blessing can well serve as spiritual markers for all who seek to be in tune with the Lord and in harmony with the Church. "This is my voice unto all," the Lord said at the close of the revelation to Emma. Perhaps we should read it as God's voice to all.

NOTES

1. Typescript of blessing in Archives, The Church of Jesus Christ of Latter-day Saints, Salt Lake City, Utah; hereafter cited as Church Archives.

2. See, for example, Linda Kay Newell and Valeen Tippetts Avery, *Mormon Enigma: Emma Hale Smith* (Garden City, New York: Doubleday, 1984); and Jill Mulvay Derr, Janath Russell Cannon, and Maureen Ursenbach Beecher, *Women of Covenant: The Story of Relief Society* (Salt Lake City: Deseret Book, 1992).

3. John Ferguson, ed., *An Illustrated Encyclopedia of Mysticism* (London: Thames and Hudson, 1976), s.v. "Catherine of Siena," 37.

4. Ferguson, *Illustrated Encyclopedia,* s.v. "Angela of Foligno," 13.

5. Ferguson, *Illustrated Encyclopedia,* s.v. "Catherine of Genoa," 36–37.

6. Ferguson, *Illustrated Encyclopedia,* s.v. "Sarah Pierrepont," 145; see also Martin Buber, *Ecstatic Confessions,* trans. Esther Cameron, ed. Paul Mendes-Flohr (San Francisco: Harper and Row, 1985); and Walter Holden Capps and Wendy M. Wright, eds., *Silent Fire: An Invitation to Western Mysticism* (San Francisco: Harper and Row, 1978).

7. Edward Tullidge, *The Women of Mormondom* (New York: Tullidge and Crandall, 1877), 42.

8. Jane Snyder Richards, "Reminiscences of Jane Snyder Richards," typescript, Church Archives.

9. Nicholas G. Morgan Sr., ed., *Eliza R. Snow, an Immortal* (Salt Lake City: Nicholas G. Morgan Sr. Foundation, 1957), 6.

10. Autobiography of Mary Gibbs Bigelow, June 26, 1809, to April 19, 1858, typescript, Church Archives.

11. Joseph Smith greeted with joy and thanksgiving this proliferation of spirituality that accompanied and indeed testified of the return of the gospel of Christ to the earth. "To witness and feel with our own natural senses, the like glorious manifestations of the power of the Priesthood, the gifts and blessings of the Holy Ghost, and the good and condescension of a merciful God," he wrote in 1830,

"combined to create within us sensations of rapturous gratitude, and inspire us with fresh zeal and energy in the cause of truth." The dreams and visions of the Saints, he wrote, strengthened his faith and he welcomed them as evidence of the last days "as foretold by the Prophet Joel" (*History of the Church of Jesus Christ of Latter-day Saints*), ed. B. H. Roberts, 2nd ed., rev. [Salt Lake City: Deseret Book, 1957], 1:85–86). Besides the numerous manuscript accounts, Carol Lynn Pearson has collected reports of many of these experiences, most of them previously published, in a volume entitled *Daughters of Light* (Salt Lake City: Bookcraft, 1973).

12. See Daniel H. Ludlow, ed., *Encyclopedia of Mormonism* (New York: Macmillan, 1992), s.v. "Elect of God," 2:448–49; see also Bible Dictionary, s.v. "Election."

13. At least thirty-six other revelations are partially or fully addressed to individuals.

14. Minutes of the Female Relief Society of Nauvoo, March 17, 1842, Church Archives; hereafter cited as Nauvoo Minutes.

15. Lucy Mack Smith, "Biographical Sketches of Joseph Smith the Prophet and His Progenitors for Many Generations," original manuscript, Church Archives, as quoted in Newell and Avery, *Mormon Enigma*, 44.

16. For mote details about the development of Latter-day Saint hymnals, see Michael Hicks, *Mormonism and Music: A History* (Urbana and Chicago: University of Illinois Press, 1989), 10–14, 18–34. A brief account is available in Karen Lynn Davidson, *Our Latter-day Hymns: The Stories and the Messages* (Salt Lake City: Deseret Book, 1988), 7–13. E. Cecil McGavin provides an early account in "Emma Smith's Collection of Hymns," *Improvement Era,* January 1936, 38.

17. Hicks, *Mormonism and Music,* 20.

18. Hicks, *Mormonism and Music,* 25–27.

19. Hicks, *Mormonism and Music,* 26–27. Emma's second hymnal was published in 1841 by Ebenezer Robinson in the place of William Phelps, who was temporarily out of favor with Church leaders. Many of the borrowed hymn texts revised by Phelps for the 1835 edition were restored to their original form, giving the 1841 edition less of a restorationist tone than either the earlier edition or the British hymnbook, which contained many of the hymns of Parley P. Pratt. Emma expanded the collection one last time in 1843, but it was never printed. In 1860 Emma Smith was commissioned by the newly formed Reorganized Church of Jesus Christ of Latter Day Saints, which her son Joseph would lead, to make a selection of hymns. A number of RLDS publications deal with her contributions. See, for instance, Fred'k. M. Smith, "Emma Smith and Her Selection of Hymns," *Saints' Herald,* 1905, 386–87; Audentia Smith

Anderson, "Emma Smith and the Church Hymns," *Saints' Herald,* May 6, 1939, 553–54; Samuel A. Burgess, "Latter Day Saint Hymns, Emma Smith," Joseph Smith, *Journal of History* 18 (July 1925): 257–60.

20. Lucy Mack Smith enjoyed the privilege once in 1845 in addressing the last conference of the Church before the departure of the Saints the following winter. See *History of the Church,* 7:470–72. For a complete version of her talk and commentary, see Ronald W. Walker, "Lucy Mack Smith Speaks to the Nauvoo Saints," *BYU Studies* 32 (Winter and Spring 1991): 276–84.

21. An interesting description of a cottage meeting is provided in Charlotte Havens, "A Girl's Letters from Nauvoo," *Overland Monthly,* December 1890, 627.

22. Dean C. Jessee, ed., *The Papers of Joseph Smith* (Salt Lake City: Deseret Book, 1992), 2:58, 86, 123.

23. For more discussion of these early blessings, see Carol Cornwall Madsen, "Mothers in Israel: Sarah's Legacy," *Women of Wisdom and Knowledge,* ed. Marie Cornwall and Susan Howe (Salt Lake City: Deseret Book, 1990), 191–92.

24. Wilford Woodruff, *Wilford Woodruff's Journal, 1833–1898 Typescript,* ed. Scott G. Kenney (Midvale, Utah: Signature Books, 1983), 3:343.

25. Nauvoo Minutes, March 17, 1842. This is a slight variation on the actual words of the revelation instructing Emma "to expound scriptures, and to exhort the Church" (D&C 25:7). In earlier times, the terms "ordain" and "set apart" were often used interchangeably, both asserting the delegation of authority. Thus Emma Smith was "ordained" to office, whereas twenty-four years later Eliza R. Snow was "set apart" to the same office. More recently, specific distinctions have been made between the two terms.

26. During its second year, because of the large enrollment, the Relief Society met as ward groups, each meeting conducted by Emma's counselors. There are only references in the minutes to Emma's attendance at the meetings.

27. Nauvoo Minutes, March 17, 1842.

28. Nauvoo Minutes, March 17, 1842.

29. Nauvoo Minutes, May 18, 1842.

30. Nauvoo Minutes, March 9 and 16, 1842.

31. Newell and Avery equivocate on the issue (see *Mormon Enigma,* 173–75). Derr, Cannon, and Beecher are more forthright (see *Women of Covenant,* 61–62).

32. Nauvoo Minutes, April 19 and 28, 1842.

33. "An Early Pioneer, Lucy Walker Kimball," in Kate B. Carter, *Our*

Pioneer Heritage (Salt Lake City: Daughters of Utah Pioneers, 1976), 19:198.

34. Nauvoo Minutes, March 24, 1842.

35. Nauvoo Minutes, August 4, 1842.

36. Hyrum M. Smith and Janne M. Sjodahl explain that "all men and women are the children of God, through Adam, who 'was the son of God' (Luke 3:38); those who receive the gospel are sons and daughters in the Kingdom of God" (*Doctrine and Covenants Commentary* [Salt Lake City: Deseret News, 1927], 173).

37. Bible Dictionary, s.v. "Election."

38. Jessee, *Papers of Joseph Smith,* 371.

39. Nauvoo Minutes, March 17, 1842.

40. Nauvoo Minutes, March 17, 1842.

41. *Woman's Exponent,* August 1, 1880, 36.

CHAPTER ELEVEN

THE LAW OF COMMON CONSENT (D&C 26)

MATTHEW O. RICHARDSON

In Latter-day Saint sacrament meetings, time may be allotted for ward business. Part of the procedure with items of business is an invitation to the congregation to sustain fellow Church members in their callings by raising their right hand. If members are opposed to the proposed action, they can also make it known in the same manner. This practice, formally known as the law of common consent, is not only a noticeable part of our meetings but also an essential principle in proper gospel government and personal progression.

Unfortunately, the law of common consent is viewed by many members as nothing more than an accompaniment to a business agenda. Perhaps because of the frequency of the event, application of the law of common consent may become an automated raising of a hand in mechanical approval. Some might say that the law of common consent is too common and therefore feel that it is a commonplace occurrence in the Church that signifies more tradition than actual function. Although common consent is familiar to Church members, it is anything but common. President J. Reuben Clark Jr. taught, "It is clear that the sustaining vote by the people is not, and is not to be regarded as, a mere matter of form, but on the contrary a matter of the last gravity."[1]

Perhaps this important gospel principle has become a matter of form to some not because of familiarity with it but because of a lack of familiarity. For example, some members may understand the

---

Matthew O. Richardson is associate dean of Religious Education at Brigham Young University.

proper procedure but have never learned, or have forgotten, the purposes of the principle. Others may be acquainted with the purposes and practices of common consent but have failed to see the doctrinal significance as emphasized in the Doctrine and Covenants and throughout Church history. As the Saints learn about the law of common consent, it becomes anything but common. Obviously it requires more than raising a hand on Sundays to become familiar with the law of common consent. To develop a deeper familiarity with this practice, it is helpful to obtain a basic understanding of Christ's government in His kingdom. Next, a historical overview of common consent reveals its historical precedence and underscores its importance and necessity. With this background, it is easier to understand the proper practice or procedure of this principle. Finally, the deep meaning of common consent is found in its intended purposes. When understood correctly, common consent becomes a meaningful rite of worship for the Saints, which ultimately brings them closer to the Savior.

THE GOVERNMENT OF THE CHURCH

To better understand common consent, it is important first to understand the workings of the government of God. Elder Harold B. Lee described the government of the kingdom of God as a theocracy but also "something like a democracy."[2] This description is a simple clarification of a seemingly complex and often misunderstood organization. Elder Lee highlighted two significant pillars in the Lord's government: theocracy and democracy. The first pillar, theocracy, accents Christ's undeniable position as head of the kingdom—the sole proprietor. The second pillar, democracy, emphasizes the people's opportunity to participate in their government. This combination of terms, however, immediately raises questions from traditional political sciences. How can a theocracy also be described as a democracy? On the surface these terms not only seem incompatible but provoke a jealous power struggle. A democracy doesn't seem to fit with a theocracy because of the world's understanding and definition of democracy. But thankfully, when this term is properly understood, the powerful second pillar not only fits but is seen for the essential principle in gospel government and doctrine it is.

The pillar of democracy that Elder Lee described in the Lord's kingdom was something *like* a democracy. In a traditional democracy, power is vested in the people and they hold participatory rights. The role of the people under a conventional theocracy, on the other hand, is being part of the kingdom rather than of its governmental process and procedure. The Lord's kingdom, unlike a conventional theocracy, allows the members to participate in its government. This unique combination in which all power is vested in the Lord (theocracy) with the participation of the people (democracy) has thus been called a theodemocracy,[3] which is a form of government in which the decisions for the kingdom of the Lord are His decisions but in which His people have been given the opportunity to exercise their presence in that kingdom. Members of the Lord's kingdom exercise their democratic presence through the principle of common consent.

THE HISTORICAL PERSPECTIVE OF COMMON CONSENT

The unique relationship between Christ and His disciples in divine government is found throughout religious history. A glimpse into the past reveals the precedence, patterns, and practice of common consent as it underscores its vitality and importance. This principle was practiced in one form or another during the lifetimes of Moses (Exodus 24:3), Joshua (Numbers 27:19–22), Peter (Acts 1:26), and Mosiah (Mosiah 29:25–26). According to Elder Bruce R. McConkie, the law of common consent "has been operative in every dispensation."[4] Thus, this principle is of necessity part of modern Church government. Common consent is another of the many witnesses that the Church of Jesus Christ has been literally restored.

The law of common consent in the modern dispensation was first revealed to Joseph Smith and Oliver Cowdery in Peter Whitmer's home in June 1829. At that time, Joseph and Oliver were instructed to ordain each other to the office of elder and then to ordain others as it was made known unto them. Their ordination was deferred, however, until "such times as it should be practicable to have our brethren, who had been and who should be baptized, assembled together, when we must have their sanction to our thus proceeding to ordain each other, and have them decide by vote whether they were willing to accept us as spiritual teachers or not."[5]

Because priesthood ordination is of obvious doctrinal importance, that historical event also teaches the relative importance of common consent and its necessity to God's kingdom. Elder Orson F. Whitney explained the significance of that event as follows: "What!—exclaims one. After these men had communed with heavenly beings and received from them commandments for their guidance; after receiving divine authority to preach the Gospel, administer its ordinances, and establish once more on earth the long absent Church of Christ! After all this must they go before the people and ask their consent to organize them and preside over them as a religious body? Yes, that was precisely the situation. Notwithstanding all those glorious manifestations, they were not yet fully qualified to hold the high positions unto which they had been divinely called. One element was lacking— the consent of the people. Until that consent was given, there could be no church with these people as its members and those men as its presiding authorities. The Great Ruler of all never did and never will foist upon any of his people, in branch, ward, stake or Church capacity, a presiding officer whom they are not willing to accept and hold."[6]

Further instruction concerning ordinations and the "vote" of brethren was later revealed to Joseph Smith in early April 1830. Joseph was instructed to organize the Church and kingdom of God. Included in those specific instructions was the "law of common consent," which reemphasized that "no person is to be ordained to any office in this church, where there is a regularly organized branch of the same, without the vote of that church" (D&C 20:65–66).

On April 6, 1830, Joseph Smith, Oliver Cowdery, and members of the Smith and Whitmer families gathered in Peter Whitmer's home in Fayette, New York, to organize the Church of Jesus Christ. It was anticipated that at this gathering Joseph and Oliver would be ordained elders. Before that ordination, however, Joseph and Oliver needed to receive a sanctioning vote from those present. "According to previous commandment [given in June 1829 and recorded in D&C 20:65–66], the Prophet Joseph called upon the brethren present to know if they would accept himself and Oliver Cowdery as their teachers in the things of the kingdom of God; and if they were willing that they should proceed to organize the church according to the commandment of the Lord. To this they consented by unanimous vote."[7] Joseph then proceeded to ordain Oliver an elder, after which Oliver likewise ordained Joseph.

The early emphasis of common consent seems centered upon the selection of ecclesiastical leadership; however, doctrinal and procedural issues were also presented before the people for their "vote." Also during the organizational meeting on April 6, 1830, those at Peter Whitmer's home were to consent to organizing the Church according to the commandments of the Lord. Three months later, in July 1830, Joseph was instructed that "all things shall be done by common consent in the church, by much prayer and faith, for all things you shall receive by faith" (D&C 26:2). This revelation has become a foundation to the government of the Lord's kingdom and defines the order of proper Church procedure.

After the events leading to the establishment of the doctrine of common consent in July 1830 (D&C 26), instructions for its operation, reemphasis of it as a principle, and evidences of its practice can be found throughout the other revelations in the Doctrine and Covenants. Some examples include the role of revelation and common consent, which was revealed in September 1830 (D&C 20:13, 63, 65, 66). Members who were appointed to service to give relief to the poor and needy or to leadership positions within the Church organization were appointed by "the voice of the church" (D&C 38:34–35; 41:9–10; 51:4, 12; see also 104:64, 71–77, 85; 124:124–44). In February 1831 the "law of the Church" (D&C 42) reemphasized that anyone possessing authority must be "known to the church" (D&C 42:11).[8] One final example found in the Doctrine and Covenants comes from the minutes of the organization of the first high council of the Church on February 17, 1834, in Kirtland, Ohio, (see D&C 102:9) and neatly sums up the law of common consent as practiced by the Saints over the previous five years. A "voting" took place to acknowledge those called by revelation in their administration "by the voice of the church" (D&C 102:9). Evidences of the law of common consent are found throughout other journals, histories, and records of the restored Church. Although there is ample historical precedent, instruction, and evidence of common consent in early religious history, some of the early Saints, like some modern Saints, still misunderstood exactly how to practice the law properly.

PRACTICE AND PROCEDURE

Many early members of the Church felt that common consent meant they would be involved in making decisions and policies and in determining the course of the Church. In other words, some of them felt that the Church would follow the standard of parliamentary procedure. After all, many of the revelations and instructions concerning common consent described this procedure as the members' opportunity to *consent* or *vote* for all things in the Church (see D&C 20:63, 65, 66; 26:2; 28:13; 102:19; 104:21, 72, 85; Official Declarations 1 and 2). These words generally summon the images of electioneering and all the trappings of politics. It was revealed that there is an "order" (see D&C 28:13; 43:3–6) that common consent follows. Members' participation according to the order of the Lord's kingdom is clearly described by President Clark, who said, "In the Church the nominating power rests in a group, the General Authorities, but the sustaining or electing power rests in the body of the Church, which under no circumstances nominates officers, the function of the Church body being solely to sustain or to elect. . . .

"The sole function of this constituent assembly today, is, as already stated, to accept or reject the General Authority or other officers proposed to them. This assembly may not propose others to be voted upon.

"Furthermore, the actual procedure for voting is normally by the uplifted hand of those present. No electioneering, no speech-making, no stating of objections, no proposing of candidates, no vocal demonstration of any kind is in order. Anyone seeking to do any of these things would not only be out of order as a matter of procedure, but would be likewise breaking the peace of the State by interrupting and disturbing a public assembly, would be subject to arrest as a disturber of the peace, and if necessary, would have to be so dealt with as a matter of public order. This assembly might be called the 'voting booth' of the Church. This will be clear to all our listeners."[9]

It is clear that the principle of common consent distinctly defines the practice and procedures of participation within Church government. Limited to "the voice of the church," or members of the Church of Jesus Christ (D&C 38:34; 41:9; 51:4; 58:49; 102:9), practice of the law of common consent is a privilege given to every member of the Church in good standing. This privilege of voting is more an act of ratifying leadership callings and decisions rather than actually making those decisions. Such decisions are left to the Lord and His anointed servants. Because politicking is not part of the process of voting within the Church, members signify their approval of a proposed action by raising their right hand. The method of manifesting a vote was a little different in earlier times. For example, Peter and the original Apostles "cast lots,"[10] and earlier procedures in the latter-day Church required members to cast their votes by standing rather than by raising their hands. Today, however, it is common practice to raise the right hand in approval or disapproval of proposed actions.

Some members are concerned whether it is appropriate for them to vote when visiting a ward or branch other than their own. Generally, members called to most Church positions are sustained by a vote of those belonging to the organization in which they will serve. For example, a stake president is sustained by his stake members, a bishop is sustained by his ward members, and an elders quorum president is sustained by those in the elders quorum rather than by the entire ward. Thus, the vote of members of a given organization (whether a deacons quorum, members of a Beehive class, or the entire Church, as at general conference) manifest their approval of the Lord's will concerning them and their governance.

CONCLUSION

When we become more familiar with the law of common consent, we understand the uncommon blessing it is in Church government and in our lives. We become more like Christ through common consent because it affords us the opportunity to recognize Christ as the sovereign King, make our will like His, sustain our fellow Saints, bind ourselves to Him through solemn covenants, and exercise our agency by choosing as He would choose. Elder Boyd K. Packer taught that "there is an obedience that comes from a knowledge of the truth that transcends any external form of control. We are not obedient because we are blind, we are obedient because we can see."[11] As Saints exercise common consent, they are in a better position to see as Christ sees.

The exercise of common consent would never be considered common by those who can see in its purpose doctrinal necessity as well as the example of the Savior. As Saints become familiar with the law of common consent, they cannot help but become more familiar with Christ. When we exercise our privilege to consent to Christ, "we shall be like him; for we shall see him as he is" (1 John 3:2). The day will come that because of this perspective, we consent to Christ's will because we have become like Him in every way.

NOTES

1. J. Reuben Clark Jr., in Conference Report, April 1940, 73.
2. Harold B. Lee, "The Place of the Living Prophet, Seer, and Revelator," in *Charge to Religious Educators,* 2nd ed. (Salt Lake City: The Church of Jesus Christ of Latter-day Saints, 1982), 105.
3. Hyrum M. Smith and Janne M. Sjodahl, *Doctrine and Covenants Commentary* (Salt Lake City: Deseret Book, 1965), 131–32.
4. Bruce R. McConkie, *Common Consent* (Salt Lake City: The Church of Jesus Christ of Latter-day Saints, 1973), 4.
5. Joseph Smith, *History of the Church of Jesus Christ of Latter-day Saints,* ed. B. H. Roberts, 2nd ed., rev. (Salt Lake City: Deseret Book, 1980), 1:61.
6. Orson F. Whitney, in Conference Report, October 1930, 45.
7. B. H. Roberts, *A Comprehensive History of The Church of Jesus Christ of Latter-day Saints* (Provo, Utah: Brigham Young University Press, 1965), 1:196.
8. The first revelation concerning proper authority was revealed in September 1830 and is recorded in Doctrine and Covenants 28. At the time, Hiram Page professed to receive revelation concerning the order of Church through a stone and thereby deceived many members. Section 28 established the order of revelation for the Church. Later, in February 1831, a Mrs. Hubble went to Kirtland, claiming to receive revelation, and confused many of the newly converted Saints. The Lord again reminded the Saints of the proper order of revelation for the Church (see D&C 43). Both incidents of deception were preceded by revelations to the Prophet of the proper procedure and the role of common consent regarding revelation and authority (see D&C 26; 42).
9. J. Reuben Clark Jr., in Conference Report, April 1940, 71–72.
10. Elder McConkie described "casting lots" as "sustaining votes" (see Bruce R. McConkie, *Doctrinal New Testament Commentary* [Salt Lake City: Bookcraft, 1971], 2:32).
11. Boyd K. Packer, "Agency and Control," *Ensign,* May 1983, 66.

CHAPTER TWELVE

THE JOSEPH SMITH TRANSLATION: A PRIMARY SOURCE FOR THE DOCTRINE AND COVENANTS

ROBERT J. MATTHEWS

The book of Doctrine and Covenants is a fact of life and deserves our most diligent study; it presents the voice of Jesus Christ speaking to us who live upon the earth now. It is a collection of sacred utterances that have been printed and bound into a volume for easy access so that those who wish to learn of their contents may do so.

The translation of the Bible by Joseph Smith is also a fact of life and is an extensive work presenting information revealed to the Prophet primarily from 1830 to 1833. The Bible translation was done at the command of the Lord and by the inspiration of the Holy Ghost. It stands along with the Book of Mormon, the Doctrine and Covenants, and the Pearl of Great Price as a tangible literary product that came from the hand of Joseph Smith. It is, with the other standard works, a witness for the Lord Jesus Christ.

Unfortunately, in some respects, even after 150 years both the Doctrine and Covenants and the Joseph Smith Translation of the Bible (JST) remain unknown books because there is so much about them that we have not understood or appreciated. This is particularly true with regard to the circumstances out of which the revelations came. Let us peel back the cover of a century and a half and obtain a

Robert J. Matthews, former dean of Religious Education, is an emeritus professor of ancient scripture at Brigham Young University.

glimpse of the Prophet Joseph Smith as he received revelation from the Lord. When we do that, we will see that there is no essential difference in the revelations that are in the JST and the revelations in the Doctrine and Covenants.

VALUE OF ORIGINAL SOURCES

One situation that has blurred our vision is that the JST is published as one book; the Doctrine and Covenants as a separate book; and the Pearl of Great Price as still another book. Having these revelations, all of which were given in the very inception of the Church, printed in separate books obscures the context and thus also the historical and doctrinal relationship between these early revelations. The books have become compartmentalized, whereas in reality the revelations in these books were revealed on a day-to-day basis in the same real-life situations. The roots of the Doctrine and Covenants and the roots of the JST are not just intertwined; they are the very same.

Every revelation that has been received was received at some specific geographical place and at some specific point in time and in connection with some specific situation. But the past becomes buried by the passage of time and the accumulation of tradition. All the while, life goes on, new experiences arise, new people come into prominence, and former leaders pass on. As a consequence, there often forms a vacuum of understanding; false concepts are gradually developed and incorrect impressions are formed. To correct this situation we often have to become literary archaeologists and dig down to the original sources so as to view them as they really are. When we do this, we will see things we had not noticed before no matter how many times we have trodden the path.

It matters not how well a person knows the *surface* of the ground and how many times he has traversed the land; he can never know what lies even close under the surface—what forms of architecture, what relics of art, and what message the past can convey—until he, or someone else, will remove the surface accumulation and examine the facts remaining from an earlier day.

It is the same way with the Doctrine and Covenants and the JST. Reading only the surface of the printed page does not give the necessary comprehension to understand the significance of some of its plainest messages. Sometimes it is only by going to sources earlier than the printed page, to the original or at least prepublication manuscripts, that one can re-create enough historical framework to see the relationships. When we see the development that has taken place, we gain a more accurate perception and appreciation for the printed page. Until we know the background, our understanding is apt to be superficial and fragmented.

In making an inquiry as to the relationships between the Doctrine and Covenants and the JST, we need to begin with a few basic dates and concepts. The Prophet Joseph Smith said that if a man could gaze into heaven for five minutes, he would learn more about heaven than by reading all that has ever been written on the subject.[1] In like manner, if we could return to 1830, 1831, or 1844 and talk with the Prophet or walk about the streets and observe conditions, we could no doubt learn something that we have so far missed about *how* and *why* some revelations were received. But as we cannot return, we are obliged to reconstruct the history as best we can with the facts that are available. This can be pleasantly rewarding because by excavation, we will begin to see things we had not seen before.

A CHRONOLOGICAL APPROACH

We will not have difficulty seeing the connection between the JST and the revelations in the Doctrine and Covenants when we sort them out chronologically. We are not accustomed to doing that because we tend to think in terms of books rather than in terms of history. Without an awareness of the context, we tend to forget, or perhaps fail to ever learn, that the gospel was revealed line upon line, precept upon precept, here and there a little at a time.

Consider what the Church was like in June 1830. What were the offices, the doctrines, and the practices of the Church in that day? It would be easier to tell what the Church was not. In June 1830 there were no wards, no stakes, no First Presidency, no Quorum of the Twelve Apostles, no patriarchs, no seventies, no bishops, no Word of Wisdom, no revelation on degrees of glory, no tithing, no welfare program, no law of consecration or united order, no priesthood quorums of any kind, no temples, no endowments, no sealings, no marriages for eternity, no real understanding of the New Jerusalem, no baptisms for the dead, no Doctrine and Covenants, no Pearl of Great Price, and no JST. How did these things come to be, which today we recognize as vital to our spiritual life and basic to the Church? They came when the time was right, in answer to prayer—the result of earnest search. Each of these things was revealed at some time, and at some place, in some situation; and one by one each became part of the doctrine and the structure of the Church. Many of the fundamental doctrines of the gospel which are contained in the Doctrine and Covenants were first made known to the Prophet Joseph Smith as he worked through the pages of the Bible in making the inspired translation.

Sequence of Events

The Book of Mormon came from the press during the week of March 18–25, 1830. In a few more days, on April 6, the Church was organized. A few weeks later, in June 1830, we have the earliest revelation associated with the JST. We are familiar with it as the "Visions of Moses" in the Pearl of Great Price, Moses chapter one.[2] We do not know the exact day in June on which the material was written, but it was in Harmony, Pennsylvania, and chronologically would be just before Doctrine and Covenants 25.[3]

Fortunately, the prepublication manuscript of the JST has been preserved. It is in the possession of the Community of Christ (formerly the RLDS Church) in Independence, Missouri, and through the graciousness of the Community of Christ Historian's Office we have been able to examine it. I have found the manuscript to be in good condition and readable. It is very informative as to the history of the translation because it contains a number of dates showing when certain portions of the Bible translation were in process. These dates, along with the varying styles of known handwriting, reflecting the services of different scribes, have enabled us to identify certain relationships with the Doctrine and Covenants that otherwise would have escaped us.

After presenting the material that we call the "Visions of Moses" (June 1830), the succeeding pages of the manuscript contain what we know as JST Genesis 1–5 (Moses 2–5), which should be placed in proximity to Doctrine and Covenants 29. Since exact dates are not given in the manuscripts of either these chapters of Genesis or Doctrine and Covenants 29, the placing of these has to be approximate. The chapters from Genesis were received and recorded sometime between June

1830 and October 1830, and thus very likely previous to the reception of section 29.

The subjects of these chapters of JST Genesis have to do with the spiritual and temporal creations, agency, the rebellion of Lucifer, the Fall of Adam, and the introduction of the gospel to Adam and his posterity. The doctrinal emphasis of these topics is clear and prominent in the JST but is almost totally lacking in any other Bible.

In the Genesis account the principles are woven into story form involving several chapters, and they tell of the events of the Garden of Eden, Satan's rebellion, his temptation of Adam and Eve, and their eating the forbidden fruit and being ushered out of the garden. In contrast, the material in Doctrine and Covenants 29:30–45 is a brief statement of doctrinal principles—without the story—actually a summary of the doctrines found in the longer narrative of JST Genesis 1–5.

A further point needs to be made in this comparison. As a Church, our main access to the early chapters of JST Genesis has been through the book of Moses in the Pearl of Great Price. When the book of Moses was printed therein, the Church did not have access to the original manuscripts and thus the text was obtained from printed sources that did not have the dates of the various chapters. In the 1880 edition of Moses, chapters 2–8 were incorrectly identified as having been received by Joseph Smith in December 1830. This dating continued in subsequent editions. This was an unfortunate error, first because no one suspected it was an error, and second because it prevented readers from seeing the true relationship that existed with the Doctrine and Covenants. Access to the originals has shown us the true dates and made the foregoing discussion relative to Doctrine and Covenants 29 possible. With the printing of the new edition of the scriptures by The Church of Jesus Christ of Latter-day Saints in 1981, the correct dates have been placed in the book of Moses. Thus, for maximum comprehension, JST Genesis 1–5 (Moses 2–5) should be read just prior to a study of Doctrine and Covenants 29, since that appears to be the order in which they were received.

The historical relationship between JST Genesis and Doctrine and Covenants 29 begins a procedure repeated in later revelations. The pattern shows that many of the concepts contained in the Doctrine and Covenants were first presented to the mind of the Prophet during his translation of the Bible, and were actually first recorded therein. Later many of these subjects were enlarged upon and appeared as parts of various sections of the Doctrine and Covenants. We will examine other examples.

THE REVELATIONS CONCERNING THE BUILDING OF A LATTER-DAY ZION

An extensive revelation about Enoch and his people was given to Joseph Smith in December 1830 while he and Sidney Rigdon were translating from the fifth chapter of the King James Version of Genesis. Chronologically this came after Doctrine and Covenants section 35 and before section 37. This revelation, called in early Latter-day Saint literature the "Prophecy of Enoch," deals with the ministry of Enoch, his faith in Jesus Christ, his preaching of the gospel, his city which was called Zion, the righteousness of his people, the fact that there were no poor among them, the taking of the people into heaven, and a declaration that they would return to the earth in the last days and be joined with the New Jerusalem that would be built upon the earth. This information about Enoch contains many items of history and doctrine of particular interest to the Latter-day Saints because it deals with the work of the Lord on the earth in our day—the establishment of latter-day Zion.

Consider the situation of the Church in December 1830. What did anyone in the Church know about Enoch, or the New Jerusalem, or the city of Zion, or any of these things at that time? We certainly cannot learn much from the King James Version about Enoch or his city of Zion, or the laws that governed the people of Zion. The King James Version does not even say Enoch had a city, or that his people were called "Zion," or that his people were translated. The entire offering in the Bible about Enoch can be read in less than two minutes and consists of only nine verses totaling thirty-eight lines of type, found in Genesis 5:18–24, Hebrews 11:5, and Jude 1:14–15. All of that together would amount to about three-fourths of one column of print in a Bible. The Book of Mormon does not mention or allude to Enoch at all.

The Church in 1830 was entirely dependent on a new revelation in order to know anything substantial about Enoch, his ministry, the people of his city (Zion), or their laws. However, the Lord was about to reveal to the Church much about Enoch and the laws pertaining to both the ancient and the future Zion. The first introduction to these things was in November and December 1830 while the Prophet was translating from Genesis. In the next few months came the revelations in Doctrine and Covenants 42–43, 45–51, and 57–59 (February–August 1831). Can you see what a marvelous prelude the prophecy of Enoch in JST Genesis chapter 7 (Moses 7) was in laying the foundation for these later revelations? In length alone it is impressive. The information about Enoch and Zion, as revealed to Joseph Smith in November and December 1830 while he was translating the Bible, is eighteen times as long as all of the Enoch material that is contained in the King James Version. Thus, if we want to get a correct historical perspective of how the Lord educated His Prophet and His people about Zion, we must first read the revelations that were received while Joseph was translating the Bible. This is perfectly proper, because that is the order in which they were given. It is only in publishing them in different books that we have created an artificial separation between JST Genesis 6–7 and Doctrine and Covenants 42–59. In other words, if one is studying the Doctrine and Covenants and wishes to get a proper orientation about the sections dealing with consecration and the establishment of Zion and the New Jerusalem, an appropriate procedure would be to first study JST Genesis 6–7 (Moses 6–7) about Enoch and his people who were called Zion, their laws, their absence of poverty, and their glory, before reading Doctrine and Covenants 38–59. From the vantage point of the information about Enoch and Zion, as first presented in the translation of the Bible, the next twenty sections or so of the Doctrine and Covenants fall neatly into place. JST Genesis 7 is an overview of the glory and greatness of Enoch's Zion given to the Church as a prelude before the Lord revealed in detail the laws and requirements that would enable the Latter-day Saints to build a similar Zion.

Note this sequence: In October 1830 (D&C 32) the Lord sends Oliver Cowdery and others to Missouri. In November and December in New York, the Lord reveals extensive information about Enoch and his Zion while the Prophet is translating Genesis. Later in December (D&C 37) the Lord tells the Prophet to move to Ohio, which he does in January 1831. In February (D&C 42) the Lord promises that in due time the exact spot for the city of Zion shall be revealed. Also, in this same revelation the law of consecration and other economic provisions that pertain to Zion are set forth. In June 1831 several of the elders are sent to Missouri. In July a conference is held in Missouri and the site for the city of Zion or the New Jerusalem is at last made known (D&C 57). Thus, we see in the winter and spring of 1830 to 1831, the Lord was about to reveal the law that pertains to Zion so that Zion could be established and the New Jerusalem could be built. That is, before He gave the particulars outlining the details of the law for use in this Church, He gave to Joseph Smith and to the Church an informative overview and historical backdrop or pattern by means of the "prophecy of Enoch" obtained in November and December 1830 while the Prophet was translating the Bible.

The Enoch material from Genesis gave them the "big picture," or the necessary perspective. This is borne out by various comments in the Doctrine and Covenants revelations. For example, there is a reference to Enoch in Doctrine and Covenants 38:4 that says, "I am the same which have taken the Zion of Enoch into mine own bosom." This passage, dated January 2, 1831, would hardly be meaningful without the information about Enoch and his translated city, which had just been obtained a few days before from the JST. Two months later, in March 1831, the Lord again makes reference to Enoch and his city. This is a very pointed reference to the JST Enoch material and says, "Wherefore, hearken ye together and let me show unto you even my wisdom—the wisdom of him whom ye say is the God of Enoch, and his brethren, who were separated from the earth, and were received unto myself—a city reserved until a day of righteousness shall come—a day which was sought for by all holy men, and they found it not because of wickedness and abominations" (D&C 45:11–12).

Both of these passages in the Doctrine and Covenants would be deprived of much of their meaning if they had not been preceded by the information in JST Genesis; without the JST these Doctrine and Covenants comments would have no reference since the King James Version offers none of this information about Enoch or his Zion.

We would have a clearer, richer, fuller and more comprehensive understanding of the way this dispensation was unfolded if we were to take the revelations received during the translation of the Bible and place them in their proper chronological order between the sections of the Doctrine and Covenants. For example, Moses 1 would be just before section 25; JST Genesis 1–5 (Moses 2–5) would be just before section 29; JST Genesis 6 (Moses 6) would be just before section 35; and JST Genesis 7 (Moses 7) would be just before section 37. We were not able to think of this idea until quite recently because we did not have access to the original JST manuscripts and did not know the dates that are written thereon.

THE AGE OF ACCOUNTABILITY

In Doctrine and Covenants 68:25–28, the age of accountability is explained as beginning at the age of eight years, at which time it is stated that baptism should be administered and that parents have a responsibility to teach this to their children. This is the only mention of this in the Doctrine and Covenants and is dated November 1831. However, the eight-year-old age of accountability is recorded in the JST in connection with Genesis 17:11. According to the dates on the JST manuscript, this was recorded sometime between February 1831 and April 1831 and was received, therefore, from six to nine months earlier than it appears in the Doctrine and Covenants.

A careful reading of Doctrine and Covenants 68:25–28 demonstrates that the declaration of the eight-year-old accountability at that instance does not sound like a "first-time" announcement anyway, but more like a reaffirmation or a reminder. And indeed that was the case, for, as we have seen, the concept was already written in the translation of the Bible many months before it was reiterated in the Doctrine and Covenants. Without the original JST manuscripts which contain the dates, we would never have been able to reconstruct this relationship which provides a broader background to this part of the Doctrine and Covenants.

PRESERVATION OF ANIMAL LIFE

A prohibition against the people of the Lord wasting or unnecessarily taking animal life is given in both the JST and the Doctrine and Covenants. The dates of these two sources are not exact, but are close together in 1831, with the stronger evidence that the JST was given first.

Genesis 9 recounts instructions from the Lord to Noah soon after the flood, dealing with human and animal life. Note the comparison of the King James Version (KJV) and the JST.

KJV, Genesis 9:

> 3 Every moving thing that liveth shall be meat for you; even as the green herb have I given you all things.
>
> 4 But flesh with the life thereof, which is the blood thereof, shall ye not eat.
>
> 5 And surely your blood of your lives will I require; at the hand of every beast will I require it, and at the hand of man; at the hand of every man's brother will I require the life of man.

JST Genesis 9:

> 9 Every moving thing that liveth shall be meat for you; even as the green herb have I given you all things.
>
> 10 But, *the blood of all flesh which I have given you for meat, shall be shed upon the ground, which taketh life thereof, and the blood* ye shall not eat.
>
> 11 And surely, *blood shall not be shed, only for meat, to save your lives; and the blood* of every beast will I require *at your hands* (Bible appendix; emphasis added).

The emphasis against wasting animal life and flesh is totally lost in the KJV but comes across clearly in the JST, and it even calls for man having to give an account for the taking of animal life.

The manuscripts of the JST place all of Genesis chapters 7–24 (which would include this material) between December 1830 and April 1831. Intervening chapters have to be within these dates. Since we know Joseph Smith did not translate during January,[4] a conclusion tends toward chapter 9 being sometime in February or March 1831.

In March 1831 the revelation now known as Doctrine and Covenants 49 was received, which contains this statement about not wasting animal life: "For, behold, the beasts of the field and the fowls of the air, and that which cometh of the earth, is ordained for the use of man for food and for raiment, and that he might have in abundance. . . . And wo be unto man that sheddeth blood or that wasteth flesh and hath no need" (D&C 49:19, 21).

Taken together, the JST and the Doctrine and Covenants give the reader a view that man has a stewardship for the animal kingdom. The dating of these two utterances draws our attention to their complementary relationship.[5]

THE VISION OF THE DEGREES OF GLORY

In the process of the translation, the Prophet, with Sidney Rigdon as scribe, came to the fifth chapter of John in the New Testament. It was while translating this chapter and pondering over verse 29 about the resurrection of the just and the unjust that the vision of the degrees of glory was revealed. The relationship of the JST to this revelation can be seen in the following excerpts. In his journal the Prophet recorded: "Upon my return from Amherst conference, I resumed the translation of the Scriptures. From sundry revelations which had been received, it was apparent that many important points touching the salvation of man had been taken from the Bible, or lost before it was compiled. It appeared self-evident from what truths were left, that if God rewarded every one according to the deeds done in the body, the term 'Heaven,' as intended for the Saints' eternal home, must include more kingdoms than one. Accordingly, while translating St. John's Gospel, myself and Elder Rigdon saw the following vision."[6]

Within the revelation we read the following: "For while we were doing the work of translation, which the Lord had appointed unto us, we came to the twenty-ninth verse of the fifth chapter of John, which was given unto us as follows—speaking of the resurrection of the dead, concerning those who shall hear the voice of the Son of Man: and shall come forth; they who have done good, in the resurrection of the just; and they who have done evil, in the resurrection of the unjust. Now this caused us to marvel, for it was given unto us of the Spirit. And while we meditated upon these things, the Lord touched the eyes of our understandings and they were opened, and the glory of the Lord shone round about" (D&C 76:15–19).

THE JST AS A FORERUNNER

Based on the line of thinking given in this article, it is evident that many of the important doctrines and practices of this Church were made known to the Prophet Joseph Smith during the course of his translation of the Bible and were subsequently incorporated into the later revelations in the Doctrine and Covenants. The reason the Kirtland period was such a great revelatory period may certainly be because it was the time in which the Prophet was engaged in the translation of the Bible. Time prohibits a discussion of each instance, but this concept includes revelations on at least the following subjects: the New Jerusalem, plural marriage, Zion, powers of the priesthood, quorums and councils in the Church, quorum organization and duties, the Fall of Adam, the Atonement of Jesus Christ, the spirit world, resurrection, exaltation, age of accountability, agency, and the nature of the devil, of man, and of God.

In addition to the doctrinal associations discussed in this paper, the Doctrine and Covenants has other close ties to the JST. The selection of Sidney Rigdon as scribe is given in Doctrine and Covenants 35:20. Interestingly, at this same time (December 1830) the manuscript of the JST begins to be in Rigdon's handwriting. Instructions to pause temporarily (see D&C 37:1), to resume translating (see D&C 73:3), to hasten the work (see D&C 93:53), or to publish the translation (see D&C 94:10; 104:58, 89) are also found in the Doctrine and Covenants. A perusal of the headnotes and the footnotes of the 1981 edition of the Doctrine and Covenants shows that there are many relationships of the Doctrine and Covenants to the JST.

CONCLUSION

What, then, is the conclusion to the whole matter? That the Prophet's work with the Bible was a primary source for much of the doctrinal content and the instructional information of the Doctrine and Covenants. Consequently, one could not adequately understand either the background or the content of those parts of the Doctrine and Covenants without an acquaintance with the history and content of the JST. The two volumes, when placed in tandem, enable the student to gain a clearer picture of how the gospel was restored in this dispensation, and they give the reader insight as to how divine revelation comes. Underlying the whole process is the bold demonstration that revelation comes through a careful study of the scriptures. As the Prophet labored with the translation of the Bible, additional revelation was given to him. That this is one of the purposes of the JST is stated in Doctrine and Covenants 45:60–62, wherein the Lord said in effect, if you want more knowledge, translate the New Testament, for in it "all these things shall be made known." Thus we see enacted a gospel truth: when we study the revelations already given, new revelation comes to enlarge our spiritual understanding. And that is, after all, our reason for searching the scriptures.

NOTES

1. Joseph Smith, *Teachings of the Prophet Joseph Smith,* comp. Joseph Fielding Smith (Salt Lake City: Deseret Book, 1938), 324.
2. The reader is reminded that the Book of Moses in the Pearl of Great Price is an extract from the JST up to JST Genesis 8:18.
3. December 1830 was the correct date for the material known as Moses 7, but chapters 2–6 were earlier and chapter 8 was later.
4. This conclusion is reached by combining the statement in Doctrine and Covenants 37:1 (December 1830), which instructed the Prophet not to translate further until he had moved to the Ohio (where he arrived on February 4, 1831). Doctrine and Covenants 42:56–58, received on February 9, 1831, instructed him to continue with the translation. Thus it appears he did not translate during January 1831.
5. At another time the Prophet expressed the view that men should not needlessly kill animals and that the animal race will not lose its vicious disposition as long as the servants of God make war upon it (see Smith, *Teachings,* 71).
6. Joseph Smith, *History of the Church of Jesus Christ of Latter-day Saints,* ed. B. H. Roberts, 2nd ed., rev. (Salt Lake City: Deseret Book, 1957), 1:245.

CHAPTER THIRTEEN

THE LAWS OF CONSECRATION, STEWARDSHIP, AND TITHING

CRAIG J. OSTLER

The Lord requires His people to consecrate their lives and temporal possessions for the building of His kingdom and to provide for the poor. In the early days of the Restoration, the Lord revealed specific laws concerning consecration of earthly property, receiving steward-ships, and payment of tithes to the Church of Jesus Christ. The Lord emphasized that the Saints must learn to obey these laws to receive an inheritance in the celestial kingdom (see D&C 105:1–5; 119:1–7). Possibly due to misunderstanding of the revelations governing these principles, there has been some confusion regarding these laws— especially their relationship to each other and our responsibility to abide by them today. One sister in the Church was heard to lament, "In my situation I can hardly make ends meet. Every month it is a struggle to pay tithing. How will I ever be able to live the law of con-secration?" A brief examination of revelations in the Doctrine and Covenants regarding the laws of consecration, stewardship, and tithing within their historical context can illuminate our under-standings of the principles underlying their purposes.[1]

THE LAWS OF CONSECRATION AND STEWARDSHIP REVEALED (D&C 42)

True principles governing the laws of consecration and steward-ship evidence the Lord's wisdom in providing for His Saints. At a con-ference of the Church held in Fayette, New York, in January 1831,

Craig J. Ostler is an associate professor of Church history and doctrine at Brigham Young University.

the Lord commanded the Saints to go to "the Ohio" where He would give them His law and where they would be endowed with power from on high (D&C 38:32). In this same revelation the Lord twice commanded the Saints, "let every man esteem his brother as himself" (D&C 38:24–25), which in essence is the spirit of the law of consecration. In February, after the Prophet Joseph Smith's arrival in Ohio, the revelation, known as "the law of the Church," was received. This revelation clarified principles governing consecration of property to the Lord and receiving stewardships to oversee consecrated land and material goods.

Some of those baptized in Kirtland, Ohio, had previously attempted to live what they believed was the law of having all things in common as found in the New Testament. That is, all property was held jointly by the community, and they referred to it as "common stock." John Whitmer, early historian for the Church, explained, "The disciples had all things common, and were going to destruction very fast as to temporal things; for they considered from reading the scripture that what belonged to a brother, belonged to any of the brethren. Therefore they would take each other's clothes and other property and use it without leave which brought on confusion and disappointments, for they did not understand the scripture."[2]

In place of the misguided attempts of the early Saints to live according to their private interpretations of New Testament passages, the Lord revealed that the Saints were to consecrate their properties to Him. The foundational principle upon which this law rests is recognition that the Lord is the Creator of the earth and therefore all property is His. "Behold, the Lord hath created the earth that it should be inhabited" Nephi explained; "and he hath created his children that they should possess it" (1 Nephi 17:36). All worldly wealth, whether it be lands or gold, is provided for the benefit of God's children during their mortal sojourn. In commanding His Saints to consecrate their temporal, earthly goods to the building up of His kingdom, the Lord is not interested in real estate, precious ores, jewels, or houses. Rather, consecration is a godly activity, and those who devote their property, time, and talents to blessing others become more godlike.

The Lord directed the means by which property was to be consecrated within His law. Basically, to consecrate property is to set it apart for sacred purposes. The Lord indicated that properties were to be consecrated or set apart "with a covenant and a deed which cannot be broken" (D&C 42:30). The covenant was a sacred promise made with God to dedicate temporal property to the Church. The deed was a legally binding document, written and signed by both the member consecrating his property and by the bishop who received the property as the Lord's authorized agent (see D&C 42:31). Thus, the covenant was binding according to both the laws of God and the laws of the land.

After deeding all of his property to the Lord's Church through his bishop, the consecrating member was appointed "a steward over his own property" (D&C 42:32). That is, after consecrating his properties the member received another legal, signed document from the bishop listing the lands, furniture, tools, and so forth that were being leased to him by deed as his stewardship. This property was held as a stewardship for the Master, Jesus Christ, Lord of the earth. This arrangement recognized that we are but stewards for the Lord and are accountable to Him for the use of our talents to bless the lives of others. The Lord clarified that the steward was to receive "as much as is sufficient for himself and family" (D&C 42:32). In other words, the stewardship property deeded to the member was to be adequate to enable him to provide for his family according to the number of children and other dependents in the household.

Such a law anticipated that some Saints would have more property to consecrate than would be necessary to be deeded back to them as a stewardship. In addition, it was hoped that those who received a stewardship would produce more than they needed and could regularly consecrate the surplus. To this end the Lord explained that "the residue shall be kept in my storehouse" (D&C 42:34). In so doing the Lord restored the principle of keeping of the Lord's storehouse, as was done anciently to provide for the poor (see Malachi 3:10). One of the most sacred trusts that are placed in the bishop's hands is that of providing for the poor and needy. In this law the bishop uses the property or goods that are surplus to provide for the needs of the members.

In addition, this law also anticipated the time of building the city of the New Jerusalem. The Lord indicated that another use for the surplus generated in the law of consecration and stewardship was "for the purpose of purchasing lands for the public benefit of the church, and building houses of worship, and building up of the New Jerusalem which is hereafter to be revealed—that my covenant people may be gathered in one in that day when I shall come to my temple" (D&C 42:35–36). Thus, there was no thought that Zion would be built up by a single individual; rather, the law of consecration was to be the law of the Lord's covenant people as a community.

IMPLEMENTING THE LAWS OF CONSECRATION AND STEWARDSHIP (D&C 51)

Often there is a gap between theory and practice in living the principles of the gospel. Such was the case with implementing the newly restored laws of consecration and stewardship. The Saints desired to obey the Lord, but the time had arrived to learn how to obey Him. By May 1831, in response to the Lord's earlier command for the Church to move to Ohio, approximately two hundred Saints living in New York sold their properties and made the move west. Their arrival called attention to the need for further instructions to implement the laws of consecration and stewardship as previously revealed. In preparation, an earlier revelation directed the Saints to purchase lands in the region near Kirtland (see D&C 48:3). In Thompson, Ohio, a new convert named Leman Copley owned a large tract of land, some 759 acres, which he consecrated for the settlement of the newly arrived Saints. Bishop Edward Partridge was responsible for dividing this property among the Saints. Consequently, he requested the Prophet Joseph Smith to inquire of the Lord for direction on the matter.

The Lord revealed that stewardships were to be given by the bishop according to the laws previously revealed and clarified that in appointing each their portions, "every man [was to be] equal according to his family, according to his circumstances and his wants and needs" (D&C 51:3). Such instructions take into consideration that no two families have exactly the same needs. In the division of properties, the number of children in a family, as well as the ages and abilities of the children, is taken into consideration. A farmer would receive farm land as his stewardship, a printer a printing office, a tanner a tannery, and a businessman a mercantile establishment (see D&C 57:8, 11; 104:19–42). "And all of this" reads a later revelation, "for the benefit of the church of the living God, that every man may improve upon his talent, that every man may gain other talents" (D&C 82:18). In this manner the needs of the poor were provided for and they were placed in a position in which they could supply their own wants and aid others in doing the same.

The principles governing who determined what was needed by each individual and family in their particular circumstances posed a challenge. The Lord designated the bishop to "appoint unto this people their portions" (D&C 51:3). However, safeguards were put in place to prevent abuses or even perceived abuses by the bishop in determining the portions given as stewardships. Instructing the bishop in the principles that would direct his decision, the Prophet explained in a letter to Bishop Partridge: "To condescend to particulars, I will tell you that every man must be his own judge how much he should receive and how much he should suffer to remain in the hands of the Bishop. I speak of those who consecrate more than they need for the support of themselves and their families.

"The matter of consecration must be done by the mutual consent of both parties; for to give the Bishop power to say how much every man shall have, and he be obliged to comply with the Bishop's judgment, is giving to the Bishop more power than a king has; and upon the other hand, to let every man say how much he needs, and the Bishop be obliged to comply with his judgment, is to throw Zion into confusion, and make a slave of the Bishop. The fact is, there must be a balance or equilibrium of power, between the Bishop and the people, and thus harmony and good will may be preserved among you.

"Therefore, those persons consecrating property to the Bishop in Zion, and then receiving an inheritance back, must reasonably show to the Bishop that they need as much as they claim. But in case the two parties cannot come to a mutual agreement, the Bishop is to have nothing to do about receiving such consecrations; and the case must be laid before a council of twelve High Priests, the Bishop not being one of the council, but he is to lay the case before them."[3]

The Lord subsequently directed that each stewardship was to be given by a legal deed, or, as stated in the revelation, the bishop was to "give unto him a writing that shall secure unto him his portion" (D&C 51:4). A few of these writings have survived to our day. They consist of both consecration deeds and stewardship deeds, which are partly printed and partly handwritten documents. The left-hand side includes the granting of property to "Edward Partridge, . . . bishop said church." A description of the consecrated property follows in handwritten form. The deed stipulated that this transaction was "for the purpose of purchasing lands, and building up the New Jerusalem, even Zion, and for relieving the wants of the poor and needy." Where the name of the individual was written, it stated that he covenanted and bound himself and his heirs forever "to release all" their "right and interest to the above described property."[4]

The right-hand side of the document read, "Be it known that I, Edward Partridge [name written by hand] of Jackson county, and state of Missouri, bishop of the church of Christ, organized according to law, and established by the revelations of the Lord, on the 6th day of April, 1830, have leased, and by these presents do lease unto [individual's name written by hand] of Jackson county, and state of Missouri, a member of said church, the following described piece or parcel of land . . . [description of property written by hand] to have and to hold the above property. . . . And it is agreed by the parties, that this lease and loan shall be binding during the life of the said [individual's name written by hand] unless he transgress, and is not deemed worthy by the authority of the church, according to its laws, to belong to the church. And in that case I the said [individual's name written by hand] do acknowledge that I forfeit all claim to the above described leased and loaned property, and hereby bind myself to give back the leased, and also pay an equivalent for the loaned, for the benefit of said church."[5]

Over a period of time, implementation of the law of consecration was clarified and adapted to meet the needs of the Saints. For example, today Doctrine and Covenants 51:5 reads differently than it does in the *Kirtland Revelation Book*. As it now reads, members who left the Church were given a deed as privately owning the stewardship property, rather than having the leased property revert back to the Church. In the original text, Bishop Partridge was instructed to retain deeds for the Church to property consecrated by its members. It read thus:

"Wherefore let my servant Edward receive the properties of this people which have covenanted with me to obey the laws which I have given and let my servant Edward receive the money as it shall be laid before him according to the covenant and go and obtain a deed or article of this land unto himself of him who holdeth it if he harden not his heart for I have appointed him to receive these things and thus through him the properties of the church shall be consecrated unto me."[6]

Accordingly, Bishop Partridge held title to the land for the Church, but members received the leased land as a stewardship. If an individual left the Church after receiving property as a stewardship, the inheritance reverted back to the hands of the Church (see D&C 51:4). It was determined, however, that this practice did not accord with the law of the land because individuals could not be deprived of property by a religious organization. Hence, Church leaders revised the practice to agree with the law of the land. In a letter to the Saints in Zion, the Prophet Joseph Smith wrote, "On the subject of giving deeds, and receiving contributions from brethren, I have nothing further to say on the subject than to recommend that you make yourselves acquainted with the commandments of the Lord, and the laws of the state, and govern yourselves accordingly."[7]

Principles of consecration extend beyond the consecration of property to consecrating all that we are. At a conference held at Orange, Cuyahoga County, Ohio, October 25–26, 1831, "very many of the brethren holding the Priesthood addressed the conference, and each one expressed his willingness to consecrate all he possessed to God and His cause."[8] When the Prophet Joseph Smith arose to address the conference, he "said that he had nothing to consecrate to the Lord of the things of the Earth, yet he felt to consecrate himself and family."[9] Thus, we see that the Prophet Joseph Smith understood early that consecration extended beyond the stipulations of property explained in the early revelations of the Doctrine and Covenants. In addition, it is evident that although they may work in conjunction with each other, consecration might be obeyed as a law apart from the laws governing stewardship of property. On the other hand, it soon became unmistakable that consecration of the individual heart is necessary to be a faithful steward for the Lord.

ORGANIZATION OF THE LITERARY FIRM (D&C 70)

The principles of consecration and stewardship afforded guidelines for providing funds to print Church publications. On the last day of a conference held in Hiram, Ohio, November 12, 1831, the Lord appointed six brethren "to be stewards over the revelations and commandments" (D&C 70:3). This was the beginning of Church-owned businesses that were to further the work of the Lord on the earth. This group—the Prophet Joseph Smith; Sidney Rigdon, the Prophet's scribe; Martin Harris and Oliver Cowdery, who both had helped in translating and publishing the Book of Mormon; John Whitmer, Church historian; and William W. Phelps, the Church printer—comprised what was known as the Literary Firm. Their stewardship was to manage the publishing of scriptures, and it eventually included publishing a Church hymnal and newspaper. The Lord further revealed that moneys collected from the sale of Church publications were to provide for the temporal needs of the members of the firm. "Nevertheless," the Lord indicated, "inasmuch as they receive more than is needful for their necessities and their wants, it shall be given into my storehouse; and the benefits shall be consecrated unto the inhabitants of Zion" (D&C 70:7–8). Thus, the Literary Firm was organized on principles of the laws of consecration and stewardship. Each member was expected to consecrate their efforts to build up the kingdom of God within their appointed sphere. Regarding the anticipated concerns over what eventually constituted full-time Church employment, the Lord explained, "He who is appointed to administer spiritual things, the same is worthy of his hire, even as those who are appointed to a stewardship to administer in temporal things" (D&C 70:12). The stewardship of spiritual concerns was deemed a sacred trust.

ORGANIZATION OF THE UNITED FIRM (D&C 78 AND 82)

Church-owned businesses help to provide for the poor and the building up of Zion. In late February or early March 1832, a group of high priests again met in Hiram, Ohio. The Lord revealed, "The time has come . . . that there [must] be an organization of my people, in regulating and establishing the affairs of the storehouse for the poor of my people, both in this place and in the land of Zion" (D&C 78:3). As originally recorded, this revelation called for the organization of "the literary and mercantile establishments of my church."[10] The Lord directed that, in addition to the previously appointed Literary Firm, the brethren were to organize a Church-owned mercantile firm referred to in Church records as the United Firm, the United Order, and also the Order of Enoch. The United Firm eventually included about a dozen Church leaders, specified by the Lord in revelation to receive responsibility as His stewards to hold legal title to Church property and buildings. Continuing the pattern revealed regarding the Literary Firm, members of the order were governed by principles of the laws of consecration and stewardship. That is, each individual member had specific responsibilities within the United Firm given them as a stewardship. Further, surplus profits generated by the firm's holdings were used for the operation of the Church, publishing scriptures and other Church materials, and purchasing lands for the inheritance of the Saints in Zion and Kirtland. On June 25, 1833, the Prophet Joseph Smith wrote to the Saints in Missouri, "The order of the Literary Firm is a matter of stewardship, which is of the greatest importance; and the mercantile establishment God commanded to be devoted to the support thereof."[11]

This simple organization laid the groundwork of the Saints' ability to "stand independent" from the world in providing for the temporal needs of the poor (D&C 78:14). Many Church-owned businesses have developed from this original command to organize the United Firm, several of which comprise the Church welfare system to provide for the poor and disadvantaged. As a result, the temporal survival of the kingdom of God is less and less dependent upon the success of worldly markets and merchandising. Neither will the ability of the Church to provide for the poor be contingent on the ability of worldly governments to rebound from natural or man-made disasters. In recent years the strength of the kingdom has been evident in its independent capacity to reach areas of turmoil and catastrophe quickly and in an organized manner. Part of the latter-day mission of the Church is to demonstrate to the world that the Church has the ability to provide help to those in need. In sum, the principles of stewardship emphasized in the revelations continue to guide the Church to the present day in supplying funds for its operation and for providing for those in need.

The Lord designated that the original three members of the United Firm were to be Newel K. Whitney, recently called as a bishop in Ohio, the Prophet Joseph Smith, and Sidney Rigdon (see D&C 78:9). In obedience to the Lord's command to "sit in council with the saints which are in Zion" (D&C 78:9), these men left Kirtland on April 1,

1832, accompanied by Peter Whitmer Jr. and Jesse Gause. The Prophet Joseph Smith and his companions arrived in Jackson County, Missouri, on April 24, 1832. The purpose of this visit was to establish a branch of the United Firm in Missouri according to the Lord's command (see D&C 78:3–4). The Lord revealed that members of the Literary Firm, previously called by the Lord, were to also be included in the organization of the United Firm. In addition, the eight members were to be joined by Bishop Edward Partridge (see D&C 82:11). The next day the council of brethren reconvened and determined that the names of the branches of the United Firm in Ohio and Missouri would be "Gilbert, Whitney & Company in Zion. And Newel K. Whitney & Company in Kirtland Geauga Co. Ohio."[12]

At a meeting of the United Firm held April 30, 1832, in Independence, Missouri, it was "Resolved That the firm [secure a] loan [of] fifteen thousand dollars for five years or longer at six per cent annually or semi-annually as the agreement can be made, & that N.K. Whitney & Co. be appointed to negotiate the same."[13] In late October 1832, the Prophet Joseph Smith and Newel K. Whitney traveled together to New York City. Brother Whitney secured loans to purchased goods for the mercantile businesses of the United Firm.[14] These goods were used to stock the Newel K. Whitney store in Kirtland, Ohio, and, most probably, the A. Sidney Gilbert store in Independence, Missouri (see D&C 57:8; 63:42–43; 64:26).

The Lord made clear that all of the members of the United Firm were "to have equal claims on the properties, for the benefit of managing the concerns of your stewardships" (D&C 82:17). The Lord further reiterated that the use of property was according to the principles of the laws of consecration and stewardship, "every man according to his wants and his needs, inasmuch as his wants are just—and all this for the benefit of the church of the living God, that every man may improve upon his talent, that every man may gain other talents, yea, even an hundred fold, to be cast into the Lord's storehouse, to become the common property of the whole church—every man seeking the interest of his neighbor, and doing all things with an eye single to the glory of God" (D&C 82:17–19).

During the months that the Prophet Joseph Smith received these revelations, March and April 1832, the Quorum of the First Presidency was also being established for the first time in this dispensation. It is worth noting that the original members of the First Presidency—Joseph Smith, Sidney Rigdon, and Jesse Gause—were appointed as stewards in the United Firm. A year later, on March 15, 1833, Frederick G. Williams was appointed to replace Jesse Gause in the Presidency. At that time the Lord declared, "I give unto the united order [United Firm], organized agreeable to the commandment previously given, a revelation and commandment concerning my servant Frederick G. Williams, that ye shall receive him into the order" (D&C 92:1). Thus, from the beginning of the Restoration, the First Presidency of the Church received the continuing stewardship to manage the temporal concerns of the Church, along with the presiding bishopric.

STEWARDSHIPS FOR HOUSES OF THE LORD (D&C 94 AND 96)

The Lord wishes to bless the Saints and endow them "with power from on high" (D&C 95:8). In late December 1832 and early January 1833, He called upon a council of high priests meeting in the translating room of the Whitney store in Kirtland to "organize yourselves; prepare every needful thing; and establish a house, even a house of prayer, a house of fasting, a house of faith, a house of learning, a house of glory, a house of order, a house of God" (D&C 88:119). Subsequently, on March 23, 1833, He directed the organization of a Church building committee to oversee this work and additionally called for them to build "a house for the presidency" and a house "for the work of the printing and the translation of my scriptures" (D&C 94:3, 10).

Further, as more and more Saints gathered to the Kirtland area, need arose to purchase lands for their settlement. In April 1833 the Church purchased a 103-acre farm from Peter French. This farm extended south from the Kirtland flats, near the Newel K. Whitney home and store, and rose up the hill to the lot upon which the Kirtland Temple now stands. The Prophet Joseph Smith wrote: "A conference of High Priests convened in the translating room in Kirtland [above the Newel K. Whitney store] . . . and took into consideration how the French farm should be [distributed]."[15] During this council the Lord revealed that He wished Bishop "Newel K. Whitney [to] take charge of the place which is named among you, upon which I design to build mine holy house" (D&C 96:2), today referred to as the Kirtland Temple. Further, a portion of the property was to be set aside "to benefit mine order [United Firm, specifically the Literary Firm] for the purpose of bringing forth my word to the children of men" (D&C 96:4).

Also, the Lord appointed that John Johnson "should become a member of the order, that he may assist in bringing forth my word unto the children of men . . . and he shall seek diligently to take away incumbrances that are upon the house named among you, that he may dwell therein" (D&C 96:8–9). That is, the purchase of a farm from Peter French included a house or inn located on the Kirtland flats on the lot south of Newel K. Whitney's home. The Lord commanded John Johnson to supply funds to help pay the debt the United Firm incurred in the purchase of the farm. John sold his home and farm in Hiram, Ohio, as part of honoring the covenant he made as a member of the order to consecrate his property to the Lord's Church. The proceeds from the sale of his farm in Hiram were combined with the money of the order and used to pay the mortgage on the Peter French farm. It was upon a portion of this land that the Kirtland Temple was built. Thus it was that the Savior gave members of the United Firm stewardship over the growing land holdings of the Church.

Much of the success of the laws of consecration and stewardship depended on wise management of temporal stewardships in producing surplus that could be consecrated for the poor and the building of the kingdom of God on earth. Similar to the Lord's parable of the wise and unwise stewards, those who were slothful in managing their stewardships incurred the displeasure of the Master (see Matthew 25:14–30). And thus it was that indolence and iniquity soon resulted in problems for the temporal progress of the kingdom. An article published in *The Evening and the Morning Star* indicated that many of the twelve hundred Saints in Zion "have been planted upon their inheritances."[16] On the other hand, it cited the covetousness of "one Bates, from New London, Ohio—who subscribed fifty dollars for the purpose of purchasing lands, and necessaries for the Saints—after his arrival here, sued (Bishop) Edward Partridge, and obtained a judgment for the same. Bates shortly after denied the faith, and ran away on Sunday, leaving debts unpaid."[17] In addition, note was made that "as yet, there has not been enough consecrated to plant the poor in inheritances, according to the regulation of the Church and the desire of the faithful. This might have been done, had such as had property been prudent."[18]

POSTPONEMENT OF THE REDEMPTION OF ZION (D&C 97, 101, 104, AND 105)

Satan will always tempt the Saints to "set at naught the counsels of God, and despise his words" (DC& 3:7). Further, he will endeavor to stir up others to anger against them. Profits from the Church-owned businesses and consecrated funds from the Saints were to meet the debts they incurred setting up the United Firm's mercantile and literary establishments, as well as their real estate acquisitions. This plan met with difficulties in the fall of 1833 when the Saints in Missouri—specifically, members of the United Firm—were unable to contribute financially to the Church because mobs had driven them from their farms and businesses in Jackson County.

On July 20, 1833, an armed mob, approved by the Missouri's lieutenant governor, Lilburn W. Boggs, demanded that all Mormons remove from Jackson County. They ransacked the home of William W. Phelps and destroyed the unbound sheets of the Book of Commandments that were in the printing office above his home. The Literary Firm's printing press was destroyed, and Brother Phelps's personal belongings were plundered. Bishop Edward Partridge and another member, Charles Allen, were taken to the County Courthouse Square, where they were stripped of their clothing and tarred and feathered. Sidney Gilbert was forced to agree to close the United Firm's mercantile store in Independence. Three days later, leaders among the Saints signed a treaty with the mob that they would leave the county.

In October the Saints decided to remain and defend their property if necessary. Consequently, the non-Mormon citizens armed themselves and forced the Saints to leave beginning October 31. By November 8, virtually all the Saints were expelled from the county. On December 16, the Lord revealed that He had "suffered the affliction to come upon them . . . in consequence of their transgressions . . . and envyings, and strifes, and lustful and covetous desires among them; therefore by these things they polluted their inheritances" (D&C 101:2, 6). Following this same theme, nearly a year afterward,

He indicated that the Saints' land in Jackson County was not restored because "they have not learned to be obedient to the things which I required at their hands, but are full of all manner of evil, and do not impart of their substance, as becometh saints, to the poor and afflicted among them" (D&C 105:3).

In addition to the troubles in Jackson County, Missouri, in Kirtland, Ohio, an apostate named Philastus Hurlburt brought a lawsuit against Hyrum Smith to obtain property owned by the United Firm. As a result, funds of the United Firm were needed to pay court costs and attorneys' fees as well as travel expenses. Further complicating the situation, the Lord called the Prophet Joseph Smith to lead a group of men known as Zion's Camp to travel to Missouri to aid the Saints who had been driven from their homes in Jackson County. Joseph felt that he could not journey to Missouri at the head of Zion's Camp until the problems concerning the United Firm's debts with New York City creditors were resolved. He realized that "if I do not go [to Missouri], it will be impossible to get my brethren in Kirtland, any of them, to go."[19] Thus, the success of Zion's Camp in restoring the Saints' property in Jackson County, Missouri, was in this way connected to the financial needs of the United Firm.

Donations were sought from members of the Church, but it soon became evident that sufficient funds would not be raised to pay the notes that were due. Members of the Firm in Kirtland met for months counseling with one another and petitioning the Lord to show the way whereby they might free themselves from debt. On April 7 the Prophet wrote, "Bishop Whitney, Elder Frederick G. Williams, Oliver Cowdery, Heber C. Kimball, and myself, met in the council room, and bowed down before the Lord, and prayed that He would furnish the means to deliver the Firm from debt, that they might be set at liberty; also, that I might prevail against that wicked man, Hurlburt, and that he might be put to shame."[20] Three days later, the Prophet recorded that "it was agreed that the Order should be dissolved, and each one have his stewardship set off to him."[21] By such a plan the property of the Church managed by the United Firm could be protected. The creditors would not have claim on property owned by individuals, but only on the property held by the United Firm. This was not to escape responsibility for paying their debts, but rather to give more time to gather the funds needed and to allow the Prophet to travel with Zion's Camp to Missouri.

The actual division of the property was postponed for two weeks in the hope that such a course might not be necessary. When the council met again on April 23, the Lord confirmed by revelation that He approved of their decision to assign properties to individuals (see D&C 104:19–46). However, rather than completely dissolving the United Firm, He commanded that they reorganize into two separate orders—one in Ohio and another in Missouri (see D&C 104:47–50). He further explained, "And this I have commanded to be done for your salvation, . . . in consequence of their [the Saints in Missouri] being driven out and that which is to come" (D&C 104:51). The Lord also gave instructions regarding the Church's assets and the obligation of members of the United Firm to pay their debts (see D&C 104:78–86).

Those who were later called to positions of trust similar to those of members of the United Firm assumed the debts and obligations entered into by their predecessors. Brigham Young accepted responsibility for the Prophet Joseph Smith's debts. "Joseph was doing business in Kirtland," Brigham explained, "and it seemed as though all creation was upon him, to hamper him in every way, and they drove him from his business, and it left him so that some of his debts had to be settled afterwards; and I am thankful to say that they were settled up; still further, we have sent East to New York, to Ohio, and to every place where I had any idea that Joseph had ever done business, and inquired if there was a man left to whom Joseph Smith, jun., the Prophet, owed a dollar, or a sixpence. If there was we would pay it. But I have not been able to find one. I have advertised this through every neighborhood and place where he formerly lived, consequently I have a right to conclude that all his debts were settled."[22]

THE LAW OF TITHING GIVEN (D&C 115, 119, AND 120)

A major weight upon the members of the United Firm was to raise funds to build the Kirtland Temple. Any surplus funds that were derived from the various stewardships were added to the Saints' contributions toward building a house of the Lord. Elder Heber C. Kimball explained, "This building [the Kirtland Temple] the Saints commenced in 1833, in poverty, and without means to do it. In 1834 they completed the walls, and in 1835–6 they nearly finished it. The cost was between sixty and seventy thousand dollars. A committee was appointed to gather donations; they traveled among the churches and collected a considerable amount, but not sufficient, so that in the end they found themselves between thirteen and fourteen thousand dollars in debt."[23]

Subsequent to their being driven from Ohio, the Lord designated Far West, Missouri, as the place of gathering for the Saints. On April 26, 1838, the Lord commanded that a temple be built in Far West. However, He also commanded the First Presidency that they were not to "get in debt any more for the building of a house unto my name" (D&C 115:13). On the other hand, attempts by the Saints to live the law of consecration had not provided for the expenses of building up the kingdom of God. Very few of the Saints at that time had many, if any, surplus goods, and of those that did very few considered their property to be surplus. President Brigham Young described the response of the Saints to consecrating surplus: "The brethren wished me to go among the Churches, and find out what surplus property the people had, with which to forward the building of the Temple we were commencing at Far West. I accordingly went from place to place through the country. Before I started, I asked brother Joseph, 'Who shall be the judge of what is surplus property?' Said he, 'Let them be the judge themselves, for I care not if they do not give a single dime. So far as I am concerned, I do not want anything they have.'

"Then I replied, 'I will go and ask them for their surplus property;' and I did so; I found the people said they were willing to do about as they were counselled, but, upon asking them about their surplus property, most of the men who owned land and cattle would say, 'I have got so many hundred acres of land, and I have got so many boys, and I want each one of them to have eighty acres, therefore this is not surplus property.' Again, 'I have got so many girls, and I do not believe I shall be able to give them more than forty acres each.' 'Well, you have got two or three hundred acres left.' 'Yes, but I have a brother-in-law coming on, and he will depend on me for a living; my wife's nephew is also coming on, he is poor, and I shall have to furnish him a farm after he arrives here.' I would go on to the next one, and he would have more land and cattle than he could make use of to advantage. It is a laughable idea, but is nevertheless true, men would tell me they were young and beginning the world, and would say, 'We have no children, but our prospects are good, and we think we shall have a family of children, and if we do, we want to give them eighty acres of land each; we have no surplus property.' 'How many cattle have you?' 'So many.' 'How many horses, &c?' 'So many, but I have made provisions for all these, and I have use for every thing I have got.'

"Some were disposed to do right with their surplus property, and once in a while you would find a man who had a cow which he considered surplus, but generally she was of the class that would kick a person's hat off, or eyes out, or the wolves had eaten off her teats. You would once in a while find a man who had a horse that he considered surplus, but at the same time he had the ringbone, was broken-winded, spavined in both legs, had the pole evil at one end of the neck and a fistula at the other, and both knees sprung."[24]

In December 1837, at Far West, Missouri, Bishop Partridge met with John Corrill and Isaac Morley as a committee to determine how the expenses of the kingdom could be sustained. They proposed "a plan wher[e]by the church of Latter Day Saints may voluntarily raise means by tithing themselves to be a fund ready at all times to assist the poor."[25] They decided to try to raise "five mills . . . upon the dollar which every man is worth."[26] This plan consisted of the Saints estimating their total assets in property and goods and paying two cents on the dollar. A further proposition was that widows and those "families not worth over seventy five dollars each, should not be required to tithe themselves and yet retain an honorable standing in the church."[27] It is evident that at this time the Saints did not have a firm understanding of the principle of tithing.

Needing further light, the Prophet Joseph Smith "inquired of the Lord, 'O Lord! Show unto thy servant how much thou requirest of the properties of thy people for a tithing.'"[28] In response the Lord declared, "I require all their surplus property to be put into the hands of the bishop of my church in Zion, for the building of mine house, and for the laying of the foundation of Zion and for the priesthood, and the debts of the Presidency of my Church. And this," He continued, "shall be the beginning of the tithing of my people. And after that, those who have thus been tithed shall pay one tenth of all their interest annually" (D&C 119:1–4). Thus, the law of tithing did not replace the principle of consecration; rather, it was added to it. Indeed, consecration was referred to as a tithing of surplus properties, and an additional tithing of ten percent was given as "a standing law unto them forever" (D&C 119:4).

It is noteworthy that the command that the Saints pay one-tenth of their increase annually often requires a greater sacrifice of property than that required by the law of consecration and stewardship, as practiced in the early days of this dispensation. To be precise, in the law of consecration of property, after the Saints lay their substance and possessions before the bishop, they receive a stewardship to provide for their needs. Later, if from their stewardship they produce more than is necessary for their support (see D&C 42:33)—or in other words, a residue or a surplus—they contribute that surplus to the Church. The great difference here is that the law of tithing requires that the Saints pay a tenth of their income annually, not the surplus after their needs have been satisfied. The law of tithing may thus be identified as a law of sacrifice. That is, in obeying the law of tithing, many Saints sacrifice their own needs to contribute to the building up of the kingdom of God.

Because of the sacrifice we offer to the Lord, He promises great blessings as we willingly pay our tithing. President Joseph F. Smith taught:

"The bishop should encourage every man, woman and child who earns and receives a return for labor, to honor the Lord and to prove obedient to the law of God by giving the one-tenth of that which he or she receives, as the Lord requires, so that they may have their names enrolled on the book of the law of the Lord, that their genealogies may be had in the archives of the Church, and that they may be entitled to the privileges and blessings of the house of God.

"I recollect most vividly a circumstance that occurred in the days of my childhood. My mother was a widow, with a large family to provide for. One spring when we opened our potato pits, she had her boys get a load of the best potatoes and she took them to the tithing office; potatoes were scarce that season. I was a little boy at the time, and drove the team. When we drove up to the steps of the tithing office, ready to unload the potatoes, one of the clerks came out and said to my mother, 'Widow Smith, it's a shame that you should have to pay tithing,' . . . and he chided my mother for paying her tithing, called her anything but wise or prudent; and said there were others who were strong and able to work that were supported from the tithing office. My mother turned upon him and said: 'William, you ought to be ashamed of yourself. Would you deny me a blessing? If I did not pay my tithing, I should expect the Lord to withhold his blessings from me. I pay my tithing, not only because it is a law of God, but because I expect a blessing by doing it. By keeping this and other laws, I expect to prosper, and to be able to provide for my family.' Though she was a widow, you may turn to the records of the Church from the beginning unto the day of her death, and you will find that she never received a farthing from the Church to help her support herself and her family; but she paid in thousands of dollars in wheat, potatoes, corn, vegetables, meat, etc. The tithes of her sheep and cattle, the tenth pound of her butter, her tenth chicken, the tenth of her eggs, the tenth pig, the tenth calf, the tenth colt—a tenth of everything she raised was paid. Here sits my brother who can bear testimony to the truth of what I say, as can others who knew her. She prospered because she obeyed the laws of God. She had abundance to sustain her family."[29]

Conclusion

The Church continues to be governed by the principles of the laws of consecration, stewardship, and tithing. Saints are expected to consecrate to build up the kingdom and provide for the poor. However, in general, the law of stewardship no longer includes temporal property. Rather, we often receive responsibilities in Church callings. There are relatively few who are given stewardship or responsibility for temporal property. Consequently, as a general rule we are still under obligation to live principles of the law of consecration but not the laws of stewardship governing temporal possessions.

Further, the kingdom of God continues to be built up by the faithful tithes and offerings of the poor, as well as those who have been blessed beyond their needs with a surplus. The millions of poor in the Church that give their tithe to the Lord follow the path taken by the widow in Christ's day, who gave two mites in her poverty and not out of her abundance but out of her faith (see Mark 12:41–44). In essence, they live the laws of consecration and sacrifice.

The consecration and stewardship of property was the Lord's

means to teach the Saints that all things are His and to rid them of the spirit of selfishness. Consecration is a higher law than tithing only when it extends beyond that which is temporal and involves dedicating all of one's time, talent, and energies that may be needed to the building up of the Lord's kingdom (see D&C 105:3–5). It then envelopes the law of tithing as individuals consecrate everything that they are and possess to the Lord and His work.

NOTES

1. Much of the research and observations in this article were previously published in commentary format in Joseph Fielding McConkie and Craig J. Ostler, *Revelations of the Restoration: A Commentary on the Doctrine and Covenants and Other Modern Revelations* (Salt Lake City: Deseret Book, 2000).

2. John Whitmer, *Book of John Whitmer*, typescript, L. Tom Perry Collections, Harold B. Lee Library, Brigham Young University, Provo, Utah, chapter 2.

3. Joseph Smith, *History of the Church of Jesus Christ of Latter-day Saints*, ed. B. H. Roberts, 2nd ed., rev. (Salt Lake City: Deseret Book, 1973), 1:364–65.

4. Original documents cited in Leonard J. Arrington, Feramorz Y. Fox, and Dean L. May, *Building the City of God* (Salt Lake City: Deseret Book, 1976), 28.

5. Cited in Arrington, Fox, and May, *Building the City of God*, 29.

6. Joseph Smith, *Joseph Smith's Kirtland Revelation Book* (Salt Lake City: Modern Microfilm, 1979), 87–88.

7. Smith, *History of the Church*, 1:341.

8. Smith, *History of the Church*, 1:219, n.

9. Donald Q. Cannon and Lyndon W. Cook, *Far West Record* (Salt Lake City: Deseret Book, 1983), 22.

10. Smith, *Kirtland Revelation Book*, 16.

11. Smith, *History of the Church*, 1:365–66.

12. Cannon and Cook, *Far West Record*, 45.

13. Cannon and Cook, *Far West Record*, 48.

14. See Smith, *History of the Church*, 1:295; Joseph Smith, *The Personal Writings of Joseph Smith*, comp. Dean C. Jessee (Salt Lake City: Deseret Book, 1984), 251–54.

15. Smith, *History of the Church*, 1:352.

16. Smith, *History of the Church*, 1:380.

17. Smith, *History of the Church*, 1:380.

18. Smith, *History of the Church*, 1:381.

19. Smith, *History of the Church*, 2:48.

20. Smith, *History of the Church*, 2:47–48.

21. Smith, *History of the Church*, 2:49.

22. Brigham Young, in *Journal of Discourses* (London: Latter-day Saints' Book Depot, 1854–86), 18:242.

23. Orson F. Whitney, *Life of Heber C. Kimball* (Salt Lake City: Bookcraft, 1945), 88.

24. Brigham Young, *Journal of Discourses*, 2:306–7.

25. Cannon and Cook, *Far West Record*, 129.

26. Cannon and Cook, *Far West Record*, 130.

27. Cannon and Cook, *Far West Record*, 129.

28. Smith, *History of the Church*, 3:44.

29. Joseph F. Smith, *Gospel Doctrine* (Salt Lake City: Deseret Book, 1986), 228–29.

CHAPTER FOURTEEN

THE DOCTRINES OF SUBMISSION AND FORGIVENESS (D&C 64)

DANIEL K JUDD

Doctrine and Covenants 64 contains doctrines essential to personal peace in this world and exaltation in the world to come. The intent of this paper is to focus specifically on the life-giving doctrines of submission and forgiveness as expounded in the scriptural and historical contexts of Doctrine and Covenants 64:1–21 and to contrast the doctrines of submission and forgiveness with the philosophies of men that permeate our culture.

SUBMISSION VERSUS SELFISHNESS

Each of the brethren to whom Doctrine and Covenants 64 was addressed—the Prophet Joseph Smith, Ezra Booth, Isaac Morley, Edward Partridge, Sidney Gilbert, Frederick G. Williams, and Newel K. Whitney—was invited to overcome the world by making his will consistent with the Lord's will for him. Section 64 begins with the Lord inviting these elders of the Church to "hearken ye and hear, and receive *my will* concerning you. For verily I say unto you, I will that ye should overcome the world; wherefore I will have compassion upon you" (D&C 64:1–2; emphasis added).

The scriptures teach repeatedly that submitting to the will of God rather than following our own wills is essential to exaltation: "For although a man may have many revelations, and have power to do

---

Daniel K Judd is the chair for the department of ancient scripture at Brigham Young University.

many mighty works, yet if he boasts in his own strength, and sets at naught the counsels of God, and follows after the dictates of his own will and carnal desires, he must fall and incur the vengeance of a just God upon him" (D&C 3:4). The Savior exemplified the doctrine of submission most poignantly in Gethsemane, saying, "Father, if thou be willing, remove this cup from me: nevertheless not my will, but thine, be done" (Luke 22:42). The Apostle Paul wrote of yielding his own desires to the needs of others: "For I am in a strait betwixt two, having a desire to depart, and to be with Christ; which is far better: nevertheless to abide in the flesh is more needful for you" (Philippians 1:23–24). Shortly before Nephi, son of Helaman, was given the sealing power, the Lord said to him, "Blessed art thou, Nephi, . . . thou . . . hast not sought thine own life, but hast sought my will, and to keep my commandments" (Helaman 10:4).

We, as well, are asked to submit and sacrifice our lives in the service of God. Although we may not be asked to die, we are asked to live and serve God in ways that may not always be convenient or consistent with our own desires. Many times those whom we are called to sacrifice for are those who give us the most reason not to. "Ye have heard that it hath been said, Thou shalt love thy neighbour, and hate thine enemy. But I say unto you, Love your enemies, bless them that curse you, do good to them that hate you, and pray for them which despitefully use you, and persecute you" (Matthew 5:43–44). Being "saviours . . . on mount Zion" (Obadiah 1:21) may require that we mercifully bear the sins and ignorance of others (see D&C 138:12–13).

Yielding our own desires to the commands of God is the key to peace in this life and exaltation in the next. President Boyd K. Packer wrote, "Perhaps the greatest discovery of my life, without question the greatest commitment, came when finally I had the confidence in God that I would loan or yield my agency to Him."[1] Not only are we to do physically as the Lord would have us do, but we must learn to put off the natural man and learn to feel as He would feel and think as He would think. "Behold, the Lord requireth the heart and a willing mind; and the willing and obedient shall eat the good of the land of Zion in these last days. And the rebellious shall be cut off out of the land of Zion, and shall be sent away, and shall not inherit the land" (D&C 64:34–35). A few years ago a friend of mine visited with a member of the Quorum of the Twelve Apostles. During their conversation on the importance of serving willingly, this Apostle taught my friend an important lesson by saying, "The day that doing the right thing became a quest and not an irritation was the day I gained power."

SELF-IMAGE VERSUS THE IMAGE OF CHRIST

The emphasis on "overcoming the world" through submission to God's will stressed in Doctrine and Covenants 64 and throughout the scriptures contrasts sharply with false educational ideas of today such as self-actualization, self-esteem, self-image, and others that are so prevalent in our culture. These ideas have "a form of godliness, but they deny the power thereof" (Joseph Smith—History 1:19). Doing "what's best for me" has generally replaced doing what God wills concerning us and our lives. Paradoxically, it is in doing the will of our Father in heaven and overcoming the world that we realize our own desires. "For whosoever will save his life shall lose it; but whosoever shall lose his life for my sake and the gospel's, the same shall save it. For what shall it profit a man, if he shall gain the whole world, and lose his own soul? Or what shall a man give in exchange for his soul?" (Mark 8:35–37).

The adversary's philosophy is one of deception. Whatever gospel truth is being taught, he provides both its opposite and its counterfeit. Personally, I have come to believe "high self-esteem" is the adversary's counterfeit of what the scriptures describe as "confidence" and is the opposite of meekness. "Low self-esteem" is the adversary's counterfeit of meekness and is the opposite of confidence.

Having "high self-esteem" or "low self-esteem" is generally based upon the prideful presence or absence of things temporal, such as physical appearance (see 1 Samuel 16:7), wealth (see Proverbs 13:7), and learning (see 2 Nephi 9:28). Godly confidence is a spiritual gift that develops from recognizing our own nothingness (see Mosiah 4:5; Moses 1:10). If we do the will of our Father in heaven, our "confidence" shall "wax strong" (D&C 121:45).

Ammon taught this same doctrinal comparison in his dialogue with his brother Aaron concerning their missionary success:

"For if we had not come up out of the land of Zarahemla, these our dearly beloved brethren, who have so dearly beloved us, would still have been racked with hatred against us, yea, and they would also have been strangers to God.

"And it came to pass that when Ammon had said these words, his brother Aaron rebuked him, saying: Ammon, I fear that thy joy doth carry thee away unto boasting.

"But Ammon said unto him: I do not boast in my own strength, nor in my own wisdom; but behold, my joy is full, yea, my heart is brim with joy, and I will rejoice in my God.

"Yea, I know that I am nothing; as to my strength I am weak; therefore I will not boast of myself, but I will boast of my God, for in his strength I can do all things; yea, behold, many mighty miracles we have wrought in this land, for which we will praise his name forever" (Alma 26:9–12).

President Ezra Taft Benson has stated: "In the scriptures there is no such thing as righteous pride. It is always considered as a sin. We are not speaking of a wholesome view of self-worth, which is best established by a close relationship with God. But we are speaking of pride as a universal sin."[2]

In place of being consumed with the selfish notion of enhancing self-image through personal, worldly pursuits, the Lord has invited the Saints, past and present, to be concerned with doing His will and thus taking upon ourselves His image. "And now behold, I ask of you, my brethren of the church, have ye spiritually been born of God? Have ye received his image in your countenances? Have ye experienced this mighty change in your hearts?" (Alma 5:14).

A comprehensive search of all the revelations in the Doctrine and Covenants reveals that the "elders of [the] church" (D&C 64:1) to whom section 64 was addressed were struggling to follow the Lord's will as they sought to overcome an array of intellectual, spiritual, and temporal trials. Following are brief analyses of the challenges these brethren faced and how they fared in overcoming the world and submitting to the will of God as represented by the Lord through the scriptures and Church history.[3]

Ezra Booth. Ezra Booth, formerly a Baptist minister, had been baptized after witnessing the Prophet Joseph Smith heal a woman of a lame arm.[4] After witnessing this miracle, Booth desired the power to "convert" others in the same manner. He soon became embittered, however, when he was confronted with the doctrine that "faith cometh not by signs, but signs follow those that believe. Yea, signs come by faith, not by the will of men, nor as they please, but by the will of God" (D&C 63:9–10). Booth later apostatized and published several articles against the Prophet Joseph and the Church in the *Ohio Star,* which provoked much opposition to the work of the Restoration.[5] Elder B. H. Roberts identified Booth as the "first apostate . . . to publish anything against the Church."[6]

Booth's preoccupation with physical manifestations of spiritual truths serves as a warning to those with similar desires. Whenever we seek to base our own faith or encourage others to base their faith on physical "proofs," emotional sentiment, or intellectual argument, our faith and theirs lack the solid foundation of personal and prophetic revelation.

Isaac Morley. Both Isaac Morley and Ezra Booth were chastised for having "evil in their hearts" (D&C 64:16), but unlike Booth, Morley repented and was forgiven. While he was also reproved for faultfinding and not selling his farm as he had been commanded (see D&C 64:15–16, 20), he proved himself a man of conviction when he later offered his life as a ransom for the safety of the Saints in Missouri.[7] Isaac Morley died in Sanpete County, Utah, after having been a great strength to the establishment of the Church in that area.[8]

Edward Partridge. The Lord described Edward Partridge as one whose "heart is pure before me, for he is like unto Nathanael of old, in whom there is no guile" (D&C 41:11). A little over a month before section 64 was given, the Lord revealed to Edward Partridge that if he did not repent of his "unbelief and blindness of heart," he would "fall" (D&C 58:15). The Lord told Edward Partridge in Doctrine and Covenants 64 that he had "sinned, and Satan [sought] to destroy his soul" (D&C 64:17). Bishop Partridge was guilty of putting "forth his hand to steady the ark of God," and if he didn't repent he would "fall by the shaft of death" (D&C 85:8; see also 2 Samuel 6:1–11). Edward Partridge did repent and was granted the promise of eternal life (see D&C 124:19).

Sidney Gilbert. Algernon Sidney Gilbert was first called by the Lord to preach the gospel and be "an agent" for the Church in its business dealings (see D&C 53:3–4). Over a year later, the Lord revealed to Joseph Smith that Brother Gilbert had "many things to repent of" (D&C 90:35). Although Sidney Gilbert was faithful in many things (at one point he, along with Isaac Morley, offered his life as a ransom for his fellow Saints), he lacked confidence in his ability to preach the gospel and died soon after turning down a mission call. The Lord had previously counseled Brother Gilbert, "Ye should learn that he only is saved who endureth unto the end" (D&C 53:7). The Prophet Joseph commented on Brother Gilbert's turning down his mission call and on his subsequent death by saying, "He had been called to preach the Gospel, but had been known to say that he 'would rather die than go forth to preach the Gospel to the Gentiles.'" Elder Heber C. Kimball remarked, "The Lord took him [Sidney Gilbert] at his word."[9]

Frederick G. Williams. Frederick G. Williams was obedient to the Lord's command to "not . . . sell his farm," which property assisted the Lord in establishing "a strong hold in the land of Kirtland" (D&C 64:21). Some two and a half years later, the Lord revealed that Frederick G. Williams had not taught his children properly and was to set his house in order: "But verily I say unto you, my servant Frederick G. Williams, you have continued under this condemnation; you have not taught your children light and truth, according to the commandments; and that wicked one hath power, as yet, over you, and this is the cause of your affliction. And now a commandment I give unto you—if you will be delivered you shall set in order your own house, for there are many things that are not right in your house" (D&C 93:41–43).

In addition to this warning to Frederick G. Williams and others of the brethren in Doctrine and Covenants 93:40–50, the scriptures contain many other warnings relative to the relationship of family and Church responsibilities. The Savior chastised the ancient Pharisees for perverting the gospel when He indicted them for abdicating the care of their families on the grounds of "Corban" (Mark 7:11). The Bible Dictionary teaches that the Pharisees "misused the opportunity of dedicating their material possessions to God, in order to avoid responsibility to care for their parents." Although this same indictment of "Corban" may or may not be true of the early brethren and their families, it is important that those facing similar challenges in the present be aware of the danger of not being as "diligent and concerned at home" (D&C 93:50) as they are in their professional or

ecclesiastical assignments. Never should serving our neighbors
become a rationalization for not serving those at home.

Frederick G. Williams continued to have difficulty and was excommunicated twice and rebaptized twice between 1837 and 1840; however, he "died as a faithful member of the Church, October 10, 1842
at Quincy, Illinois."[10]

Newel K. Whitney. Newel K. Whitney was obedient to the Lord's
command not to sell his "store and . . . possessions" (D&C 64:26).
Three years later Brother Whitney was also admonished to "set in
order his family, and see that they are more diligent and concerned at
home" (D&C 93:50). After being called to be the second bishop of the
Church (Edward Partridge being the first), Bishop Whitney was
admonished by the Lord to forsake his worldly ways and devote more
time to his duties as a bishop: "Let my servant Newel K. Whitney be
ashamed of the Nicolaitane band and of all their secret abominations,
and of all his littleness of soul before me, saith the Lord, and come up
to the land of Adam-ondi-Ahman, and be a bishop unto my people,
saith the Lord, not [only] in name but [also] in deed, saith the Lord"
(D&C 117:11). There are no scriptural details available about why the
Lord chastened Newel K. Whitney for his involvement in the
"Nicolaitane band," but the scriptures do give us some clues. The designation "Nicolaitane" apparently was derived from "Nicolas," mentioned in Acts 6:5. Nicolas was one of seven men designated to
administer the temporal affairs of the Church during New Testament
times. Apparently, Nicolas used his position in the Church for personal gain; hence, the Lord stated in Revelation 2:6 that He "[hated]
the deeds of the Nicolaitans." Elder Bruce R. McConkie taught that
those who involve themselves in Nicolaitane interests are "members
of the Church who [are] trying to maintain their church standing
while continuing to live after the manner of the world."[11]

Whether it be Nicolas of biblical times, Newel K. Whitney, or those
of us in the present, there is much to be lost by those who use their
membership in the Church for their own selfish interests. This self-
interest is a form of priestcraft, which Nephi described: "For, behold,
priestcrafts are that men preach and set themselves up for a light unto
the world, that they may get gain and praise of the world; but they
seek not the welfare of Zion" (2 Nephi 26:29). Those of us involved in
the Church Educational System or various other academic disciplines

need to be ever aware of the danger of selling our spiritual birthrights for the sake of being true to academic traditions. It is possible we can become as the scribes and Pharisees of old who were rebuked by the Savior for such practices: "Full well ye reject the commandment of God, that ye may keep your own tradition" (Mark 7:9).

The Prophet Joseph Smith. John Taylor wrote: "Joseph Smith, the Prophet and Seer of the Lord, has done more, save Jesus only, for the salvation of men in this world, than any other man that ever lived in it" (D&C 135:3). Scriptural perspectives relative to the weaknesses of the Prophet Joseph are few, but the Prophet himself has offered some insight. He wrote of his adolescence: "I was left to all kinds of temptations; and, mingling with all kinds of society, I frequently fell into many foolish errors, and displayed the weakness of youth, and the foibles of human nature; which, I am sorry to say, led me into divers temptations, offensive in the sight of God. In making this confession, no one need suppose me guilty of any great or malignant sins. A disposition to commit such was never in my nature. But I was guilty of levity, and sometimes associated with jovial company, etc., not consistent with that character which ought to be maintained by one who was called of God as I had been. But this will not seem very strange to any one who recollects my youth, and is acquainted with my native cheery temperament" (Joseph Smith—History 1:28).

The Lord chastened the Prophet Joseph for allowing himself to be influenced by the "persuasions of men" and fearing "man more than God" (D&C 3:6–7). This rebuke came as a consequence of Joseph's yielding to Martin Harris's repeated request to show the Book of Mormon manuscript to others whom the Lord had not designated.

From Doctrine and Covenants 64:7 we learn that the Prophet Joseph had sinned but had repented and been forgiven: "Nevertheless, he [Joseph] has sinned; but verily I say unto you, I, the Lord, forgive sins unto those who confess their sins before me and ask forgiveness, who have not sinned unto death."

From Doctrine and Covenants 93:47–49 we learn that the Prophet Joseph and his family had sins and weaknesses to overcome: "And now, verily I say unto Joseph Smith, Jun.—You have not kept the commandments, and must needs stand rebuked before the Lord; your family must needs repent and forsake some things, and give more earnest heed unto your sayings, or be removed out of their place. What I say unto one I say unto all; pray always lest that wicked one have power in you, and remove you out of your place."

Joseph Smith "lived great, and he died great in the eyes of God and his people" (D&C 135:3). While recognizing there are many greater than I who have testified of the prophetic call of the Prophet Joseph Smith, I add my personal witness of his call and ministry as a prophet of God.

FORGIVENESS

The brethren of the Restoration were counseled concerning the dangers of hardening their hearts toward one another: "My disciples, in days of old, sought occasion against one another and forgave not one another in their hearts; and for this evil they were afflicted and sorely chastened" (D&C 64:8; see also Acts 15:1–11, 36–40; Galatians 2:11–14). These brethren were also taught that forgiveness of those who had offended them was a requisite for their own forgiveness and exaltation: "Wherefore, I say unto you, that ye ought to forgive one another; for he that forgiveth not his brother his trespasses standeth condemned before the Lord; for there remaineth in him the greater sin. I, the Lord, will forgive whom I will forgive, but of you it is required to forgive all men" (D&C 64:9–10).

An account from the writings of President Heber J. Grant illustrates that the "disciples" in the recent past have also "sought occasion against one another" (D&C 64:8) but then went on to understand and live the divine command to forgive. At the time this incident took place, Heber J. Grant was a junior member of the Quorum of Twelve Apostles. He participated in a Church court in which a fellow member of the Quorum of the Twelve was excommunicated. In the ensuing years, this man came several times before the court to ask for rebaptism. His request was denied each time, but eventually every member of the Quorum of Twelve consented to rebaptism except Elder Grant. Elder Grant felt that because of the magnitude of the sin (adultery) and this man's former position in the Church, he should never be forgiven. At this time Elder Grant was brought to truly understand Doctrine and Covenants 64:10. Following is Elder Grant's own description of how this came about: "I was reading the Doctrine and Covenants through for the third or fourth time systematically, and I had my bookmark in it, but as I picked it up, instead of opening where the bookmark was, it opened to D&C 64:10: 'I, the Lord, will forgive whom I will forgive, but of you it is required to forgive all men.' I closed the book and said: 'If the devil applies for baptism, and claims that he has repented, I will baptize him.'

"After lunch I returned to the office of President Taylor and said, 'President Taylor, I have had a change of heart. One hour ago I said, never while I live did I expect to ever consent that Brother So and So should be baptized, but I have come to tell you he can be baptized, so far as I am concerned.' President Taylor had a habit, when he was particularly pleased, of sitting up and laughing and shaking his whole body, and he laughed and said, 'My boy, the change is very sudden, very sudden. I want to ask you a question. How did you feel when you left here an hour ago? Did you feel like you wanted to hit that man squarely between the eyes and knock him down?'

"I said, 'That is just the way I felt.' He said, 'How do you feel now?' 'Well, to tell you the truth, President Taylor, I hope the Lord will forgive the sinner.' He said, 'You feel happy, don't you, in comparison? You had the spirit of anger, you had the spirit of bitterness in your heart toward that man, because of his sin and because of the disgrace he had brought upon the Church. And now you have the spirit of forgiveness and you really feel happy, don't you?' And I said, 'Yes, I do . . . now I feel happy.'"

President Taylor explained to Elder Grant: "Forgiveness is in advance of justice, where there is repentance, and that to have in your heart the spirit of forgiveness and to eliminate from your hearts the spirit of hatred and bitterness, brings peace and joy; that the gospel of Jesus Christ brings joy, peace and happiness to every soul that lives it and follows its teachings."[12]

JUSTICE AND MERCY

The doctrines of justice and mercy are to be understood and lived by each of us. These doctrines do, however, have their counterfeits. I have come to believe that a blaming and punishing attitude is the adversary's counterfeit of justice. Indulgence is the adversary's counterfeit of mercy. Punishment is laden with anger, resentment, and blame, whereas justice denotes charity—a heartfelt desire to help another repent. Indulgence is doing what comes easily, whereas mercy requires personal, loving sacrifice. Punishment and indulgence are both selfish. Justice and mercy are selfless. Negative, accusing feelings such as anger and resentment, although "natural" (Mosiah 3:19), are not of God, no matter the reasons we may have for harboring them (see 3 Nephi 12:22; Matthew 5:22; JST Matthew 5:25).

Although the scriptures speak of the Savior's anger, His anger is much different from ours. His only concern is that we attain "immortality and eternal life" (Moses 1:39). As He dealt with the Pharisees, He "looked round about on them with anger, being grieved for the hardness of their hearts" (Mark 3:5). His anger is selfless.

THE GREATER SIN

Doctrine and Covenants 64:9 teaches that we have the "greater sin" if we do not forgive another. How is this possible especially if others have sinned against us in a most loathsome and degrading way? How can such sins as adultery, incest, and rape be lesser sins than the sin of an offended person not forgiving the offender? Perhaps the following account can teach us the truth of the matter: "As a child I was abused by my older brother. At the time I knew what my brother did was wrong, yet I still loved him. As I grew older, however, I learned to hate him. As I came face to face with the everyday problems of life, I didn't accept the responsibility for my own mistakes and faults. I looked for an excuse—a way out. I looked for someone or something else to blame. I began having problems with my physical health, but when I began to get well I refused to accept it. I didn't want to return to the everyday problems that would be waiting for me. That was when the hate for my brother really grew. In my mind, all of my problems were his fault. I realize now, it was then that it became my sin. My hate, my anger was what hurt me—it made me sick. The hate for my own brother had grown so strong and fierce that it left him behind. I hated myself, my family, my friends, this earth, and its creator. I think that when you hate everyone, the void is so powerful that if you don't find love, if you don't give love, you die. That's where the gospel came in. That was when I finally realized there was something more to life than my bitterness. Being part of the Church had never really been important to me. It became worthless, because I didn't do my part. So I began for the first time to work, to really live the gospel. I found that in return

Heavenly Father began to give more to me than anything I could ever give him. My happiness and peace became his gift to me. With each day of my life as I give all that I can give, I can't even comprehend the blessings he gives me."[13]

This young woman came to understand that it was her sin and not her brother's that was consuming her life. Even though she had been receiving counsel from a host of professionals either to "vent" or to "control" her anger, she found peace only when she began to understand and live the gospel of Jesus Christ. She found that the peace she was seeking did not come either in expressing her anger or in controlling it, but peace came as she repented of the hate she harbored. If one were to take incest and hate without regard to context, incest would obviously be the greater sin. But within the context of our own lives, it is what we do, not what others do to us, that either blesses us or condemns us. Lehi taught that individuals are free "to act for themselves and not to be acted upon" (2 Nephi 2:26). The Book of Mormon prophet Samuel also taught this truth: "And now remember, remember, my brethren, that whosoever perisheth, perisheth unto himself; and whosoever doeth iniquity, doeth it unto himself; for behold, ye are free; ye are permitted to act for yourselves; for behold, God hath given unto you a knowledge and he hath made you free" (Helaman 14:30; see also Mark 7:15).

President Spencer W. Kimball wrote: "If we have been wronged or injured, forgiveness means to blot it completely from our minds. To forgive and forget is an ageless counsel. 'To be wronged or robbed,' said the Chinese philosopher Confucius, 'is nothing unless you continue to remember it.' . . . Man can overcome. Man can forgive all who have trespassed against him and go on to receive peace in this life and eternal life in the world to come."[14]

Many of the brethren mentioned in Doctrine and Covenants 64 overcame the challenges they faced and died faithful to the covenants they had made to the Lord. Those who were faithful eventually yielded "to the enticings of the Holy Spirit, and [put] off the natural man and [became] a saint through the atonement of Christ the Lord, and [became] as a child, submissive, meek, humble, patient, full of love, willing to submit to all things which the Lord [saw] fit to inflict upon [them], even as a child doth submit to his father" (Mosiah 3:19).

The gospel of Jesus Christ contains the answers to life's problems. The scriptures, the words of our living prophets, and individual revelation can teach us the doctrines that will enable us to overcome the sins and deceptions of this world and receive exaltation in the next. It is my prayer that we, as individuals and families, teachers and faculties, will overcome the world and do the will of Him who sent us. Let us review the words of our Savior: "Behold, I stand at the door, and knock: if any man hear my voice, and open the door, I will come in to him, and will sup with him, and he with me. To him that overcometh will I grant to sit with me in my throne, even as I also overcame, and am set down with my Father in his throne" (Revelation 3:20–21).

NOTES

1. Boyd K. Packer, *That All May Be Edified* (Salt Lake City: Bookcraft, 1982), 256–57.

2. Ezra Taft Benson, "Cleansing the Inner Vessel," *Ensign*, May 1986, 6.

3. These analyses reflect the Lord's perspective of these men's problems and not their own or another mortal's (see Ether 12:27). Scriptural commentary outside the general time period of D&C 64 was based on the assumption that these men's strengths and weaknesses remained fairly consistent over time.

4. See Joseph Smith, *History of the Church of Jesus Christ of Latter-day Saints*, ed. B. H. Roberts, 2nd ed., rev. (Salt Lake City: Deseret Book, 1957), 1:215.

5. See Smith, History of the Church, 1:241.

6. See Smith, History of the Church, 1:216.

7. See Smith, History of the Church, 1:394.

8. See Andrew Jensen, *Latter-day Saint Biographical Encyclopedia* (Salt Lake City: Western Epics, 1971), 1:235–36.

9. Smith, *History of the Church*, 2:118.

10. Jensen, *Latter-day Saint Biographical Encyclopedia*, 1:51–52.

11. Bruce R. McConkie, *Doctrinal New Testament Commentary* (Salt Lake City: Bookcraft, 1975), 3:446.

12. Heber J. Grant, in Conference Report, October 1920, 2–11.

13. Personal correspondence with the author.

14. Spencer W. Kimball, *The Miracle of Forgiveness* (Salt Lake City: Bookcraft, 1969), 299–300.

CHAPTER FIFTEEN

SIX VISIONS OF ETERNITY (D&C 76)

MONTE S. NYMAN

Perhaps the most comprehensive vision of this dispensation, as well as others, was given to Joseph Smith and Sidney Rigdon on February 16, 1832, at Hiram, Ohio, in the upper story of the Johnson home. Perhaps others have seen the same or similar vision, but there are only two other men recorded in our present-day scriptures to whom this great revelation was revealed: Jacob, the father of the twelve tribes of Israel (see Genesis 28:10–12), and Paul, the Apostle to the Gentiles (see 2 Corinthians 12:1–7). And even our knowledge of these two men having seen such a vision is dependent upon a statement by the Prophet Joseph Smith.

"Paul ascended into the third heavens, and he could understand the three principal rounds of Jacob's ladder—the telestial, the terrestrial, and the celestial glories or kingdoms, where Paul saw and heard things which were not lawful for him to utter."[1]

While several men have seen a vision of the beginning of the world to the end thereof (for example, see 1 Nephi 14:26), Joseph Smith's vision went beyond the scope of this world and into the eternal worlds of varying degrees of glory. It is also possible that Joseph Smith was the one privileged to record this vision for the inhabitants of this telestial world just as John the Revelator was the one ordained to record the vision to the end of the world (see 1 Nephi 14:25, 27). Although the brother of Jared also recorded his vision of the beginning of the world to the end thereof (see 2 Nephi 27:6–11), his record

---

Monte S. Nyman is an emeritus professor of ancient scripture at Brigham Young University.

is apparently reserved for the Millennium, when only those of a terrestrial or celestial nature will be living on the earth. Although Jacob saw a vision of the degrees of glory, the present text of Genesis provides only this meager account: "And he dreamed, and behold a ladder set up on the earth, and the top of it reached to heaven: and behold the angels of God ascending and descending on it" (Genesis 28:12).

Paul's account is not much fuller, and although it sounds as if he is speaking of someone else, a careful reading of verses 5 through 7 reveals this man to be himself. "And I knew such a man, (whether in the body, or out of the body, I cannot tell: God knoweth;) How that he was caught up into paradise, and heard unspeakable words, which it is not lawful for a man to utter" (2 Corinthians 12:3–4).

Although Paul mentions a third heaven, the Prophet Joseph's explanation does much to clarify what he intended. Paul's treatise of the three different types of resurrection, recorded in 1 Corinthians chapter 15, was undoubtedly based on his vision. Note also that Paul was forbidden to reveal his revelation. It should again be acknowledged that since Joseph and Sidney were working on "the translation of the Scriptures" when this vision was given, this knowledge could have once been in the Bible and was being restored through Joseph (see the preface to section 76). Whether Joseph was the only one who recorded it or if he was restoring knowledge that had previously been recorded, the fact remains that he is the one who has given this generation the knowledge of the varying degrees of glory.

In language almost identical to Isaiah's opening sentence (see Isaiah 1:2), the Lord addresses the inhabitants of the heavens as well as the earth. As to why the inhabitants of the heavens are included one can only speculate; however, inasmuch as they are invited to rejoice, it seems the Lord may be making them aware that He is revealing information to the earth's inhabitants that has long been withheld from them. Certainly those in the heavens are desirous that the earth's inhabitants know that "the term 'Heaven' . . . must include more kingdoms than one" (preface to section 76).

Another purpose for including the heavens is implied in verses 5 through 7, which state that the Lord honors those who serve Him and will reward those who do so by revealing the mysteries of the kingdom to them. If the heavens, as used here, refers to beings who once lived on this earth and now serve the Lord as His messengers but have not yet received their eternal status or blessings, it may be that they are also being shown and enlightened by the power of the Lord's spirit (see D&C 76:10).

Before analyzing the recorded portion of this vision, it should be noted that Joseph and Sidney wrote very little of what they actually saw and heard. Over eleven years later, the Prophet said, "I could explain a hundred fold more than I ever have of the glories of the kingdoms manifested to me in the vision, were I permitted, and were the people prepared to receive them."[2] Importantly, some parts of the vision were recorded while yet in the Spirit (see D&C 76:28, 80, and 113) and under the Lord's command (see D&C 76:115), while other parts were not recorded by direction of the Lord's command (see D&C 76:115). Either those things that were not recorded were unlawful for man to utter, or man was incapable of receiving them; such things are only seen and understood by the power of the Holy Spirit (see D&C 76:115–16). Rather than worrying about what *was not* recorded, we should carefully ponder what *is* recorded. Are the inhabitants of the earth, and particularly the members of the Church, prepared to receive what is recorded? What some people today may esteem as deep doctrine that should not be discussed was considered by the Lord to be basic doctrine necessary to prepare the people for some of the actual deeper doctrines of the gospel of Jesus Christ. These deeper doctrines the Lord would readily reveal if the people were prepared to receive it. The more basic doctrines will be analyzed in this paper.

The interpretation of these basic doctrines may also need to be clarified. What one may consider to be a fundamental doctrine taught in the revelation, another may consider to be an erroneous interpretation of doctrine. Correct interpretations can be ascertained by appealing to other revelations in the Doctrine and Covenants, the other standard works, and modern Apostles and prophets. In addition to these sources, there is another primary source from which one may confirm interpretation. In a reply to a poem written by W. W. Phelps, the Prophet Joseph dictated a poetic answer based upon the revelation of the three degrees of glory.[3] The wording of this poem often confirms or dictates the interpretation that should be given to the revelation. With this background, an analysis of the vision may be undertaken.

As indicated in the title of this paper, "the Vision" is really a series of six visions. The first of these visions is a vision of the glory of the Son on the right hand of the Father. Very little is said about what they saw; the emphasis is upon what they heard. What they saw, however, is important. Verse 20 states that they "received of his fulness." From the poetic version published in the *Times and Seasons*, we learn that this meant that they saw the Son was "in a fulness of glory and holy applause," not that Joseph and Sidney received of the fulness. Second, they saw that those giving the holy applause consisted of holy angels and those who were sanctified. While this may sound like Hebrew parallelism, the poetic version qualifies that these are two separate groups: holy angels (implying those who were assigned to this world) and "sanctified beings from worlds that have been." This is the first indication of the vision including other worlds. What Joseph and Sidney heard further enlightens this concept. They testify that through the Only Begotten other worlds were created, and the inhabitants of those worlds were also saved. The poetic version is even more descriptive:

> By him, of him, and through him, the worlds were all made,
> Even all that career in the heavens so broad.
> Whose inhabitants, too, from the first to the last,
> Are sav'd by the very same Saviour of ours;
> And, of course, are begotten God's daughters and sons.
> By the very same truths and the very same powr's.[4]

The fact that other worlds were created by Jesus Christ, under the Father's direction, is a prevalent New Testament teaching, although it is often not recognized (see John 1:3, 10; Colossians 1:16–17; Hebrews 1:1–2). This doctrine is also confirmed in the Pearl of Great Price (see Moses 1:33), which source also reminds us, "Only an account of this earth and the inhabitants thereof, give I [the Lord] unto you" (Moses 1:35). Perhaps this is why nothing is said in the New Testament about the Atonement covering the inhabitants of other worlds. On the other hand, perhaps it did originally but was lost with many other plain and precious things (see 1 Nephi 13:24–29). The Doctrine and Covenants confirms that Jesus Christ atoned for other worlds as well. In speaking of the many kingdoms and the inhabitants thereof existing in the universe, the Lord likened them unto a man having a field, sending his servants into the field, and promising to visit each man in his own hour and in his own order (see D&C 88:37, 51–61). After quoting these verses in section 88, President John Taylor wrote: "That is, each kingdom, or planet, and the inhabitants thereof, were blessed with the visits and presence of their Creator, in their several times and seasons."[5] Also, in the 1879 edition of the Doctrine and Covenants, Elder Orson Pratt wrote the following footnotes to verses 51 and 61: "Each planetary kingdom is visited by its Creator in its time and season," and "The inhabitants of each planet [are] blessed with the presence and visits of their Creator." Therefore, just as the Nephite prophets had their prophecies and signs of Christ's birth and Atonement verified by the Savior's visit among them, it seems logical that the other planets or kingdoms that were created and covered by the Savior and His Atonement received a verification of the Atonement when He visited them. Recognizing that the Lord has through His vision enlarged our understanding of the Savior's mission, let us examine another of the visions.

Joseph and Sidney next behold the fall of Lucifer from the presence of God. Although this fall is documented in the Bible (see Isaiah 14:12; Revelation 12:7–9), and in the Pearl of Great Price (see Moses 4:14; Abraham 3:27–28), there are many additional things about Satan and his fall revealed in section 76. That he was in a position of authority in the beginning is amplified in the poetic version by the descriptive "authority great." The titles given him in section 76 are revealing. That he was called "Perdition" explains why the heavens wept over him. According to the dictionary, the word means utter destruction, loss, eternal damnation, hell."[6] As Isaiah also said, he was Lucifer, a "son of the morning" (Isaiah 14:12). According to President Joseph Fielding Smith, *Lucifer* means "a torchbearer."[7] "Son of the morning" is usually interpreted to mean he was one of the early-born spirit children of Elohim. Thus, as one of the older of the children of God and someone in a position of authority, the title of Lucifer implies he was not only rebelling against God but was also leading others to do likewise; therefore, he is designated a torchbearer or crusader against God. In fact, as both Isaiah (Isaiah 14:13–14) and this section teach, he "sought to take the kingdom of our God and his Christ" (D&C 76:28). To do this "he maketh war with the saints of God, and encompasseth them round about" (verse 29). In other words, his primary function on the earth is to oppose the work of the Church and its members. He spends considerable time and effort upon Church members. Therefore, we may be assured that whenever members of the Church are individually or collectively assembled to further their own spiritual progress or that of the Church, the devil will be there in opposition. In the words of Joseph Smith, "In relation to the kingdom of God, the devil always sets up his kingdom at the very same time in opposition to God."[8]

Having seen the glory of God and the fall of Satan, Joseph and Sidney are now shown the eternal destinies of the earth's inhabitants in a series of four visions. The order of the next four visions is interesting. As members of the Church, we usually speak of the various kingdoms in the descending order of celestial, terrestrial, telestial, and those who qualify for none of the above, the sons of perdition. In this revelation, the sons of perdition are treated first and then the celestial, terrestrial, and telestial kingdoms. There may be purpose for this order. The sons of perdition had known and experienced the principles of exaltation necessary for the celestial kingdom and had rejected them, choosing to follow Satan. Therefore, laws designed for exalting God's children will result in one's becoming a son of perdition if he meets the requirements for exaltation and then commits the unpardonable sin. This concept is supported by the insertion of a definition of the gospel (see D&C 76:40–43) within the description of the vision concerning the sons of perdition. By comparison, the division of the terrestrial and telestial peoples is caused by their following or failing to follow lesser portions of the laws that are given to make men honorable but not like unto God.

What was seen in the vision of those who were overcome by Satan (sons of perdition) was not recorded. However, what the Lord said about the vision was recorded. From the Lord's description, we learn that those who were overcome had not only come to a *knowledge* of the power of the Lord but had *experienced* that power in their lives. The Lord also explained that these people had *chosen* to follow Satan; they had suffered (allowed) themselves to be overcome. The poetic version says they were guilty of "despising my [Christ's] name."

Having had such a spiritual experience, their rebellion means they "deny the truth and defy my power." This further substantiates their willful disobedience.

Many years after he had seen this vision, the Prophet Joseph commented:

"The contention in heaven was—Jesus said there would be certain souls that would not be saved; and the devil said he could save them all, and laid his plans before the grand council, who gave their vote in favor of Jesus Christ. So the devil rose up in rebellion against God, and was cast down, with all who put up their heads for him.

"All sins shall be forgiven, except the sin against the Holy Ghost; for Jesus will save all except the sons of perdition. What must a man do to commit the unpardonable sin? He must receive the Holy Ghost, have the heavens opened unto him, and know God, and then sin against Him. After a man has sinned against the Holy Ghost, there is no repentance for him. He has got to say that the sun does not shine while he sees it; he has got to deny Jesus Christ when the heavens have been opened unto him, and to deny the plan of salvation with his eyes open to the truth of it; and from that time he begins to be an enemy. This is the case with many apostates of the Church of Jesus Christ of Latter-day Saints.

"When a man begins to be an enemy to this work, he hunts me, he seeks to kill me, and never ceases to thirst for my blood. He gets the spirit of the devil—the same spirit that they had who crucified the Lord of Life—the same spirit that sins against the Holy Ghost. You cannot save such persons; you cannot bring them to repentance; they make open war, like the devil, and awful is the consequence."[9]

In describing the fate of the sons of perdition, the Lord uses several New Testament phrases (see Matthew 26:24; 12:32; Hebrews 6:6; Revelation 19:20), and concludes with the declaration these are "the only ones on whom the second death shall have any power; yea, verily, the only ones who shall not be redeemed" (D&C 76:37–38). Some conclude from this declaration that the sons of perdition will not be resurrected, basing their conclusion on the next verse, which states that "all the rest shall be brought forth by the resurrection of the dead" (verse 39). A careful reading of section 88 shows that redemption as used here refers to receiving a degree of glory after the Resurrection and not the Resurrection per se (see verses 25–32). The

New Testament and Book of Mormon also repeatedly teach a universal resurrection, and modern-day prophets have confirmed that sons of perdition will be resurrected.[10]

The Lord concluded His remarks about what Joseph and Sidney had seen concerning the sons of perdition by declaring that only those "who are made partakers thereof" (verse 46) or "are ordained unto this condemnation" (verse 48) will ever know the torment, the misery, and the end of such punishment. Therefore, we should not speculate concerning these things. Our goal is to achieve the celestial kingdom, and we would profit more by seeking understanding of how to attain this goal than by speculating about the sons of perdition. Those who are striving for this celestial goal will naturally avoid the pitfalls that lead to becoming a son of perdition. Although a candidate for the celestial kingdom is also a candidate for becoming a son of perdition (if he rebels and defies God), as long as he seeks knowledge and gives heed to the commandments, he will attain salvation. Joseph Smith described it this way:

"A man cannot commit the unpardonable sin after the dissolution of the body, and there is a way possible for escape. Knowledge saves a man; and in the world of spirits no man can be exalted but by knowledge. So long as a man will not give heed to the commandments, he must abide without salvation. If a man has knowledge, he can be saved; although, if he has been guilty of great sins, he will be punished for them. But when he consents to obey the Gospel, whether here or in the world of spirits, he is saved.

"A man is his own tormenter and his own condemner. Hence the saying, They shall go into the lake that burns with fire and brimstone. The torment of disappointment in the mind of man is as exquisite as a lake burning with fire and brimstone. I say, so is the torment of man.

"I know the Scriptures and understand them. I said, no man can commit the unpardonable sin after the dissolution of the body, nor in this life, until he receives the Holy Ghost; but they must do it in this world. Hence the salvation of Jesus Christ was wrought out for all men, in order to triumph over the devil; for if it did not catch him in one place, it would in another; for he stood up as a Savior. All will suffer until they obey Christ himself."[11]

The knowledge and heed which a person must achieve to receive a celestial glory was shown to Joseph and Sidney in their fourth vision, concerning those "who shall come forth in the resurrection of the just," (verse 50), or as stated in the poetic version, "in the first resurrection of Christ." The description of these people is based upon what Joseph and Sidney saw and heard. Twelve descriptions of qualifications for people who will be in the celestial kingdom are recorded, each introduced with the introductory phrase "they are they" or "these are they" (see verses 51–70).

The first qualification is receiving and following the principles of the gospel. In the words of President Harold B. Lee: "Conversion must mean more than just being a 'card carrying' member of the Church with a tithing receipt, a membership card, a temple recommend, etc. It means to overcome the tendencies to criticize and to strive continually to improve inward weaknesses and not merely the outward appearances."[12]

The poetic version stresses the trials that have been faced and overcome:

> For these overcome, by their faith and their works,
> Being tried in their life-time, as purified gold.
> And seal'd by the spirit of promise to life,
> By men called of God, as was Aaron of old.

Their being sealed to (eternal) life corresponds with Doctrine and Covenants 131:5: "(May 17th, 1843.) The more sure word of prophecy means a man's knowing that he is sealed up unto eternal life, by revelation and the spirit of prophecy, through the power of the Holy Priesthood." Therefore, those people who attain the celestial glory are those who fully live the gospel after receiving it and endure to the end.

Having considered the division of those who know and experience the principles for exaltation, let us examine the division brought about through the lesser portions of the law. The fifth vision shown to Joseph and Sidney was of the terrestrial world. The description of these beings is much shorter, and mention is made only of seeing, not of hearing. Only six qualifications of terrestrial beings are enumerated or recorded, although there may be more. These are likewise introduced with the phrase "these are they who." Only two of these categories will receive some comment here. Those who "died without law" (D&C 76:72) are further described in the poetic version as "the heathen of ages that never had hope." Thus the law must refer to the law of Christ, and those described in this category are those who were never exposed to that law while living upon the earth. This group included those who were visited in the spirit prison where the gospel was preached to them to give them the opportunity they had missed on the earth. They "received not the testimony of Jesus in the flesh, but afterwards received it" (verse 74).

Some have erroneously interpreted this verse as saying that those who were preached to in the spirit world could attain no higher than the terrestrial kingdom. However, a careful reading will show that these people did not accept the gospel in the spirit world but only received the testimony of Jesus. A person may receive a testimony of Jesus but reject the principles and ordinances of His gospel. Those in the celestial kingdom accepted both (see verses 51–53). Note also that those in the telestial kingdom are described as receiving not the gospel neither the testimony of Jesus (see verse 82). In other words, the celestial kingdom requires a testimony of Jesus and an acceptance of the gospel, while all that is required for the terrestrial order is to receive a testimony of Jesus either in this life or in the spirit world. Those who reject both the gospel and the testimony of Jesus will be in the telestial kingdom. It is only logical then that those who receive both the testimony of Jesus and the gospel in the spirit world will be able to enter the celestial kingdom when the vicarious work is done for them.

The other description that seems to need some explanation is those "who are not valiant in the testimony of Jesus" (verse 79). This may sound like those who are not keeping the commandments. But those who do not keep the commandments are candidates for the telestial kingdom, not the terrestrial, unless they repent. The word *valiant* means "possessing or acting with bravery or boldness: courageous."[13] Therefore, it is probably not what they do but what they don't do. In the words of Elder Bruce R. McConkie: "Members of the church who have testimonies and who live clean and upright lives, but who are not courageous and valiant, do not gain the celestial kingdom. Theirs is a terrestrial inheritance."[14] Those who break the commandments and fail to live the lesser portions of the law are described next.

The sixth and final vision shown to Joseph and Sidney was the glory of the telestial kingdom. The description of what they saw is written in twelve qualifications for people who will be in the telestial kingdom. These are introduced again with the phrase "these are they who." That these rejected both the gospel and the testimony of Jesus has already been stressed. The other eleven qualifications are easily understood and are not controversial. There are some interesting additions in the poetic version. Those who say they are of various men—Paul, Apollos, Cephas, and others—must be in a different category than the honorable men spoken of in the terrestrial world. In the poetic version, there are some additional names of men whom they followed; namely, "For Luther and Calvin, and even the Pope." These telestial men were apparently justifying their actions through what they claimed Paul or others had taught. This is implied in both the scriptural and the poetic version. The poetic version states, "They went their own way, and have their reward." These were obviously not honorable men. The scriptural account again confirms that they received not the gospel nor the testimony of Jesus, and also adds that they did not receive the prophets, neither the everlasting covenant (see D&C 76:101). The poetic version also repeats that they rejected the gospel and the prophetic spirit of the Lord (the testimony of Jesus). It also qualifies the everlasting covenant as that "which Jacob once had."

The great number of people who will be in this degree of glory is "as innumerable as the stars in the firmament of heaven, or as the sand upon the seashore" (D&C 76:109). While these will all eventually acknowledge the Savior and have to go through the judgments of God for one thousand years, they will yet receive the glory of the telestial kingdom. But even this glory surpasses all understanding by earth standards and can only be known by revelation (see D&C 76:89–90) "in a world vain as this" (poetic version). The poetic version also gives an interesting comparison of the kingdoms:

> The glory celestial is one like the sun;
> The glory terrestrial is one like the moon;
> The glory telestial is one like the stars,
> And all harmonize like the parts of a tune.
> As the stars are all different in lustre and size,
> So the telestial region is mingled in bliss;

>   From the least unto greatest, and greatest to least,
>   The reward is exactly as promised in this.

The vision of the telestial kingdom concludes with a declaration that these will "be servants of the Most High; but where God and Christ dwell they cannot come, worlds without end" (D&C 76:112). This seems to say that there is no progression from one kingdom to another, at least from the telestial. And if there is no progression from the telestial, it is only logical that the same is true from other kingdoms. In spite of the apparent varying statements among past and present Church leaders, all that will be considered here is what the scriptures state. Modern scripture lends further support to there being no progression. Section 88 describes a qualitative resurrection for the earth's inhabitants. Those who attain the celestial kingdom are quickened by a celestial glory to bring about their resurrection. Those who attain either of the lesser kingdoms are quickened by the glory which they attain. This enables them to abide in that kingdom in which they are resurrected. Their spirits and the elements of their bodies are thus inseparably connected (see D&C 93:33); "they can die no more; their spirits uniting with their bodies, never to be divided; thus the whole becoming spiritual and immortal" (Alma 11:45). This implies a permanent status, and while it could be suggested that a higher glory could infuse the already permanent body, there is no scriptural evidence to substantiate this. Until further information is revealed "by the power of the Holy Spirit" to those who are granted the "privilege of seeing and knowing for themselves" (D&C 76:116–17), the concept of no progression from kingdom to kingdom is more scriptural. But first we must grasp the great amount of knowledge about these visions that Joseph was permitted to record.

The last vision shown and recorded was of the telestial kingdom. The end of the revelation concerning the visions that they had seen is a proclamation of the greatness and glory of the Lord. Joseph Smith provided a fitting conclusion in his history following the recording of this revelation:

"Nothing could be more pleasing to the Saints upon the order of the kingdom of the Lord, than the light which burst upon the world through the foregoing vision. Every law, every commandment, every promise, every truth, and every point touching the destiny of man, from Genesis to Revelation, where the purity of the Scriptures remains unsullied by the folly of men, go to show the perfection of the theory [of different degrees of glory in the future life] and witness the fact that the document is a transcript from the records of the eternal world. The sublimity of the ideas; the purity of the language; the scope for action; the continued duration for completion, in order that the heirs of salvation may confess the Lord and bow the knee; the rewards for faithfulness, and the punishments for sins, are so much beyond the narrow-mindedness of men, that every man is constrained to exclaim: 'It came from God.'"[15]

NOTES

This chapter is used by permission from a book titled *Even Great Revelations—An Analysis of the "Most Important" Revelations of the Doctrine and Covenants* (Bountiful, Utah: Horizon Publishers, 2004).

1. Joseph Smith, *Teachings of the Prophet Joseph Smith,* comp. Joseph Fielding Smith (Salt Lake City: Deseret Book, 1976), 304–5.
2. Smith, *Teachings,* 305.
3. See Joseph Smith, *History of the Church of Jesus Christ of Latter-day Saints* (Salt Lake City: Deseret Book, 1932–51), 5:288.
4. In 1843 the Prophet Joseph Smith published a poetic version of Doctrine and Covenants 76 as "The Answer," *Times and Seasons,* February 1, 1843, 82–85. All citations are to this version.
5. John Taylor, *Mediation and Atonement* (Salt Lake City: Steven & Wallis, 1950), 77.
6. *Webster's Tenth New Collegiate Dictionary,* s.v. "Perdition."
7. See Joseph Fielding Smith, *Church History and Modern Revelation* (Salt Lake City: Deseret Book, 1953), 1:281.
8. Smith, *Teachings,* 365.
9. Smith, *Teachings,* 357–58.
10. See Joseph Fielding Smith, *Answers to Gospel Questions* (Salt Lake City: Deseret Book, 1993), 2:169.
11. Smith, *Teachings,* 357.
12. Harold B. Lee, in Conference Report, April 1971, 92.
13. *Webster's Tenth New Collegiate Dictionary,* s.v. "Valiant."
14. Bruce R. McConkie, in Conference Report, October 1974, 44.
15. See Smith, *History of the Church,* 1:252–53.

CHAPTER SIXTEEN

THE SECOND COMING OF CHRIST: QUESTIONS AND ANSWERS

ROBERT L. MILLET

The Doctrine and Covenants is a sacred book of scripture that provides literally thousands of answers—answers to questions that have plagued the religious world for centuries. It is a treasure-house of doctrinal understanding.

WHAT IS THE SECOND COMING?

Jesus came to earth as a mortal being in the meridian of time. He taught the gospel, bestowed divine authority, organized the Church, and suffered and died as an infinite atoning sacrifice for the sins of the world. He stated that He would come again, would return not as the meek and lowly Nazarene but as the Lord of Sabaoth, the Lord of Hosts, the Lord of Armies. His Second Coming is thus spoken of as His coming "in glory"—meaning, in His true identity as the God of all creation, the Redeemer and Judge. His Second Coming is described as both *great* and *dreadful*—great for those who have been true and faithful and therefore look forward to His coming, and dreadful to those who have done despite to the spirit of grace and who therefore hope against hope that He will never return. The Second Coming in glory is in fact "the end of the world," meaning the end of worldliness, the destruction of the wicked (Joseph Smith—Matthew 1:4, 31).[1] At this coming the wicked will be destroyed, the

Robert L. Millet is the Richard L. Evans Professor of Religious Understanding and former dean of Religious Education at Brigham Young University.

righteous quickened and caught up to meet Him, and the earth transformed from a fallen telestial orb to a terrestrial, paradisiacal sphere. We will live and move about among new heavens and new earth. The Second Coming will initiate the millennial reign.

Does Christ Himself Know When He Will Come?

This question comes up occasionally, perhaps because of what is stated in the Gospel of Mark: "Heaven and earth shall pass away: but my words shall not pass away. But of that day and that hour knoweth no man, no, not the angels which are in heaven, *neither the Son*, but the Father" (Mark 13:31–32; emphasis added). The phrase "neither the Son" is not found in Matthew or Luke. Christ knows all things; He possesses the fulness of the glory and power of the Father (see D&C 93:16–17). Surely He knows when He will return. If He did not know the exact day or time of His return in glory when the Olivet prophecy was uttered, then certainly after His Resurrection and glorification He came to know. It is worth noting that the Joseph Smith Translation of this verse omits the disputed phrase.

Will All Be Surprised and Caught Unaware?

The scriptures speak of the Master returning as "a thief in the night" (1 Thessalonians 5:2; 2 Peter 3:10). It is true that no mortal man has known, does now know, or will yet know the precise day of the Lord's second advent. That is true for prophets and Apostles as well as the rank and file of society and the Church. The Lord did not reveal to Joseph Smith the precise day and time of His coming (D&C 130:14–17). Elder M. Russell Ballard, speaking to students at Brigham Young University, observed: "I am called as one of the Apostles to be a special witness of Christ in these exciting, trying times, and I do not know when He is going to come again. As far as I know, none of my brethren in the Council of the Twelve or even in the First Presidency knows. And I would humbly suggest to you, my young brothers and sisters, that if we do not know, then *nobody* knows, no matter how compelling their arguments or how reasonable their calculations. . . . I believe when the Lord says 'no man' knows, it really means that no man knows. You should be extremely wary of anyone who claims to be an exception to divine decree."[2] On the other hand, the Saints are promised that if they are in tune with the Spirit, they can know the time and the season. The Apostle Paul chose the descriptive analogy of a pregnant woman about to deliver. She may not know the exact hour or day when the birth is to take place, but one thing she knows for sure: it will be soon. It *must* be soon! The impressions and feelings and signs within her own body so testify. In that day, surely the Saints of the Most High, the members of the body of Christ, will be pleading for the Lord to deliver the travailing earth, to bring an end to corruption and degradation, to introduce an era of peace and righteousness. And those who give heed to the words of scripture, and especially to the living oracles, will stand as the "children of light, and the children of the day," those who "are not of the night, nor of darkness" (1 Thessalonians 5:2–5). In a modern revelation the Savior declared: "And again, verily I say unto you, the coming of the Lord draweth nigh, and *it overtaketh the world as a thief in the night*—therefore, gird up your loins, that you may be the children of light, and that day shall not overtake you as a thief" (D&C 106:4–5; emphasis added).

To certain brethren who would soon be called to the first Quorum of the Twelve Apostles in this dispensation, the Lord said: "And unto you it shall be given to know the signs of the times, and the signs of the coming of the Son of Man" (D&C 68:11). As we move closer to the end of time, we would do well to live in such a manner that we can discern the signs of the times; we would be wise also to keep our eyes fixed and our ears riveted on those called to direct the destiny of this Church. The Prophet Joseph Smith pointed out that a particular man who claimed prophetic powers "has not seen the sign of the Son of Man as foretold by Jesus. Neither has any man, nor will any man, till after the sun shall have been darkened and the moon bathed in blood. For the Lord hath not shown me any such sign, and as the prophet saith, so it must be: 'Surely the Lord God will do nothing, but he revealeth his secret unto his servants the prophets.'"[3]

Is It True That Not Everyone Will Know When the Savior Has Come?

Once in a while we hear something in the classes of the Church to the effect that not all people will know when the Lord returns. Let us be clear on this matter. There may be some wisdom in speaking of the second *comings* of the Lord Jesus Christ, three of which are preliminary appearances, or comings, to select groups, and one of which is to the whole world. The Lord will make a preliminary appearance to His temple in Independence, Jackson County, Missouri. This seems to be a private appearance to those holding the keys of power in the earthly kingdom. Elder Orson Pratt, in speaking of this appearance, said: "All of them who are pure in heart will behold the face of the Lord and that too before he comes in his glory in the clouds of heaven, for he will suddenly come to his Temple, and he will purify the sons of Moses and of Aaron, until they shall be prepared to offer in that Temple an offering that shall be acceptable in the sight of the Lord. In doing this, he will purify not only the minds of the Priesthood in that Temple, but he will purify their bodies until they shall be quickened, renewed and strengthened, and they will be partially changed, not to immortality, but changed in part that they can be filled with the power of God, and they can stand in the presence of Jesus, and behold his face in the midst of that Temple."[4] Charles W. Penrose observed that the Saints "will come to the Temple prepared for him, and his faithful people will behold his face, hear his voice, and gaze upon his glory. From his own lips they will receive further instructions for the development and beautifying of Zion and for the extension and sure stability of his Kingdom."[5]

The Lord will make an appearance at Adam-ondi-Ahman, "the place where Adam shall come to visit his people, or the Ancient of Days shall sit" (D&C 116). This grand council will be a large sacrament meeting, a time when the Son of Man will partake of the fruit of the vine once more with His earthly friends. And who will be in attendance? The revelations specify Moroni, Elias, John the Baptist, Elijah, Abraham, Isaac, Jacob, Joseph, Adam, Peter, James, John, "and also," the Savior clarifies, "all those whom my Father hath given me out of the world" (D&C 27:5–14), multitudes of faithful Saints from the beginning of time to the end. This will be a private appearance in that it will be unknown to the world. It will be a leadership meeting, a time of accounting, an accounting for priesthood stewardships. The Prophet Joseph Smith explained that Adam, the Ancient of Days, "will call his children together and hold a council with them to prepare them for the coming of the Son of Man. He (Adam) is the father of the human family, and presides over the spirits of all men, and all that have had the keys must stand before him in this grand council. . . . The Son of Man stands before him, and there is given him [Christ] glory and dominion. Adam delivers up his stewardship to Christ, that which was delivered to him as holding the keys of the universe, but retains his standing as head of the human family."[6]

President Joseph Fielding Smith observed: "This gathering of the children of Adam, where the thousands, and the tens of thousands are assembled in the judgment, will be one of the greatest events this troubled earth has ever seen. At this conference, or council, all who have held keys of dispensations will render a report of their steward-ship. . . . We do not know how long a time this gathering will be in session, or how many sessions will be held at this grand council. It is sufficient to know that it is a gathering of the Priesthood of God from the beginning of this earth down to the present, in which reports will be made and all who have been given dispensations (talents) will declare their keys and ministry and make report of their stewardship according to the parable [the parable of the talents; Matthew 25]. Judgment will be rendered unto them for this is a gathering of the righteous. . . . It is not to be the judgment of the wicked. . . . This will precede the great day of destruction of the wicked and will be the preparation for the Millennial Reign."[7]

Elder Bruce R. McConkie has likewise written: "Every prophet, apostle, president, bishop, elder, or church officer of whatever degree—all who have held keys shall stand before him who holds all of the keys. They will then be called upon to give an account of their stewardships and to report how and in what manner they have used their priesthood and their keys for the salvation of men within the sphere of their appointments. . . . There will be a great hierarchy of judges in that great day, of whom Adam, under Christ, will be the chief of all. Those judges will judge the righteous ones under their jurisdiction, but Christ himself, he alone, will judge the wicked."[8]

The Savior will appear to the Jews on the Mount of Olives. It will be at the time of the battle of Armageddon, at a time when His people will find themselves with their backs against the wall. During this period, two prophets will stand before the wicked in the streets of Jerusalem and call the people to repentance. These men, presum-ably members of the Quorum of the Twelve Apostles or the First Presidency—holding the sealing powers—"are to be raised up to the

Jewish nation in the last days, at the time of the restoration," and will "prophesy to the Jews after they are gathered and have built the city of Jerusalem in the land of their fathers" (D&C 77:15; see also Revelation 11:4–6).[9] They will be put to death by their enemies, their bodies will lie in the streets for three and a half days, and they will then be resurrected before the assembled multitude (Revelation 11:7–12).

At about this time, the Savior will come to the rescue of His covenant people: "Then shall the Lord go forth, and fight against those nations, as when he fought in the day of battle. And his feet shall stand in that day upon the mount of Olives, which is before Jerusalem on the east, and the mount of Olives shall cleave in the midst thereof toward the east and toward the west, and there shall be a very great valley; and half of the mountain shall remove toward the north, and half of it toward the south" (Zechariah 14:3–4). Then shall come to pass the conversion of a nation in a day, the acceptance of the Redeemer by the Jews. "And then shall the Jews look upon me and say: What are these wounds in thine hands and in thy feet? Then shall they know that I am the Lord; for I will say unto them: These wounds are the wounds with which I was wounded in the house of my friends. I am he who was lifted up. I am Jesus that was crucified. I am the Son of God. And then shall they weep because of their iniquities; then shall they lament because they persecuted their king" (D&C 45:51–53; see also Zechariah 12:10; 13:6).

Finally, and we would assume not far removed in time from His appearance on the Mount of Olives, is Christ's coming in glory. He comes in glory. All shall know. "Be not deceived," the Master warned in a modern revelation, "but continue in steadfastness, looking forth for the heavens to be shaken, and the earth to tremble and to reel to and fro as a drunken man, and for the valleys to be exalted, and for the mountains to be made low, and for the rough places to become smooth" (D&C 49:23). "Wherefore, prepare ye for the coming of the Bridegroom; go ye, go ye out to meet him. For behold, he shall stand upon the mount of Olivet, and upon the mighty ocean, even the great deep, and upon the islands of the sea, and upon the land of Zion. And he shall utter his voice out of Zion, and he shall speak from Jerusalem, and *his voice shall be heard among all people;* and it shall be a voice as the voice of many waters, and as the voice of a great thunder, which shall break down the mountains, and the valleys shall not be found" (D&C 133:19–22; emphasis added).

WHEN THE LORD COMES, WHO WILL COME WITH HIM?

The righteous dead from ages past—those who qualify for the first resurrection, specifically those who died true in the faith since the time the first resurrection was initiated in the meridian of time—will come with the Savior when He returns in glory. The Prophet Joseph corrected a passage in Paul's first epistle to the Thessalonians as follows: "I would not have you to be ignorant, brethren, concerning them which are asleep, that ye sorrow not, even as others which have no hope. For if we believe that Jesus died and rose again, even so them also which sleep in Jesus will God bring with him. For this we say unto you by the word of the Lord, that they who are alive at the coming of the Lord, shall not prevent [precede] them who remain unto the coming of the Lord, who are asleep. For the Lord himself shall descend from heaven with a shout, with the voice of the archangel, and with the trump of God; and the dead in Christ shall rise first; then they who are alive, shall be caught up together into the clouds with them who remain, to meet the Lord in the air; and so shall we be ever with the Lord" (JST 1 Thessalonians 4:13–17).

WHAT HAPPENS TO THOSE LIVING ON EARTH WHEN HE COMES?

Those who are of at least a terrestrial level of righteousness shall continue to live as mortals after the Lord returns. The Saints shall live to "the age of man"—in the words of Isaiah, the age of one hundred (see Isaiah 65:20)—and will then pass through death and be changed instantly from mortality to resurrected immortality. "Yea, and blessed are the dead that die in the Lord, . . . when the Lord shall come, and old things shall pass away, and all things become new, they shall rise from the dead and shall not die after, and shall receive an inheritance before the Lord, in the holy city. And he that liveth when the Lord shall come, and hath kept the faith, blessed is he; nevertheless, it is appointed to him to die at the age of man. Wherefore, children shall grow up until they become old"—that is, no longer shall little ones die before the time of accountability; "old men shall die; but they shall not sleep in the dust, but they shall be changed in the twinkling of an eye" (D&C 63:49–51). President Joseph Fielding Smith pointed out that "the inhabitants of the earth will have a sort of translation. They will be transferred to a condition of the terrestrial order, and so they will have power over disease and they will have power to live until they get a certain age and then they will die."[10]

IS THE BURNING SPOKEN OF IN SCRIPTURE LITERAL?

Malachi prophesied that "the day cometh, that shall burn as an oven; and all the proud, yea, and all that do wickedly, shall be stubble: and the day that cometh shall burn them up, saith the Lord of hosts, that it shall leave them neither root nor branch" (Malachi 4:1; see also 2 Nephi 26:4; D&C 133:64). In 1823 Moroni quoted this passage differently to the seventeen-year-old Joseph Smith: "And all the proud, yea, and all that do wickedly shall burn as stubble; for *they that come* shall burn them, saith the Lord of Hosts" (Joseph Smith—History 1:37; emphasis added). In the Doctrine and Covenants the Lord of Armies declares: "For the hour is nigh and the day soon at hand when the earth is ripe; and all the proud and they that do wickedly shall be as stubble; and *I will burn them up,* saith the Lord of Hosts, that wickedness shall not be upon the earth" (D&C 29:9; emphasis added), "for after today cometh the burning," a day wherein "all the proud and they that do wickedly shall be as stubble; and *I will burn them up,* for I am the Lord of Hosts; and I will not spare any that remain in Babylon" (D&C 64:24; emphasis added).

The Second Coming of Christ in glory is a day in which "every corruptible thing, both of man, or of the beasts of the field, or of the fowls of the heavens, or of the fish of the sea, that dwells upon all the face of the earth, shall be consumed; and also that of element shall melt with fervent heat; and all things shall become new, that my knowledge and glory may dwell upon all the earth" (D&C 101:24–25; see also 133:41; 2 Peter 3:10). President Joseph Fielding Smith wrote: "Somebody said, 'Brother Smith, do you mean to say that it is going to be literal fire?' I said, 'Oh, no, it will not be literal fire any more than it was literal water that covered the earth in the flood.'"[11]

WHY WILL THE SAVIOR APPEAR IN RED APPAREL?

Red is symbolic of victory—victory over the devil, death, hell, and endless torment. It is the symbol of salvation, of being placed beyond the power of all one's enemies.[12] Christ's red apparel will also symbolize both aspects of His ministry to fallen humanity—His mercy and His justice. Because He has trodden the winepress alone, "even the wine-press of the fierceness of the wrath of Almighty God" (D&C 76:107; 88:106), He has descended below all things and mercifully taken upon Him our stains, our blood, or our sins (see 2 Nephi 9:44; Jacob 1:19; 2:2; Alma 5:22). In addition, He comes in "dyed garments" as the God of justice, even He who has trampled the wicked beneath His feet. "And the Lord shall be red in his apparel, and his garments like him that treadeth in the wine-vat. And so great shall be the glory of his presence that the sun shall hide his face in shame, and the moon shall withhold its light, and the stars shall be hurled from their places. And his voice shall be heard: I have trodden the wine-press alone, and have brought judgment upon all people; and none were with me; and I have trampled them in my fury, and I did tread upon them in mine anger, and their blood have I sprinkled upon my garments, and stained all my raiment; for this was the day of vengeance which was in my heart" (D&C 133:48–51).

WHEN DOES THE MILLENNIUM BEGIN? WHY WILL IT BEGIN?

The Second Coming of Jesus Christ in glory ushers in the Millennium. The Millennium does not begin when Christ comes to His temple in Missouri, when He appears at Adam-ondi-Ahman, or when He stands on the Mount of Olives in Jerusalem. The Millennium will not come because men and women on earth have become noble and good, because Christian charity will have spread across the globe and goodwill is the order of the day. The Millennium will not come because technological advances and medical miracles will have extended human life or because peace treaties among warring nations will have soothed injured feelings and eased political tensions for a time. The Millennium will be brought in by power, by the power of Him who is the King of Kings and Lord of Lords. Satan will be bound by power, and the glory of the Millennium will be maintained by the righteousness of those who are permitted to live on earth (see 1 Nephi 22:15, 26).

WHAT ARE THE TIMES OF THE GENTILES? THE FULNESS OF THE GENTILES?

In the meridian of time, by command of the Savior, the gospel of Jesus Christ was delivered first to the Jews and then later to the Gentiles. In our day, the gospel was delivered first to Joseph Smith and the Latter-day Saints, those of us who are "identified with the Gentiles" (D&C 109:60), those who are Israelite by descent (see D&C 52:2; 86:8–10) and Gentile by culture. The gospel is given to us, and we bear the responsibility to take the message of the Restoration to the descendants of Lehi and to the Jews (see 1 Nephi 22:7–11). We therefore live in "the times of the Gentiles." "And when the times of the Gentiles is come in, a light shall break forth among them that sit in darkness, and it shall be the fulness of my gospel" (D&C 45:28). It is a time, in the words of President Marion G. Romney, in which "in this last dispensation, the gospel is to be preached primarily to the non-Jewish people of the earth."[13]

In a day yet future, a time when the Gentiles—presumably those outside the Church as well as some from within the fold—sin against the fulness of the gospel and reject its supernal blessings, the Lord will take away these privileges from the Gentile nations and once again make them available primarily to His ancient covenant people (see 3 Nephi 16:10–11). This will be known as the fulfillment, or the "fulness of the times of the Gentiles," or simply the "fulness of the Gentiles." Because the people of earth no longer receive the light of gospel fulness and turn their hearts from the Lord because of the precepts of men, "in that generation shall the times of the Gentiles be fulfilled" (D&C 45:29–30). In the purest sense, this will not take place until Jesus sets His foot upon Olivet and the Jews acknowledge their long-awaited Messiah. Thus the fulness of the Gentiles is millennial.[14]

WHAT ARE WE TO EXPECT ABOUT THE RETURN OF THE TEN TRIBES?

As we all know, there have been numerous legends, traditions, vague reminiscences, and a myriad of folktales that deal with the location and eventual return of the ten lost tribes, those from the northern part of Israel who were taken captive by the Assyrians in 721 B.C. During my youth in the Church, I was brought up to believe a whole host of things: that the lost tribes were in the center of the earth, on a knob attached to the earth, on another planet, and so forth. Each of these traditions had its own source of authority. Since that time, and particularly since I discovered the Book of Mormon, I have concluded simply that the ten tribes are scattered among the nations, lost as much to their identity as to their whereabouts (see 1 Nephi 22:3–4). Thus it seems to me that the restoration, or gathering, of the ten tribes consists in scattered Israel—descendants of Jacob from such tribes as Reuben, Gad, Asher, Naphtali, Zebulun, and, of course, Joseph—coming to the knowledge of the restored gospel, accepting Christ's gospel (see 1 Nephi 15:14), coming into the true church and fold of God (see 2 Nephi 9:2), congregating with the faithful, and receiving the ordinances of the house of the Lord.[15] That is to say, the ten tribes will be gathered as all others are gathered—through conversion.

The risen Lord explained to the Nephites that after His Second Coming, once He has begun to dwell on earth with His faithful, "then shall the work of the Father"—the work of the gathering of Israel—"commence at that day, even when this gospel shall be preached among the remnant of this people. Verily I say unto you, at that day shall the work of the Father commence among all the dispersed of my people, yea, even the tribes which have been lost, which the Father hath led away out of Jerusalem" (3 Nephi 21:25–26). It will commence in the sense that its magnitude will be of such a nature as to cause earlier efforts at gathering to pale into insignificance. The return of the ten tribes is spoken of in modern revelation in majestic symbolism: "And the Lord, even the Savior, shall stand in the midst of his people, and shall reign over all flesh" (D&C 133:25). Further, those who are descendants of the northern tribes shall respond to the gospel message, come under the direction of those prophets or priesthood leaders in their midst, traverse that highway we know as the "way of holiness" (Isaiah 35:8), and eventually participate in those temple ordinances that make of us kings and queens, priests and priestesses before God; they will "fall down and be crowned with glory, even in Zion, by the hands of the servants of the Lord, even the children of Ephraim," those who are entrusted with the keys of salvation (D&C 133:26–32).[16] In addition to that portion of the record of the ten tribes in our possession that we know as the Doctrine and Covenants—the record of God's dealings with modern Ephraim—we thrill in the assurance that other sacred volumes chronicling our Redeemer's ministry to the lost tribes shall come forth during the Millennium (see 2 Nephi 29:13).

Must Every Person Living on Earth Hear the Gospel Before the Lord Can Come?

In November 1831 the early elders of the Church were authorized to preach the gospel: "Go ye into all the world, preach the gospel to every creature, acting in the authority which I have given you, baptizing in the name of the Father, and of the Son, and of the Holy Ghost" (D&C 68:8). "For, verily, the sound must go forth from this place into all the world, and unto the uttermost parts of the earth—the gospel must be preached unto every creature, with signs following them that believe" (D&C 58:64). It is true that every person must have the opportunity to hear the gospel, either here or hereafter. Eventually "the truth of God will go forth boldly, nobly, and independent, till it has penetrated every continent, visited every clime, swept every country, and sounded in every ear, till the purposes of God shall be accomplished, and the Great Jehovah shall say the work is done."[17]

Not all, however, will have that privilege as mortals, and not all will have that privilege before the Second Coming. Jesus had spoken to the Twelve about the last days as follows: "And again, this Gospel of the Kingdom shall be preached in all the world, for a witness unto all nations, and then shall the end come, or the destruction of the wicked" (Joseph Smith—Matthew 1:31). As we have seen, the great day of gathering—the day when millions upon millions will come into the true fold of God—is millennial. But there is more. Elder McConkie explained that before the Lord Jesus can return in glory, two things must take place: "The first . . . is that the restored gospel is to be preached in every nation and among every people and to those speaking every tongue. Now there is one immediate reaction to this: Can't we go on the radio and preach the gospel to . . . the nations of the earth? We certainly can, but that would have very little bearing on the real meaning of the revelation that says we must preach it to every nation, kindred, and people. The reason is the second thing that must occur before the Second Coming: The revelations expressly, specifically, and pointedly say that when the Lord comes the second time to usher in the millennial era, he is going to find, in every nation, kindred, and tongue, and among every people, those who are kings and queens, who will live and reign a thousand years on earth (Revelation 5:9–10).

"That is a significant statement that puts in perspective the preaching of the gospel to the world. Yes, we can go on the radio; we can proclaim the gospel to all nations by television or other modern invention. And to the extent that we can do it, so be it, it's all to the good. But that's not what is involved. What is involved is that the elders of Israel, holding the priesthood, in person have to trod the soil, eat in the homes of the people, figuratively put their arms around the honest in heart, feed them the gospel, and baptize them and confer the Holy Ghost upon them. Then these people have to progress and advance, and grow in the things of the Spirit, until they can go to the house of the Lord, until they can enter a temple of God and receive the blessings of the priesthood, out of which come the rewards of being kings and priests.

"The way we become kings and priests is through the ordinances of the house of the Lord. It is through celestial marriage; it is through the guarantees of eternal life and eternal increase that are reserved for the Saints in the temples. The promise is that when the Lord comes He is going to find in every nation and kindred, among every people speaking every tongue, those who will, at that hour of his coming, have already become kings and priests. . . . All this is to precede the Second Coming of the Son of Man."[18]

The revelations declare: "Prepare ye the way of the Lord, and make his paths straight, for the hour of his coming is nigh—when the Lamb shall stand upon Mount Zion, and with him a hundred and forty-four thousand, having his father's name written on their foreheads" (D&C 133:17–18). This group of 144,000 are high priests after the holy order of God, men who have themselves received the promise of exaltation and godhood and whose mission it is to bring as many as will come into the Church of the Firstborn, into that inner circle of men and women who have passed the tests of mortality and have become the elect of God.[19] I have often thought that the 144,000 high priests called in the last days to bring men and women into the Church of the Firstborn (see D&C 77:11) is a symbolic reference: in that day of division, of unspeakable wickedness and consummate righteousness, temples will dot the earth, be accessible to the Lord's covenant people everywhere, and thus the fulness of those temple blessings will be sealed upon millions of the faithful Saints worldwide by those holding those transcendent powers.

Is the Time of Christ's Coming Fixed, or May It Be Altered by Us?

We hear once in a while the plea for us as Latter-day Saints to repent and improve so that the Lord may come quickly to us. It is true that we are under obligation to be faithful to our covenants, to deny ourselves of every worldly lust and cross ourselves as to the pulls of a decaying society, and to live as becometh Saints. It is true that our labor is to build up the kingdom of God and establish Zion, all in preparation for the Second Coming. The full redemption of Zion depends on the urgency with which the Saints of the Most High pursue their sacred duty. Further, our righteous obsession to be a light to a darkened world assures our own readiness to receive the Savior. But the time of His coming is a constant, not a variable. It may not be postponed because of the Saints' tardiness or sloth any more than it can be hastened through a burst of goodness. The Father and the Son know when the King of Zion (see Moses 7:53) shall return to earth to assume the scepter and to preside over the kingdom of God. As was the case with His first coming to earth in the meridian of time, so it is in regard to His Second Coming. The Nephite prophets, for example, did not encourage the people to be faithful so that the Lord could come; rather, they stated forthrightly that in six hundred years He would come (see, for example, 1 Nephi 10:4; 19:8; 2 Nephi 25:19)—ready or not! It will be a time. It will be a specific day, a designated hour. That day and that hour are known. The time is set. It is fixed.[20]

How Can We Know Who Are False Christs and False Prophets?

We must keep our eyes fixed on those charged with the direction of this Church, the prophets, seers, and revelators of our day. What they stress in their instruction to us should be what we stress. Any who come before the Saints claiming some special insight, gift, training, or commission to elucidate detail concerning the signs of the times beyond that which the Brethren have set forth is suspect, is running before his or her leaders. Their teachings are not to be trusted or received. Truly, "it shall not be given to any one to go forth to preach my gospel, or to build up my church, except he be ordained by some one who has authority, and it is known to the church that he has authority and has been regularly ordained by the heads of the church" (D&C 42:11).

With the exception of those few deluded persons who claim to be Jesus, when we speak of false Christs we speak not so much of individuals as of false spirits, false doctrines, false systems of salvation. Latter-day Saints who "stick with the Brethren," who study and teach from the conference reports, the official pronouncements and proclamations, and the monthly First Presidency messages in the *Ensign*— these are they who treasure up the word of the Lord, who will not be deceived or led astray at the last day (Joseph Smith—Matthew 1:37). President Boyd K. Packer declared: "There are some among us now who have *not* been regularly ordained by the heads of the Church and who tell of impending political and economic chaos, the end of the world. . . . Those deceivers say that the Brethren do not know what is going on in the world or that the Brethren approve of their teaching but do not wish to speak of it over the pulpit. Neither is true. The Brethren, by virtue of traveling constantly everywhere on earth, certainly know what is going on, and by virtue of prophetic insight are able to read the signs of the times."[21]

WHAT ARE THE BEST SOURCES FOR UNDERSTANDING THE EVENTS INCIDENT TO THE SAVIOR'S COMING?

At the October 1972 and April 1973 conferences of the Church, President Harold B. Lee warned the Latter-day Saints about what he called "loose writings" by members of the Church in regard to the signs of the times. "Are you . . . aware of the fact," President Lee inquired, "that we need no such publications to be forewarned, if we were only conversant with what the scriptures have already spoken to us in plainness?" He then provided what he termed "the sure word of prophecy on which [we] should rely for [our] guide instead of these strange sources." He instructed the Saints to read the Joseph Smith Translation of Matthew 24 (what we have in the Pearl of Great Price as Joseph Smith—Matthew), and also sections 38, 45, 101, and

133 of the Doctrine and Covenants.[22] It is of interest to me that President Lee cited primarily the revelations of the Restoration. He did not refer the Church to Isaiah or Ezekiel or Daniel or Revelation. In 1981 President Romney explained: "In each dispensation, . . . the Lord has revealed anew the principles of the gospel. So that while the records of past dispensations, insofar as they are uncorrupted, testify to the truths of the gospel, still each dispensation has had revealed in its day sufficient truth to guide the people of the new dispensation, independent of the records of the past.

"I do not wish to discredit in any manner the records we have of the truths revealed by the Lord in past dispensations. What I now desire is to impress upon our minds that the gospel, as revealed to the Prophet Joseph Smith, is complete and is the word direct from heaven to this dispensation. It alone is sufficient to teach us the principles of eternal life. It is the truth revealed, the commandments given in this dispensation through modern prophets by which we are to be governed."[23]

Even given the divine direction of living oracles and the words of sacred scripture brought forth in this final age, we really cannot plot or calculate the signs of the times or lay out a precise scheme of events. That is, as one Apostle pointed out, "It is not possible for us . . . to specify the exact chronology of all the events that shall attend the Second Coming. Nearly all of the prophetic word relative to our Lord's return links various events together without reference to the order of their occurrence. Indeed, the same scriptural language is often used to describe similar events that will take place at different times."[24]

CONCLUSION

We obviously could go on and on. But these feeble efforts at providing answers point us to the glorious reality that modern revelation, especially the Doctrine and Covenants, represents, in the language of Parley P. Pratt, "the dawning of a brighter day."[25] The Doctrine and Covenants is indeed, as President Ezra Taft Benson explained, the "capstone" of our religion.[26] It is truly "the foundation of the Church in these last days, and a benefit to the world, showing that the keys of the mysteries of the kingdom of our Savior are again entrusted to man" (D&C 70, headnote).

The early elders of the Church were instructed: "Wherefore, be of good cheer, and do not fear, for I the Lord am with you, and will stand by you; and ye shall bear record of me, even Jesus Christ, that I am the Son of the living God, that I was, that I am, and that I am to come" (D&C 68:6). Answer after answer after divine answer concerning such matters as the divine sonship of Christ, His infinite and eternal atoning sacrifice, the principles of His eternal gospel—these things are made known with great power and persuasion. In addition, the revelations testify—that He will come again to reign among the Saints and to come down in judgment upon Idumea, or the world (see D&C 1:36); that He will gather His faithful as a mother hen and enable them to partake of the waters of life (see D&C 10:64–66; 29:2; 33:6); that Satan and the works of Babylon will be destroyed (see D&C 1:16; 19:3; 35:11; 133:14); that this dispensation of the gospel represents His last pruning of the vineyard (see D&C 24:19; 33:2–3; 39:17; 43:28); that the elect in the last days will hear His voice; they will not be asleep because they will be purified (see D&C 35:20–21); that we will have no laws but His laws when He comes; He will be our ruler (see D&C 38:22; 41:4; 58:22); that from the Lord's perspective, according to His reckoning, His coming is nigh (see D&C 63:53); He comes tomorrow (see D&C 64:24); He comes quickly, suddenly (see D&C 33:18; 35:27; 36:8; 39:24; 41:4; 68:35).

Mine is a certain witness as to the divine calling of the Prophet Joseph Smith and of the keys of authority that have continued in rightful apostolic succession to our own day. I know as I know that I live that The Church of Jesus Christ of Latter-day Saints is, in the language of the revelation, "the only true and living church upon the face of the whole earth" (D&C 1:30). Truly, "the keys of the kingdom of God are committed unto man on the earth, and from thence shall the gospel roll forth unto the ends of the earth, as the stone which is cut out of the mountain without hands shall roll forth, until it has filled the whole earth" (D&C 65:2).

That we will follow the Brethren, search the scriptures, pray mightily for discernment and for awareness and understanding of the signs of the times is my hope. That we will be wise, receive the truth, take the Holy Spirit for our guide, and thereby have our lamps filled (see D&C 45:56–57) is my prayer. "Wherefore, be faithful, praying always, having your lamps trimmed and burning, and oil with you, that you may be ready at the coming of the Bridegroom—for behold, verily, verily, I say unto you, that I come quickly" (D&C 33:17–18). In harmony with the soul cry of John the Revelator, we exclaim, "Even so, come, Lord Jesus" (Revelation 22:20).

NOTES

1. Joseph Smith, *Teachings of the Prophet Joseph Smith,* comp. Joseph Fielding Smith (Salt Lake City: Deseret Book, 1976), 101.
2. M. Russell Ballard, "When Shall These Things Be?" Brigham Young University devotional address, Provo, Utah, March 12, 1996, 2.
3. *Times and Seasons,* March 1, 1843, 113.
4. Orson Pratt, in *Journal of Discourses* (London: Latter-day Saints' Book Depot, 1854–86), 15:365–66.
5. *Millennial Star,* September 10, 1859, 582–83.
6. Joseph Smith, *Teachings,* 157.
7. Joseph Fielding Smith, *The Progress of Man* (Salt Lake City: Deseret Book, 1964), 481–82; see also Joseph Fielding Smith, *The Way to Perfection* (Salt Lake City: Deseret Book, 1970), 288–91.
8. Bruce R. McConkie, *The Millennial Messiah* (Salt Lake City: Deseret Book, 1982), 582, 584.
9. Bruce R. McConkie, *Doctrinal New Testament Commentary* (Salt Lake City: Deseret Book, 1974), 3:509.
10. Joseph Fielding Smith, *The Signs of the Times* (Salt Lake City: Deseret Book, 1942), 42.
11. Smith, *The Signs of the Times,* 41.
12. Joseph Smith, *Teachings,* 297, 301, 305.
13. Marion G. Romney, in Conference Report, October 1971, 69.
14. McConkie, *Millennial Messiah,* 241.
15. Joseph Smith, *Teachings,* 307.
16. McConkie, *Millennial Messiah,* 214–17, 325–26.
17. Joseph Smith, *History of the Church of Jesus Christ of Latter-day Saints,* ed. B. H. Roberts, 2nd ed. rev. (Salt Lake City: Deseret Book, 1972), 4:540.
18. Cited in Spencer J. Palmer, *The Expanding Church* (Salt Lake City: Deseret Book, 1978), 141–42.
19. Orson Pratt, in *Journal of Discourses,* 14:242–43; 16:325; 18:25.
20. McConkie, *Millennial Messiah,* 26–27, 405.
21. Boyd K. Packer, in Conference Report, October 1992, 102.
22. Harold B. Lee, in Conference Report, October 1972, 128.

23. Marion G. Romney, "A Glorious Promise," *Ensign,* January 1981, 2.

24. McConkie, *Millennial Messiah,* 635.

25. *Hymns of The Church of Jesus Christ of Latter-day Saints* (Salt Lake City: The Church of Jesus Christ of Latter-day Saints, 1985), no. 1.

26. Ezra Taft Benson, *A Witness and a Warning* (Salt Lake City: Deseret Book, 1988), 30–31.

CHAPTER SEVENTEEN

THE OATH AND COVENANT OF THE PRIESTHOOD (D&C 84)

S. BRENT FARLEY

"When we receive the Melchizedek Priesthood, we enter into a covenant with the Lord. It is the covenant of exaltation. . . . There neither is nor can be a covenant more wondrous and great."[1] Thus testified Elder Bruce R. McConkie of the Quorum of the Twelve Apostles.

The core of revelation focusing upon the oath and covenant of the priesthood is found in Doctrine and Covenants 84:33–48. This nucleus of information is rich with doctrine which, like the hub of a great wheel, is connected with and extends out to the circumference of the entire gospel. It is the purpose of this paper to examine that hub, or nucleus, in a verse-by-verse analysis so that we may achieve a greater and clearer understanding of this pivotal covenant that affects the eternities.

Doctrine and Covenants 84:33. "For whoso is faithful unto the obtaining these two priesthoods of which I have spoken, and the magnifying their calling, are sanctified by the Spirit unto the renewing of their bodies."

The two priesthoods are the Aaronic and Melchizedek, and *obtaining* means "to be ordained to." The key word that precedes *obtaining* is *faithful.* One must live so as to be judged worthy of receiving each of these priesthoods. President Joseph Fielding Smith explained that

---

S. Brent Farley is the manager of Church Educational System College Curriculum.

"the Aaronic Priesthood is a preparatory priesthood to qualify us to make the covenant and receive the oath that attends this higher priesthood."[2]

In the course of personal priesthood development, men are to magnify their callings. To what are they called? Alma repeatedly associates the word *called* or *calling* with the priesthood itself (as contrasted with particular priesthood assignments), teaching that men are "called by this holy calling, and ordained unto the high priesthood of the holy order of God" (Alma 13:6). The way to magnify that calling to priesthood authority is beautifully illustrated by the Lord as He explains why "there are many *called,* but few are chosen" (D&C 121:34; emphasis added). One who magnifies his calling to the priesthood will understand that "the rights of the priesthood are inseparably connected with the powers of heaven, and that the powers of heaven cannot be controlled nor handled only upon the principles of righteousness." He will know that "no power or influence can or ought to be maintained by virtue of the priesthood, only by persuasion, by long-suffering, by gentleness and meekness, and by love unfeigned; by kindness, and pure knowledge, which shall greatly enlarge the soul without hypocrisy, and without guile" (D&C 121:36, 41–42).

One whose service is characterized by those qualities is magnifying his calling to the priesthood, and he has the foundation for success for the varied priesthood tasks and offices he may hold throughout his life. He will also use these principles in his home, for, President Harold B. Lee stated, "The most important of the Lord's work that you will ever do will be the work you do within the walls of your own home. . . . God will never ask any man to sacrifice his family in order to carry out his other duties in the kingdom."[3]

What does it mean to magnify a calling? Elder McConkie explained: "Now, to magnify as here used means to enlarge or increase, to improve upon, to hold up to honor and dignity, to make the calling noble and respectable in the eyes of all men by performing the mission which appertains to the calling in an admirable and successful manner."[4]

Elder Carlos E. Asay of the Seventy listed ways that one magnifies a priesthood calling: "By learning one's duty and executing it fully (see D&C 107:99–100). By giving one's best effort in assigned fields of labor. By consecrating one's time, talents, and means to the Lord's work as called upon by our leaders and the whisperings of the Spirit. . . . By teaching and exemplifying truth."[5]

In referring to magnifying one's calling, President Marion G. Romney of the First Presidency said: "I am persuaded that it requires at least the following three things: 1. That we obtain a knowledge of the gospel. 2. That we comply in our personal living with the standards of the gospel. 3. That we give dedicated service."[6]

Faithful priesthood holders are "sanctified by the Spirit unto the renewing of their bodies" (D&C 84:33). To be sanctified is to be made clean through the power of the Holy Ghost and then to have its operative power giving guidance for life's activities. Such influence has a positive effect upon the body. *Renew* is defined as something that restores to a good state, rebuilds, repairs, confirms, revives, makes fresh and vigorous, transforms, implants holy affections, etc.[7] It is not necessarily that the body is visibly transformed (though this could be the case at times), but the positive effects of the Spirit support and invigorate physical and mental well-being. In connection with the oath and covenant of the priesthood, the renewal of the body refers to an eternal effect as well as a mortal one. Ultimately, the one who is faithful to the oath and covenant will have the body renewed in celestial glory in the Resurrection (see D&C 88:28–29).

Doctrine and Covenants 84:34. "They become the sons of Moses and of Aaron and the seed of Abraham, and the church and kingdom, and the elect of God."

Sonship denotes belonging to a family and having certain rights as a member and as an heir. We speak of becoming sons and daughters of Jesus Christ when we are converted, or born again, to the things of the Spirit. In this gospel conversion sense, becoming a son implies the acceptance of the person and principles of the one designated as the father. To become a son of Moses and Aaron, then, would imply accepting them and their principles so that we would have a relationship and as heirs, receive certain rights, including the rights of the priesthood.

Moses was called of God as the prophet to gather Israel, lead them from Egyptian bondage, and establish them as an independent and strong people (see Exodus 3:10–17). He was the prophet, the mouthpiece of the Lord to Israel; by following his inspired direction the people could obtain exaltation. Those who become sons of Moses today are those who accept the mouthpiece of the Lord who has been called to deliver modern Israel from the bondage of worldliness in order to become established as a strong and independent people and be led toward exaltation. They too participate in the gathering of Israel, the keys of which Moses committed to Joseph Smith and Oliver Cowdery in the latter-day restoration (see D&C 110:11).

The sons of Moses have a right to the holy priesthood, "which priesthood continueth in the church of God in all generations, and is without beginning of days or end of years" (D&C 84:17). Moses sought diligently to prepare his people for this right to be worthy of the presence of God through the authority, ordinances, and power of the priesthood (see D&C 84:19–23). The sons of Moses today hearken to the one called of God to guide them in their preparation to behold His presence.

Aaron was a spokesman for Moses and an assistant to him, Moses having the greater calling and Aaron the lesser. The lesser, or preparatory, priesthood was named after Aaron (see D&C 84:18, 26–27). The sons of Aaron today are those who accept the preparatory, or Aaronic, priesthood and live its principles, thus proving worthy of greater blessings as they enter the order of the Melchizedek Priesthood. They learn to accept all who are called as spokesmen (those other local and General Authorities who help accomplish the Lord's work) under the direction of the prophet. They are also willing themselves to serve as spokesmen in priesthood capacities when called to do so.

Thus, the sons of Moses and of Aaron today are faithful priesthood holders. In the course of their progress, they will become worthy temple recommend holders. They will "offer an acceptable offering and sacrifice in the house of the Lord" (D&C 84:31) by receiving their own temple endowment and performing work for the dead. "And the sons of Moses and of Aaron shall be filled with the glory of the Lord, upon Mount Zion in the Lord's house, whose sons are ye; and also many whom I have called and sent forth to build up my church" (D&C 84:32).

The mention of the temple is most significant, for it is through the ordinances of the Lord's house that we prepare to achieve the goal sought by Moses for his people: to enter the Lord's presence. Elder

McConkie noted that "the greatest blessings are reserved for those who obtain 'the fulness of the priesthood,' meaning the fullness of the blessings of the priesthood. These blessings are found only in the temples of God."[8] The oath and covenant of the priesthood includes all of the covenants made in the temple.

In similitude of the mission of Moses to gather Israel and establish them as a people, the Lord revealed a latter-day mission of the "sons of Moses": "Yea, the word of the Lord concerning his church, established in the last days for the restoration of his people, as he has spoken by the mouth of his prophets, and for the gathering of his saints" (D&C 84:2). The corollary between the mission of Moses in ancient Israel and the mission of the sons of Moses in modern Israel is not coincidental.

Doctrine and Covenants 84:34 specifies that "they become . . . the seed of Abraham." The literal house of Israel all descended from Abraham, but as Paul explained, "they are not all Israel, which are of Israel: Neither, because they are all children of Abraham, are they the seed. . . . But the children of the promise are counted for the seed" (JST Romans 9:6–8). In other words, faithfulness to the principles the patriarch taught (the gospel) determines heirship and acceptance— literal descent is not enough. Abraham became a model for all Saints, eventually achieving godhood (see D&C 132:37). The blessings of the gospel are often referred to in connection with the Abrahamic covenant, which is, as explained by Elder McConkie, "that Abraham and his seed (including those adopted into his family) shall have all of the blessings of the gospel, of the priesthood, and of eternal life,"[9] including eternal increase. The Lord revealed, "This promise is yours also, because ye are of Abraham," and said that we should "go . . . therefore, and do the works of Abraham" (D&C 132:31–32).

Elder McConkie noted that "what we say for Abraham, Isaac, and Jacob we say also for Sarah, Rebekah, and Rachel, the wives . . . who with them were true and faithful in all things,"[10] for, as President Joseph Fielding Smith taught, "the Lord offers to his daughters every spiritual gift and blessing that can be obtained by his sons."[11]

In order to enjoy the full blessings of the oath and covenant of the priesthood, a man must marry for time and eternity in the house of the Lord (see D&C 131:1–3). Elder McConkie explained that "this covenant, made when the priesthood is received, is renewed when the recipient enters the order of eternal marriage."[12] Further, "when he is married in the temple for time and for all eternity, each worthy member of the Church enters personally into the same covenant the Lord made with Abraham. This is the occasion when the promises of eternal increase are made, and it is then specified that those who keep the covenants made there shall be inheritors of all the blessings of Abraham, Isaac, and Jacob."[13]

Those taking the covenant of the priesthood are included in "the church and kingdom, . . . of God" (D&C 84:34). They are members of "the only true and living church upon the face of the whole earth" (D&C 1:30). Their king is the Savior, and the church and kingdom upon the earth is a type for the heavenly kingdom yet to be obtained.

Elder Harold B. Lee referred to "the church and kingdom of God" as "the church of the firstborn."[14] Not all members of The Church of Jesus Christ of Latter-day Saints are members of the Church of the Firstborn, however, for as Elder McConkie explained, "the Church of the Firstborn is made up of . . . those who are destined to be joint-heirs with Christ in receiving all that the Father hath."[15] Hence, that church membership includes those who are now proving or who will in the future prove themselves worthy of that exalted society.

Those upon earth who are living worthy of such future attainment are also called "the elect of God" (D&C 84:34). Elder McConkie defined these as "the portion of church members who are striving with all their hearts to keep the fulness of the gospel law in this life so that they can become inheritors of the fulness of gospel rewards in the life to come.

"As far as the male sex is concerned, they are the ones, the Lord says, who have the Melchizedek Priesthood conferred upon them and who thereafter magnify their callings and are sanctified by the Spirit."[16]

Those who receive the Lord's priesthood and His servants are accepting both the Lord and the Father who sent Him (see D&C 84:35–37), for the Father and Son are one in purpose and mission. Such unity was the Savior's desire when He prayed: "Holy Father, keep through thine own name those whom thou hast given me, that they may be one, as we are. . . . Father, I will that they also, whom thou hast given me, be with me where I am; that they may behold my glory, which thou hast given me" (John 17:11, 24). The oath and covenant of the priesthood is the means for the fulfillment of that prayer.

Doctrine and Covenants 84:38. "And he that receiveth my Father receiveth my Father's kingdom; therefore all that my Father hath shall be given unto him."

Herein is the fulfillment of heirship, "Wherefore, all things are theirs. . . . These shall dwell in the presence of God and his Christ forever and ever. . . . They who dwell in his presence are the church of the Firstborn; . . . and he makes them equal in power, and in might, and in dominion" (D&C 76:59, 62, 94–95).

Elder Asay said of this promise of heirship, "Few of us, I suppose, can comprehend all that this promise means. Even though we know that it includes eternal life, or the inheritance of exaltation, still it is so great and so wonderful that it defies proper explanation."[17] Of this the scripture testifies, "Eye hath not seen, nor ear heard, neither have entered into the heart of man, the things which God hath prepared for them that love him" (1 Corinthians 2:9).

Two key words mentioned in the oath and covenant serve as a foreshadowing of this great blessing of eternal life: *calling* (D&C 84:33) and *elect* (D&C 84:34). Elder McConkie testified that "brethren whose calling and election is made sure always hold the holy Melchizedek Priesthood. Without this delegation of power and authority they cannot be sealed up unto eternal life."[18] President Romney also gave witness that "we talk about making our callings and elections sure. The only way we can do this is to get the priesthood and magnify it."[19]

The Prophet Joseph Smith taught that "Abraham, Isaac, and Jacob had the promise of eternal life confirmed to them by an oath of the Lord, but that promise or oath was no assurance to them of their salvation. But they could, by walking in the footsteps and continuing in the faith of their fathers, obtain for themselves an oath for confirmation that they were meet to be partakers of the inheritance with the saints in light.

"If the saints in the days of the Apostles were privileged to take the saints for example and lay hold of the same promises and attain to the same exalted privileges of knowing that their names were written in the Lamb's book of life and that they were sealed there as a perpetual memorial before the face of the Most High, will not the same faith bring the same assurance of eternal life and that in the same manner to the children of men now in this age of the world?"[20]

Thus, those priesthood holders accounted as the seed of Abraham may receive the same blessings as their faithful forebears.

Doctrine and Covenants 84:39–40. "And this is according to the oath and covenant which belongeth to the priesthood. "Therefore, all those who receive the priesthood, receive this oath and covenant of my Father, which he cannot break, neither can it be moved."

Who makes the oath? What is the oath? Who makes the covenant, and what are the terms?

President Romney defined an oath as "a sworn attestation to the inviolability of the promises in the agreement."[21] President Joseph Fielding Smith explained that "to swear with an oath is the most solemn and binding form of speech known to the human tongue."[22] In the oath and covenant of the priesthood, it is the Father who makes the oath. Elder McConkie taught that the oath is "that everyone who keeps the covenant made in connection with the Melchizedek Priesthood shall inherit, receive, and possess all things in his everlasting kingdom, and shall be a joint-heir with that Lord who is his Only Begotten. . . . God swore with an oath that Christ would be exalted, and he swears anew, at the time each of us receives the Melchizedek Priesthood, that we will have a like exaltation if we are true and faithful in all things."[23] This oath is as eternal as the priesthood, and always accompanies it, signifying its validity in providing for the exaltation of God's faithful children.

President Romney explained that "a covenant is an agreement between two or more parties. . . . In the covenant of the priesthood the parties are the Father and the receiver of the priesthood."[24]

For the preparatory Aaronic Priesthood, Elder McConkie stated, "Those who receive the Aaronic Priesthood covenant and promise to magnify their callings, to serve in the ministry of the Master, to forsake the world, and to live as becometh Saints. In return, the Lord covenants and promises to enlarge the standing and station of all who keep their Aaronic covenant. He promises to give them the Melchizedek Priesthood, out of which eternal life comes. [The oath from God accompanies the Melchizedek Priesthood.] Those who receive the Melchizedek Priesthood covenant and promise, before

God and angels, to magnify their callings, to 'live by every word that proceedeth forth from the mouth of God' (D&C 84:44), to marry for time and all eternity in the patriarchal order, and to live and serve as the Lord Jesus did in his life and ministry."[25]

Elder Asay noted that God's covenant to faithful priesthood holders includes the following promises: "Promise 1: We Will Be Sanctified by the Spirit. . . . Promise 2: We Will Be Numbered with the Elect of God. . . . Promise 3: We Will Be Given All That God Has."[26] Elder McConkie explained that to be given all that God has includes exaltation and godhood and admittance to "his eternal patriarchal order, an order that prevails in the highest heaven of the celestial world, an order that assures its members of eternal increase, or in other words of spirit children in the resurrection. (See D&C 131:1–4)."[27]

Doctrine and Covenants 84:41. "But whoso breaketh this covenant after he hath received it, and altogether turneth therefrom, shall not have forgiveness of sins in this world nor in the world to come."

This is a solemn declaration. According to Elder McConkie, "this has never been interpreted by the Brethren to mean that those who forsake their priesthood duties, altogether turning therefrom, shall be sons of perdition; rather, the meaning seems to be that they shall be denied the exaltation that otherwise might have been theirs."[28]

President Joseph Fielding Smith explained that there is a chance to repent if a man has not altogether turned from the priesthood. If he does altogether turn from it, however, there is no forgiveness. "That does *not* mean that man is going to become a son of perdition, but the meaning is that *he will never again have the opportunity of exercising the priesthood and reaching exaltation.* That is where his forgiveness ends. He will not again have the priesthood conferred upon him, because he has trampled it under his feet; but as far as other things are concerned, he may be forgiven."[29]

Doctrine and Covenants 84:42. "And wo unto all those who come not unto this priesthood."

As the priesthood is the only source and channel through which exaltation may be obtained from the Lord, it follows that those who avoid it also avoid their only chance for eternal happiness in the celestial kingdom.

"And even I have given the heavenly hosts and mine angels

charge concerning you" (D&C 84:42). Worthy priesthood holders have the right to the ministering of angels (see D&C 13), which may come as direct visitations or as communications via the Holy Ghost, for "angels speak by the power of the Holy Ghost" (2 Nephi 32:3; see also 1 Nephi 17:45). Worthy priesthood holders also have the rights of fellowship and communion "with the general assembly and church of the Firstborn" (D&C 107:19), meaning those faithful members whose names "are written in heaven" (Hebrews 12:23), referring to Saints on both sides of the veil.

Doctrine and Covenants 84:43. "And I now give unto you a commandment to beware concerning yourselves, to give diligent heed to the words of eternal life."

This verse is a key verse within the oath and covenant of the priesthood. It leads one to an understanding of how to obtain the fulness of the oath and covenant of the priesthood.

Doctrine and Covenants 84:44. "For you shall live by every word that proceedeth forth from the mouth of God."

The words of eternal life have God as their source; how one receives these words is next explained in a chain of logic.

Doctrine and Covenants 84:45. "For the word of the Lord is truth, and whatsoever is truth is light, and whatsoever is light is Spirit, even the Spirit of Jesus Christ."

Doctrine and Covenants 84:46. "And the Spirit giveth light to every man that cometh into the world; and the Spirit enlighteneth every man through the world, that hearkeneth to the voice of the Spirit."

Elder McConkie explained that the Light of Christ "is the instrumentality and agency by which Deity keeps in touch and communes with all his children, both the righteous and the wicked. It has an edifying, enlightening, and uplifting influence on men. One of its manifestations is called conscience, through which all men know right from wrong.

"It is the means by which the Lord invites and entices all men to improve their lot and to come unto him and receive his gospel."[30]

Doctrine and Covenants 84:47. "And every one that hearkeneth to the voice of the Spirit cometh unto God, even the Father."

Elder McConkie explained: "By following the light of Christ, men are led to the gospel covenant, to the baptismal covenant, to the church and kingdom. There they receive the Holy Ghost."[31] Those who are sensitive to the Holy Ghost continue to learn the words of God and direct their lives according to His counsel. Faithful brethren are led by this process to the oath and covenant of the priesthood.

Doctrine and Covenants 84:48. "And the Father teacheth him of the covenant which he has renewed and confirmed upon you."

This is the apex, the grandest key in understanding the oath and covenant of the priesthood: a man who holds and honors the Melchizedek Priesthood will be taught of that holy covenant by revelation from God.

Elder McConkie testified: "This doctrine, this doctrine of the priesthood—unknown in the world and but little known even in the Church—cannot be learned out of the scriptures alone. It is not set forth in the sermons and teachings of the prophets and Apostles, except in small measure.

"The doctrine of the priesthood is known only by personal revelation. It comes, line upon line and precept upon precept, by the power of the Holy Ghost to those who love and serve God with all their heart, might, mind, and strength."[32]

In revealing the proper use of the priesthood, the Lord directed: "Let thy bowels also be full of charity towards all men, and to the household of faith, and let virtue garnish thy thoughts unceasingly; then shall thy confidence wax strong in the presence of God; *and the doctrine of the priesthood shall distil upon thy soul as the dews from heaven*" (D&C 121:45; emphasis added). By this means, one progresses within the oath and covenant of the priesthood.

Sufficient scriptural information is given to place a brother upon the pathway of exaltation, but the printed word in the standard works is not the culmination point. It is an aid in helping one to progress to the point where revelation is the key in magnifying a calling and in learning more about the oath and covenant of the priesthood. And one may progress through this medium to a certain point where he is considered to have received sufficient light and knowledge from God that to turn away would incur the awful penalty of no forgiveness (see D&C 84:41). This opens the very real possibility that some might indeed suffer the fate of sons of perdition, having progressed to such a degree in tutelage from God that to turn away then would condemn them to that eternal fate.

The concept of worthiness to be directed by God through personal revelation also relates to Joseph Smith's teaching regarding one's knowing that his calling and election is sure. Elder Romney testified: "To do this one must receive a divine witness that he will inherit eternal life."[33] Alma recorded a similar witness from God: "And whosoever doeth this, and keepeth the commandments of God from thenceforth, the same will remember that I say unto him, yea, he will remember that I have said unto him, he shall have eternal life, according to the testimony of the Holy Spirit, which testifieth in me" (Alma 7:16).

Another illustration is the following revelation to the Prophet Joseph Smith: "For I am the Lord thy God, and will be with thee even unto the end of the world, and through all eternity; for verily I seal upon you your exaltation, and prepare a throne for you in the kingdom of my Father, with Abraham your father" (D&C 132:49).[34] As the Lord confirmed the priesthood by His own voice out of the heavens to His servants (see D&C 84:42), so may He confirm the promise of eternal life, whether in this life or the next.

The fulfillment of that promise of eternal life is the grand purpose of the oath and covenant of the priesthood. Every worthy priesthood holder may qualify if he will keep the covenants of the priesthood. President Joseph Fielding Smith said, "It is perfectly clear that there are no more glorious promises that have or could be made than those that came to us when we accepted the privilege and assumed the responsibility of holding the holy priesthood and of standing as ministers of Christ."[35] Herein is brought to pass the noblest goal of existence, according to Moses 1:39, "For behold, this is my work and my glory—to bring to pass the immortality and eternal life of man."

NOTES

1. Bruce R. McConkie, *A New Witness for the Articles of Faith* (Salt Lake City: Deseret Book, 1985), 312–13.

2. Joseph Fielding Smith, in Conference Report, October 1970, 92.

3. Harold B. Lee, as cited in *Prepare Ye the Way of the Lord: Melchizedek Priesthood Study Guide, 1978–79* (Salt Lake City: The Church of Jesus Christ of Latter-day Saints, 1978), 127.

4. Bruce R. McConkie, *Mormon Doctrine,* 2nd ed. (Salt Lake City: Bookcraft, 1966), 481–82.

5. Carlos E. Asay, in Conference Report, October 1985, 57.

6. Marion G. Romney, in Conference Report, October 1980, 64.

7. See *American Dictionary of the English Language* (San Francisco: The Foundation for American Christian Education, 1985); s.v. "renew."

8. McConkie, *Mormon Doctrine,* 482.

9. McConkie, *New Witness,* 505.

10. Bruce R. McConkie, "Mothers in Israel and Daughters of Zion," *New Era,* May 1978, 37.

11. Joseph Fielding Smith, in Conference Report, April 1970, 59.

12. McConkie, *New Witness,* 313.

13. McConkie, *New Witness,* 508.

14. Harold B. Lee, in Conference Report, April 1950, 99.

15. McConkie, *Mormon Doctrine,* 139.

16. McConkie, *Mormon Doctrine,* 217.

17. Asay, in Conference Report, October 1985, 59.

18. Bruce R. McConkie, *The Promised Messiah* (Salt Lake City: Deseret Book, 1978), 587.

19. Romney, in Conference Report, April 1974, 115.

20. Joseph Smith, *The Personal Writings of Joseph Smith,* comp. Dean C. Jessee (Salt Lake City: Deseret Book, 1984), 300; spelling and punctuation standardized.

21. Romney, in Conference Report, April 1962, 17.

22. Smith, in Conference Report, October 1970, 92.

23. Bruce R. McConkie, in Conference Report, April 1982, 49.

24. Romney, in Conference Report, April 1962, 17.

25. McConkie, in Conference Report, April 1982, 49.

26. Asay, in Conference Report, October 1985, 58–59.

27. McConkie, in Conference Report, April 1982, 49.

28. McConkie, *New Witness,* 232.

29. Joseph Fielding Smith, *Doctrines of Salvation,* comp. Bruce R. McConkie (Salt Lake City: Bookcraft, 1954–56), 3:141–42.

30. McConkie, *New Witness,* 259.

31. McConkie, *New Witness,* 260.

32. McConkie, in Conference Report, April 1982, 47.

33. Marion G. Romney, in Conference Report, October 1965, 20.

34. Elder Bruce R. McConkie cited this as a classic example for our day of one who was sealed up unto eternal life (see *Doctrinal New Testament Commentary* [Salt Lake City: Bookcraft, 1981], 3:348).

35. Smith, in Conference Report, October 1970, 92.

CHAPTER EIGHTEEN

LIGHT, TRUTH, AND GRACE: THREE THEMES OF SALVATION (D&C 93)

RICHARD D. DRAPER

The revelation contained in section 93 of the Doctrine and Covenants was received May 6, 1833. The specific circumstances that generated it are obscure; the general conditions, however, are clear. During the few months before Joseph Smith received this informative masterpiece, the energy of the leaders of the Church was focused on making Kirtland, Ohio, a major stake of Zion. Since March 1833, efforts had been made to buy several farms for Church use.[1] These efforts had met with success, and some of the Saints had begun to settle on various pieces of land. During that same period Sidney Rigdon and Frederick G. Williams were ordained to the office of Presidents of the high priesthood, were given the keys of the kingdom, and became Joseph Smith's counselors.[2] President Williams was assigned to rent one of the pieces of property and to care for it for the benefit of the Church.[3]

At a meeting on May 4, these men presided. The meeting focused on how best to raise funds for a meetinghouse for the School of the Prophets.[4] Rented halls and homes had been used up to this point, but the Lord had instructed the Prophet that the time was right for the school to have its own house in which important instruction on both temporal and spiritual matters could be given. He emphasized

---

Richard D. Draper is a professor of ancient history at Brigham Young University and the managing director of publications at the Religious Studies Center.

individual worthiness to assure the success of the endeavor. Just two months before, the Lord had warned:

"Be admonished in all your high-mindedness and pride, for it bringeth a snare upon your souls.

"Set in order your houses; keep slothfulness and uncleanness far from you. . . .

"Search diligently, pray always, and be believing, and all things shall work together for your good, if ye walk uprightly and remember the covenant wherewith ye have covenanted one with another" (D&C 90:17–18, 24).

In this revelation we see concern expressed over pride and slothfulness, and admonitions given for the Saints to pray, to be believing, and to set their homes in order. The latter was needed even at the highest levels of Church leadership. Because this admonition was not followed immediately, circumstances arose that the revelation recorded in Doctrine and Covenants 93 addressed.

During the settling period, rather serious family problems had beset President Williams. Just what these were is unknown, but apparently he had discussed them with the Prophet. The revelation given on May 6, 1833, now recorded in section 93, identified the source of the troubles that were besetting President Williams: "You have not taught your children light and truth, according to the commandments; and that wicked one hath power, as yet, over you, and this is the cause of your affliction" (D&C 93:42). The revelation then instructed all the members of the First Presidency as well as the bishop of Kirtland, Newel K. Whitney, to set their houses in order. The revelation explained the value and necessity of doing so and in the process provided deeper understanding of certain aspects of salvation, among them light, truth, and grace. The purpose of this paper is to investigate the contribution this revelation makes to our understanding of the relationship of these concepts in the work of salvation.

"THE GLORY OF GOD IS INTELLIGENCE"

The Lord commanded President Williams to bring up his children in "light and truth" (D&C 93:42), having already elaborated on the importance of these two elements. In His elaboration the Lord explained, "The glory of God is intelligence, or, in other words, light and truth" (D&C 93:36). Observe that light and truth are shown to be constituent elements of intelligence, which constitutes the glory of God.

The concept of glory is very prominent in the scriptures, especially as something bestowed on the faithful as part of their final reward. But what is glory? A modern dictionary gives as definitions "fame, honor, distinction, and renown."[5] Over the centuries many Christian theologians, such as Milton, Johnson, and Thomas Aquinas, have felt that this was the sense of the scriptural use. Specifically, *glory* denoted appreciation or approval from God.[6] Thus, the glory of God was the favor and respect He granted those who met with His divine approbation.

The definition given in section 93 goes beyond such a definition, at least so far as the glory associated with God is concerned. His glory, as defined under inspiration, is something associated with His very nature, not just something He bestows upon others. Moses not only saw but also shared in the glory of God. The account in Moses 1:2 states, "And he saw God face to face, and he talked with him, and the glory of God was upon Moses; therefore Moses could endure his presence." There is no doubt that Moses was in the favor of God, but this revelation shows that God's glory was a capacitating agent that made it possible for Moses to bear God's actual presence. But that was not all. Through that power Moses was endowed with sufficient intellect to understand to a degree the nature of God's work. The Lord stated that He would show Moses the workmanship of His hands, "but not all, for my works are without end, and also my words, for they never cease." He then explained why He would not show Moses all His works: "No man can behold all my works," He said, "except he behold all my glory; and no man can behold all my glory, and afterwards remain in the flesh on the earth" (Moses 1:4–5). This scripture suggests that it is God's glory that gives Him the capacity to be all-seeing. Further, the ability to behold all that glory would require a change in the basic constitution of man that would make him more than mortal.

LIGHT AS AN ASPECT OF GLORY

A modern dictionary gives a secondary definition of *glory* as "a ring or spot of light";[7] glory is therefore associated with radiance. The dictionary gives one the feeling that such association is very limited; that, however, is not the case in a dictionary available to Joseph Smith. According to that dictionary, *glory* is first and foremost "brightness, luster, and splendor." Only in a secondary sense is it fame or praise. That dictionary notes that in a scriptural sense, glory is a manifestation of the presence of God.[8] This meaning accords much better with Joseph Smith's use of the term. For example, while recounting his First Vision he wrote, "I saw a pillar of light exactly over my head, above the brightness of the sun, which descended gradually until it fell upon me. . . . I saw two Personages, whose brightness and glory defy all description" (Joseph Smith—History 1:16–17). Writing of this experience on another occasion, he stated, "I was enwrapped in heavenly vision, and saw two glorious personages, who exactly resembled each other in features and likeness, surrounded with a brilliant light which eclipsed the sun at noon day."[9] In these passages, glory is directly associated with radiance. This association fits nicely with the idea expressed in Doctrine and Covenants 93 that light is a constituent part of glory.

To ancient Israel, one of the important aspects of God was His ability to display His power through the manifestation of burning light. Indeed, Israel stood in awe of the display of a brilliance like a devouring inferno on the top of Sinai (see Exodus 24:17). Moses proclaimed, "The Lord thy God is a consuming fire" (Deuteronomy 4:24). His presence was made manifest on more than one occasion by a pillar of fire, which gave light to Israel but vexed the Egyptians (see Exodus 13:21; 14:24). The cloud of His glory dwelt upon the tabernacle, while its radiance filled the court (see Exodus 40:34). The fact that this idea has continued into the present can be seen in the promise to the early Saints that "this generation shall not all pass away until an house shall be built unto the Lord, and a cloud shall rest upon it, which cloud shall be even the glory of the Lord, which shall fill the house" (D&C 84:5).

Like Moses, the Prophet Joseph Smith knew well the glory associated with the presence of the Lord. Of His appearance in the Kirtland Temple, the Prophet reported, "His eyes were as a flame of fire; . . . his countenance shone above the brightness of the sun" (D&C 110:3). We are told that when He comes the second time He will be "clothed in the brightness of his glory" (D&C 65:5). These are only a few of many references suggesting that light and radiance are important aspects of glory.

LIGHT AND THE PROCESS OF SALVATION

Radiance in the normative sense is related to light. But what is light? A careful look at the way the term is used in the scriptures suggests that it is more than mere luminosity. We get a glimpse of the breadth of meaning ascribed to the word when the Lord states, "The light which shineth, which giveth you light, is through him who enlighteneth your eyes, which is the same light that quickeneth your understandings" (D&C 88:11). This phrase defines *light* not only as something that makes vision possible but also as that force which activates and stimulates the intellect. Further, light "is in all things," gives "life to all things," and "is the law by which all things are governed" (D&C 88:13). Thus, a more full definition would make light an ever-present, life- and law-giving power that manifests itself, among other ways, as natural light, intellectual activity, and the living energy in all things. The scriptures declare that this "light proceedeth forth from the presence of God to fill the immensity of space" and that it is "the power of God who sitteth upon his throne, who is in the bosom of eternity, who is in the midst of all things" (D&C 88:12–13).

These scriptures suggest that the term *light* is used to describe that aspect of the nature of God which radiates out from Him, expanding with His work and will, enlightening, organizing, capacitating, and quickening as it does.

In sum, light is the ever-present, life- and law-giving, intellectually and spiritually quickening aspect of the power of God. Perhaps the best definition would be living and capacitating energy. Thus, a scripture states, "That which is of God is light; and he that receiveth light, and continueth in God, receiveth more light; and that light groweth brighter and brighter until the perfect day" (D&C 50:24). This scripture suggests that the continual reception of this living energy endows one with ability. Thus, the Lord states, "If your eye be single to my glory, your whole bodies shall be filled with light, and there shall be no darkness in you; and that body which is filled with light comprehendeth all things" (D&C 88:67). As we increase in light, we increase in ability until we are able to comprehend all things.

THE RELATIONSHIP BETWEEN LIGHT AND TRUTH

One is not, however, glorified in light, or as here defined, power or energy. Glorification is contingent upon the reception of glory's other all-important element. Section 93 teaches us, "He that keepeth [God's] commandments receiveth truth and light, until he is glorified *in truth* and knoweth all things" (D&C 93:28; emphasis added). The glorifying principle is truth. Defining truth,[10] the scripture states, "Truth is knowledge of things as they are, and as they were, and as they are to come" (D&C 93:24). In other words, truth is knowledge of what a Latter-day Saint hymn proclaims as "the sum of existence."[11] Truth defined in this way is always associated with light because truth can only be acquired through the power or the capacitating force of light. Without the faculty created by light, a fulness of truth could never be gained.

The acquisition of both light and truth is dependent on obedience. Explaining the need and the reason for obedience, the Lord stated, "You shall live by every word that proceedeth forth from the mouth of God" (D&C 84:44). The explanation is simple: obedience is requisite for eternal life. Again the Lord explains why: "For the word of the Lord is truth, and whatsoever is truth is light, and whatsoever is light is Spirit, even the Spirit of Jesus Christ" (D&C 84:45). The factors of life—light and truth—are equated with the Spirit of Christ, because He alone controls their dissemination through the bestowal of His Spirit. Therefore, He can stipulate the means by which they are granted. Thus, obedience to His will is absolutely requisite for those who would gain life.

According to Doctrine and Covenants 131:7–8, all spirit is matter. If this includes the Spirit of Christ, then its bestowal upon an individual would be an imparting of actual celestial substance—actual elements producing higher power, higher capacity, higher life. The result of its infusion would be spiritual and intellectual capacitation, which would allow the individual to progress to the point that He could enjoy eternal life.

But the capacitating force of light would have to precede the possession of this celestial substance. The scripture continues, "And the

Spirit giveth light to every man that cometh into the world; and the Spirit enlighteneth every man through the world, that hearkeneth to the voice of the Spirit. And every one that hearkeneth to the voice of the Spirit cometh unto God, even the Father" (D&C 84:46–47). Light, the capacitating power, and enlightenment, or truth, are received by acquisition of celestial element through the Spirit of Christ to those who obey the word. But first comes obedience to the word, then light, and finally truth.

Thus, all things—word, light, truth, Spirit—become one. They are inseparably welded together so man cannot be touched by one without being touched by all. Accordingly, the scripture states, "My voice is Spirit; my Spirit is truth; truth abideth and hath no end; and if it be in you it shall abound" (D&C 88:66). As noted already, that body which is filled with light—the power of God—can comprehend all things: truth.

For emphasis, let me say again that truth is the basis of glorification. Section 93 helps us understand why. In verse 30 we read, "All truth is independent in that sphere in which God has placed it, to act for itself, as all intelligence also; otherwise there is no existence." The very essence of existence is the ability of truth and intelligence to act for themselves. But how can truth, which has been defined earlier as knowledge, act? It would be more comprehensible if the scripture stated that truth impels or causes righteous action. But that is not what this verse states. And what does the scripture mean by "all truth"? Is there more than one kind of truth?

Understanding comes from the latter part of verse 30, which states that "all intelligence" is free to act for itself. As noted above, intelligence is equated with the glory of God—in other words, light and truth. But intelligence is also equated with a specific primal substance. Verse 29 of section 93 states, "Intelligence, or the light of truth, was not created or made, neither indeed can be."[12] Thus, intelligence has two scriptural definitions. One is an abstraction designated as "light and truth," conveying the idea of mental acuity by which existence is cognized. The other is more concrete. It designates the primal substance of being, which is called "the light of truth." The context of verse 30 suggests that intelligence should be understood in the latter sense. Thus, all intelligence, or the primal substance from which man is created, is free to act within the bounds in which God has placed it.

Intelligence, then, has two definitions. So may *truth.* The Lord says *all* truth is independent in the sphere in which He has placed it. If truth is the knowledge of the sum of existence, then *all truth* would seem to define existence itself.[13] Thus, all existence (or all things that exist—that is, truth) has a measure of independence in which it is free to act. Of this totality, that portion designated as intelligence and associated expressly with man is also free to act. Because it is a portion of the whole of reality, it is designated as the spirit part of truth.

In sum, "all intelligence," as I see it, identifies a component of the spirit aspect of existence. The phrase *all truth* defines the whole of that existence. The condition for glorification is cognition of that whole. Cognition comes only with obedience and the acquisition of light, which allows truth to follow as the capstone and seal. Thus, one is glorified in truth.

Note that God is the one who sets the bounds and conditions that make cognition possible. He has determined that man will be glorified only as he receives truth. But man can receive a fulness of truth only as he receives a fulness of light. Emphasizing this point are the verses that state: "Behold, here is the agency of man, and here is the condemnation of man; because that which was from the beginning [truth] is plainly manifest unto them, and they receive not the light [or capacitating power]. And every man whose spirit receiveth not the light is under condemnation" (D&C 93:31–32). Intelligence is free to choose or reject light. When it willfully rejects light, it is rejecting truth, and condemnation follows.

WHY MAN CAN RECEIVE LIGHT AND TRUTH

Section 93 explains why man is capable of receiving a fulness of light and truth. The Savior states, "I was in the beginning with the Father" (D&C 93:21); "I am the Spirit of truth, and John bore record of me, saying: He received a fulness of truth, yea, even of all truth" (D&C 93:26). Because Christ is of God (I take this to mean that He was the literal Son of God and so was of the genus of the Gods), He had the ability to do what the race of the Gods do, and that includes possessing all truth. One purpose of John's record, as preserved in section 93, was to bear testimony that this potential was indeed realized in the Lord.

But the Savior was not the only descendant of the Gods. He tells us that He was but the firstborn of many brethren (see Romans 8:29). Therefore, concerning mankind, He further explains, "Ye were also in the beginning with the Father; that which is Spirit, even the Spirit of truth" (D&C 93:23). Here we learn that as Christ was in the beginning with the Father, so too was man. Further, both man and Christ are the Spirit of truth. They are therefore of the same genus, their primal nature being identical. Accordingly, what the Savior was able to realize is likewise within the potential of man. This is emphasized in the verses that state, "Verily I say unto you, I was in the beginning with the Father, and am the Firstborn; and all those who are begotten through me are the partakers of the glory of the same, and are the church of the Firstborn" (D&C 93:21–22). We can receive glory, even the same glory as the Savior, because we are of the same origin and stock.

CHRIST AS THE SOURCE OF LIGHT AND TRUTH

But what is the process by which mortals receive the glory of Christ? The Savior has answered, "I am the way, the truth, and the life: no man cometh unto the Father, but by me" (John 14:6). Here He emphasizes that the only way is through Him, and He explains the reason, stating that He will appoint nothing unto man "except it be by law, even as I and my Father ordained unto you, before the world was." Going on, He states, "I am the Lord thy God; and I give unto you this commandment—that no man shall come unto the Father but by me or by my word, which is my law, saith the Lord" (D&C 132:11–12).

Here we see the central role that the word of Christ plays in the process of salvation. Man can only come to know God through the word of the Lord. But we have already seen that His word is equated with spirit, light, and truth. Therefore, the reception of the word is the reception of light and truth. The Savior's objective is to bring obedient souls to a fulness of glory. He knows how, for He followed the way set down by the Father. And if man receives glory, it will be in the same way through which Christ received it.

God's glory consists of a fulness of light and truth. Christ was glorified as He too came to possess a fulness of light and truth. It did not happen all at once. Section 93 states, "I, John, saw that he received not of the fulness at the first, but received grace for grace; and he received not of the fulness at first, but continued from grace to grace, until he received a fulness" (D&C 93:12–13).

THE ROLE OF GRACE

The role played by grace in the process through which the Lord received a fulness of the glory of the Father was twofold: He received grace for grace, and He went from grace to grace. But what does it mean to receive grace for grace and to go from grace to grace? The answer lies in the very nature of grace. The word denotes favor, kindness, and goodwill. Out of this comes the theological definition: "the free unmerited love and favor of God," which brings divine assistance to His chosen ones.[14] The key expressions here are love, favor, and unmerited assistance. To receive grace for grace is to receive assistance on the condition of giving assistance. But not just any kind of assistance can be given. What transforms assistance into grace is the kindness and favor felt by the giver and extended to the receiver when such service is totally unmerited. But grace does not have to be given without condition. Indeed, an important aspect of the word is reciprocity. The scripture states specifically that man receives "grace for grace" (D&C 93:20). Thus, the extension of favor is meant to obligate the recipient so that he will extend the same. As he meets this condition, more grace is extended to him, which further obligates him to greater assistance of others.

Apparently, it was necessary for the Lord to grow through this process. In order to do so, He first received grace, or divine assistance, from the Father. This grace He extended to His brethren. As He did so, He received even more grace. The process continued until He eventually received a fulness of the glory of the Father. The implication of this process is interesting: in a very real way, Christ Himself was saved by grace.

Such a concept sheds light on certain aspects of the Savior's teachings. "The Father hath not left me alone," He stated, "for I do always those things that please him" (John 8:29). Here He acknowledged the contingent relationship that existed between Him and His Father. He was totally dependent upon the Father for power and knowledge. By doing God's will, the Savior enjoyed communion with the Father, through which God gave grace to the Son. This association anchored the Savior's profound abilities to teach and to do. He insisted, "The Son can do nothing of himself," but "the Father that dwelleth in me, he doeth the works" (John 5:19; 14:10). Thus, the grace of God was, of necessity, upon the Son. But note that it was truly grace, for the Atonement did not effect the Father's salvation. Otherwise, any assistance God rendered could not be considered an act of grace but of necessity.

In a very real way, the Savior has the same relation to the Father as we have to Christ. He stated, "As the branch cannot bear fruit of itself, except it abide in the vine; no more can ye, except ye abide in me. I am the vine, ye are the branches: He that abideth in me, and I in him, the same bringeth forth much fruit: for without me ye can do nothing" (John 15:4–5).

These verses suggest another important aspect of grace, that of impartation. Whenever grace is extended, something is imparted. This imparting results in increased ability in the recipient. In the scriptures the reception of grace is expressed in two ways: a loss of the very propensity for sin and the accompanying ability to live God's laws. Paul taught this concept, saying, "What shall we say then? Shall we continue in sin, that grace may abound? God forbid. How shall we, that are dead to sin, live any longer therein? . . . For sin shall not have dominion over you: for ye are not under the law, but under grace" (Romans 6:1–2, 14).

The Savior Himself had to have power to live His Father's law. According to Joseph Smith, "None ever were perfect but Jesus; and why was He perfect? Because He was the Son of God, and had the fullness of the Spirit, and greater power than any man."[15] This power came through grace, even the grace of God.

Just what was imparted to Christ and, by inference, to man? Doctrine and Covenants 93 makes clear that it is light and truth. The possession of light and truth allows one to forsake the evil one and to be protected against his machinations. Further, light and truth enable their recipient to progress toward a fulness of the glory of God. This was the case with the Lord. Through His benevolence, He received grace. Additional powers of light and truth were continually being extended to Him such that He went from grace to grace. In other words, He went from one power level to another, from one capacity to a greater, until He received a fulness of the Father.

Receiving these life-giving principles of God allowed the Lord to become the spiritual Son of the Father.[16] John seems to have been communicating this idea when he stated, "And *thus* he was called the Son of God, because he received not of the fulness at the first" (D&C 93:14; emphasis added). The Father confirmed that sonship had been accomplished when He stated, "This is my beloved Son" (D&C 93:15). The fulness of sonship was contingent upon receiving the fulness of grace or, in other words, light and truth. The Savior did receive this fulness, and John testified, "He received a fulness of the glory of the Father; and he received all power, both in heaven and on earth, and the glory of the Father was with him, for he dwelt in him" (D&C 93:16–17).

Thus, section 93 is clear about the way the Savior gained the glory of the Father. Since He is the way, the course He pursued must be the way all must follow. Section 93 is emphatic that this is the case. The Savior states, "I give unto you these sayings that you may understand, . . . that you may come unto the Father in my name, and in due time receive of his fulness. For if you keep my commandments you shall receive of his fulness, and be glorified in me as I am in the Father; therefore, I say unto you, you shall receive grace for grace" (D&C 93:19–20).

Expressing the same thought, the Prophet Joseph Smith stated, "You have got to learn how to be Gods yourselves, and to be kings and priests to God, the same as all Gods have done before you, namely, by going from one small degree to another, and from a small capacity to a great one; from grace to grace, from exaltation to exaltation, until you attain to the resurrection of the dead, and are able to dwell in everlasting burnings, and to sit in glory, as do those who sit enthroned in everlasting power."[17]

CONCLUSION

An essential part of the glory of God is light, or living, life-giving energy. Light is a capacitating power through which man is given the faculty to receive truth. Possession of truth is the condition that must be met for glorification. A fulness of truth, or the knowledge of the sum of existence, requires the acquisition of the fulness of light. The grace of God plays a direct part in the reception of light and truth. Grace expresses itself through impartation. That which is imparted is light. The agency of man is expressed in choosing or rejecting light. But he is not free to choose or reject God's initial endowment of grace. Grace comes to all men freely, as it is the unmerited favor that God holds for all His children. Grace allows light to flow unto man. Thus, light, through grace, is freely manifest unto man. When we reject light, we reject God's favor and cut ourselves off from truth. Thus, we stand under condemnation. When we accept grace by choosing light, we are capacitated to receive truth. As we continue from grace to grace by giving grace for grace, we receive more light and truth until we are eventually glorified in truth.

NOTES

1. Joseph Smith, *History of the Church of Jesus Christ of Latter-day Saints,* ed. B. H. Roberts (Salt Lake City: The Church of Jesus Christ of Latter-day Saints, 1932–51), 1:335.

2. Smith, *History of the Church,* 334.

3. Smith, *History of the Church,* 336.

4. Smith, *History of the Church,* 342–43.

5. *Webster's New Collegiate Dictionary,* s.v. "glory."

6. C. S. Lewis, *The Weight of Glory* (Grand Rapids, Michigan: William B. Eerdmans, 1949), 8–9.

7. *Webster's New Collegiate Dictionary,* s.v. "glory."

8. Noah Webster, *American Dictionary of the English Language,* 3rd ed. of the reprint of the 1829 ed. (San Francisco: Foundation of American Christian Education, 1983), s.v. "glory."

9. Smith, *History of the Church,* 4:536.

10. *American Dictionary,* in standard use during Joseph Smith's lifetime, defines *truth* as "conformity to fact or reality; exact accordance with that which is, or has been, or shall be" (s.v. "truth").

11. John Jaques, "Oh Say, What Is Truth?" *Hymns* (Salt Lake City: The Church of Jesus Christ of Latter-day Saints, 1985), no. 272.

12. The Prophet Joseph Smith elaborated on this thought, stating, "Intelligence is eternal and exists upon a self-existent principle. It is a spirit from age to age, and there is no creation about it" (*Teachings of the Prophet Joseph Smith,* comp. Joseph Fielding Smith [Salt Lake City: Deseret Book, 1939], 354). B. H. Roberts believed this referred to the primal substance from which man's spirit was organized (see Smith, *Teachings,* 354 n. 9; see also 158 n. 5).

13. This is the definition in "Oh Say, What Is Truth?" (*Hymns,* no. 272).

This hymn, as a piece of poetry, was once a part of the Pearl of Great Price. It was set to music and placed in the Latter-day Saint hymnal.

14. *American Dictionary*, s.v. "grace."

15. Smith, *Teachings*, 187–88.

16. The Savior was already the spirit Son of God. He was also the physical Son. But it was the reception of the divine attributes of light and truth by which He was glorified and gained eternal life. Accordingly, He became the spiritual or eternal Son of God when He received of the fulness of the Father.

17. Smith, *Teachings*, 346–47.

CHAPTER NINETEEN

Zion's Camp: A Study in Obedience, Then and Now

DAVID F. BOONE

The first Latter-day Saints to arrive in Independence, Jackson County, Missouri, were the missionaries to the Lamanites, arriving probably in late January 1831. In July 1831 Church leaders visited Jackson County, Missouri, and the Lord identified Independence as the center place of Zion (see D&C 57), suggesting a spot of great historical significance and one of future Church importance. Within weeks, several groups were called to Independence to settle the region, including the Colesville Branch of Latter-day Saints from New York, who arrived in the latter part of July 1831, and other converts from New York and Kirtland, Ohio. Within the next two years, hundreds of Latter-day Saints likewise settled in Independence, Missouri, eager, it seems, to harvest blessings by virtue of being in an area rich in spiritual heritage.

All did not go well for the settlers, however. As time passed, boastful and overzealous colonizers tended to anger the old settlers with unnecessary claims that the land had been given to Latter-day Saints through divine favor and that others would be removed by force, if necessary, to fulfill the Lord's promises for the region. The old settlers resisted and resorted to a show of force in an unsuccessful effort to intimidate the Mormons. When they did not respond to the satisfaction of the Jackson County Missourians, mob violence erupted in

---

David F. Boone is an associate professor of Church history and doctrine at Brigham Young University.

1833, and by November the Latter-day Saints were forcibly removed from their homes and lands.

The Need for Zion's Camp

The violent expulsion of Latter-day Saints from their homes and lands in Jackson County, Missouri, precipitated the need for specific action. The action that ultimately came was a force of Saints organized militarily but for the most part without formal experience; that group is referred to in Church history as Zion's Camp. Mobs, bent on brutality and destruction despite the organization of Zion's Camp, publicized their intent to drive all Latter-day Saints beyond the Missouri borders.

Church leaders in Kirtland, specifically the Prophet Joseph Smith, sought assistance from the courts, from the Missouri governor, from the president of the United States, and from other parties whose sympathies may have favored the Mormon position. By mid-December, the Prophet Joseph had received a revelation (D&C 101) that outlined the reasons why the Lord had allowed the Saints to be expelled from their homes and lands, a timetable for what must be done before they could redeem their personal property, and specific instructions for the Saints to rectify the situation. An important part of this revelation was a parable depicting the plight of the Missouri Saints. Referred to since as the parable of the nobleman (see D&C 101:43–64), the parable described specifically the literal and ultimate redemption of the Latter-day Saints to their homes and property.

Sidney B. Sperry's insights into the meaning of the parable are valuable. In his Compendium he noted: "It would seem that the parable is to be interpreted in this way: the nobleman is the Lord, whose choice land in His vineyard is Zion in Missouri. The places where the Saints live in Zion are the olive trees. The servants are the Latter-day Saint settlers, and the watchmen are their officers in the Church. While yet building in Zion, they become at variance with each other and do not build the tower or Temple whose site had been dedicated as early as 3 August 1831. Had they built it as directed, it would have been a spiritual refuge for them, for from it the Lord's watchmen could have seen by revelation the movements of the enemy from afar. This foreknowledge would have saved them and their hard work when the enemy made his assault.

"But the Saints in Missouri were slothful, lax, and asleep. The enemy came, and the Missouri persecutions were the result. The Lord's people were scattered and much of their labors wasted. The Almighty rebuked His people, but He commanded one of His servants (vs. 55), Joseph Smith (103:21), to gather the 'strength of mine house' and rescue His lands and possessions gathered against them.

"Subsequently, the Prophet and his brethren in the famous Zion's Camp did go to Missouri in 1834 in an attempt to carry out the terms of the parable. Before they went, additional revelation was received (see 103:21–28) concerning the redemption of Zion. The brethren were instructed to try to buy land in Missouri, not to use force; and if the enemy came against them, they were to bring a curse upon them. Zion was not redeemed at that time, but we may look for it in the not-too-distant future. Verily, it will be redeemed when the Lord wills it."[1]

Although given as instruction to the Church, the revelation was published and distributed to others, including Missouri governor Daniel Dunklin. A part of the revelation carried a promise of armed redemption from Church leaders and members in Kirtland, Ohio, to the exiled Jackson County Saints: "And the lord of the vineyard said unto one of his servants: Go and gather together the residue of my servants, and take all the strength of mine house, which are my warriors, my young men, and they that are of middle age also among all my servants, who are the strength of mine house, save those only whom I have appointed to tarry;

"And go ye straightway unto the land of my vineyard, and redeem my vineyard; for it is mine; I have bought it with money.

"Therefore, get ye straightway unto my land; break down the walls of mine enemies; throw down their tower, and scatter their watchmen" (D&C 101:55–57).

By mid-December, the Prophet Joseph responded to Church members' concerns by saying that "he was going to Zion, to assist in redeeming it." He called for a sustaining vote of the council in Kirtland to support his decision, which was given; and in response to his request for volunteers to assist him, thirty or forty of the men of the council agreed to go.[2]

Later that same day, the Lord revealed to the Prophet Joseph specific instructions relating to the formation and execution of the march to be taken by Zion's Camp (see D&C 103). This revelation provided the Prophet and the Church with such detailed information as the number of participants the Lord expected (see D&C 103:30–34), the demographic makeup of the expedition (see D&C 103:21–22), how the group was to be financed (see D&C 103:23), how the force was to be organized (see D&C 103:30–31), and who its principal leaders were to be (see D&C 103:35–40).

Initially, Zion's Camp was intended to protect the rights of the Latter-day Saints after the state militia made possible the return of the exiles to their confiscated homes and other property. Before the Saints could complete their recruiting, financing, and purchasing of supplies for the camp, however, the Missouri governor reconsidered involving the state militia in the operation. Governor Dunklin, who in November 1833 had suggested such a military organization on the part of the Church, waffled because of public outcry. Dunklin ultimately withdrew his support for involving any state military force.

Meanwhile, the Saints' preparations continued, and Mormon recruits departed from Kirtland in the main body of Zion's Camp on May 5, 1834. The leaders of Zion's Camp did not learn that Governor Dunklin had reversed his position until the expedition was underway. Upon his arrival at the Mississippi River, Elder Parley P. Pratt recalled: "We had an interview with the Governor, who readily acknowledged the justice of the demand, but frankly told us he dare not attempt the execution of the laws in that respect, for fear of deluging the whole country in civil war and bloodshed. He advised us to relinquish our rights, for the sake of peace, and to sell our lands from which we had been driven."[3]

As well intentioned as the governor may have been in this affair, it is apparent that he did not understand the position of the Latter-day Saints. Had Jackson County not been designated as the center place of Zion and the gathering place for the Saints, it would have been less of a sacrifice for the Saints to leave; in fact, the Saints would likely not have settled there to start with. But the Lord had so declared and the Saints had been obedient to settle the region in 1831 and to buy the land, which gave them legal right to their property. That was all according to instruction from the Lord to the earliest Saints who settled in the area of Independence, Jackson County, Missouri: "But unto him that keepeth my commandments I will give the mysteries of my kingdom, and the same shall be in him a well of living water, springing up unto everlasting life. And now, behold, this is the will of the Lord your God concerning his saints, that they should assemble themselves together unto the land of Zion, not in haste, lest there should be confusion, which bringeth pestilence" (D&C 63:23–24).

The protection of the state militia was necessary to enforce the return of the exiled Saints to their homes in Missouri; without it, the Church paramilitary force could not ensure their safety. The politically expedient change in the governor's position had to do with the Missourians' intense feelings against the Saints. Their united bitterness exacerbated the situation, for many in the state's militia were also antagonists in the Mormon relocation question. Without the support of the state's chief executive or the militia he commanded, there was little left for the Church leaders and Zion's Camp participants to do except disband and return to their homes. They did not do so, however, until the Prophet received a revelation (D&C 105) on June 22, 1834, that the Lord accepted the sacrifice of the Saints and deferred the redemption of Zion to a later date. The disbanding of the camp came on June 25, less than six months after hostilities necessitated its creation and after a march of eight hundred to a thousand miles from Kirtland to Clay County. The camp members' hardships were severe. Hunger, thirst, unseasonable cold, disease, milk sickness, and inadequate dress combined to create suffering.

CONTRIBUTIONS OF ZION'S CAMP

Because Zion's Camp was dissolved before achieving its expressed objectives, the whole mission has been labeled a failure by many authors from 1834 to the present. Nonetheless, the expedition made numerous lasting contributions to the Church. The following are but some of those contributions.

Doctrines and teachings. A great deal of official Church doctrine came as a result of the instructions the Lord gave for the organization of Zion's Camp. Doctrine and Covenants 101, 103, and 105 are replete with insights on such doctrinal themes as obedience, patience, testing, trust in the Lord, sacrifice, mankind's dependence upon the Lord, God's intervention in mankind's dealings, signs of the Second Coming of the Lord, millennial conditions on the earth, the judgments of God upon the earth, continuing instructions concerning the establishment of Zion, characteristics of a Zion people, and the divine involvement in the establishment of the United States Constitution. Numerous other instructions were also given, including revelation to assist with the challenges facing the Latter-day Saints in Missouri. All of this comforted, encouraged, and brought hope to the hearts of Latter-day Saints who desired to learn from their experiences.

Obedience and sacrifice. Although perhaps not fully recognized as such by its participants, one purpose of Zion's Camp was to determine who would be obedient to the Lord's counsel. Obedience often includes sacrifice, and sacrifice is not divinely recognized without obedience to eternal laws. (Saul learned from the Lord that obedience is far better than sacrifice; see 1 Samuel 15:22). The experience of traveling to Missouri was a test for each of the camp's participants. Many failed a part of the test through willful disobedience; in other words, they did not realize all that was potentially theirs if they had been obedient. Although some failed because of their attitude and unwillingness to be taught, the only real losers were those who refused to go when called to serve. If there was failure in Zion's Camp, it was attributable in part to lack of support from Church members. Elder B. H. Roberts wrote, "Had the Saints in the eastern branches had more faith—faith to send up to Zion more men and more money with which to strengthen the hands of the Saints . . . the history of Zion's Camp might have been different."[4]

Additional Church members were needed, but some had good reasons to stay behind. Dennis Lake and Albert Miner drew straws to determine who would go to Missouri and who would stay home to care for both of their families. Lake went with Zion's Camp. When he returned, disenchanted with the experience, he apostatized. Apparently he was so bitter that he later sued the Prophet for sixty dollars, the value of the three months' work that he had missed. Elder Brigham Young was unable to pacify Lake, but as a part of his official assignment, he told Brother Miner, "he would receive his blessings" as a result of his staying home and doing his part. That greatly satisfied Brother Miner.[5]

It appears that from the outset some participants understood the higher principles that brought them together. Others went simply because they were asked to go. Nonetheless, those individuals went, whereas others elected not to.

Brother Nathan Bennett Baldwin's journal entry revealed a higher law for participation. He spoke of consecrating that which he owned to the service of the Lord, as did others.[6] Levi Hancock wrote, "Our money was then thrown together."[7] The law of consecration was first revealed to the Church in February 1831 (see D&C 42:3034), only three years before the calling of Zion's Camp. Furthermore, some areas of the Church in Ohio and in Missouri practiced this law. It is interesting, therefore, to note the references to individual participation as a result of obedience to that particular law.

Some men gave reasons why they could not go. But when the Prophet chided one man, "Now that you have a wife, don't say you can't go," the man responded: "I said my wife shan't hinder me and went and bought me a rifle and sword. I armed myself for battle." His wife's support continued during his absence. He wrote later: "My wife had managed to get along with the baby without running me in debt. Some had to pay many dollars for their wives debts. I felt thankful for this and loved her dearly."[8]

A more significant contribution is a principle usually overlooked about these individuals who accompanied the Prophet: all the individuals went with the realization that their lives could be forfeited for the gospel cause. Despite the potential for loss, they were nevertheless obedient to the call.

On May 4, 1834, the Prophet spoke in Kirtland to the assembled Saints, many of whom would shortly become members of Zion's Camp. "He impressed upon them the necessity of being humble, exercising faith and patience and living in obedience to the commands of the Almighty, and not murmur at the dispensations of Providence. He bore testimony of the truth of the work which God had revealed through him and promised the brethren that if they all would live as they should, before the Lord, keeping His commandments, and not, like the children of Israel murmur against the Lord and His servants, they should all safely return and not one of them should fall upon the mission they were about to undertake, for if they were united and exercised faith, God would deliver them out of the hands of their enemies, but should they, like the children of Israel, forget God and His promises and treat lightly His commandments, He would visit them in His wrath, and vex them in his sore displeasure."[9]

True to the Prophet's promise to the Saints, the Lord did protect them, usually in ways that they could not comprehend. One of the best examples of divine intervention came in mid-June on the banks of the Big and Little Fishing Rivers. The camp had been under constant threat of attack from Missourians who had assembled to destroy the Mormon marchers. On the morning of Thursday, June 19, an agitated African-American woman warned Luke Johnson that a large company was planning to destroy the Mormon camp. A farmer confirmed the report later that day. The camp hastily moved forward, believing that they could receive assistance from Latter-day Saints in Clay County, Missouri, but several incidents hindered their progress: a wagon broke down and had to be repaired before the camp could proceed, and the wheels ran off at least two others. None of the delays was particularly significant in itself, but combined, they hampered progress significantly.

Zion's Camp was forced to stop "on an elevated piece of land between the forks of the Big and Little Fishing Rivers." While the main group pitched their tents, five members of the mob rode across the river and threatened the Saints that they would "see hell before morning."[10] Shortly thereafter it began raining. It rained in torrents throughout the night, "the thunder and lightning exceeded all description."[11] Heber C. Kimball related that there was continual lightning throughout the night, bright enough to see to pick up a pin. Another account suggests that small hail fell in the camp;[12] many others indicate that hail the size of eggs fell only outside camp. Many of the brethren took refuge in a local church house, but others remained in their tents. Their enemies hid under wagons. One of the mob was reportedly killed by lightning, and another's hand was torn off by a fractious horse frightened by the storm.[13] Tree limbs as large as four inches in diameter were torn from trees. The storm disorganized the Missourians, which curtailed their achieving their destructive objectives. They left, having failed in their intent to destroy Zion's Camp.

Many of the camp members perceived the terrible storm to be providential intervention. Nathan B. Baldwin recorded: "The Lord had previously said He would fight the battles of His Saints; and it seemed as though the mandate of heaven had gone forth from his presence to apply the artillery of heaven in defense of his servants. Some small hail fell in the camp but from a half mile to one mile around, we were told by inhabitants that the hail stones were as big as tumblers; and the appearance of their destructiveness showed that their size was not overestimated. Limbs of trees were broken off, fence rails were marred and splintered, and the growing corn was cut down into shreds. But the casualties were all on the side of our enemies."[14]

Elder George A. Smith further declared: "I have ever felt thankful to my Heavenly Father that He by this storm and sudden rise of the streams prevented our having a bloody conflict with our enemies, who were thereby prevented from attacking us." The stream rose to a depth of between thirty and forty feet. After leaving camp and seeing the destruction caused by the severe hailstorm, the brethren once again prayerfully expressed gratitude for their divine preservation.[15]

Like the children of Israel, members of Zion's Camp were sobered by the experience and repentant, and they did better for a time. But, like the Nephites, they regressed from sincere repentance and the blessing of improved conditions to murmuring and complaining, again to be rebuked and chastened by the Lord until they returned to a more humble, teachable condition. Neither was the value of their experience lost on those who intended to destroy the Saints after the rise of the river. Wilford Woodruff reported that the captain of the mob noted how strange it was that nothing could be done against the Mormons but that some calamity prevented them from being successful. Elder Woodruff editorialized, "But they did not feel disposed to acknowledge that God was fighting our battles."[16]

Others, however, did make such an acknowledgment: "They [the mob] declared that if that was the way God fought for the Mormons, they [themselves] might as well go about their business."[17] Colonel Sconce, a militia leader, also remarked, "I see that there is an Almighty power that protects this people, for I started from Richmond, Ray county, with a company of armed men, having a fixed determination to destroy you, but was kept back by the storm."[18]

The Saints learned again that the chastening hand of God is a great blessing to His people. With the numbers of the assembled mob and the comparative weakness of the camp, little but divine intervention could have kept the mob from destroying the Saints.

Despite these warnings to the Saints, many participants failed to follow the Prophet's advice. Repeatedly through the Zion's Camp march, the Prophet had to warn, exhort, reprimand, and encourage the participants to greater faithfulness. He reminded them of their duty; he encouraged their obedience; and he chastised them for their laxness in keeping the commandments. Through it all, many listened and as a result believed, and their view of spiritual things expanded. Others picked up a few truths and were better for their effort but did not live up to their potential. And still others, like Brother Dennis Lake, felt their time was wasted and even heaped future indignation upon themselves by creating dissension within the Church and apostatizing.

Some Church members apostatized because the Prophet instructed the Camp of Israel to take up arms. "They did not believe it right to arm themselves, or fight in self defense."[19] Luke Johnson, on the other hand, though he believed it wrong to take up arms, nevertheless was obedient and followed the Prophet. He recorded: "May 1st 1834 I started with some of the brethren for Missouri for the 1st time [in my life] that I had consented to take firearms to go into the field of battle."[20]

Some camp members complained about the lack of bread at mealtime,[21] about the butter, the meat, the horses or the lack of them, about the company they were forced to keep, and about almost every other imaginable problem. Others endured every privation, every setback, every challenge and opportunity with self-respect and fortitude.

Through it all, the Prophet was reassuring, correcting, and pacifying many of the men. On Saturday, May 17, the Prophet warned that "they would meet with misfortunes, difficulties and hindrances as the certain result of giving way to such a [rebellious and contentious] spirit and said, 'you will know it before you leave this place.' He exhorted them to humble themselves before the Lord and become united, that they might not be scourged."[22]

When the camp awakened the next morning, they discovered that almost every horse in the camp was foundered, a debilitating condition often caused by overfeeding. The condition hindered movement by the animal, but movement was essential to the animal's survival.

When the Prophet Joseph realized the condition of their horses, he said to the men "that for a witness that God overruled and had His eye upon them, all those who would humble themselves before the Lord, should know that the hand of God was in this misfortune, and their horses should be restored to health immediately."[23] Most of the men complied, and "by noon the same day, the horses were as nimble as ever." One man who had a "rebellious spirit" and would not be humbled found his horse dead soon afterward. Such experiences for the camp were numerous and poignant, teaching the brethren their duty and responsibility to the Lord.[24]

Within days of the experience on the Fishing Rivers, another example of divine protection unfolded but once again neither its severity nor its final result could have been anticipated. Partially as a result of disobedience, contention, and murmurings within the camp and partially because of the further need for protection from the mobs, the Camp of Israel was smitten with the dreaded cholera. Cholera is a gastrointestinal disorder that causes severe cramping, vomiting, and a weakening of the victim because of the inability to keep down or process nutrients. Hyrum Smith indicated that "it seized [us] like the talons of a hawk."[25]

Joseph Bates Noble was stricken but lived to share the following description of his painful ordeal: "I there was violently seized with the Cholera, vomiting and purging powerfully, then cramping from head to foot in the most powerful manner, with a burning fever in my bowels. In this situation I lay forty hours, my voice and my hearing had nearly left me. While in this situation, Bros. Brigham Young, [and others] . . . prayed for me. . . . While praying in this situation the veil became very thin between me and my God and I noticed things that I never before thought of. Such was the blessing of God upon me that I nearly had an open vision. Through the faith of my brethren that was exercised for me, I got up and with their assistance put on my clothes. . . . Never had I experienced such manifestations of the blessings of God as at this time."[26]

Cholera struck quickly. George A. Smith recorded that "many of the brethren were violently attacked . . . some falling to the ground while they were on guard."[27] The disease spread quickly in the unsanitary conditions and, not uncommonly, by and to those who cared for those already infected. The numbers reported of casualties from the disease in Zion's Camp vary. Most sources suggest thirteen or fourteen; one indicates that as many as twenty died from the disease. Burial was quick because of the rapid decomposition of the bodies and the potential for the further spread of the dreaded and highly contagious disease. Many wrote of this incident, regretting that they couldn't do more for their fallen comrades. Joseph Bates Noble, who had been caring for his dear friend, Elbur Wilcox, lamented: "Never in my life did I feel to mourn like as on this occasion. I was sensible that a strong chord of friendship bound us together, but I did not know that our hearts were so completely knit together as they were."[28] Heber C. Kimball wrote, "We felt to sit and weep over our brethren, and so great was our sorrow that we could have washed them with our tears."[29]

Three weeks earlier, the Prophet had warned the camp of repercussions from their disobedience: "The Lord had revealed to me that a scourge would come upon the camp in consequence of the fractious and unruly spirits that appeared among them, and they should die like sheep with the rot."[30] He further said that "the scourge must come; repentance and humility may mitigate the chastisement, but cannot altogether arrest it."[31]

One bright spot in an otherwise dismal situation was that the mob's fear of the sickness kept them at bay. Elder Heber C. Kimball noted: "This was our situation, the enemies around us, and the destroyer in our midst."[32] Six months later, in conversation with some of the veterans of the march, the Prophet Joseph indicated he had received a vision of those who had given their lives as a part of Zion's Camp. "I have seen those men who died of the cholera in our camp; and the Lord knows, if I get a mansion as bright as theirs, I ask no more." As the Prophet shared this experience, he wept and was unable to speak for some time.[33]

MISSIONARY LABORS

Another aspect of Zion's Camp has long been neglected and usually completely omitted: the missionary efforts of Zion's Camp participants. Missionary work has been characterized as the lifeblood of the Church. Rarely will you find assembled Latter-day Saints who are not affecting the lives of others, either as examples of Christlike living or in active proselyting efforts. Zion's Camp was no exception. Three brief examples will suffice, although others are available.

The old wagon road that Zion's Camp was to travel through Missouri passed immediately by the three-hundred-twenty-acre farm of William Adams Hickman, approximately eleven miles east of Huntsville, Missouri, near present-day Missouri State Highway 24. Hickman was a prosperous young farmer, only about twenty years old. He and his wife, Bernetta, noted the approach of Zion's Camp with interest. Although there was an air of secrecy surrounding the advancing company, it was extremely difficult to hide the identity of such a large contingent of fighting men. Hickman and his wife knew the camp's identity and were hospitable to the weary marchers when they arrived.

Bernetta's brother, Greenlief Burchardt, also knew who they were, but he was antagonistic and even hostile toward the camp. Apparently the differences of opinion between the two men were expressed, and in the passion of the moment, William Hickman challenged his brother-in-law Greenlief to a fistfight in defense of his right to entertain the Mormons on his farm. There is no evidence that the fight ever took place, but there is reason to believe that William and Bernetta treated the Mormon marchers kindly. Sources suggest that the Hickmans invited some of the marchers into their home for dinner, and evidence shows that the Mormons received fresh water, a scarce commodity, from their benefactors' well.

Undoubtedly as a result of this early introduction and apparently strengthened by the defense of the members of Zion's Camp, William Adams Hickman, Bernetta Burchardt Hickman, and their young family threw in their lot with the Latter-day Saints by being baptized members of the Church. During the expulsion of the Mormons from Missouri in 1838, the Hickmans sold their spacious farm and joined the Saints in Commerce, Illinois.[34]

Nathan and John Joshua Tanner traveled with Zion's Camp. They heard the Prophet Joseph prophesy, teach, and exhort the Saints to faithfulness. They saw him act in his prophetic role and recognized the significance of his teaching. Their father, the venerable John Tanner, a recent convert himself, "put in very near half the money that paid the expenses of Zion's Camp."[35]

Upon their arrival in Missouri and the ultimate disbanding of

Zion's Camp, the two younger Tanners remained for a time in the land of Zion before attempting to return to Kirtland. Even though there was plenty of money at home, the two ran into financial trouble on the return journey. Fiscally embarrassed, they relied on the kindness of the local citizenry. Nathan and John attempted to find work, but wet weather prevented their consistent employment. They continued toward home until they were literally down to their last dime. A local farmer named Eldredge inquired where they were from and where they were going. Upon their reply the inquisitor said, "Then I take it you are Mormons" and invited them to dinner. At the end of the meal Eldredge presented them with a sizable contribution to help them home. They refused it and instead offered to borrow the money if their benefactor would trust them to send it back upon their arrival home. Eldredge indicated he would be in their region during the coming fall and would collect his money then.

The young men continued their journey, and within a few weeks the farmer visited the John Tanner home and stayed two weeks. In addition to receiving his money, Eldredge and his son John were baptized members of the restored Church. But the story does not end there. As a result of contact with returning members of Zion's Camp, the gospel was taken to the rest of the widowed farmer's family: at least one other son, Horace S. Eldredge, embraced the faith of the Latter-day Saints. Horace became a General Authority in 1854, and he was also a successful Utah merchant, marshall, brigadier general in the Utah militia, legislator, banker, and twice a financial agent and emigration representative for the Church in the East.[36]

William Taylor was also a farmer by trade. He moved his large family from Bowling Green, Kentucky, to Clay County, Missouri. Taylor purchased six hundred forty acres of rich farmland between the forks of the Big and Little Fishing Rivers. This was the area of Clay County where the camp stopped to repair the wagons during the horrific storm that protected the Saints.

The raised levels of the Little and Big Fishing Rivers that protected the Saints likewise prevented them from continuing their journey. Throughout Saturday and Sunday, the Zion's Camp marchers were obliged to remain there. Many of the marchers were forced to seek shelter in the local Baptist meetinghouse. Later, they also learned that it was the house of worship for William Taylor, his family, and many of his neighbors. On Sunday morning, June 21, the worshippers assembled and, finding Camp members already there, encouraged them to preach. The gospel was taught. "Having heard one sermon, William Taylor was converted." Before the camp moved on the following Tuesday (June 22), William Taylor, his wife, Elizabeth, eight of their fourteen children, and some eighteen others were baptized in the same river that four days earlier had held the persecutors at bay. "Two days after meeting Joseph Smith, William Taylor manifested his confidence in the Prophet by fitting up his own son and his son in law with provisions, munitions, and equipment to [themselves] become members of Zion's camp."[37] He was ordained an elder and soon thereafter proselyted for the Church.

Descendants of the Taylor family, like those of the Eldredge and Hickman families, are still in the Church. John Taylor of Snowflake, Arizona, is a great-grandson of William. John, like many other family members, continues the legacy of faith and devotion begun by William and Elizabeth in 1834. John has been a bishop, stake president, and mission president, and currently serves as a patriarch. His civic career is no less distinguished. Yet, who could know in 1834 that the example and teachings of faithful Latter-day Saint marchers could create a legacy of adherence to the saving principles of the gospel. As a result of the Prophet's teachings then, Saints today are likewise benefited and blessed by that experience.

THE SANCTITY OF LIFE

On numerous occasions the Prophet Joseph was compelled to rebuke the members of Zion's Camp for their carelessness of the value of life. In Elder George A. Smith's reminiscence, for example, at least seven incidents were noted between men and rattlesnakes. Apparently the natural tendency of the men was to destroy the reptile and be done with the threat. The Prophet repeatedly upbraided the brethren: "How will the serpent ever lose his venom, while the servants of God possess the same disposition, and continue to make war on it? Men must become harmless, before the brute creation; and when men lose their vicious dispositions and cease to destroy the animal race, the lion and the lamb can dwell together."[38]

The teaching of the Prophet Joseph apparently had some effect, because in several future episodes the men carefully relocated unwanted serpents from their immediate campsites. Solomon Humphrey, being older than many of the camp members, became fatigued by the exertion of the march and the heat of the day. Humphrey lay down and napped but upon his awakening found a large rattlesnake coiled just a short distance from his head. Some of the men hurried to his rescue, bent on killing the snake, but Humphrey, undoubtedly remembering the earlier counsel of the Prophet, rebuffed his protectors, exclaiming, "No, I'll protect him [the snake]; you shan't hurt him, for he and I had a good nap together."[39] In addition to the comic relief that the experience provided in a tense situation, it further suggests that some were "hearing" and taking seriously the counsel of their prophet-leader.

Others did not learn so quickly or so well. These individuals continued in their old ways despite what the Prophet had taught them. Those who maintained their independence and their disposition to ignore prophetic counsel had cause to regret their decision, some of them immediately. On Wednesday, June 4, as a result of the scarcity of food, the men went searching for almost anything edible. That created a dangerous situation because enemies of the Church lingered close to the camp. With the men scattered, the whole camp was more vulnerable to attack, not to mention the individuals who were out searching for food.

Some men found on a sandbar some eggs they believed to be turtle eggs and highly edible. The Prophet Joseph, however, said that they were not turtle eggs but snake eggs, which, if consumed, would make the men ill. The men preferred their own reasoning to the Prophet's counsel. Again the Prophet warned the men against eating the eggs, but they persisted, probably driven to disobedience because of hunger as well as an unwillingness to hearken to prophetic counsel. The men who ate the eggs provided again substantial evidences of the prophetic role of Joseph Smith, because they became violently ill upon consuming the eggs.[40]

The Prophet also protected forms of life other than snakes. Men were sometimes required to walk rather than continually overburden the horses. Sylvester Smith, the "chronic complainer" of the camp, was enraged when a dog in the camp snarled at him. His emotions out of control, he threatened to kill the dog if it bit him.

The Prophet, having already dealt with Sylvester's insolence on several previous occasions, promised him that if he killed the dog, he, the Prophet, would whip him.[41] Further, the Prophet warned Smith that he had a wicked spirit, which if it continued unchecked, would lead to the literal as well as the spiritual destruction of Sylvester Smith. Although Sylvester continued to be the camp's self-appointed critic, complainer, and gadfly, finally, after the camp was disbanded, he did repent, made himself available, and was useful in further Church service.

Although these examples are in some respects simple and perhaps largely insignificant to the outcome of Zion's Camp as a whole, they demonstrate that the Prophet was attempting to teach lessons with far greater value and significance to the individuals than it might seem at first. The lessons he was teaching included valuable information that his followers could use the rest of their lives.

The Prophet was determined to teach the marchers the sin and senselessness of unnecessary and wasteful killing of harmless animals. He recorded: "I came up to the brethren who were watching a squirrel on a tree, and to prove them and to know if they would heed my counsel, I took one of their guns, shot the squirrel and passed on, leaving the squirrel on the ground. Brother Orson Hyde, who was just behind, picked up the squirrel, and said, 'We will cook this, that nothing may be lost.' I perceived that the brethren understood what I did it for, and in their practice gave more heed to my precept than to my example, which was right."[42]

The Prophet's teachings were important to those who were willing to learn; however, not all had ears to hear. Upon the arrival of the camp in Missouri and the declaration by the Lord through the Prophet that the time had not yet come for the redemption of Zion (see D&C 105:9), some of the men expressed great anger and resentment at the prospect of not being allowed to destroy the life of another human being. "Soon after this revelation was given several of the brethren apostatized because they were not going to have the privilege of fighting."[43] They had not heard the Lord's counsel; neither had they learned the important lesson of the sanctity of life. Instead, as Nathan Tanner recorded, they felt that "they would rather die than return without a fight." Instead of making necessary preparations to return to Kirtland, Ohio, to family, friends, and additional service to the Church, some of the unhappy participants "became angry . . . drew their swords and went a short distance from the camp and gave vent to their wrath on a patch of Pawpaw brush, and mowed them down like grass."[44]

JOSEPH SMITH AS A LATTER-DAY MOSES

Zion's Camp, often called the Camp of Israel, has been compared to the camp of the former-day children of Israel, so it seems fair to compare the latter-day Prophet Joseph Smith to the great prophet Moses. The Lord does just that in citing the call and affirming the work of the latter-day Joseph (see D&C 28:2; 1 Nephi 22:20; D&C 103:16).

In reading journals and other materials on Zion's Camp, I am impressed, as were the journalists, with the great spiritual prowess of the Prophet Joseph, whose spiritual magnanimity was evidenced in his travels with Zion's Camp. A few insights into his spiritual attributes will benefit us all either by way of hearing them for the first time or in reviewing the experiences again.

Already recounted are the experiences of protection and intervention by the Lord to protect His covenant people. The Prophet was likewise protected, generally along with the others, but more specifically as the Lord's anointed. During the outbreak of cholera, the Prophet's sympathies were with those who were afflicted. Already recounted are the grief and tender feelings he had for those who succumbed to the disease—he loved them in spite of their having brought down upon themselves the judgments of God. The Prophet's sympathies were such that he seems to have interfered with the directed course of Deity, and as a result he suffered severe consequences.

"June 24. This night the cholera burst forth among us, and about midnight it was manifested in its most virulent form. Our ears were saluted with cries and moanings, and lamentations on every hand. . . . At the commencement, I attempted to lay on hands for their recovery, but I quickly learned by painful experience, that when the great Jehovah decrees destruction upon any people, and makes known His determination, man must not attempt to stay His hand. The moment I attempted to rebuke the disease I was attacked, and had I not desisted in my attempt to save the life of a brother, I would have sacrificed my own. The disease seized upon me like the talons of a hawk, and I said to the brethren: 'If my work were done, you would have to put me in the ground without a coffin.'"[45]

The same reasoning could also be used to explain the preservation of the Saints by means of the terrific storms while they were camped between the Fishing rivers. The Prophet Joseph had a promise of life until his work was finished, and his allusion to his life being spared because his work was not yet finished is significant.

Miracles. Holy writ and modern prophets alike testify that miracles will attend the administration of a true prophet. Several participants referred in their journals to examples of the miracles that attended the camp. From the *Juvenile Instructor* in 1883 come the reminiscences of marcher Hiram Winters. Brother Winters recorded: "About four days before we were disbanded, our company ran short of provisions. We ate the last bite for breakfast. I applied at the commissary wagon for something for dinner, but received nothing, for the very good reason that it was empty. During the day, however, Joseph Hancock, while hunting, killed a deer, and, just after coming into camp at night, sent us about two pounds of venison. This, together with a two-pound loaf of bread . . . had to serve as supper for twelve men.

"The meat and bread were divided into equal parts [about 2.6 ounces each] and passed to the company. By the blessing of the Lord we all ate till we were satisfied, and there was some left."[46]

Warnings. Frequently the Prophet was warned about the precarious position of the camp. At times he would wake up his fellow marchers and insist that they move to a better location. On other occasions, he would go to the woods or other natural covering and beseech the Lord for safety, returning to the camp with the prophetic assurance that all would be well through the night, even though the enemies of the Saints lurked about them.[47] Luke Johnson recounted, "Our enemies oft tried to come upon us and destroy us, but the Lord by his providence as oft defeated them."[48]

Prophecy. The gift of prophecy likewise played an important role in the survival of the camp of Israel and in their success. On numerous occasions the Prophet would prophesy. "At dinner time some of the brethren expressed considerable fear on account of milk sickness, with which the people were troubled along our route. Many were afraid to use milk or butter, and appealed to me to know if it was not dangerous. I told them to use all they could get, unless they were told it was 'sick.' Some expressed fears that it might be sold to us by our enemies for the purpose of doing us injury. I told them not to fear; that if they would follow my counsel, and use all they could get from friend or enemy, it should do them good, and none be sick in consequence of it."[49]

With this promise and others that he gave the camp, the Prophet warned men not to trifle with the principle or to tempt the Lord. The Prophet recorded, "Although we passed through neighborhoods where many of the people and cattle were infected with the sickness, yet my words were fulfilled."[50]

Healing. Except for when the Prophet was seized with sickness while trying to heal another, he manifested a great ability to heal and be healed. Brother Burr Riggs was taken ill while standing guard over the camp. His military supervisor recounted: "I was sergeant of the night-guards, with instructions to see each guard every fifteen minutes, and speak to him in a whisper and receive a reply.

"The last night, about twelve o'clock, in going the third round, Burr Riggs was missing from his post. I found his body behind a log that lay about a rod away, as stiff as the log itself. Calling to Alexander Whiteside, I asked him to carry the body to his tent while I went for Joseph. We lifted the body to his shoulder and it still remained perfectly straight. I soon found Joseph and Hyrum and F. G. Williams, who administered to him; and it was not over fifteen minutes from the time I found him till he was back at his post."[51]

Visions. "Where there is no vision, the people perish" (Proverbs 29:18). Several visions of the Prophet are recounted during the march toward Missouri. One example was related by Nathan Tanner: "I had the pleasure of seeing him in a vision when he saw the country over which we had traveled in a high state of cultivation. This was while he was riding, and when he camped, he had a wagon run out in the middle of the corral of wagons, and got up into it, and told the camp what he had seen while in the Spirit. It was glorious and grand to hear."[52] There may have been many other such events that were not recorded or even known by most in the camp.

Prophetic insight. Other instances represent the spiritual and prophetic powers of Joseph Smith. Young George A. Smith remembered: "I got into the wagon to ride a short distance with Presidents

Joseph and Hyrum Smith and Brother Ezra Thayer. We were traveling through a thicket of small timber of recent growth. Brother
Joseph said, 'I feel very much depressed in spirits; there has been a
great deal of bloodshed here at some time. When a man of God
passes through a place where much blood has been shed he will feel
depressed in spirits and feel lonesome and uncomfortable.'"⁵³

The cause of the Prophet's depression later was determined by the
finding of a large hill covered with holes exposing human bones.
Brother Hyrum Smith suggested that "he believed that a great army
had some time been slain and piled up and covered with earth, an
ancient manner of burying the dead from a battlefield. The country
around for miles was level."⁵⁴

Example. A final illustration of Joseph Smith's prophetic stature
and standing within the camp of Israel was his example to the other
members of the camp. Despite discouragement, disobedience, grum-
bling, sickness, and low morale the Prophet never seemed to lose perspective. "In addition to the care of providing for the camp and
presiding over it, he [Joseph] walked most of the time and had a full
proportion of blistered, bloody, and sore feet, which was the natural
result of walking from 25 to 40 miles a day in a hot season of the
year."⁵⁵ On one occasion, the Prophet gave a pair of shoes to his
cousin George A. Smith, who was ill prepared for the march.

"During the entire trip he [Joseph] never uttered a murmur or
complaint, while most of the men in the Camp complained to him
of sore toes, blistered feet, long drives, scanty supply of provisions,
poor quality of bread, bad corn dodger, frouzy butter, strong honey,
maggoty bacon and cheese, &c., even a dog could not bark at some
men without their murmuring at Joseph. If they had to camp with
bad water it would nearly cause rebellion, yet we were the Camp of
Zion, and many of us were prayerless, thoughtless, careless, heedless,
foolish or devilish and yet we did not know it. Joseph had to bear
with us and tutor us, like children. There were many, however, in the
Camp who never murmured and who were always ready and willing
to do as our leaders desired."⁵⁶

Like King David or Alexander the Great, the Prophet Joseph
would not allow himself special privileges that were not also available to his men. He ate the same food they ate, he walked the same
distances they walked, he slept in the same tents they used, and he

refused special treatment for himself or others unless through empathy he attempted to make another's burden lighter. "At noon, the Prophet discovered that a part of [the] mess had been served with sour bread, while he had received good sweet bread from the same cook, whom he reproved for this partiality, saying, 'He wanted his brethren to fare as well as he did, and preferred to eat his portion of sour bread with them.'"[57] Further, we have accounts of the Prophet eating meat that others believed to be spoiled and taking his turn at difficult tasks, in addition to his rigorous responsibilities of leadership.

The Lord through the Prophet promised the Saints protection and preservation if certain things were accomplished. Most of the marchers adhered to some of the conditions, and a few of the marchers met most of the conditions, but as a camp they were not obedient to all of the particulars.

A few of the participants apostatized after Zion's Camp. They had various reasons, including not getting to fight, personal disgruntlements, disillusionment, and so forth, but the great majority of the camp members remained faithful and many of them became very productive leaders in the Church. Approximately seven months later, in February 1835, the Prophet, having returned to Kirtland with most of the marchers, asked Brigham and Joseph Young to assemble the veterans of Zion's Camp for a mission reunion of sorts. Incidentally, this practice, although interrupted for a time, was reinstituted after the Saints arrived in the West, and the reunions were held for several years while there was a sizable group of its participants still living. From the assembled veterans in February 1835, the Prophet laid his hands on the heads of the Three Witnesses to the Book of Mormon, whose responsibility it was to select the Twelve Apostles.[58] After the blessing, the witnesses retired from the group for about an hour and then returned with the names of those chosen. Nine of the original Twelve Apostles in this dispensation had served faithfully during the trek of Zion's Camp.

Conclusion

The success of Zion's Camp cannot be determined solely by whether or not its initial objectives were met. Other important factors must be considered. We believe that Zion will yet be redeemed in the Lord's wisdom and on His timetable. During the weeks that Zion's Camp marched toward Missouri, the Lord convincingly manifested sufficient power through the elements and through His servants to show that He could redeem Zion at any time if the redemption of Zion simply meant returning the Saints to their lands. The timetable was His, the means of fulfillment were known to Him, and He showed that neither the mobs nor anyone else was a match for His power. Independence, Missouri, was the desired destination, but the creation of a Zion society seems to be the ultimate objective. According to Elder Neal A. Maxwell, "God is more concerned with growth than with geography. Thus, those who marched in Zion's Camp were not exploring the Missouri countryside but their own possibilities."[59] Looked at in this light, then, we may conclude that Zion's Camp was ideally named because—

1. The camp was made up of a group of Latter-day Saints who were individually committed to creating Zion by establishing the kingdom of God on earth. Furthermore, they willingly consecrated all that they had, including their lives if necessary, to see the Lord's ideal realized.
2. Participants were obedient in agreeing to go to the revealed center place of Zion to fulfill the will of the Master as revealed by His servant, the Prophet Joseph Smith.
3. Camp members were taught and tested on such principles as unity, obedience to counsel, consecration, brotherly love, sacredness of life, and so forth. These characteristics were necessary prerequisites to living together in peace, whether or not the ultimate objectives were realized at that time. These principles are likewise necessary wherever the Lord's people live.
4. The participants in Zion's Camp were being tried, stretched, refined, tutored, and tested like Abraham of old to determine their obedience to the Lord in all things. Abraham was obedient to the Lord's command, and likewise, the participants in Zion's Camp were generally obedient.

Furthermore, the march of Zion's Camp was a veritable "School of the Prophets," for many of the marchers later became leaders. They received virtually the same instruction, manifestations, and spiritual outpouring as did the members of the School of the Prophets held in the Whitney Store in Kirtland.

Zion's Camp was to the dispensation of the fulness of times as the camp of the children of Israel was to the dispensation of the days of Moses. Both experiences showed the extent of God's patience and His love in bringing a covenant people from where they were to where they needed to be. Both experiences exemplify that "of him unto whom much is given much is required" (D&C 82:3).

The expedition of Zion's Camp illustrated that God will fight the battles of His chosen people and intervene for their welfare upon the condition of obedience.

The march of Zion's Camp was a preparatory phase, in which future Church leaders were tutored against a day when specific skills and personalities were needed to—

1. Lead the Saints from Ohio to Missouri in a group known as Kirtland Camp.
2. Lead the Saints from Illinois to settlements in Iowa and Nebraska in a group known as the Camp of Israel.
3. Lead the Saints from Winter Quarters, Nebraska, to the Great Basin.
4. Provide a pattern for leadership for many thousands of emigrant Saints to follow in subsequent years as they came from all parts of the earth.

Zion's Camp was a means of identifying, teaching, and testing future leaders of the Church. Of the first twenty-five Apostles of this dispensation, including four future Church Presidents, fourteen (56 percent) were members of Zion's Camp; seven of that number were not yet members of the Church, and two others were already in Missouri. Of those available to serve, fourteen of sixteen (88 percent) participated in Zion's Camp. The leadership skills gained from Zion's Camp spanned the Church's history from 1834, when they marched, until after the dawning of the twentieth century.

When asked what they had gained by their extended absence from family, business, and personal concerns, Brigham Young responded that they had accomplished everything in Zion's Camp that they had set out to do. "I would not exchange the knowledge I have received this season for the whole of Geauga County [Ohio]."[60]

Similarly, Wilford Woodruff observed on December 12, 1869: "When the members of Zion's Camp were called, many of us had never beheld each other's faces; we were strangers to each other and many had never seen the prophet. . . . We were young men, and were called upon in that early day to go up and redeem Zion, and what we had to do we had to do by faith. . . . God accepted our works as he did the works of Abraham. We accomplished a great deal. . . . We gained an experience that we never could have gained in any other way. We had the privilege of beholding the face of the prophet, and we had the privilege of travelling a thousand miles with him, and seeing the workings of the spirit of God with him, and the revelations of Jesus Christ unto him and the fulfilment of those revelations. . . . Had I not gone up with Zion's Camp I should not have been here today, and I presume that would have been the case with many others in this Territory."[61]

A great blessing to the Church from these experiences is that the descendants of these participants are still members of the Church and are still providing support and strength for the kingdom. Those individuals were obedient then and their descendants are still being obedient to the Lord's anointed today.

Zion's Camp was the composite of some two hundred individuals' personal experiences, and, as such, the experience as a whole was greater than the sum of all of their individual experiences. In addition to the redemption of Zion, an important objective of the march was to focus the Saints involved on still higher purposes of building the kingdom of God on earth. They fought their good fight, and they have their reward. The value of Zion's Camp today as a legacy of obedient adherence to the commandments of God is determined by what we can learn from their faithfulness and the efforts we will expend in further building the kingdom in our day.

NOTES

1. Sidney B. Sperry, *Doctrine and Covenants Compendium* (Salt Lake City: Bookcraft, 1960), 521–22.
2. Joseph Smith, *History of the Church of Jesus Christ of Latter-day Saints*, ed. B. H. Roberts, 2nd ed., rev. (Salt Lake City: The Church of Jesus Christ of Latter-day Saints, 1932–51), 2:39.
3. Parley P. Pratt, *Autobiography of Parley P. Pratt*, ed. Parley P. Pratt Jr. (Salt Lake City: Deseret Book, 1985), 94.

4. Smith, *History of the Church*, 2:123, n.

5. Tamma Durfee Miner Autobiography, typescript, L. Tom Perry Special Collections, Harold B. Lee Library, Brigham Young University, Provo, Utah, 2; hereafter cited as Special Collections.

6. Nathan B. Baldwin Journal, typescript, Special Collections, 9; see also Elijah Fordham's Journal, Tuesday, June 10, 1834, Special Collections.

7. Levi Hancock Journal, Special Collections, 53.

8. Levi Hancock Journal, 53, 57.

9. "George Albert Smith's History of Zion's Camp," May 4, 1834, 1.

10. "George Albert Smith's History of Zion's Camp," June 19, 1834, 21.

11. "George Albert Smith's History of Zion's Camp," June 19, 1834, 22.

12. Nathan B. Baldwin Journal, 12.

13. "George Albert Smith's History of Zion's Camp," June 19, 1834, 22.

14. Nathan B. Baldwin Journal, 12.

15. "George Albert Smith's History of Zion's Camp," June 19, 1834, 22.

16. Smith, *History of the Church*, 2:104, n.

17. Smith, *History of the Church*, 2:105.

18. Smith, *History of the Church*, 2:106.

19. "George Albert Smith's History of Zion's Camp," 1.

20. Raymond P. Draper, "The Early Life of Luke S. Johnson: From the Absolute Beginning to Oct. 11, 1836," entry for May 1, 1834, 3. Typescript in possession of the author.

21. "George Albert Smith's History of Zion's Camp," May 14, 1834, 3.

22. "George Albert Smith's History of Zion's Camp," May 14, 1834, 5.

23. "George Albert Smith's History of Zion's Camp," May 14, 1834, 5.

24. "George Albert Smith's History of Zion's Camp," May 18, 1834, 56.

25. Smith, *History of the Church*, 2:114.

26. As quoted in Michael Jay Noble, "Joseph Bates Noble," 4.

27. "George Albert Smith's History of Zion's Camp," June 25, 1834, 23.

28. As quoted in Noble, "Joseph Bates Noble," 4.

29. Heber C. Kimball, in *Times and Seasons*, March 15, 1845, 839.

30. Smith, *History of the Church*, 2:80.

31. Smith, *History of the Church*, 2:107.

32. Kimball, in *Times and Seasons*, March 15, 1845, 839.

33. Smith, *History of the Church*, 2:181, n.

34. In *Church News*, October 7, 1984, 7.

35. George S. Tanner, *John Tanner and His Family* (Salt Lake City: John Tanner Family Association, 1974), 382.

36. Lawrence R. Flake, *Mighty Men of Zion: General Authorities of the Last Dispensation* (Salt Lake City: Karl D. Butter, 1974), 410–11.

37. Lella Marler Hogan, "William Taylor," 1; see also *Family Group Record for William and Elizabeth Patrick Taylor*.

38. Smith, *History of the Church*, 2:71.

39. Smith, *History of the Church*, 2:7374.

40. Smith, *History of the Church*, 2:82, n.

41. "George Albert Smith's History of Zion's Camp," June 6, 1834, 16.

42. Smith, *History of the Church*, 2:72.

43. "George Albert Smith's History of Zion's Camp," June 22, 1834, 23.

44. Tanner, *John Tanner and His Family*, 382.

45. Smith, *History of the Church*, 2:114.

46. Hiram Winters, in *Juvenile Instructor*, March 15, 1883, 86.

47. Smith, *History of the Church*, 2:114.

48. Draper, "Luke S. Johnson," May 1, 1834, 3.

49. Smith, *History of the Church*, 2:114.

50. Smith, *History of the Church*, 2:66–67.

51. Winters, in *Juvenile Instructor*, March 15, 1883, 86.

52. Tanner, *John Tanner and His Family*, 382–83.

53. "George Albert Smith's History of Zion's Camp," May 16, 1834, 3.

54. "George Albert Smith's History of Zion's Camp," May 16, 1834, 3–4.

55. "George Albert Smith's History of Zion's Camp," June 25, 1834, 23.

56. "George Albert Smith's History of Zion's Camp," June 25, 1834, 23–24.

57. "George Albert Smith's History of Zion's Camp," May 29, 1834, 9.

58. Smith, *History of the Church*, 2:186–87; see also D&C 18:37–39.

59. Neal A. Maxwell, in Conference Report, October 1976, 16.

60. Brigham Young, in *Journal of Discourses* (London: Latter-day Saints' Book Depot, 1854–86), 2:10.

61. Wilford Woodruff, in *Journal of Discourses*, 13:158.

CHAPTER TWENTY

"Exalt Not Yourselves": The Revelations and Thomas B. Marsh, an Object Lesson for Our Day

RONALD K. ESPLIN

Our purpose here is to understand the historical setting for several revelations related to the Quorum of the Twelve Apostles in 1837 and 1838, most notably Doctrine and Covenants 112, but also 114, 118, and the very short 126 (dated July 1841); and, aided by that understanding, better understand the revelations. At the same time, in the spirit of Nephi, who "did liken all scriptures unto us, that it might be for our profit and learning" (1 Nephi 19:23), we will see the relevance for today of inspired counsel from the 1830s. Reviewing how Thomas B. Marsh responded to challenges and adversity provides profitable reminders for the conduct of our own lives.

What follows is a chapter in the early history of the Quorum of the Twelve Apostles that transpired before Joseph Smith, in 1841, formally invited them to take their place next to the First Presidency in governing the whole Church. Before that, especially in Kirtland, the Twelve had neither prominence nor precedence (over, for example, the Kirtland High Council), though revelation and inspired counsel from the beginning made clear that this was their potential. This lack

Ronald K. Esplin is a professor of Church history at Brigham Young University.

of status or formal authority within organized stakes rankled some and contributed to misunderstandings and disharmony, but in retrospect we can see it as an important period of testing and preparation before greater responsibility was given to the Twelve. In Doctrine and Covenants 112, which we will examine in detail, the Lord says of the Twelve specifically that "after their temptations, and much tribulation, behold, I, the Lord, will feel after them" *if* they harden not their hearts (D&C 112:13). Their history provides a specific example of the general principle that "after much tribulation come the blessings" (D&C 58:4; see also 103:12; Ether 12:6).

On Sunday, September 6, 1857, in Salt Lake City, Thomas B. Marsh, who had been called in 1835 as an Apostle and as President of the first Quorum of the Twelve Apostles, stood before the Saints for the first time in nearly two decades. A broken man, a shadow of his former self, he felt acutely the pain of opportunities and blessings irretrievably lost. Among lost blessings was his health. A once vigorous man, Marsh now referred to himself as old and infirm, and so he appeared—a dramatic illustration of the toll of apostasy and disobedience. Standing comparatively young and robust, President Young pointed out that Thomas was his senior by less than two years. For his part Marsh acknowledged faults that led him first to jealousy and anger and finally to apostasy, which brought only misery and affliction.[1] Four months earlier he had confessed to Heber C. Kimball: "I have sined [*sic*] against Heaven and in thy sight. . . . I deserve no place . . . in the church even as the lowest member; but I cannot live long . . . without a reconciliation with the 12 and the Church whom I have injured O Bretheren once Bretheren!! How can I leave this world without your forgiveness Can I have it Can I have it? Something seems to say within yes. . . . can you speak one word of comfort to me. . . . Can I find peace among you?"[2]

What he sought now, and what the audience voted unanimously to extend, was not office or position but simply fellowship with the Saints. In the 1830s he had aspired to much more.

When the Quorum of the Twelve Apostles was organized in February 1835, Thomas B. Marsh became president because he was the eldest of those selected, though thereafter, seniority would be determined by date of ordination, not age. A member since 1830, when the Church was still in New York, and an effective missionary,

Marsh appeared to be a reasonable choice to head the new quorum. David Whitmer had baptized him, Oliver Cowdery had ordained him an elder, he had been one of the first to receive the high priesthood in 1831, and in 1834 he had become a member of the first high council organized in Zion, or Missouri. An 1831 revelation declared that he would be "a physician unto the church" (D&C 31:10).

But there were also warning signs, or at least foreshadowings, of possible trouble. The Quorum of the Twelve was uniquely charged to carry the gospel to all the world, and from the Church's beginning members looked toward the day they could begin that work abroad by preaching in England, yet the same 1831 revelation that named Marsh a "physician unto the church" warned that he could not be a physician "unto the world, for they will not receive you" (D&C 1:10). Furthermore, an impressive charge to the new Apostles in February 1835, delivered by Oliver Cowdery in Kirtland before Marsh had arrived from Missouri, stressed the need for brotherhood and unity within the Twelve and warned the Apostles to cultivate humility, beware of pride, and give all credit to God. Rather than playing to natural strengths, these requirements challenged Marsh where he was weakest, for he tended toward officiousness and an overblown concern about appearances and position. The 1831 revelation concerning him had ended with a warning and a promise. "Pray always, lest you enter into temptation and lose your reward," Marsh was told, but "be faithful unto the end, and lo, I am with you" (D&C 31:12–13).

A YOUNG QUORUM

Members of a new quorum with scriptural precedents but without institutional memory or living example to rely on, the Apostles at first struggled to understand their proper role and to develop effective ways of working together as a quorum and in harmony with other leaders. In preparation for their first mission—again even before Marsh had arrived from Missouri—Joseph instructed them by counsel and by revelation. In March 1835, feeling unprepared and unworthy, they had petitioned the Prophet to "inquire of God for us, and obtain a revelation, (if consistent) that our hearts may be comforted."[3] The significant revelation "on priesthood" (see D&C 107) was the result. Among its instructions was the declaration that the Quorum of the Twelve Apostles "form a quorum, equal in authority and power" to the presidency of the Church—but only when they are united and in harmony as a quorum—along with a reminder, accompanied with a promise, that relationships within the quorum must be characterized by "lowliness of heart, meekness and long suffering, and . . . temperance, patience, godliness, brotherly kindness and charity" (D&C 107:24, 30). Despite such guidelines, only with time and experience could these men learn in detail what it meant to be Apostles. In the meantime, understandably, they would occasionally grope and stumble.

As it turned out, both inexperience and personality made it difficult for Thomas Marsh to lead the new quorum effectively. In terms later used by Joseph Smith in writing about priesthood leadership, too easily do pride, vain ambition, and even compulsion enter into relationships that should be based only on persuasion, long-suffering, gentleness, meekness, and love unfeigned (see D&C 121:31, 41). For Thomas Marsh and others like him—young men in a young church, uneducated, inexperienced as leaders—the style demanded by such principles remained a distant ideal. Faced with opportunities for growth and improvement, for the moment Marsh was part of the committed but struggling generation in Missouri whose "jarrings, and contentions, and envyings, and strifes, and lustful and covetous desires," in the words of revelation, brought them into difficulties (D&C 101:6). Here, clearly, was a man of ability. But it was less clear that he would learn to govern his feelings enough to reach his potential or learn to meet challenges and snubs with patience and love rather than "jarrings and strife."

The new Apostles spent that summer of 1835 traveling together in the East on their first (and only) missionary undertaking under President Marsh as a full quorum. With pointed counsel and revelation vividly in mind, they conscientiously labored to carry out their commission, and the result was a successful mission. But that fall they returned home not to accolades but to accusations, and these they handled much less well. What should have been minor difficulties arising from affronts or simple miscommunication aroused intense feelings, and soon the new Quorum of the Twelve found itself immersed in charges and countercharges with the First Presidency, concerns about position and precedence with the High Council, and divisive complaints among its own members.[4]

President Marsh generally met these challenges in a manner that stressed rights, justice, and his (or his quorum's) prerogatives more than brotherhood or humble submission to counsel. The difficulties cannot all be attributed to Marsh, of course. All of the Apostles were inexperienced, none yet fully understood their calling, and some others shared Marsh's unfortunate focus on potential authority and prestige greater than the actual. Moreover, the Prophet Joseph Smith ruffled the feelings of his sensitive Apostles as often as he soothed them. Whether this was a conscious ploy to teach that humility and service must precede authority, as Brigham Young came to believe, or simply a consequence of his own style, the results were the same. Anxious to be powerful men in the kingdom, some of the Apostles bristled and complained at every slight.

For the Apostles and other Church leaders in Kirtland, the fall of 1835 should have been a joyful season devoted to preparing hearts and spirits for long-awaited blessings in the nearly completed Kirtland Temple. Instead, hurt feelings required that council after council be dedicated to airing complaints, soothing feelings, and generally working to reestablish brotherhood.[5] These efforts did bear fruit, however, and as far as records reveal, by November comparative harmony seemed to prevail. Then, without clarifying explanation, on November 3 the Prophet recorded in his diary the following: "Thus came the word of the Lord unto me concerning the Twelve [saying] behold they are under condemnation, because they have not been sufficiently humble in my sight, and in consequence of their covetous desires, in that they have not dealt equally with each other." The revelation named several of the Apostles as offenders and then concluded that "all must humble themselves before me, before they will be accounted worthy to receive an endowment."[6]

Understandably this caused a stir among the Apostles. The only other revelation addressing them specifically had been the great revelation on priesthood, and now, only months later, this. Records do not preserve President Marsh's response to this chastisement, though we can surmise that he took it personally and was not pleased, but Joseph did record that Elders Hyde and McLellin, two of those named, stopped by to express "some little dissatisfaction." Brigham Young, on the other hand, "appeared perfectly satisfied" with the chastisement.[7] Perhaps he felt no need to take it personally or, if he did, remembered the inspired counsel of the June 1833 revelation that became Doctrine and Covenants 95: "Whom I love I also chasten that their sins may be forgiven, for with the chastisement I prepare a way for their deliverance in all things out of temptation" (D&C 95:1).

No doubt Brigham Young also recognized the justice of the rebuke. Not only had the Apostles clashed with other Church officials but they had also experienced disunity, jealousy, and pettiness within their own quorum. Years later Young characterized the Kirtland Twelve as "continually sparring at each other." To illustrate, he told of once being summoned to answer for having accepted an invitation to preach. By what authority, demanded his fellow Apostles, had he "presumed to appoint a meeting and preach" without consulting them? Under Thomas Marsh the Twelve met very often, Young continued, "and if no one of them needed cleaning, they had to 'clean' some one any how."[8] On another occasion President Young contrasted his own style as President, trying to be a father to all, with President Marsh's: "like a toad's hair comb[ing] up and down."[9]

There is no doubt that the personality of Thomas Marsh contributed to the pettiness and self-concern that plagued his quorum. Because of his concern about prerogatives, his leadership could be intrusive and officious. He was also impatient with criticism and tended to view a difference of opinion or even initiative by others as a challenge to his leadership. And he was impatient about the status of the Twelve in Kirtland. According to Brigham Young, he was among those who, when Joseph "snubbed" the Apostles, exclaimed, "We are apostles[!] it's an insult for us to be so treated."[10] Brigham, on the other hand, came to see the snubbing, the trials, in a way Thomas never did: as a testing, a necessary preparation, before they were ready for power. This he once explained to Marsh when he complained of their treatment. "If we are faithful," insisted Brigham Young, "we shall see the day . . . that we will have all the power we shall know how to wield before God."[11]

JOY AND TROUBLE IN KIRTLAND

Although it took until January 1836, the Apostles eventually settled important differences and came to enjoy both increased unity within their quorum and general harmony with other leaders. Thus prepared, they shared with other Kirtland Saints the extraordinary blessings and manifestations associated with the Kirtland Temple in early 1836.

But for the Quorum of the Twelve, unity, harmony, and new spiritual strength did not last. Instead of moving the quorum to Missouri, as earlier contemplated once the temple was finished, Joseph Smith announced that they were now free to move or not, as they chose; and instead of another quorum mission, he suggested that each was free to preach where he would—though each understood his duty to take the gospel abroad as soon as possible. Thomas Marsh and David Patten, the two senior Apostles, returned to Missouri, whereas most of the others continued to call Kirtland home. Within a year the Twelve would be as divided spiritually as they were geographically.

In 1837 dissension and rebellion swept the Church, especially among the leaders. Although most retained faith in the Book of Mormon and believed in the necessity of restored authority, not everyone shared the Prophet's enthusiasm for the ancient order of things. To some, a society modeled after ancient Israel, where prophetic authority directed all aspects of life (not just the religious), portended a reduction in cherished social and economic freedoms. Too Papist, they declared, too un-American. Those concerns underlay the discontent of many who ostensibly blamed Joseph for meddling in the Kirtland Bank, which ultimately failed, or who had other complaints against his conduct of economic or civic affairs.[12] While most members trusted the Prophet and continued to remain loyal even if they did not yet fully understand his vision, a rift developed between Joseph and many leaders, including some in the Presidency and in the Twelve, who were certain they understood more, or at least better, than he did. Of the Apostles in Kirtland, only Brigham Young and Heber C. Kimball expressed unwavering support for Joseph Smith and his program.

When news of the rebellion reached President Marsh in Missouri, he was appalled. Word that several of his own quorum members were prominent among dissenters especially humiliated him. He had envisioned leading a united quorum abroad to introduce the gospel to Great Britain, and now this. He was also distressed to learn that an impatient Parley P. Pratt (and perhaps others) intended to leave on a foreign mission without him. Hurt, angry, and determined, Marsh hoped to "right-up" the Twelve and reestablish himself as an effective leader by holding a dramatic meeting with his quorum in Kirtland in which he would interject himself vigorously into the fray on the side of the Prophet. On May 10 he and Elder Patten dispatched an urgent letter to Parley P. Pratt, advising him not to depart for England: "The 12 must get together difficulties must be removed & love restored, we must have peace within before we can wage a successful war without. . . . Shall the 12 apostles of the Lambe be a disorganised body pulling different ways, Shall one [go] to his plough another to his merchandise, another to England &c. No! I even I Thomas will step in (if their [*sic*] is none other for it is my right in this case) and give council to you."[13]

The letter appointed July 24 for an extraordinary council "to break through every obstacle" and prepare for their mission abroad.

Since at least February 1837, Kirtland Apostles had spoken of a summer mission to England; Parley Pratt was not alone in this. But amid dissension and the continuing absence of President Marsh, the mission appeared doubtful. Heber Kimball was thus shocked when the Prophet told him in early June that "for the salvation of His church" the mission must go forth without delay and that he must head it.[14] Joseph needed Brigham Young in Kirtland, he insisted, Parley had joined the others in rebellion, and they could not wait for Marsh and Patten. Begging forgiveness, Orson Hyde sought reconciliation the very day Kimball was set apart for his mission and requested permission to accompany him. Thus it was that Elders Kimball and Hyde, not Marsh and Patten, left Kirtland June 13 to open the work abroad.[15]

A few days later, after Brigham Young tried but failed to reconcile him with Joseph, Parley Pratt suddenly departed for Missouri. Providentially, Marsh and Patten encountered Parley en route, and they succeeded (where Brigham had not) in turning him around.

As soon as they reached Kirtland, Brigham Young briefed Elders Marsh and Patten on the perplexing problems. Marsh then went directly to Joseph's home—his headquarters during his Kirtland stay—and set to work reconciling the disaffected. (David Patten, meanwhile, visited first the dissenters and, according to Brigham, "got his mind prejudiced" and insulted Joseph. The Prophet reacted strongly to the affront, which, in Young's view, "done David good," and quickly returned him to his senses.)[16] The Prophet arranged a special meeting at his home for several of the prominent malcontents, no doubt including Apostles. Marsh "moderated" and, he reported later, "a reconciliation was effected between all parties."[17] Without question President Marsh contributed to the healing and reconciliation in Kirtland that summer. He labored with the "merchant apostles," Lyman Johnson and John Boynton, and with Constable Luke Johnson. Following his arrival, Elders Orson Pratt and Parley Pratt, among others, made public confessions and expressions of support for Joseph. Although neither Marsh nor the Prophet swept away the basic differences in outlook that had brought dissent, as President of the Twelve, Marsh was able to return a modicum of civility and unity to his quorum. An early departure for England seemed out of the question, however, and there is no evidence that Marsh convened the "extraordinary meeting" he had earlier proposed for July 24.

Despite modest success, President Marsh was still troubled— troubled that members of his quorum had rebelled and also troubled that missionary work abroad was proceeding without him. Concerned about his own status and wondering if the Lord could still accept the Twelve, he went to Joseph on July 23, the day before his extraordinary council would have been held, to discuss his concerns. That evening the Prophet dictated as Thomas wrote "the word of the Lord unto Thomas B. Marsh, concerning the Twelve Apostles of the Lamb" (headnote to D&C 112).

The revelation acknowledged Marsh's prayerful concern for his quorum and counseled him to continue to pray for them and, as needed, to admonish them sharply, for "after their temptations, and much tribulation . . . I, the Lord, will feel after them, and if they harden not their hearts . . . they shall be converted, and I will heal them" (verse 13). It admonished the Twelve—"Exalt not yourselves; rebel not against my servant Joseph" (verse 15)—and counseled Marsh to be more faithful and humble, at the same time reaffirming his position as President of the Twelve. The revelation also approved Marsh's residence in Missouri, where he worked with the printing office, "for I, the Lord, have a great work for thee to do, in publishing my name among the children of men" (verse 6).

With that background, we are now ready to closely examine

Doctrine and Covenants 112, given on July 23, 1837, for Thomas Marsh and the Twelve, noting how it applied to them and how it might apply to us. "I have heard thy prayers," says verse 1, "in behalf of those, thy brethren, who were chosen to bear testimony . . . abroad . . . and ordained through the instrumentality of my servants." Though we are not of their quorum, this passage describes a duty common to many priesthood holders, especially missionaries.

In verse 2, President Marsh is told that "there have been some few things" in his heart and with him with which the Lord is not pleased. Again, this is something that applies to us all.

Verse 3 tells Marsh that because he has humbled himself he can still be exalted and his sins are forgiven. (*Abase* means to humble, which is a universal requirement for forgiveness and reconciliation.)

So, in verse 4, President Marsh is told to let his heart be of good cheer, and—now this was what he was *really* concerned about—he is told, "thou shalt [still, despite all the problems] bear record of my name" and "send forth my word unto the ends of the earth." Even though Elders Kimball and Hyde had departed, Thomas Marsh might yet have his day.

Therefore, says verse 5, "Contend thou, therefore, morning by morning; and day after day let thy warning voice go forth"—a good description of what we all should be about.

More specifically, verse 6 says that President Marsh is not to move his household from Missouri, for from there, as printer, he is to publish the word abroad.

Verse 7 warns Marsh, "Therefore, gird up thy loins for the work. Let thy feet be shod also, for thou art chosen" to do this work. Where? "Among the mountains" (a hint of the Rocky Mountains?[18]) and "among many nations" (which because of apostasy he failed to fulfill).

Verses 8 and 9 indicate that Marsh's word will bring down the exalted and exalt the lowly and that he will rebuke the transgressor. Priesthood leaders generally share this responsibility to rebuke when so inspired. Given the history of his quorum, one might conclude that these two verses apply to counseling his brethren, but because a reminder about that specific responsibility begins with verse 12, this reference appears to be more general.

Verse 10 preserves one of the great promises in scripture, one that surely can be adopted as a general principle and applied to all: "Be thou humble; and the Lord thy God shall lead thee by the hand, and give thee answer to thy prayers." This and related scriptural promises (see, for example, Romans 8:28 and D&C 90:24) all include qualifications. To claim the promised blessings, we must be humble and faithful, love God, and honor His commandments. With us, as with President Marsh, worthiness determines whether we can claim the promise.

Verses 11–14 contain pleadings and admonitions for the Twelve. Here the Lord tells President Marsh that He knows his heart and has heard his prayers for his brethren. As president it is his right and duty to be concerned, of course, and to express and extend love, but the Lord reminds him, "Let thy love be for them as for thyself; and let thy love abound unto all men, and unto all who love my name" (verse 11). Again, though we may each have specific responsibilities, beyond that, we must learn to love all men.

Marsh should, of course, continue to "pray for [his] brethren of the Twelve" and "admonish them sharply" for their sins. But likewise (harking back to verse 2, where he is reproved), he is told, "Be ye faithful before me" (verse 12).

Reprove them as required, Marsh is told, for "after their temptations, and much tribulation," there is still a promise: "I, the Lord, will feel after them, and if they harden not their hearts, and stiffen not their necks against me, they shall be converted, and I will heal them" (112:13). Note that even though they were Apostles, these men—young, inexperienced, in transgression—needed to be converted anew. Similarly, we should search our own hearts about where we stand. When we find ourselves stumbling or kicking against the pricks, this verse reminds us of the way back.

The passage concludes with this counsel to President Marsh, counsel that the Lord says "unto all the Twelve" (and to us): "Gird up your loins, take up your cross, follow me, and feed my sheep" (verse 14). For the Twelve in 1837, this charge specifically meant that they should prepare to take the gospel abroad to His sheep in other lands.

Then follows, in verses 15 through 22, counsel clarifying the roles and duties of the First Presidency and the Twelve. After President Marsh had been specifically warned in verse 10 to be humble, here all the members of the Twelve are told, "Exalt not yourselves." The warning was not against general pride alone but against a tendency to place themselves above their leaders: "Rebel not against my servant Joseph; for verily I say unto you, I am with him" (verse 15). We can now understand why that was essential counsel to them at that time—as well as a reminder for us. Verse 15 goes on to clarify, as do earlier revelations, that while both the First Presidency and the Twelve have keys, the Prophet Joseph is the head: "My hand shall be over him," and his keys "shall not be taken from him till I come."

Verses 16 and 17 are at the heart of what weighed heavily on President Marsh's mind when he approached the Prophet seeking the word of the Lord: "Verily I say unto you, my servant Thomas, thou art the man whom I have chosen to hold the keys of my kingdom, as pertaining to the Twelve [still, despite the difficulties], abroad among all nations" (even in England!) and "to unlock the door of the kingdom in all places."

Unfortunately, instead of humbly accepting this assurance as a renewed opportunity, Thomas immediately visited Vilate Kimball and, backed by this affirmation, told her that Heber could not open an "effectual door" in England because *he,* Thomas, had not sent him! The Prophet had assured him, Marsh explained, that since proclaiming the gospel abroad was his special responsibility, the door could not be "effectually" opened until *he* sent someone or went himself.

In pressing this point, Thomas Marsh once again missed the mark, as the revelation itself makes clear. That very verse continued: Marsh held the keys "to unlock the door of the kingdom in all places *where my servant Joseph*" and his counselors, in other words, the First Presidency, "cannot come"; and, said verse 18, *"On them* have I laid the burden of *all* the churches for a little season. Wherefore, whithersoever they shall send you [or Heber Kimball and Orson Hyde or *whomever*], go ye, and I will be with you; and in whatsoever place ye shall proclaim my name an effectual door shall be opened unto you, that they may receive my word" (112:17–19; emphasis added). Stated again: the Prophet's keys held precedence even over those of the President of the Quorum of the Twelve.

Heber understood that principle. When he learned in England of Marsh's claim, he was philosophical, allowing that "Brother Joseph sed it was all right to prepare the way . . . so we have come to prepare the way before Brother Thomas. And we have baptised a good lot of them."[19] Even so, he added, Brother Marsh would have to do some of the work himself if he intended to claim some of the credit.

As if that were not clear enough, and apparently it was not for Marsh, verse 20 tries still again to clarify: "Whosoever receiveth my word receiveth me, and whosoever receiveth me, receiveth these, the First Presidency, whom I have sent, whom I have made counselors . . . unto you." Others also have power—especially the Twelve with their special calling and responsibility to take the gospel abroad—but it is all under the First Presidency.

Verse 21 adds: "And again, I say unto you, that whosoever ye shall send in my name *by the voice of your brethren,* the Twelve" (that is, President Marsh was not to act alone; compare to the principle of unity and unanimity in D&C 107:27–38), "shall have power to open the door of my kingdom unto any nation whithersoever ye shall send them" (112:21). Any nation? Always? "Inasmuch as they shall humble themselves before me, and abide in my word, and hearken to the voice of my Spirit" (verse 22).

Verses 23–26 shift the focus. These verses warning of a day of weeping, desolation, and mourning that "cometh speedily" (verse 24) may speak of things yet to occur; certainly the principles are more broadly applicable than merely Kirtland in 1837. But they also had a specific application to Kirtland, and it is that connection that we will examine.

Why will there be troubles? Because, says verse 23, "darkness covereth the earth, and gross darkness the minds of the people, and all flesh has become corrupt." (That sounds like a description of today.) *Where* will there be troubles? "Upon my house shall it begin, and from my house shall it go forth" (verse 25). *Who* will suffer? Those who "have professed to know my name and have not known me, and have blasphemed against me in the midst of my house" (verse 26). Surely some of the wayward Apostles, soon to be cut off, could be among that number. Why "my house"? Already there had been difficulties and soon there would be riots, disorder, and blasphemy *in the temple* in Kirtland, and perpetrators would include John Boynton, Apostle, and Warren Parrish, recently Joseph Smith's private secretary.

"Therefore"—therefore what? Therefore the Twelve should labor at home where the problems are and try to straighten things up? No! Verses 27 and 28 tell the Apostles: "Therefore, see to it that ye trouble not yourselves concerning the affairs of my church in this place, saith the Lord," but rather purify *your hearts* and then go about *your* labor, which is, of course, to take the gospel to all the world.

The message seems to be that the Lord Himself can care for His house, and moreover, as verses 28–33 suggest, what can be more important for the Twelve than to preach divine truth with power and authority? They are to preach to every creature who has not received the gospel, either to their damnation or to their salvation, for "unto you, the Twelve, and those, the First Presidency, who are appointed with you to be your counselors and your leaders [again the emphasis on order, everyone under the First Presidency], is the power of this priesthood given, for the last days and for the last time" (verse 30). These are the same keys which "have come down from the fathers" (verse 32). The Lord tells them, "Verily . . . behold how great is your calling" (verse 33).

A Trial of Faith in Missouri

So great is the calling that they—and we—must cleanse themselves and do their duty "lest the blood of this generation be required at your hands" (verse 33). But—and the revelation closes with this in verse 34—for the faithful, the Lord says, "My reward is with me to recompense every man according as his work shall be."

Despite the best efforts of Joseph, Sidney, Thomas, David, and Brigham, the Church could not be saved in Kirtland. Up to this point, the Prophet had patiently worked with dissenters, bringing back many, but when open rebellion broke out again in the fall of 1837, patience was no longer a virtue and backsliders were cut off. Anger mounted, division deepened, apostates grew bolder, and by year's end Brigham Young, the most vigorous and outspoken among the Prophet's defenders, was forced to flee for his life. In early January, Joseph Smith and Sidney Rigdon followed, their families close behind, and by spring most of the faithful were on their way to Missouri.

Joseph Smith arrived in Far West, Missouri, in March 1838. After firming up local organization and leadership, he then set about the business in Kirtland of removing apostates. At the April 7 conference,

David Patten reviewed the status of each of the Twelve; there were concerns about William Smith, and he was unable to recommend Elders McLellin, Boynton, Johnson, and Johnson at all. At proceedings that commenced April 12, the four Apostles, along with Oliver Cowdery and David Whitmer, were each formally tried and cut off. After months of concern and labor with his quorum, Thomas's twelve were now eight, and one of those could not be relied upon. Feeling deep concern for their quorum, no doubt Marsh and the remaining Apostles were cheered by a revelation for David Patten received April 7.

In Doctrine and Covenants 114, given April 7, 1838, verse 1 advised Patten to prepare himself, saying, "He may perform a mission unto me next spring, in company with others, even twelve including himself, to testify of my name and bear glad tidings unto all the world." What twelve, including himself? There were no longer twelve Apostles in his quorum, nor had any ever been added since its organization more than three years before. Verse 2 supplied the answer: "For verily . . . inasmuch as there are those among you who deny my name, others shall be planted in their stead and receive their bishopric." By noting that fallen brethren would be replaced and by commanding Elder Patten to prepare, after all, for a mission "with others, even twelve," this short revelation foreshadows several of the key points made more explicitly three months later.

On July 8, in answer to the query "Show us thy will, O Lord, concerning the Twelve" (headnote to D&C 118), another revelation, now Doctrine and Covenants 118, imparted firm direction and new life to the Quorum of the Twelve. "Let men be appointed to supply the place of those who are fallen," declared the revelation (verse 1). Thomas Marsh was to "remain for a season in the land of Zion," where he was now coeditor of the *Elder's Journal* with Joseph, "to publish my word" (verse 2). The others were to resume preaching and, as a quorum, prepare for a spring 1839 mission abroad. They would depart, continued the revelation, from the Far West temple site on April 26, the very day an earlier revelation had named for laying the temple cornerstone (see D&C 115).

Verse 1 of Doctrine and Covenants 118, given July 8, 1838, announced: "Let a conference be held immediately; let the Twelve be organized; and let men be appointed to supply the place of those who are fallen."

Verse 2 then authorized President Marsh to remain in Far West, Missouri, "for a season." This was not a choice between Kirtland and Missouri, as before in Doctrine and Covenants 112, but between staying for a time in Far West and going abroad immediately. Verse 3 instructed "the residue," the other Apostles who had remained faithful or who had returned to full fellowship, to "continue to preach from that hour." It promised that if they would do this "in all lowliness of heart, in meekness and humility, and long-suffering," they could still fulfill their divine mission (that is, despite disaster and division they had not yet lost the possibility of fulfilling their destiny) "and an *effectual door* shall be opened for them, from henceforth" (emphasis added; see also D&C 112:19).

Moreover, if they were thus faithful they had another promise, that while they were serving abroad, the Lord would "provide for their families" (D&C 118:3).

Verses 4 and 5 instructed, "Next spring let them [the residue and the new] depart to go over the great waters, and there promulgate my gospel [in Britain]. . . . Let them take leave of my saints in the city of Far West, on the twenty-sixth day of April next, on the building-spot of my house, saith the Lord."

The revelation closed, with verse 6, by naming those "appointed to fill the places of those who have fallen": John Taylor, John E. Page, Wilford Woodruff, and Willard Richards.

The following day, the Apostles, for the first time in months, held a formal quorum meeting. They agreed to notify immediately the four new Apostles, none of whom were in Far West, and to prepare for their mission abroad. The anticipated ordination of new Apostles, the return of Elders Kimball and Hyde from England later in the month, and this renewal of their commission to carry the gospel to the nations seemed to portend a new day for Marsh's shattered quorum. The command had been given, the date was known: finally President Marsh would have the opportunity to lead his colleagues abroad.

But it was not to be. Before the spring mission, indeed even before existing vacancies could be filled, there would be two more, one when David Patten was killed during the violence that soon erupted in northern Missouri, and the other caused by the disaffection of

President Marsh himself, in some ways a by-product of that same Missouri conflict.

Marsh's disillusionment and decision to leave the Church were the result of many factors, having to do with pride, misunderstanding, hurt feelings, suspicion, and, in Marsh's own later words, stubbornness and a loss of the Spirit.[20] Troubled of mind and spirit, feeling himself wavering, he humbled himself before the Lord in his printing shop long enough to receive a revelation about what course he should take. After sharing it with Heber Kimball and Brigham Young, he promptly went out and did the opposite, becoming bitter against the Church. Once his face was set, the stubborn, inflexible Thomas was not a man who could be turned. By removing himself from the Saints, he escaped the violence that soon decimated Far West and drove his coreligionists from Missouri, but at what cost? As he eventually came to acknowledge, his loss was the greater.

From Liberty Jail, the Prophet named George A. Smith to fill the vacancy created by the death of Elder Patten, but Marsh's position remained vacant for nearly three years. In the meantime, under the direction of President Brigham Young, now senior Apostle, the available Apostles—William Smith was not to be found, Parley Pratt was in prison, and Willard Richards was in England—boldly returned to Missouri, whence they had so recently escaped, to fulfill the July 1838 revelation requiring them to depart April 26, 1839, from "the building-spot of my house" in Far West (D&C 118:5).

Enemies had boasted that the revelation proved Joseph Smith a false prophet because it could not be fulfilled. So certain were they that no one would attempt it that they did not even bother to post a guard. Perhaps, under the circumstances, the Lord would "take the will for the deed," some Latter-day Saints urged, but Brigham Young and his associates would not allow even supposed failure to stand as a witness against Joseph. In the predawn hours they and a small group of Saints sang hymns, ordained two Apostles, laid a symbolic cornerstone, excommunicated dissidents, and departed before the first surprised anti-Mormon reached the site.

NEW HOPE IN NAUVOO

From Far West the Apostles returned to the new city being built in Illinois on the banks of the Mississippi to complete their preparations and to situate their families as well as possible before departing. Instead of keeping them at arm's length as had often been the case in Kirtland, Joseph Smith embraced them, instructed them, blessed them, and participated fully in their preparations. None, however, had means to help their families. Destitute after the Missouri tragedy, without adequate shelter or provisions, everyone suffered—the more so when summer diseases befell them in the damp, sickly hollows along the river. Consequently, it was a great test of faith to leave their families in such circumstances in order to fulfill their mission. Because they understood that the Church could provide little help, they essentially left their families in the hands of God to embark on a mission that could not be postponed and which would eventually transform the Church. The Apostles did not forget that the revelation commanding their departure also declared, "I . . . give unto them a promise that I will provide for their families" (D&C 118:3). As Brigham Young wrote to his wife from England, though he longed to be able to administer to their needs, he had faith enough not to be unduly concerned: "The Lord said by the mouth of Brother Joseph, that they should be provided for, and I believed it."[21]

The result of this sacrifice, of obedience in difficult circumstances, and of diligent efforts to labor together with unity and harmony was perhaps the most successful single mission in the history of the Church. As Elder Jeffrey R. Holland noted after reading a recent book on the subject, after this mission, "neither this group of men, the British Isles, nor the Church would ever be the same again."[22] Finally the Twelve had fulfilled the promise inherent in their calling that had so eluded them during the years under President Marsh.

The rewards for service are many and often individualized. No doubt each of the Apostles received assurances and blessings fitted to his needs, as suggested by Doctrine and Covenants 82:10: "I, the Lord, am bound when ye do what I say; but when ye do not what I say, ye have no promise." Doctrine and Covenants 126, the last section in our story, preserves one example—the knowledge that service is acceptable to the Lord: "My servant Brigham," began the revelation, given July 9, 1841, "it is no more required at your hand to leave your family as in times past, for your offering is acceptable to me." Verse 2 affirmed that "I have seen your labor and toil . . . for my name" and, verse 3: "I therefore command you to *send* my word abroad [from now on *send,* rather than take it], and take especial care of your family."

Under Brigham Young, the "new" Quorum of the Twelve proved competent and fiercely loyal to Joseph and his principles and rendered extraordinary service at great sacrifice. After shared experiences in Britain molded this new quorum into an effective, united body of power, they returned home at a time when the Prophet's needs for loyal assistance had multiplied. The result, announced by Joseph Smith on August 16, 1841, was a significant realignment of assignment and authority, with the Twelve taking their place next to the First Presidency in managing all Church affairs. The ambiguity between the high councils and the Twelve that had so vexed Thomas Marsh and the Apostles in Kirtland was over. The Apostles had completed their preparation, and the Prophet judged them, to use Brigham Young's phrase, "fit for power." What Thomas Marsh had dreamed of was now reality.

Throughout his service as President of the Twelve, Thomas Marsh had thought it his special mission to lead his quorum in taking the gospel abroad, and the July 1838 revelation, a few months before his apostasy, reaffirmed that mission (see D&C 118). His 1857 letter to Heber Kimball pleading for readmission revealed that nineteen years later he still remembered: "I know what I have done a mission was laid upon me & I have never filled it and now I fear it is too late but it is filled by another, I see, the Lord could get along very well without me and He has lost nothing by my falling out of the ranks; But O what have I lost?"[23]

Had Thomas B. Marsh remained faithful in 1838, he would have led the Quorum of the Twelve to England instead of Brigham Young and he would have presided over the "new quorum" and the "new role"—the one he had so impatiently longed for—that resulted from that mission. All this occurred, instead, without him.

NOTES

1. Brigham Young and Thomas B. Marsh, in *Journal of Discourses* (London: Latter-day Saints' Book Depot, 1854–86), 5:206–10.
2. Thomas B. Marsh to Heber C. Kimball, May 5, 1857, Heber C. Kimball Papers, Archives, The Church of Jesus Christ of Latter-day Saints, Salt Lake City, Utah; hereafter cited as Church Archives.

3. Minutes, March 28, 1835, Kirtland Record Book, 198, Church Archives.

4. See Ronald K. Esplin, "The Emergence of Brigham Young and the Twelve to Mormon Leadership, 1830–1841," PhD diss., Brigham Young University, 1981, 166ff.

5. For details, see chapter 4 in Esplin, "Emergence of Brigham Young."

6. Joseph Smith Diary, November 3, 1835, in Dean C. Jessee, ed., *The Papers of Joseph Smith* (Salt Lake City: Deseret Book, 1992), 2:63–64.

7. Joseph Smith Diary, November 5, 1835, in Jessee, *Papers of Joseph Smith,* 2:65–66.

8. Historian's Office Journal, February 16, 1859, Church Archives.

9. Minutes, February 12, 1849, Church Archives.

10. Minutes, November 30, 1847, Brigham Young Papers, Church Archives.

11. Brigham Young, in *Journal of Discourses,* 8:197.

12. For details of the Kirtland crisis, see chapters 5 through 7 in Esplin, "Emergence of Brigham Young," and chapters 17 and 18 in Milton V. Backman Jr., *The Heavens Resound: A History of the Latter day Saints in Ohio, 1830–1838* (Salt Lake City: Deseret Book, 1983); details not otherwise documented are from Esplin, "Emergence of Brigham Young."

13. Thomas B. Marsh and David Patten to Parley P. Pratt, May 10, 1837, Joseph Smith letterbook, Joseph Smith Papers, Church Archives.

14. Joseph Smith, *History of the Church of Jesus Christ of Latter-day Saints,* ed. B. H. Roberts, 2nd ed., rev. (Salt Lake City: The Church of Jesus Christ of Latter-day Saints, 1932–51), 2:489.

15. The story of Kimball's call and of the Kimball-Hyde mission is told in James B. Allen, Ronald K. Esplin, and David J. Whittaker, *Men with a Mission: The Quorum of the Twelve Apostles in the British Isles, 1837–1841* (Salt Lake City: Deseret Book, 1992), 23–53.

16. Wilford Woodruff Diary, June 25, 1857, LDS Church Archives.

17. Marsh autobiography published in *Deseret News,* March 24, 1858.

18. If this is the allusion, it would not necessarily be an anachronism. Discussion of and prophecies about a destiny in the Rocky Mountains can now be demonstrated long before Nauvoo.

19. Esplin, "Emergence of Brigham Young," 313–44.

20. Esplin, "Emergence of Brigham Young," 339ff.

21. Brigham Young to Mary Ann Young, October 16, 1840, in Allen, Esplin, and Whittaker, *Men with a Mission,* 399.

22. Jeffrey R. Holland to Allen, Esplin, and Whittaker, July 31, 1992.

23. Thomas B. Marsh to Heber C. Kimball, May 5, 1857, Heber C. Kimball Papers, Church Archives.

CHAPTER TWENTY-ONE

STRENGTHENING MARRIAGE AND FAMILY RELATIONSHIPS— THE LORD'S WAY

DOUGLAS E. BRINLEY

The Doctrine and Covenants and the prophets of the Restoration have had much to say about marriage and family, for celestial marriage is a doctrine of major significance. The Creator ordained the family as the basic unit of His kingdom, both in this life and beyond. He has an interest in how families function, for the plan of salvation was designed to exalt His family. Jesus Christ made it possible for us to live forever as male and female beings; therefore it is only natural that after years in marriage and parenting roles, our greatest interest would be the continuation of these relationships when we are resurrected beings in the hereafter. In truth, that is the plan God ordained for His children. Exaltation, the highest of eternal opportunities, is the continuation of marriage and family relationships beyond this brief span of mortality (see D&C 131:1–4). We came to this earth to qualify for eternal life, and marriage is one of the requirements. The highest degree of glory is a family kingdom (see D&C 131:4). The Apostle Paul said, "Neither is the man without the woman, neither the woman without the man, in the Lord" (1 Corinthians 11:11). Such a lofty ideal is of little value, however, if our family relationships are not strong and healthy in this life. Does it not seem inconsistent to think

Douglas E. Brinley is a professor of Church history and doctrine at Brigham Young University.

that our dislike for each other in this life will suddenly change at death, and we then will be forever deeply committed to each other?

The Lord's way of strengthening marriage and family relationships is to reveal to His children the doctrine of their origin and potential. Doctrine is the basis for ethical or Christlike behavior, because what we believe determines how we behave. When people comprehend their relationship to Deity and understand their potential for exaltation, they tend to use their agency to make choices that lead to eternal life. Therefore, it is doctrine that provides a theory or framework to keep marriage and family relationships "on course." President Boyd K. Packer explained the link between doctrine and personal actions: "True doctrine, understood, changes attitudes and behavior. The study of the doctrines of the gospel will improve behavior quicker than a study of behavior will improve behavior."[1]

Knowing that marriage is eternal influences us not only to exercise care in our mate selection but also to do all in our power to ensure the success of this newly formed partnership. How we feel about each other, how we treat each other, and how we meet each other's needs are factors that contribute to marital satisfaction; how willingly and how well we function in our marital roles is grounded in our doctrinal framework.

We also need to understand the importance of marriage and family in the eternal plan. In a general conference address, Elder Bruce R. McConkie explained: "From the moment of birth into mortality to the time we are married in the temple, everything we have in the whole gospel system is to prepare and qualify us to enter that holy order of matrimony which makes us husband and wife in this life and in the world to come.

"Then from the moment we are sealed together . . . everything connected with revealed religion is designed to help us keep the terms and conditions of our marriage covenant, so that this covenant will have efficacy, virtue, and force in the life to come. . . .

"There is nothing in this world as important as the creation and perfection of family units of the kind contemplated in the gospel of Jesus Christ."[2]

From this perspective, it is clear why prophet-leaders have made statements that give such a high priority to family life. President David O. McKay: "No other success can compensate for failure in the home."[3] President Harold B. Lee: "The most important work you will ever do will be within the walls of your own home."[4] President Spencer W. Kimball: "Our success [as a people, as a Church] will largely be determined by how faithfully we focus on living the gospel in the home."[5] President Ezra Taft Benson: "No other institution can take the place of the home or fulfill its essential function."[6]

DOCTRINES THAT INFLUENCE OUR ACTIONS IN MARRIAGE AND FAMILY RELATIONSHIPS

Doctrines that can generate in our hearts a desire to be effective marriage partners and parents include the following:

1. The premortal life and the purpose of mortality.
2. Eternal marriage.
3. The three degrees of glory.
4. The damnation and curse of Lucifer.
5. Rearing the children of God.

These doctrines provide meaning and perspective to marriage. Covenants strengthen commitment, and Christlike behavior (patience, meekness, charity, kindness, and forgiveness, for example) prepares us for exaltation. It is a dynamic process to move from understanding doctrinal principles to gaining exaltation, and the Atonement of Christ makes the plan operational.

THE PREMORTAL LIFE AND THE PURPOSE OF MORTALITY

The doctrine of the premortal life proclaims us to be the literal offspring of heavenly parents. We lived before this life, in their presence, as their male and female spirit children. Our spirit bodies were similar in appearance to our mortal bodies (see Ether 3:16–17); however, these bodies in the premortal state were not capable, at least to our knowledge, of reproduction, and therefore marriage was not possible. In fact, one of the primary purposes in our coming to this "second estate" was to obtain a body of element—flesh and blood—to begin, for the first time, our stewardship in marriage and parenthood. The Lord explains that marriage was ordained of Him and that the earth was created so that His children could fulfill their destiny:

"I say unto you, that whoso forbiddeth to marry is not ordained of God, for marriage is ordained of God unto man. Wherefore . . .

they twain shall be one flesh, and all this [marriage] that the earth might answer the end of its creation; and that [the earth] might be filled with the measure of man, *according to his creation before the world was made"* (D&C 49:15–17; emphasis added).

This earth, then, becomes the residence for our spirit bodies, which are united with a body of element in a probationary state. Here we are born as infants and grow to be adult men and women. Ideally, we marry and exercise our divine powers to create and bear offspring. For the first time in our existence, we are privileged to marry and participate in a functional sex role whereby we can reproduce "after our kind."

In the premortal life, each of us was a single adult, a spirit son or daughter of God, and we lived in His presence for some time. President Brigham Young explained our relationship: "You are well acquainted with God our Heavenly Father, or the great Elohim. You are all well acquainted with him, for there is not a soul of you but what has lived in his house and dwelt with him year after year. . . .

"There is not a person here to-day but what is a son or a daughter of that Being. In the spirit world their spirits were first begotten and brought forth, and they lived there with their parents for ages before they came here."[7]

In the premortal realm, the only family relationships we experienced were those of sons or daughters of God and brothers or sisters to each other. There we were never intimately involved with one of the opposite sex in a marriage relationship, possessing the ability to create children.

Consider how long each of us anticipated this opportunity to come to earth to marry and become parents. It has been almost six thousand years since Adam and Eve brought about the Fall; at least seven thousand years were required to create the earth (using the most conservative estimates from Abraham 3:4, 9); there was a period from the beginning of the earth's creation backward to the Council in Heaven; and even further back was our birth as spirit children and a maturing period to become an adult male or female spirit before the Council in Heaven. Even a conservative estimate of these earlier periods (and perhaps it was really eons of time) makes it evident that we waited a substantial period of time as "single adults" to come to this earth to experience marriage and the privilege of beginning our own family life.

In comparison to this lengthy premortal period of time as single adults, we are married for only a brief period here in this probation—fifty to perhaps eighty years at most. Yet the staggering reality is that the quality of our marriage and family relationships in this life greatly influences whether these privileges will be extended into eternity. Here we have the privilege to form an eternal partnership if we are faithful to the laws and covenants upon which this relationship is based. How important it is that we build an eternal foundation under marriage and family relationships.

ETERNAL MARRIAGE

In the Doctrine and Covenants, we learn that "the spirit and the body are the soul of man. And the resurrection from the dead is the redemption of the soul" (D&C 88:15–16). The soul is two separate "bodies," born of two different sets of parents—one mortal, the other immortal. Our flesh and blood bodies were created by parents who transmitted to us the effects of the Fall. Neither our bodies, nor those of our children, will escape death and dissolution. But the parents of our spirit body are immortal, resurrected parents, and therefore our spirit bodies are not subject to death.[8] Sexual relations, conception, and birth are important elements in the creation of a soul, for these processes bring together our two bodies for an earthly probation. Through the power of procreation, we assist our Heavenly Father in bringing His children to their mortal state. At death the mortal body and eternal spirit separate. Mortal remains are committed to the earth, while our spirit, the "real" us, inhabits the "spirit world."[9] When resurrected, there is no further separation of the body and spirit, for a resurrected person cannot die (see Alma 11:45).

Concerning the spirits who were awaiting the Resurrection, the Lord explained, "Their sleeping dust was to be restored unto its perfect frame, bone to his bone, and the sinews and the flesh upon them, the spirit and the body to be united never again to be divided, that they might receive a fulness of joy" (D&C 138:17).

Clearly we are in a very important phase of our eternal existence. The Savior's Atonement makes possible our resurrection with "a body of flesh and bones as tangible as man's" (D&C 130:22). Our resurrection enables our eternal spirit to be restored to its former body of "dust" (now refined and purified) with male or female attributes. Exalted beings have bodies capable of generating life.[10] Our association as husband and wife in that sphere will be "coupled with eternal glory, which glory we do not now enjoy" (D&C 130:2). Priesthood keys restored by Elijah to Joseph Smith allow the organization of eternal families through sealings for time and eternity (see D&C 110:13).

If a couple in mortality are married by priesthood authority (the authority of an eternal being), are faithful to their covenants, and become Christlike in nature, they will come forth in the resurrection clothed with immortality and eternal lives, meaning that they shall continue to bear children. "Then shall they be gods, because they have no end; therefore shall they be from everlasting to everlasting, because they continue" (D&C 132:20). As resurrected beings, husband and wife will have the power to beget spirit children. On June 30, 1916, the First Presidency and the Council of the Twelve Apostles explained the principle of "eternal lives": "So far as the stages of eternal progression and attainment have been made known through divine revelation, we are to understand that only resurrected and glorified beings can become parents of spirit offspring. Only such exalted souls have reached maturity in the appointed course of eternal life; and these spirits born to them in the eternal worlds will pass in due sequence through the several stages or estates by which the glorified parents have attained exaltation."[11]

THE THREE DEGREES OF GLORY

Another tenet intertwined with the doctrine of eternal marriage is that of the assignment of souls to degrees of glory. In eternity, the power to beget children is limited to those who reach the highest degree of glory (see D&C 131:4). Elder Melvin J. Ballard explained the meaning of "eternal increase": "What do we mean by endless or eternal increase? We mean that through the righteousness and faithfulness of men and women who keep the commandments of God they will come forth with celestial bodies, fitted and prepared to enter into their great, high and eternal glory in the celestial kingdom of God; and unto them, through their preparation, there will come spirit children. I don't think that is very difficult to comprehend. The nature of the offspring is determined by the nature of the substance that flows in the veins of the being. When blood flows in the veins of the being the offspring will be what blood produces, which is tangible flesh and bone; but when that which flows in the veins is spirit matter, a substance which is more refined and pure and glorious than blood, the offspring of such beings will be "spirit children."[12]

The Doctrine and Covenants explicitly states that only those who attain to the highest degree of glory remain married and possess the power of increase or "eternal lives": "In the celestial glory there are three heavens or degrees; and in order to obtain the highest [degree], a man must enter into this order of the priesthood (meaning the new and everlasting covenant of marriage); and if he does not [enter this order of marriage], he cannot obtain it [the highest degree of glory]. He may enter into the other [degrees], but that is the end of his kingdom; he cannot have an increase" (D&C 131:1–4).

This scripture confirms that those who retain the powers of increase in the next life are those who inherit the highest degree of glory. A temple sealing confers keys to allow a man and woman to come forth in the Resurrection and retain these life-giving powers. At the time of marriage, they enter into the same covenant as did Abraham, in which he was promised innumerable seed (see Abraham 2:9–11). Elder Bruce R. McConkie said, "Those portions of [the Abrahamic covenant] which pertain to personal exaltation and eternal increase are renewed with each member of the house of Israel who enters the order of celestial marriage."[13] Those keys were restored by Elias, who appeared to Joseph Smith in the Kirtland Temple on April 3, 1836. He restored the "dispensation of the gospel of Abraham, saying that in us and our seed all generations after us should be blessed [with the gospel and the priesthood]" (D&C 110:12). In the Resurrection, with death no longer a factor, our seed shall be as innumerable as the "sand upon the seashore" (D&C 132:30).

THE DAMNATION AND CURSE OF LUCIFER

Another doctrine that adds to our perspective of marriage and parenthood is that of the limitations placed upon Lucifer for his rebellion in the premortal world. His damnation consists of his never being allowed to marry or have posterity. He is single and impotent forever, and he wants all of mankind to be as he is. He does not want any who kept their first estate, who now are in their "second estate," to retain the powers of procreation beyond this life. He realizes that we have these powers in mortality, but he knows that if he can prevent us from using these powers within the bounds God has set, or if we fail to build marriages worthy of exaltation, we will lose these powers when we die. Elder Orson Pratt wrote of Satan's limitations and of those who attain to lower degrees of glory: "God . . . has ordained that the highest order and class of beings that should exist in the eternal worlds should exist in the capacity of husbands and wives, and that they alone should have the privilege of propagating their species. . . . Now it is wise, no doubt, in the Great Creator to thus limit this great and heavenly principle to those who have arrived or come to the highest state of exaltation . . . to dwell in His presence, that they by this means shall be prepared to bring up their spirit offspring in all pure and holy principles in the eternal worlds, in order that they may be made happy. Consequently, He does not entrust this privilege of multiplying spirits with the terrestrial or telestial, or the lower order of beings there, nor with angels. But why not? Because they have not proved themselves worthy of this great privilege."[14]

Individuals who suffer "deaths" (D&C 132:25) are those who no longer are able to propagate their own kind after resurrection. On another occasion Elder Orson Pratt wrote on a similar theme: "Could wicked and malicious beings, who have irradicated every feeling of love from their bosoms, be permitted to propagate their species, the offspring would partake of all the evil, wicked, and malicious nature of their parents. . . .

" . . . *It is for this reason that God will not permit the fallen angels to multiply:* it is for this reason that God has ordained marriages for the righteous only [in eternity]: it is for this reason that God will put a final stop to the multiplication of the wicked after this life: it is for this reason that none but those who have kept the celestial law will be permitted to multiply after the resurrection: . . . for they alone are prepared to beget and bring forth [such] offspring."[15]

From these statements we understand what a great privilege it is to come to earth to obtain a physical body, to learn self-discipline, to be valiant sons and daughters (faithful to eternal principles), to marry, and to rear a posterity. Satan will do his best to destroy the plan of God by destroying families. He can destroy us if we are careless or fail to keep our covenants.

Rearing the Children of God

When we speak of "our children," we mean the spirit children of our Heavenly Father. He places a great trust in us when He assigns His children to our custody. We are honored by the stewardship we are given to create bodies for His spirit children. Because women conceive, carry to term, and bear His offspring, their importance to God's plan is critical. The Lord explains: "For [a wife is] given unto [her husband] to multiply and replenish the earth, according to my commandment, and to fulfil the promise which was given by my Father before the foundation of the world, and for [her] exaltation in the eternal worlds, that [she] may bear the souls of men; for herein is the work of my Father continued, that he may be glorified" (D&C 132:63).

If couples were to decide not to have children (and many in our society are making that decision), the Father's plan would cease to function. We are privileged to assist God in His great work to "bring to pass the immortality and eternal life" of His children (Moses 1:39). We bring them to this earth to fulfill their eternal destiny, the same as our parents have done for us.

Could there be a greater trust given to two people than to have the children of God assigned to them with the responsibility to prepare them for exaltation? Certainly our heavenly parents have a great interest in how their children are reared during their probationary state. An understanding of this doctrine would surely prevent the physical, verbal, and mental abuse of many of these children in our day.

Doctrine Leads to the Development of Christlike Attributes

The five doctrines discussed above can create in us a broader vision of the purpose of life, of marriage, and of our purpose in mortality. We realize that to succeed in these stewardships, our example, our model, must be Christ, for He taught the qualities that are essential to succeed in family relationships. Not only did Christ make the

Father's plan operational through His Atonement, but He also came to the earth to teach us the character traits that are necessary if we are to be part of a celestial society. Gospel doctrine and our faithful observance of covenants make it more probable that we will develop Christlike traits in our character. The Doctrine and Covenants lists a number of these traits that would undoubtedly make a remarkable difference in our marriage and family behavior if we were to incorporate them into our nature: repentance, charity, humility, kindness, temperance, diligence, faith, hope, love, a spirit of meekness, an eye single to the glory of God, virtue, knowledge, patience, brotherly kindness, and godliness. We are taught to be one with God and man, ask, knock, keep the commandments, seek to bring forth and establish the cause of Zion, seek not for riches but for wisdom, assist in bringing forth God's work, do good, hold out faithful to the end, inquire of God, be sober, doubt not, fear not, be faithful, murmur not, resist temptation, study it out in our mind, pray always, harden not our hearts, read the scriptures, seek counsel from Church leaders, guard against hypocrisy and guile, allow virtue to garnish our thoughts unceasingly, possess a broken heart and a contrite spirit, love our husband or wife with all our heart, live together in love, practice virtue and holiness before the Lord, have the Holy Ghost as a constant companion, and endure to the end.

How could a marriage fail if each spouse made these traits his or her creed to live by? Such attributes would make us more attractive, lovable, and competent marriage partners. On the other hand, when we emulate Satan's traits (temper, anger, contention, bickering), we become repulsive, and relationships suffer. Our goal must be to strive to be like the Savior in every way—emotionally, spiritually, mentally, and physically. If we follow His example, our marriages will be stronger and our children may be more likely to choose to adopt our values and follow our example.

Understanding His Atonement and Resurrection brings an appreciation for Christ, not only for what He did to remit sins but also for how, in overcoming both physical and spiritual death, He made it possible for marriage and family life to be eternal. The Resurrection restores our bodies of element and spirit, male and female attributes in those bodies, and relationships organized by the sealing power to be forever. In the Resurrection we retain all of the deep affections of the heart we have come to prize in this life. Elder Parley P. Pratt marveled at this doctrine: "It was at this time that I received from him [Joseph Smith] the first idea of eternal family organization, and the eternal union of the sexes in those inexpressibly endearing relationships which none but the highly intellectual, the refined and pure in heart, know how to prize, and which are at the very foundation of everything worthy to be called happiness. . . .

"It was from [Joseph] that I learned that the wife of my bosom might be secured to me for time and all eternity; and that the refined sympathies and affections which endeared us to each other emanated from the fountain of divine eternal love. It was from him that I learned that we might cultivate these affections, and grow and increase in the same to all eternity. . . .

"I had loved before, but I knew not why. But now I loved—with a pureness—an intensity of elevated, exalted feeling, which would lift my soul from the transitory things of this groveling sphere and expand it as the ocean."[16]

MARRIAGE AND FAMILY LIFE—PRACTICAL IMPLICATIONS

These five doctrines should influence in a practical way how well our families function. Knowing the importance of marriage in this life and that we anticipated this experience; knowing that Christ's Atonement and Resurrection restore bodies and sexuality; knowing that the Judgment assigns individuals to kingdoms of no marriage and family if they do not function well in marital roles; realizing that Lucifer's damnation was the denial of marriage and the impossibility of his ever becoming a father, thus explaining his relentless efforts to destroy us and prevent us from having these blessings beyond this life; and realizing that our children are lent to us by eternal parents who expect us to rear them in righteousness—all these should provide us with powerful reasons and incentives to build strong families.

Practically speaking, how could a person who understands these principles abuse a spouse or child? How could a person with an eternal perspective of family life, who has made sacred covenants with the Author of the plan, use anger to control or manipulate or intimidate a spouse or child when it is obvious he is using Satan's techniques? Could an unrepentant person who had violated a position of trust as spouse or parent ever, in all eternity, be allowed those roles again, especially if that person was no longer subject to death so that his evil influence would never end? It is not reasonable that God would allow a being with that temperament to remain married or continue in a parenting role. A degree of glory with no marriage or children would best satisfy justice. The powers of increase for such a person would be removed at the time of death.

These doctrines should have another effect—that of humbling us. We know so little about marriage or parenting during our brief experience here. Why do we think we are experts on marriage matters or parenting practices when we have been in these roles for such a short period of time? As we look back on a lifetime of parenting, we all realize that we could have done some things better. Marriage is a commitment to learn and work together if we are to succeed in this adventure. We must be good students of marriage and family life as we learn from our spouse and children their perceptions, feelings, and responses, which often vary from ours. Parents must teach, be firm, and insist on obedience to commonsense rules because they are responsible for the direction of the family and they have been down the road a little farther; but even then, our teaching should be charitable and kind to those we are helping along the path. If we choose to be angry or careless through our own spiritual immaturity and offend others, when we regain our senses (perspective), surely we would seek forgiveness as we realize the destructive nature of our actions. We would want to restore our relationships through apologies and repentance. We would make things right with the most important people in our lives. How relieved we would be to know that an atonement had been made that allows us to repent and seek forgiveness of God and others for our mistakes and misjudgments; for when we offend members of our family, we offend God. Anger causes a withdrawal of the Spirit, and that departure should serve as a further reminder to us of our need to repent and repair damaged relationships in seeking a return of the Spirit.

Furthermore, a Christlike attitude would cause us, if others were thoughtless towards us, to quickly forgive, for we realize how shallow it would be to take offense when none was intended and we realize that we too have offended. The Golden Rule would apply. How easily we would forgive little children or an eternal companion for any "offense." In fact, how could a man or woman take offense at the words or actions of any other family member when he or she understands the nature of relationships in the plan of salvation?

It sounds simple, doesn't it? But why shouldn't this be the outcome? Perhaps we fail to follow this model because we do not review these doctrines of marriage and family periodically, or we have lost our eternal perspective. If we have never had the vision, or if we lose the ideal of marriage, then we allow the carnal side of our natures to prevail. When our vision is clouded, we act more like the "natural man," and if we are not careful we will follow Lucifer more than the Savior. When we "lose our temper" or say hurtful things or make statements that devastate others, we need to stop that behavior and begin using skills that will bless and strengthen others. The gospel is repentance-oriented; perhaps that is why the Lord has us renew our covenants with Him each week through the sacrament. A time for rethinking, or renewal, serves to remind us of our origins and our dependence on Him if we expect to gain eternal life. When we do not take the sacrament or renew our eternal perspective and make needed changes (repent), we lose the Spirit of the Lord, turn inward, and become insensitive to the needs and feelings of others, and our family relationships suffer.

We complicate repentance by justifying and defending our behavior or resorting to blaming others for our failures. An arrogant attitude, personal pride, and selfishness may prevent us from humbly reviewing our family relationships to help us make needed changes.

When doctrine guides our minds and hearts, we will not allow anger or negative feelings to generate in the first place. We *are* free agents. We *can* choose how we respond to events. We *can* prevent our interpretation of external events from being used to devastate family members. We surely had that ability to choose responses when we were in our dating years. If a date misses a golf or tennis ball, we laugh; in contrast, when a family member misses the ball, we may be sarcastic and critical. Who does not remember being angry and upset with a family member about some matter, only to have a friend call and we answer with a different voice and demeanor? Somehow, it seems, we have the ability to act more civilized with strangers who have no eternal connections to us than we do with those of our own household whom we have invited to join our eternal family! When people date, seek affection or intimacy, try to impress customers in business, or visit close friends, they go out of their way not to offend or take offense because they realize that to act on negative emotions brings undesirable consequences. At such times we are able to exercise self-discipline—clear evidence that these responses are within our control.

The Savior was made perfect because of this ability to choose. Though He was "in all points tempted like as we are" (Hebrews 4:15), He chose not to respond destructively or in ways that hurt others. (Occasionally the hypocrisy of His enemies made it necessary for Him to confront them, in which case they chose to take offense rather than repent.) His understanding of doctrine and His role as the Son of God in the plan of salvation gave Him a perspective and love for His brothers and sisters that made it possible for Him not to sin against people.

Modern prophets have emphasized selfishness and pride as common reasons we take offense, delay repentance, or remain unforgiving—traits never part of Christ's nature. Our sins are a result of our carelessness in losing our eternal perspective and becoming entangled in worldliness. At times we act as if we enjoy being offended so that we have an excuse to retaliate. Or we hold grudges against others to justify our position, not evaluating righteously the circumstances. It seems, at times, as if we prefer being cantankerous rather than exercising charity and forgiveness. When we choose to behave in this manner, we act more like Satan than like Christ.

The Lord told His disciples, "Ye ought to forgive one another; for he that forgiveth not his brother his trespasses standeth condemned before the Lord; *for there remaineth in him the greater sin.* I, the Lord, will forgive whom I will forgive, but of you it is required to forgive all men. And ye ought to say in your hearts—let God judge between me and thee, and reward thee according to thy deeds" (D&C 64:9–11). How could disciples who knew gospel principles and had the vision of eternity do otherwise? No wonder repentance is at the heart of the gospel and the Atonement is so critical to our spiritual progress.

When individuals understand how the doctrines of the gospel apply to their family life and have a vision of eternity, they are able to establish a Zion society—a place not only where people are physically cared for but also where they love each other as they understand their relationships to one another and help each other to obtain eternal life. This condition existed for some time after the visit of the resurrected Lord to the American continent:

"There were no envyings, nor strifes, nor tumults, nor whoredoms, nor lyings, nor murders, nor any manner of lasciviousness; and surely there could not be a happier people among all the people who had been created by the hand of God. There were no robbers, nor murderers. . . . And how blessed were they! For the Lord did bless them in all their doings; yea, even they were blessed and prospered . . . And there was no contention in all the land" (4 Nephi 1:16–18).

This condition results when people possess a doctrinal perspective on the purposes of mortality, their hearts are softened, and they are under covenant to honor God and to bless their fellow beings. Applying Christlike principles in family relationships is natural under these conditions, thanks to the knowledge and commitment of the participants to the plan of salvation and the place of marriage and family in their lives.

MARRIAGE AND FAMILY—A PERSONAL EXPERIENCE

When we talk of marriage and family, we touch on the things of eternity, for we are eternal beings. We touch on the true source of happiness, on the fountain of life, on feelings and emotions. God established that man and woman should not be alone. It is through marriage that we develop companionship and intimate relationships that are sacred and divine.

To share my own feelings on this matter, the longer I am married to my wife, the more I love her and cherish our association. The more we share our feelings and experiences, the stronger my love and appreciation for her grows. The more intertwined our lives become through our children, finances, intimacy, and a host of things we must do in life to live together, as we learn to meet each other's needs and deal with mortal limitations (including aging factors), the more I care about her.

Given our intimate association, would I want to worship a God who designed a plan of salvation that has me come to earth, gain a mortal body, marry and have children, spend all of my mortal years in a family, and then, after all the cherished experiences and emotional affiliations gained through such associations, allowed me to die and lose my family connections and ties in the grave? Without any hesitation my answer would be no. If that were the result of this mortal experience, I would want nothing to do with so-called religion. What an uninspired ending! If the Atonement of Jesus Christ had not the power to restore to me a resurrected body and my family associations (knowing that I must be worthy), I could not worship the God who implemented it. Such a theology would cause us to live in constant fear that we might lose our life and cut our family associations short. The death of a loved one would be tragic. Every honest soul would ask himself, under such assumptions, "Why would God perpetrate such a hoax? Why would a Being who knows all things and who has all power instigate such a useless and wasteful plan?" Surely one would be compelled to ask, "What was the purpose of it all?" "Why marry?" "Why bear and rear children?" As the song says, "If love never lasts forever, tell me, what's forever for?"[17]

I feel the same about my children. I find myself deeply involved in their lives, wanting to know how to help and assist them without interfering. Each child is important to me and contributes to my happiness. It must be my work (and perhaps my glory) to bring to pass their eternal life in any way that I can. I know in some small degree from my own limited experience with my little kingdom how my Heavenly Father must feel about each of His children. And would not these feelings about marriage and parenting cause any husband or wife, mother or father, to control his or her own reactions and responses?

President George Q. Cannon summarized the potential of this noble adventure of marriage and family: "We believe that when a man and woman are united as husband and wife and they love each other, their hearts and feelings are one, that that love is as enduring as eternity itself, and that when death overtakes them it will *neither extinguish nor cool that love, but that it will brighten and kindle it to a purer flame,* and that it will endure through eternity; and that if we have offspring they will be with us and our mutual associations will be one of the chief joys of the heaven to which we are hastening. . . . God has restored the everlasting priesthood, by which ties can be formed, consecrated and consummated, which shall be as enduring as we ourselves are enduring, that is, as our spiritual nature; and husbands and wives will be united together, and they and their children will dwell and associate together eternally, and this, as I have said, will constitute one of the chief joys of heaven; and we look forward to it with delightful anticipations."[18]

That is one of the "plain and precious" truths restored in the present dispensation (1 Nephi 13:34). The Lord told Joseph Smith: "And verily I say unto you, let this house be built unto my name, that I may reveal mine ordinances therein unto my people; for I deign to reveal unto my church things which have been kept hid from before the foundation of the world, things that pertain to the dispensation of the fulness of times" (D&C 124:40–41).

One of the "things" that have been revealed in our day is the eternal nature of the family, information apparently lost during the Great Apostasy. Marriage and family life were meant to be eternal, for we ourselves are eternal.

Adam and Eve made mortality possible in order for us to experience marriage and have children, and Jesus Christ made it possible for marriage to never end. No wonder we shouted for joy in the premortal existence at the prospect of earth life. This is our opportunity to marry, and it provides us the privilege to plumb the depths of another soul in an outpouring and sharing of feelings and passion while participating in the miracle of conception and birth. What a profound experience for a husband to watch his wife bring forth their offspring—to bring into mortality another being, a kindred spirit, with similar desires to accept this mortal stewardship to fashion his or her own eternal family unit. Marriage connects our past eternity of singleness to a never-ending future of marriage and family life. Never again will we be without the companionship of our spouse. Our theology blesses married couples.

CONCLUSION

When we understand clearly the doctrines associated with marriage and family and the priority of marriage and family in the plan of salvation, we are struck with the desire to live in harmony with doctrines that will exalt. Doctrines place in perspective the purpose and meaning of marriage and family; priorities keep us on the path to our potential, which is eternal life. With a vision of eternity, we are more likely to monitor prayerfully and carefully each relationship in our family because we know our potential. We are more interested and sensitive to the needs of our spouse and children because of our long-range commitment. We are eager to develop bonds of affection and caring when we understand the "big picture." We are more willing to communicate and share information, our lives, and our feelings to strengthen our relationships with each other when we know we are building for eternity.

When we comprehend the doctrine of eternal families, we gain the power to discipline ourselves (repent) to be the kind of husbands and wives, fathers and mothers, who will develop Christlike traits and characteristics essential to qualify to live together in love and happiness in this life as a prelude to eternal life.

The Lord's solution to marriage and family problems is for each of us to understand and practice the doctrines of the gospel as they apply to marriage and family life. These doctrines place in perspective mortality and the Atonement. We come to know how God would have us live and act if we are to achieve eternal life—the kind of life that He lives. What would be more natural than for two married people to desire to be as their heavenly parents? As God's children we have that right, if we will abide the laws, covenants, and principles of the gospel. If we will repent, the Atonement clears the way for us to be an eternal family. With an eternal perspective we can fulfill our destiny of gaining immortality and "eternal lives."

NOTES

1. Boyd K. Packer, "Do Not Fear," *Ensign,* May 2004, 79.
2. Bruce R. McConkie, "Salvation Is a Family Affair," *Improvement Era,* June 1970, 43–44.
3. David O. McKay, in *Improvement Era,* June 1964, 445.
4. Harold B. Lee, *Stand Ye in Holy Places* (Salt Lake City: Deseret Book, 1974), 255.
5. Spencer W. Kimball, "Let Us Move Forward and Upward," *Ensign,* May 1979, 83.
6. Ezra Taft Benson, "The Values by Which to Live," *Leaders Magazine,* October–November 1984, 154.
7. Brigham Young, *Discourses of Brigham Young,* comp. John A. Widtsoe (Salt Lake City: Deseret Book, 1951), 50.
8. When we speak of a spirit body, it is, nevertheless, a body of matter. "There is no such thing as immaterial matter. All spirit is matter, but it is more fine or pure, and can only be discerned by purer eyes; we cannot see it [in our finite, mortal state]; but when our bodies

are purified [resurrected] we shall see that it is all matter" (D&C 131:7–8). Thus bodies formed in the premortal life were bodies of celestial matter.

9. The "spirit world" is here on this earth. "The earth and other planets of a like sphere, have their inward or spiritual spheres, as well as their outward, or temporal [spheres]. The one is peopled by temporal tabernacles, and the other by spirits. A veil is drawn between the one sphere and the other, whereby all the objects in the spiritual sphere are rendered invisible to those in the temporal" (Parley P. Pratt, *Key to the Science of Theology*, 9th ed. [Salt Lake City: Deseret Book, 1965], 126–27).

10. In mortal life we create bodies that are subject to death and dissolution. In the Resurrection, however, since we will no longer be subject to death, we will have the power to organize bodies that will never die—an endowment greater than that given us in mortal life.

11. James R. Clark, comp., *Messages of the First Presidency* (Salt Lake City: Bookcraft, 1971), 5:34.

12. M. Russell Ballard, *Melvin J. Ballard—Crusader for Righteousness* (Salt Lake City: Bookcraft, 1966), 211.

13. Bruce R. McConkie, *Mormon Doctrine*, 2nd ed. (Salt Lake City: Bookcraft, 1966), 13.

14. Orson Pratt, in *Journal of Discourses* (London: Latter-day Saints' Book Depot, 1854–86), 13:186.

15. Orson Pratt, in *The Seer*, January 1853, 156–57; emphasis added.

16. Parley P. Pratt, *Autobiography of Parley Parker Pratt*, ed. Parley P. Pratt Jr., 3rd ed. (Salt Lake City: Deseret Book, 1970), 297–98.

17. Rafe Vanhoy, "What's Forever For" (Nashville: Hal Leonard, 1978).

18. George Q. Cannon, in *Journal of Discourses*, 14:320–21; emphasis added.

CHAPTER TWENTY-TWO

THE VISION OF THE REDEMPTION OF THE DEAD (D&C 138)

ROBERT L. MILLET

In an address to Church educators in 1977, President Boyd K. Packer stressed that we live in a day of great events relating to the scriptures. He reminded us that it has only been a short time since two revelations were added to the standard works, both of which have salvation for the dead as a central theme. President Packer continued: "I was surprised, and I think all of the Brethren were surprised, at how casually that announcement of two additions to the standard works was received by the Church. But we will live to sense the significance of it; we will tell our grandchildren and our great grandchildren, and we will record in our diaries, that we were on the earth and remember when that took place."[1] The two revelations to which President Packer made reference are sections 137 and 138 of the Doctrine and Covenants. This article will discuss the historical setting and doctrinal significance of section 138, President Joseph F. Smith's vision of the redemption of the dead.

During the last six months of his life, President Joseph F. Smith suffered from the effects of advancing years (he was in his eightieth year) and spent much of his time in his own room in the Beehive House. However, President Smith did manage to garner enough strength to attend the 89th Semiannual General Conference of the Church (October 1918). At the opening session of the general

Robert L. Millet is Richard L. Evans Professor of Religious Understanding and former dean of Religious Education at Brigham Young University.

conference (Friday, October 4), he arose to welcome and address the Saints, and with a voice filled with emotion[2] he spoke the following:

"As most of you, I suppose, are aware, I have undergone a siege of very serious illness for the last five months. It would be impossible for me, on this occasion, to occupy sufficient time to express the desires of my heart and my feelings, as I would desire to express them to you. . . .

"I will not, I dare not, attempt to enter upon many things that are resting upon my mind this morning, and I shall postpone until some future time, the Lord being willing, my attempt to tell you some of the things that are in my mind, and that dwell in my heart. *I have not lived alone these last five months. I have dwelt in the spirit of prayer, of supplication, of faith and of determination; and I have had my communication with the Spirit of the Lord continuously.*"[3]

According to the President's son, Joseph Fielding Smith, the prophet was here expressing (albeit in broadest terms) the fact that during the past half-year he had been the recipient of numerous manifestations, some of which he had shared with his son both before and after the conference. One of these manifestations, the vision of the redemption of the dead, had been received just the day before, on October 3, and was recorded immediately following the close of the conference.[4]

PREPARATION FOR THE VISION

The state of the world in early 1918 was cause for serious reflection upon such matters as the purpose of life and death. World War I, the "war to end all wars," cast its ominous shadow upon the globe, and Latter-day Saints were not immune from its broadening effects. By early January 1919, approximately fifteen thousand members of the Church were involved in the military services.[5] Revolutions in Russia and Finland further intensified the anxieties and confirmed the fears that truly war had begun to be poured out upon all nations (see D&C 87:2). By October an influenza epidemic began to spread throughout the land, leaving death and sorrow in its wake.

A few reminders about the status of the Church during the closing years of President Smith's administration may also help to place things into perspective. At the close of 1916, there were 819 wards, 73 stakes, and 21 missions with just over 1,300 full-time missionaries.

The new Church office building on 47 East South Temple was nearing completion, and the first temples outside the continental United States were under construction in Canada and Hawaii.[6]

Nowhere do we see the critical preparation and readiness for the vision more than in the life and ministry of Joseph F. Smith. The son of Hyrum the Patriarch and nephew of Joseph the Seer, Joseph F. possessed the blood of the prophets. He was foreordained to serve the Lord in the leading councils of the Church, and he spent the last fifty years of his life realizing that election, actively involved as a legal administrator in the kingdom. Young Joseph F. was called while in his teens to serve as a missionary to Hawaii. At twenty-seven he was called to the Apostleship by Brigham Young, and he served as a counselor in the First Presidency to Presidents Young, Taylor, Woodruff, and Snow before assuming the office of President of the Church in 1901. Intimate associations and personal searchings over several decades distilled and solidified principles and doctrines in the mind of Joseph F. Smith. By the time of his death, he had spoken and written upon a myriad of subjects and came to represent a leader grounded in the doctrines of the Restoration. One of the greatest compliments paid to President Smith was a simple statement by a successor, Harold B. Lee. Brother Lee, himself no novice in gospel understanding, said: "When I want to seek for a more clear definition of doctrinal subjects, I have usually turned to the writings and sermons of President Joseph F. Smith."[7]

Joseph F.'s attention was drawn to the world beyond mortality by his frequent confrontation with death. His parents, Hyrum and Mary Fielding Smith, both died while he was a young man. Among the great trials of his life, none was more devastating than the passing of many of his children into death. President Smith was possessed of an almost infinite capacity to love, and the sudden departure of dear ones brought extreme anguish and sorrow. Joseph Fielding has written, "When death invaded his home, as frequently it did, and his little ones were taken from him, he grieved with a broken heart and mourned, not as those mourn who live without hope, but for the loss of his 'precious jewels' dearer to him than life itself."[8]

On January 20, 1918, Hyrum Mack Smith, oldest son of Joseph F. and then a member of the Quorum of the Twelve Apostles, was taken to the hospital for a serious illness, where the physicians diagnosed a ruptured appendix. Despite constant medical attention and repeated prayers, Hyrum—then only forty-five years of age and at the time with a pregnant wife—died on the night of January 23. This was a particularly traumatic affliction for the President. Hyrum had been called as an Apostle at the same conference wherein his father had been sustained as the Church's sixth President (October 1901).

Hyrum was a man of depth and wisdom beyond his years, and his powerful sermons evidenced his unusual insight into gospel principles. Heber J. Grant explained at the funeral services: "In all my travels, week after week, no man of our quorum has ever fed me the bread of life, touched my heart, and caused me to rejoice more in the gospel of Jesus Christ . . . than did our dearly beloved brother whose remains lie before us today. His death comes as a great shock to each and every member of the Council to which he belonged."[9] In speaking of Hyrum's sermons and spirituality, his father remarked: "His mind was quick and bright and correct. His judgment was not excelled, and he saw and comprehended things in their true light and meaning. When he spoke, men listened and felt the weight of his thoughts and words." Finally, President Smith observed: "He has thrilled my soul by his power of speech, as no other man ever did. Perhaps this was because he was my son, and he was filled with the fire of the Holy Ghost."[10] Already in a weakened physical condition due to age, the prophet's sudden sense of loss caused him "one of the most severe blows that he was ever called upon to endure." He cried out in anguish: "My soul is rent asunder. My heart is broken, and flutters for life! O my sweet son, my joy, my hope! . . . And now what can I do! O what can I do! My soul is rent, my heart is broken! O God, help me!"[11] In regard to the passing of Hyrum, it is worth attending to the remarks of Elder James E. Talmage at the funeral service:

"He has gone. Elders are needed on the other side, and apostles of the Lord Jesus Christ are wanted there. . . . I read of the Lord Jesus Christ going, as soon as his spirit left his pierced and tortured body on the cross, to minister unto the spirits on the other side. . . . I *cannot think of Hyrum M. Smith as being otherwise employed.* I cannot conceive of him as being idle. I cannot think of him having no regard for those among whom he is called to associate.

"And where is he now? . . . He has gone to join the apostles who departed before him, to share with them in the work of declaring the glad message of redemption and salvation unto those who for lack of opportunity, or through neglect, failed to avail themselves of those wondrous and transcendent blessings upon the earth."[12]

AN EVENTFUL THIRTY MONTHS

Even though President Smith indicated in October 1918 that the preceding months had been a season of special enrichment, in fact it may be shown that the last thirty months of his life (specifically, from April 1916 to October 1918) represent a brief era of unusual spiritual enlightenment, in which the prophet delivered to the Church some of the most important and inspiring insights of this dispensation.

At the April 1916 general conference, President Smith delivered a remarkable address, the thrust of which established a theme for the next thirty months of his life and laid the foundation for his final doctrinal contribution—the vision of the redemption of the dead. In his opening sermon, entitled "In the Presence of the Divine," Joseph F. spoke of the nearness of the world of spirits and of the interest and concern for us and our labors exercised by those who have passed beyond the veil. He stressed that those who labored so diligently in their *mortal* estate to establish the cause of Zion would not be denied the privilege of "looking down upon the results of their own labors" from their *postmortal* estate. In fact, the president insisted, "they are as deeply interested in our welfare today, if not with greater capacity, with far more interest, behind the veil, than they were in the flesh." Perhaps the keynote statement in this sermon was the following: *"Sometimes the Lord expands our vision from this point of view and this side of the veil, so that we feel and seem to realize that we can look beyond the thin veil which separates us from that other sphere."*[13] This remark, both penetrating and prophetic, set the stage for the next two and one-half years.

In June of 1916 the First Presidency and the Twelve released a doctrinal exposition in pamphlet form entitled *The Father and the Son.* This document was delivered to alleviate doctrinal misunderstandings concerning the nature of the Godhead, specifically the role and scriptural designation of Jesus Christ as "Father."[14]

One of the most significant fruits of this segment of time was a talk delivered by President Smith at a temple fast meeting in February 1918 entitled "The Status of Children in the Resurrection." In this address we gain an insight into the power and prophetic stature of one schooled and prepared in doctrine; in addition, we are allowed a brief glimpse into the heart of a noble father who, having lost little ones to death and having mourned their absence, rejoices in the sure knowledge that (1) mortal children are immortal beings, spirits who continue to live and progress beyond the veil, and (2) as taught by the Prophet Joseph Smith, children will come forth from the grave as children and will be nurtured and reared to physical maturity by worthy parents. "O how I have been blessed with these children," exulted President Smith, "and how happy I shall be to meet them on the other side!"[15]

Further evidence that the veil had become thin for Joseph F. Smith is found in his recording (on April 7, 1918) of a dream or vision he had actually received many years earlier while on his first mission. The dream had served initially to strengthen the faith and build the confidence of a lonely and weary fifteen-year-old on the slopes of Haleakala on the isle of Maui; it had, through the years that followed, served to chart a course for Joseph F. and give to him the assurance that his labors were acceptable to the Lord, and that he also had the approbation of his predecessors in the presidency of the Church. In the dream young Joseph encountered his uncle, the Prophet, and was fortified in his desire to remain free from the taints of the world. In addition, he learned at an early age that the separation between mortality and immortality is subtle and that the Lord frequently permits an intermingling of the inhabitants of the two spheres. "That vision, that manifestation and witness that I enjoyed at that time," Joseph F. explained, "has made me what I am, if I am anything that is good, or clean, or upright before the Lord if there is anything good in me. That has helped me out in every trial and through every difficulty." Finally, "I know that that was a reality, to show me my duty, to teach me something, and to impress upon me something that I cannot forget."[16]

THE VISION: RECEPTION AND ANNOUNCEMENT

In 1862 President Brigham Young explained that despite the passing of years and the decay of the mortal body, one who opens himself to the realm of divine experience—though loosening his grip upon the here and now—may begin to tighten his grasp upon the things of eternity. "If we live our holy religion," stated President Young, "and let the Spirit reign," the mind of man "will not become dull and stupid, but as the body approaches dissolution *the spirit takes a firmer hold on the enduring substance behind the veil,* drawing from the depths of that eternal Fountain of Light sparkling gems of intelligence which surround the frail and sinking tabernacle with a halo of immortal wisdom."[17] This poignant principle was beautifully demonstrated in the life of President Joseph F. Smith. Here was a man who met death and sorrow and persecution head on, and thus through participating in the fellowship of Christ's suffering was made acquainted with the things of God. As a modern Apostle has explained: "In the agonies of life, we seem to listen better to the faint, godly whisperings of the Divine Shepherd."[18] Of President Smith it was said by Charles W. Nibley, Presiding Bishop of the Church: "He lived in close communion with the Spirit of the Lord, and his life was so exemplary and chaste that the Lord could easily manifest himself to his servant." Bishop Nibley concluded that "the heart of President Smith was attuned to the celestial melodies—he could hear and did hear."[19]

On Thursday, October 3, 1918, President Smith, largely confined to his room because of illness, sat meditating over matters of substance. No doubt because of the world situation, his own suffering, and the loss of loved ones, it has been suggested that "he had long pondered the problems connected with making family ties complete in the patriarchal lineages."[20] On this day, the prophet specifically began to read and ponder upon the universal nature of the Atonement and the Apostle Peter's allusions to Christ's postmortal ministry. The stage was set: preparation of a lifetime and preparation of the moment were recompensed with a heavenly endowment—the vision of the redemption of the dead. In the words of the President: "As I pondered over these things which are written, the eyes of my understanding were opened, and the Spirit of the Lord rested upon me, and I saw the hosts of the dead, both small and great" (D&C 138:11).

The vision was dictated to Joseph Fielding and recorded immediately after the close of the general conference.[21] It is interesting that Joseph Fielding delivered a discourse, "Salvation for the Living and the Dead," at the genealogical conference on the afternoon of Monday, October 7. In this sermon there is no mention of his father's visionary experience of only four days before, nor are any of the doctrinal particulars from the vision voiced in the talk. It would appear that Joseph Fielding knew well the principle of allowing the prophet the opportunity to deal properly with a matter of new revelation before the contents are put forward to the Church as a whole. In the Saturday afternoon (October 5) session of conference, President Joseph F. Smith had said simply, "When the Lord reveals something to me, I will consider the matter with my brethren, and when it becomes proper, I will let it be known to the people, and not otherwise."[22]

President Smith saw fit to "consider the matter" of the vision in the Thursday Council Meeting of October 31. Because of his weakened condition, the President was not in attendance, but asked his son, Joseph Fielding, to present the vision to the combined gathering of the counselors in the First Presidency, the Twelve Apostles, and the Patriarch to the Church. Note the following journal entry from Anthon H. Lund, first counselor to President Smith: "In our Council Joseph F. Smith Jr. read a revelation which his father had had in which he saw the spirits in Paradise and he also saw that Jesus organized a number of brethren to go and preach to the spirits in prison, but did not go himself. It was an interesting document and the apostles accepted it as true and from God."[23] Elder James Talmage of the Quorum of the Twelve recorded the following in his personal journal regarding this occasion: "Attended meeting of the First Presidency and the Twelve. Today President Smith who is still confined to his home by illness, sent to the Brethren the account of a vision through which, as he states, were revealed to him important facts relating to the work of the disembodied Savior in the realm of departed spirits, and of the missionary work in progress on the other side of the veil. By united action the Council of the Twelve, with the Counselors in the First Presidency, and the Presiding Patriarch accepted and endorsed the revelation as the Word of the Lord. President Smith's signed statement will be published in the next issue (December) of the *Improvement Era,* which is the organ of the Priesthood quorums of the church."[24]

The text of the vision first appeared in the November 30 edition of the *Deseret News,* eleven days after the passing of President Smith on November 19. It was printed in the December *Improvement Era,* and in January 1919 editions of the *Relief Society Magazine,* the *Utah Genealogical and Historical Magazine,* the *Young Women's Journal,* and the *Millennial Star.*

President Smith's physical condition worsened during the first weeks of November 1918. On Sunday, November 17, he was taken with an attack of pleurisy, which finally developed into pleuro-pneumonia. Tuesday morning, November 19, 1918, his work in mortality was completed. It was fitting that at the April 1919 general conference Elder Talmage should deliver the following touching and appropriate tribute to the president. Elder Talmage asked, "Well, where is he now?" and then answered, *"He was permitted shortly before his passing to have a glimpse into the hereafter, and to learn where he would soon be at work.* He was a preacher of righteousness on earth, he is a preacher of righteousness today. He was a missionary from his boyhood up, and *he is a missionary today amongst those who have not yet heard the gospel,* though they have passed from mortality into the spirit world. I cannot conceive of him as otherwise than busily engaged in the work of the Master."[25]

DOCTRINAL SIGNIFICANCE OF THE VISION

The vision of the redemption of the dead is central to the doctrine of the Latter-day Saints because it confirms and expands upon earlier prophetic insights concerning work for the dead; it also introduces doctrinal truths not had in the Church before October 1918.

While pondering upon the infinite Atonement of Christ and particularly upon Peter's testimony of the same in the third and fourth chapters of his first epistle, President Joseph F. Smith was enlightened by the Spirit and power of God. He saw within the veil and viewed the proceedings within the world of spirits (see D&C 138:1–11). He first saw "an innumerable company of the spirits of the just" (verse 12), that is to say, the righteous dead from the days of Adam to the meridian of time. They were anxiously awaiting the advent of the Christ into their dimension of life and were exuberant in their joy over an imminent resurrection (see verses 12–17). Having consummated the atoning sacrifice on Golgotha, the Lord of the living and the dead passed in the twinkling of an eye into the world of the departed. The dead, having "looked upon the long absence of their spirits from their bodies as a bondage" (verse 50; see also D&C 45:17), are in a sense in prison. Yes, even the righteous seek "deliverance" (verses 15, 18); the Master came to declare "liberty to the captives who had been faithful" (verse 18). As Peter had said, Christ went beyond the veil to preach "unto the spirits in prison" (1 Peter 3:19). Joseph Smith had taught that "Hades, Sheol, paradise, spirits in prison, are all one; *it is a world of spirits.*"[26] And as Elder Bruce R. McConkie has explained, in the vision "it is clearly set forth that the whole spirit world, and not only that portion designated as hell, is considered to be a spirit prison."[27]

To the congregation of the righteous the Lord appeared, and "their countenances shone, and the radiance from the presence of the Lord rested upon them" (verse 24). President Smith observed the Lord teaching "the everlasting gospel, the doctrine of the resurrection and the redemption of mankind from the fall, and from individual sins on conditions of repentance" (verse 19). In addition, Christ extended to the righteous spirits "power to come forth, after his resurrection from the dead, to enter into his Father's kingdom, there to be crowned with immortality and eternal life" (verse 51).

It is while pondering the question of how the Savior could have taught the gospel to so many in the spirit world in so short a time (approximately thirty-eight to forty hours) that President Smith received what may well be the most significant doctrinal insight of the entire vision. The president understood "that the Lord went not in person among the wicked and disobedient"—those in hell or outer darkness—but rather "organized his forces and appointed messengers, clothed with power and authority," that such representatives might carry the message of the gospel "unto whom he [the Lord] could not go personally, because of their rebellion and transgression" (verses 29–30, 37; see also verses 20–22, 25–29). Christ's mission to the world of spirits was thus seen to be largely organizational, as well as instructional. The chosen messengers declared "the acceptable day of the Lord" (verse 31). They carried the gospel message to those who had no opportunity in mortality to accept or reject the truth, and also to those who rejected the message on earth. These (who are visited by the messengers) are taught the first principles and ordinances of the gospel (including vicarious ordinances), in order that the inhabitants of the spirit world might be judged and rewarded by the same divine standards as those who inhabit the world of mortals (see verses 31–34).

In this vision the Lord saw fit to add "line upon line, precept upon precept" to the understanding of the Latter-day Saints relative to the work of redemption beyond the grave. The insight that Christ did not personally visit the disobedient is a doctrinal matter introduced to the Church for the first time in October 1918 and does much to broaden our scope and answer questions with regard to the work within that sphere. In the words of Elder Orson F. Whitney in the February 20, 1919, issue of the *Millennial Star:* "The new light here thrown upon the subject proceeds from the declaration that when the Savior visited the inhabitants of the Spirit World, it was by proxy and not in person so far as the wicked were concerned. He ministered to the righteous directly, and to the unrighteous indirectly, sending to them His servants bearing the authority of the Priesthood and duly commissioned to speak and act in His name and stead. President Smith's pronouncement is a modification of the view commonly taken, that the Savior's personal ministry was to both classes of spirits."[28] President Smith's pronouncement as a "modification of the view commonly taken" is evident if we simply note that in a major doctrinal standard, *Jesus the Christ* (which had been published three years earlier, in 1915), Elder Talmage had taken a traditional approach to the subject.[29] The revolutionary but inspiring nature of this particular contribution is also manifest in the fact that President Smith himself had taught on previous occasions of Christ's postmortal ministry to the wicked and unbelieving.[30] In this sense the doctrine was truly a "revelation" to the Prophet, as well as to the people.

By the power of the Holy Ghost, President Smith perceived the identity of many of the noble and great from the beginning of time, including Adam, Seth, Noah, Abraham, Isaiah, the Nephite prophets before Christ, and many more. In addition, the president recognized Mother Eve and many of her faithful daughters (see verses 38–49). Joseph F. had taught several years earlier that women minister to women in the spirit world, even as they do in holy places on earth.[31]

Suddenly the vision seems to shift in time—from a first-century

A.D. gathering to a gathering of workers in the spirit world during the final gospel dispensation. A change in time frame is common in visions, as can be seen from the experiences of Nephi (see 1 Nephi 13–14), John the Apostle (see Revelation 11–12), and Joseph Smith (see D&C 76). President Smith sees in the spirit world his predecessors in the presidency of the restored Church and other noble leaders who played such a critical role "in laying the foundations of the great latter-day work" (verse 53).

It may be that the vision shifts again in time, allowing President Smith a glimpse into the premortal world. He observes that the great leaders of the latter-day Church were "among the noble and great ones who were chosen in the beginning to be rulers in the Church of God," and becomes aware of their premortal lessons, preparation, and foreordination (verse 55).

President Joseph F. Smith's vision confirms another doctrine that had been taught by Joseph Smith—that the faithful in this life continue to teach and labor in the world of spirits in behalf of those who did not know God. As recorded in George Laub's journal under the date of May 12, 1844, the Prophet Joseph proclaimed: "Now all those die in the faith goe [sic] to the prison of Spirits to preach to the ded [sic] in body, but they are alive in the Spirit & those Spirits preach to the Spirits that they may live according to god in the Spirit and men do minister for them in the flesh."[32] Joseph F. had himself taught this doctrine on a number of occasions;[33] here he becomes an eyewitness of the same.

President Smith then reconfirms the law concerning the dead and the preaching of the gospel. Gaining salvation is by individual decision, and God will force exaltation upon no man. Those spirits that repent and accept the gospel and the vicarious ordinances "shall receive a reward according to their works, for they are heirs of salvation" (verse 59).[34]

Having laid before us his remarkable vision, "a complete and comprehensive confirmation of the established doctrine of the church where salvation for the dead is concerned,"[35] President Smith climaxes his doctrinal contribution with a testimony: "Thus was the vision of the redemption of the dead revealed to me, and I bear record, and I know that this record is true, through the blessing of our Lord and Savior, Jesus Christ, even so. Amen" (verse 60).

From Scripture to Canon

In 1919 the writings and sermons of President Joseph F. Smith were compiled and published under the title *Gospel Doctrine,* a work intended originally as a course of study for Melchizedek Priesthood quorums. The vision of the redemption of the dead was contained in chapter 24 of that volume, the chapter entitled "Eternal Life and Salvation." The vision was therefore readily available to those Saints who made the book *Gospel Doctrine* a part of their Church library or who turned to the book in their doctrinal studies. Reference was made to the vision after 1919, and excerpts were occasionally quoted by Church leaders in articles or conference addresses.[36]

In the Saturday afternoon session of conference on April 3, 1976, President N. Eldon Tanner made the following announcement:

"President Kimball has asked me to read a very important resolution for your sustaining vote.

"At a meeting of the Council of the First Presidency and the Quorum of the Twelve held in the Salt Lake Temple on March 25, 1976, approval was given to add to the Pearl of Great Price the two following revelations:

"First, a vision of the celestial kingdom given to Joseph Smith the Prophet in the Kirtland Temple, on January 21, 1836, which deals with the salvation of those who die without a knowledge of the Gospel; second, a vision given to President Joseph F. Smith in Salt Lake City, Utah, on October 3, 1918, showing the visit of the Lord Jesus Christ in the spirit world, and setting forth the doctrine of the redemption of the dead.

"It is proposed that we sustain and approve this action and adopt these revelations as part of the standard works of the Church of Jesus Christ of Latter-day Saints.

"All those in favor manifest it. Those opposed, if any, by the same sign.

"Thank you. President Kimball, the voting seems to be unanimous in the affirmative."[37]

The vision of the redemption of the dead thus became a part of the standard works, specifically an addition to the Pearl of Great Price.[38] The First Presidency and the Twelve had discussed including the revelations in the standard works on a number of occasions prior to March 1976. Elder McConkie, a member of the Twelve, divided the two visions into verses, as we now have them. In a letter to me regarding the canonization of President Joseph F. Smith's vision, Elder McConkie explained: "President Kimball and all the Brethren thought it should be formally and officially recognized as scripture so that it would be quoted, used, and relied upon more than the case would have been if it had simply been published as heretofore in various books. By putting it in the Standard Works formally, it gets cross referenced and is used to better advantage by the saints."[39] To take the lead in accomplishing what Elder McConkie has suggested above, President Kimball did a most unusual but impressive thing not long after the vision was added to the collection of holy writ. In a meeting with the General Authorities and regional representatives, he read the entire text of the vision of the redemption of the dead as a part of his own address.[40]

In June 1979 by administrative decision and "as a very direct outgrowth of the [new] scripture project,"[41] the two revelations approved in April 1976 were shifted to the Doctrine and Covenants, becoming sections 137 and 138, respectively.[42]

There can be no question but that the vision of the redemption of the dead was scripture before April 3, 1976; it was certainly spoken by the power of the Holy Ghost, and it represented the will, mind, word, and voice of the Lord (see D&C 68:4). The First Presidency, Quorum of the Twelve, and Patriarch in 1918 recognized and acknowledged it as "true and from God." Once it had been voted upon and accepted by the membership of the Church, however, it shifted in significance from *scripture* to *canonized scripture*. Prior to April 3, 1976, it represented a theological document of inestimable worth to the Saints, one that deserved the study of those interested in spiritual things; on that date it was circumscribed into the standard works, and thus its message—principles and doctrines—became binding[43] upon the Latter-day Saints, the same as the revelations of Moses or Jesus or Alma or Joseph Smith. The vision of the redemption of the dead became a part of the canon, the rule of faith and doctrine and practice, the written measure by which we discern truth from error. And at a time and in a day when the First Presidency has specifically defined three specific means for accomplishing the mission of the Church (to invite all to come unto Christ)—proclaiming the gospel, perfecting the Saints, and redeeming the dead[44]—it seems fitting that we focus greater attention upon a significant revelation that provides a spiritual justification for the Church's continued thrust in family history research and temple work. President Joseph F. Smith's vision has expanded our vision "from this point of view and this side of the veil," so that now, better than ever before, "we can look beyond the thin veil which separates us from that other sphere."[45]

NOTES

1. Boyd K. Packer, "Teach the Scriptures," address delivered to CES personnel, October 14, 1977, Salt Lake City, in *Charge to Religious Educators* (Salt Lake City: The Church of Jesus Christ of Latter-day Saints, 1981), 21.
2. In reporting the address, the *Improvement Era* recorded: "He was *visably* [sic] *affected* when he arose to make his opening speech which was listened to with profound silence." See "Editor's Table" in *Improvement Era,* November 1918, 80.
3. Joseph F. Smith, in Conference Report, October 1918, 2; emphasis added.
4. See Joseph Fielding Smith, *The Life of Joseph F. Smith* (Salt Lake City: Deseret Book, 1969), 466.
5. See Joseph Fielding Smith, *Essentials in Church History* (Salt Lake City: Deseret Book, 1967), 516–17.
6. See Conference Report, April 1917, 8–9.
7. Harold B. Lee, in Conference Report, October 1972, 18.
8. Joseph Fielding Smith, *Life of Joseph F. Smith,* 455.
9. "In Memoriam," *Improvement Era,* March 1918, 380.
10. Quoted in Joseph Fielding Smith, *Life of Joseph F. Smith,* 474.
11. Quoted in Joseph Fielding Smith, *Life of Joseph F. Smith,* 474.
12. "In Memoriam," *Improvement Era,* March 1918, 384; emphasis added.
13. Joseph F. Smith, in Conference Report, April 1916, 1–8; emphasis added.
14. See "The Father and Son," *Improvement Era,* March 1916, 934–72; James R. Clark, comp., *Messages of the First Presidency* (Salt Lake City: Bookcraft, 1971), 5:23–34.
15. Joseph F. Smith, "Status of Children in the Resurrection," *Improvement Era,* November 1919, 16–17; Clark, *Messages of the First Presidency,* 5:99–101; Smith, *Life of Joseph F. Smith,* 445–47.
16. Joseph F. Smith, "A Dream that Was a Reality," *Improvement Era,* May 1918, 567–74; Clark, *Messages of the First Presidency,* 5:90–98.

17. Brigham Young, *Journal of Discourses* (Liverpool: Latter-day Saint Book Depot, 1862), 9:288.

18. James E. Faust, in Conference Report, April 1979, 77.

19. Charles W. Nibley, "Reminiscences of President Joseph F. Smith," in *Improvement Era,* January 1919, 198.

20. "Family Life, An Eternal Unit-Joseph F. Smith," *Relief Society Magazine,* January 1941, 57.

21. Joseph Fielding Smith, in his father's biography, stated that Joseph F. saw to it that the vision was "written *immediately following the close of that conference*" (*Life of Joseph F. Smith,* 466). Joseph Fielding Smith Jr. and John J. Stewart, in their biography of Joseph Fielding, wrote: "This vision [Joseph F.] received on October 3, 1918, the day before General Conference convened. *Two weeks later* Joseph Fielding wrote the vision as his father dictated it to him" (*The Life of Joseph Fielding Smith* [Salt Lake City: Deseret Book, 1972], 201; emphasis added).

22. Joseph F. Smith, in Conference Report, October 1918, 57.

23. Anthon H. Lund Journal, Archives of The Church of Jesus Christ of Latter-day Saints, Salt Lake City, Utah; under date of October 31, 1918.

24. James E. Talmage Journal, Harold B. Lee Library, Brigham Young University, Provo, Utah; under date of October 31, 1918.

25. James E. Talmage, in Conference Report, June 1919, 60; emphasis added.

26. Joseph Smith, *History of the Church of Jesus Christ of Latter-day Saints,* comp. B. H. Roberts, 2nd ed., rev. (Salt Lake City: Deseret Book, 1957), 5:425; emphasis added.

27. Bruce R. McConkie, "A New Commandment: Save Thyself and Thy Kindred," *Ensign,* August 1976, 11.

28. Orson F. Whitney, *Latter-day Saints' Millennial Star,* February 20, 1919, 116.

29. See James E. Talmage, "The Living and the Dead," *Utah Genealogical and Historical Magazine,* July 1918, 126. The article contains the following statement: "While in the bodiless state our Lord ministered among the departed, both in Paradise and in the prison realm where dwelt in a state of durance the spirits of the disobedient." See also James E. Talmage, *Jesus the Christ* (Salt Lake City: Deseret Book, 1972), 672.

30. Joseph F. Smith quotes first from Peter's epistle and then remarks: "This may seem strange to some, that Jesus should go to preach the Gospel unto the wicked, rebellious antedeluvians, . . . nevertheless it is true." In the same sermon, he said: "Thus we see those wicked, unrepentant antedeluvians who even had the privilege of hearing

the Gospel in the flesh, as preached by Noah, . . . were actually visited in the 'prison house' by the Savior himself, and heard the Gospel from his own mouth after he was 'put to death in the flesh'" (*Journal of Discourses,* 18:92; October 6, 1875). See also Joseph F. Smith, "Redemption Beyond the Grave," *Improvement Era,* December 1901, 145–47.

31. See Joseph F. Smith, *Young Women's Journal,* 1911, 128–32; *Gospel Doctrine* (Salt Lake City: Deseret Book, 1971), 461.

32. Andrew F. Ehat and Lyndon W. Cook, comp., *The Words of Joseph Smith* (Provo, Utah: Religious Studies Center, Brigham Young University, 1980), 370. From the Samuel W. Richards Record: "The sectarians have no charity for me but I have for them. *I intend to send men to prison to preach to them*" (Ehat and Cook, *The Words of Joseph Smith,* 371; emphasis added).

33. See, for example, Joseph F. Smith, *Gospel Doctrine,* 134–35, 460–61.

34. Joseph Fielding Smith taught that Christ, in the meridian of time, bridged the gulf between paradise and hell or outer darkness (see Luke 16:26). "From that time forth this gulf is bridged so that the captives, after they have paid the full penalty of their misdeeds, satisfied justice, and have accepted the gospel of Christ, having the ordinances attended to in their behalf by their living relatives or friends, receive the passport that entitles them to cross the gulf" (*Doctrines of Salvation* [Salt Lake City: Bookcraft, 1954–56], 2:158).

35. McConkie, "A New Commandment," 11.

36. See, for example, Joseph L. Wirthlin, April 1945 conference; Marion G. Romney, April 1964 conference; Spencer W. Kimball, September 1966 conference; Boyd K. Packer, October 1975 conference; see also *Instructor,* March 1961, November 1963.

37. N. Eldon Tanner, in Conference Report, April 1976, 29.

38. The complete statement of President Boyd K. Packer at the beginning of this paper is as follows: "We live in a day of great events relating to the scriptures. It has been only a short time, something more than a year, since two revelations were added to the scriptures, to the standard works, both of these to the Pearl of Great Price. Some have asked, 'Why did they go in the Pearl of Great Price? Why not the Doctrine and Covenants?' They could have gone either place; they were put in the Pearl of Great Price" (from a tape recording of an address to CES personnel, October 14, 1977).

39. Bruce R. McConkie, letter to Robert L. Millet, October 5, 1983.

40. See Spencer W. Kimball, address in Regional Representatives Seminar, September 30, 1977.

41. Boyd K. Packer, in Conference Report, October 1982, 75–76. In a letter to the author of this paper, Elder McConkie stated: "As to

whether it [the vision of the redemption of the dead] should be in the Pearl of Great Price or the Doctrine and Covenants, that is simply an administrative decision. A number of our revelations have been published in both places over the years. It seems to me that it is properly placed in the Doctrine and Covenants" (McConkie, Millet, October 5, 1983).

42. See *Church News,* June 2, 1979, 3.

43. Note a statement to this effect by President George Q. Cannon at the time of the canonization of the Pearl of Great Price (Conference Report; October 1880; see also McConkie, "A New Commandment," 7).

44. See Spencer W. Kimball, in Conference Report, April 1981, 3.

45. Joseph F. Smith, in Conference Report, April 1916, 1–8.

CHAPTER TWENTY-THREE

OFFICIAL DECLARATION—2: REVELATION ON THE PRIESTHOOD

E. DALE LeBARON

As a young boy in Primary memorizing the ninth article of faith, I never imagined that I would live to see the Lord reveal anything as "great and important" as the revelation of June 1978, which extended priesthood and temple blessings to all worthy male members of the Church. Elder Bruce R. McConkie, who was present when this revelation was received, stated:

"It was a revelation . . . that would reverse the whole direction of the Church, procedurally and administratively; one that would affect the living and the dead; one that would affect the total relationship that we have with the world. . . . This affects what is going on in the spirit world. . . . This is a revelation of tremendous significance."[1]

As far as we know, this was the first time since Cain and Abel that all the blessings of the gospel of Jesus Christ were made available to all people of all races living upon this earth. And it was the first time that temple ordinances could be performed for all people back to the beginning of time.

On September 30, 1978, at the 148th Semiannual General Conference of The Church of Jesus Christ of Latter-day Saints, President N. Eldon Tanner, First Counselor in the First Presidency, read Official Declaration—2, which included the following:

"In early June of this year, the First Presidency announced that a

E. Dale LeBaron is an emeritus professor of Church history and doctrine at Brigham Young University.

revelation had been received by President Spencer W. Kimball extending priesthood and temple blessings to all worthy male members of the Church. . . . This revelation . . . came to him after extended meditation and prayer in the sacred rooms of the holy temple. . . .

"We have pleaded long and earnestly in behalf of these, our faithful brethren [from whom the priesthood has been withheld), spending many hours in the Upper Room of the Temple supplicating the Lord for divine guidance.

"He has heard our prayers, and by revelation has confirmed that the long-promised day has come when every faithful, worthy man in the Church may receive the holy priesthood, with power to exercise its divine authority, and enjoy with his loved ones every blessing that flows therefrom, including the blessings of the temple. . . .

"Recognizing Spencer W. Kimball as the prophet, seer, and revelator, and president of The Church of Jesus Christ of Latter-day Saints, it is proposed that we as a constituent assembly accept this revelation as the word and will of the Lord. . . .

"The vote to sustain the foregoing motion was unanimous in the affirmative."

Of the revelations now in the Doctrine and Covenants, this is the only one received within the past eighty-five years. Because this important revelation is so relevant to us today, it should receive our careful and prayerful study. It should have a deep, spiritual influence upon our souls and lives. The manner in which the revelation on the priesthood was revealed and accepted is powerful evidence of the Church's inspired leadership, the Lord's divine direction, and the members' discipleship.

BEFORE THE REVELATION ON THE PRIESTHOOD

Clearly, the gospel is intended for all people. In the preface to the Doctrine and Covenants, the Lord declared, "For verily the voice of the Lord is unto all men. . . . And the voice of warning shall be unto all people. . . . Wherefore the voice of the Lord is unto the ends of the earth" (D&C 1:2, 4, 11). Then, in the appendix to this book of scripture, the Lord stated: "And this gospel shall be preached unto every nation, and kindred, and tongue and people" (D&C 133:37). There are seventy-eight references in the Doctrine of Covenants pertaining to the Lord's dealings with every nation or with the nations of the earth.

Modern prophets have echoed that message. For example, Elder McConkie taught that before the Second Coming of the Savior, stakes will be organized in Red China, Russia, and other nations where the gospel was not then established.[2] President Spencer W. Kimball said in a great visionary message:

"'Go ye into all the world, and preach the gospel to every creature' (Mark 16:15.) . . .

" . . . Surely there is significance in these words! There was a universal need and there must be universal coverage. . . .

" . . . It seems to me that the Lord chose his words when he said 'every nation,' 'every land,' 'uttermost bounds of the earth,' 'every tongue,' 'every people,' 'every soul,' 'all the world,' 'many lands.'"[3]

The gospel has not always been sent to all people, however. From the beginning, the Lord has sent the gospel to people according to His priorities, and the priesthood has been given selectively. During the fourteen centuries from Moses to Christ, only the house of Israel had the gospel. Only the tribe of Levi was permitted to hold the Aaronic Priesthood, and a few others were chosen to hold the Melchizedek Priesthood. Elder McConkie observed, "Not only is the gospel to go, on a priority basis and harmonious to a divine timetable, to one nation after another, but the whole history of God's dealings with men on earth indicates that such has been the case in the past; it has been restricted and limited where many people are concerned."[4]

Early in this dispensation, the Lord revealed that those of the black race were not to receive the priesthood and temple blessings. In 1949 the First Presidency reaffirmed the Lord's position: "The attitude of the Church with reference to the Negroes remains as it has always stood. It is not a matter of the declaration of a policy but of direct commandment from the Lord, on which is founded the doctrine of the Church from the days of its organization, to the effect that Negroes may become members of the Church but that they are not entitled to the priesthood at the present time."[5]

That position has not always been understood or accepted, even by some in the Church. Because it did not receive specific scriptural status in the Doctrine and Covenants, some question its origin; however, not all revelations are made public. In 1977 President Kimball said, "We testify to the world that revelation continues and that the vaults and files of the Church contain these revelations which come month to month and day to day."[6]

Statements by the prophets in this dispensation suggest that there were some unanswered questions relating to blacks and the priesthood. Fifteen years before receiving the revelation, Elder Spencer W. Kimball expressed his views about this delicate and difficult matter: "The things of God cannot be understood by the spirit of men. . . . I have wished the Lord had given us a little more clarity in the matter. But for me, it is enough. The prophets for 133 years of the existence of the Church have maintained the position of the prophet of the Restoration that the Negro could not hold the priesthood nor have the temple ordinances which are preparatory for exaltation. . . . The doctrine or policy has not varied in my memory. . . . I know the Lord could change his policy. . . . If the time comes, that he will do, I am sure."[7]

Then Elder Kimball caustically rebuked members of the Church who were pressuring Church leaders to make a change regarding blacks and the priesthood: "These smart members who would force the issue, and there are many of them, cheapen the issue and certainly bring into contempt the sacred principle of revelation and divine authority."[8]

In 1973, when President Kimball became President of the Church and was asked about the position of the Church regarding the blacks and the priesthood, he answered: "I am not sure that there will be a change, although there could be. We are under the dictates of our Heavenly Father, and this is not my policy or the Church's policy. It is the policy of the Lord who has established it, and I know of no change, although we are subject to revelations of the Lord in case he should ever wish to make a change."[9]

A few months later President Kimball gave a powerful and visionary address. He spoke of "armies of missionaries" taking the gospel to areas of the world, even to lands where the Church had never been. But no mention was made of one continent—Africa. The revelation on the priesthood had to precede the gospel message being spread throughout Africa. David M. Kennedy, who served as a special representative of the First Presidency to help move the gospel to foreign nations, told of a large atlas that President Kimball kept in his office. When they studied it together, Brother Kennedy would place his hand over Africa, saying, "We can't go there unless they have the priesthood." Returning from the temple after receiving the revelation of June 1978, President Kimball stopped at David Kennedy's office and said, "You can take your hand off that map, David. We can now go to Africa!"[10]

In this dispensation some Church leaders believed the blacks would not receive the priesthood before the Millennium. Similarly, the prophets and Apostles at Jesus' time did not fully comprehend some of the basic principles of the gospel or the Lord's timetable. It wasn't until after glorious revelations were received that they completely understood the doctrines of the Atonement, of the Resurrection, or of taking the gospel to all nations. Elder McConkie said that because the gospel had been only for the house of Israel, the earliest Apostles were not able to envision that after the Resurrection the gospel should then go to all the world.[11] Even Peter had to receive a vision before he fully understood that the gospel was to be taken to the Gentiles at that time.

In this dispensation, some Church leaders spoke from limited understanding regarding when the priesthood would be given to the blacks. Elder McConkie said:

"There are statements in our literature by the early brethren that we have interpreted to mean that the Negroes would not receive the priesthood in mortality. I have said the same things. . . . We spoke with a limited understanding and without the light and knowledge that now has come into the world.

"We get our truth and our light line upon line and precept upon precept. We have now had added a new flood of intelligence and light on this particular subject, and it erases all the darkness and all the views and all the thoughts of the past. They don't matter any more."[12]

REVELATION BY THE POWER OF GOD

Typically, before a large worldly organization makes a significant change in direction, philosophy, or practice, the leaders carefully ensure that their constituency will continue to support them. That is true of political, business, and most religious organizations. They first participate in studies, surveys, conferences, pilot testing, debates,

Vatican councils, or bishops synods to determine whether change is advisable. When changes are made, they are usually implemented carefully and gradually.

For example, a Canadian newspaper reported on challenges facing the newly appointed moderator of the United Church of Canada (Canada's largest Protestant denomination): "The church was just concluding what could arguably be termed the most difficult four months in its 60-year history because of the outcry over a report which recommended the church sanction the ordination of homosexual clergy.

"Smith's first duty as moderator was to chair the fractious debate on what to do about the issue."[13]

Similarly, under the heading, "Episcopal Church report asks sanction of non-marital sex," an American newspaper reported: "The Episcopal Church should recognize and bless committed non-marital sexual relationships between homosexuals, young adults, the divorced and widowed, a report from the church's Newark diocese urges. . . .

"The report by the diocese's Task Force On Changing Patterns of Sexuality and Family Life aims to ignite a new debate on sexual ethics among leaders of the nation's 3 million Episcopalians in hopes they will amend church doctrine to embrace all believers."[14]

The Church of Jesus Christ of Latter-day Saints is subject to the Lord, not to popular opinion. The Church has used some research methods before implementing such programs as family home evening and the consolidated meeting schedule; however, when it comes to doctrines, principles, or ordinances of the gospel, change is a matter of revelation from the Lord to His prophet.

At the time of the revelation on the priesthood, my wife and I were presiding over the South Africa Johannesburg Mission, then the only mission on the continent of Africa. About six months before the revelation came, I received a copy of a letter from the First Presidency that was sent to all priesthood leaders. The letter restated the Lord's position with regard to the blacks' being denied the priesthood and temple blessings. I heard no more about this matter until the announcement of the revelation. The brethren did not survey the feelings of the Church membership or do studies to determine the effects that such a change might have. To observe the Church make such a sudden and major change of course so smoothly is a miracle of incredible proportions.

President N. Eldon Tanner observed that President Kimball had defended the position of the Church for some thirty years as a member of the Twelve, yet when the revelation came, he immediately reversed himself.[15] As an Apostle and then as the prophet, President Kimball traveled throughout the Church. His sensitive spirit reached out in love to all people, especially to those deprived of priesthood and temple blessings because of lineage. He noted: "This matter had been on my mind all these years. We have always considered it."[16] President Kimball described his sacred struggle: "Day after day I went alone and with great solemnity and seriousness in the upper rooms of the temple, and there I offered my soul and offered my efforts to go forward with the program. I wanted to do what he wanted. I talked about it to him and said, 'Lord, I want only what is right. We are not making any plans to be spectacularly moving. We want only the thing that thou dost want, and we want it when you want it and not until.'"[17]

Unknown to anyone except the First Presidency and the Twelve, President Kimball had asked each of them to carefully research the scriptures and statements of the earlier Brethren, to make an exhaustive study of all that had been recorded concerning this issue. For months before the revelation, the First Presidency and the Quorum of the Twelve discussed these sacred matters at length in their temple meetings. He also met privately with each of the Brethren to learn their feelings on the matter.[18]

On Thursday, June 1, 1978, the General Authorities held their regular monthly fast and testimony meeting. The members of the Seventy and the Presiding Bishopric were then excused, and President Kimball, his two counselors, and ten of the Apostles remained (Elder Mark E. Petersen was in South America, and Elder Delbert L. Stapley was in the hospital).

Before offering the prayer that brought the revelation, President Kimball asked each of the Brethren to express his feelings and views on this important issue. For more than two hours, they talked freely and openly. Elder David B. Haight, the newest member of the Twelve, observed:

"As each responded, we witnessed an outpouring of the Spirit which bonded our souls together in perfect unity—a glorious experience. In that bond of unity we felt our total dependence upon heavenly direction if we were to more effectively accomplish the Lord's charge to carry the message of hope and salvation to *all* the world.

"President Kimball then suggested that we have our prayer at the altar. Usually he asked one of us to lead in prayer; however, on this day he asked, 'Would you mind if I be voice at the altar today?' This was the Lord's prophet asking us. Such humility! Such meekness! So typical of this special servant of all.

" . . . The prophet of God pour[ed] out his heart, pleading eloquently for the Lord to make his mind and will known to his servant, Spencer W. Kimball. The prophet pleaded that he would be given the necessary direction which could expand the Church throughout the world by offering the fullness of the everlasting gospel to all men, based solely upon their personal worthiness without reference to race or color."[19]

In response to a prophet's humble prayer of faith, united with those of twelve other prophets, seers, and revelators, the Lord poured out His Spirit—and His answer—in a most powerful way. Elder McConkie testified:

"It was during this prayer that the revelation came. The Spirit of the Lord rested mightily upon us all; we felt something akin to what happened on the day of Pentecost and at the dedication of the Kirtland Temple. From the midst of eternity, the voice of God, conveyed by the power of the Spirit, spoke to his prophet. . . . And we all heard the same voice, received the same message, and became personal witnesses that the word received was the mind and will and voice of the Lord.

" . . . On this occasion, because of the importuning and the faith, and because the hour and the time had arrived, the Lord in his providences poured out the Holy Ghost upon the First Presidency and the Twelve in a miraculous and marvelous manner, beyond anything that any then present had ever experienced."[20]

In an attempt to stifle speculation, Elder McConkie also explained what did not happen:

"The Lord could have sent messengers from the other side to deliver it, but he did not. He gave the revelation by the power of the Holy Ghost. . . . And maybe some . . . would like to believe that the Lord himself was there, or that the Prophet Joseph Smith came to deliver the revelation. . . . Well, these things did not happen. The stories that go around to the contrary are not factual or realistic or true."[21]

President Gordon B. Hinckley described his impressions as follows: "There was a hallowed and sanctified atmosphere in the room. For me, it felt as if a conduit opened between the heavenly throne and the kneeling, pleading prophet of God who was joined by his Brethren. . . .

"It was a quiet and sublime occasion. . . .

" . . . There was a Pentecostal spirit, for the Holy Ghost was there. . . .

" . . . Not one of us who was present on that occasion was ever quite the same after that. Nor has the Church been quite the same. . . .

" . . . There was perfect unity among us in our experience and in our understanding."[22]

Elder Haight related the events immediately following the historic revelation: "President Kimball arose from the altar. (We surrounded it according to seniority, I being number twelve.). . . . He turned to his right, and I was the first member of the circle he encountered. He put his arms around me, and as I embraced him I felt the beating of his heart and the intense emotion that filled him. He then continued around the circle, embracing each of the Brethren. No one spoke. Overcome with emotion, we simply shook hands and quietly went to our dressing rooms."[23]

The manner in which this revelation came is unique in our Church history because of the power with which it came, the numbers who received it, and the powerful effects it would have upon so many. Both President Kimball and President Benson said that they had never "experienced anything of such spiritual magnitude and power" as this revelation.[24] The reason the Lord chose to reveal this to the First Presidency and the Twelve, rather than only to His prophet, is due to the tremendous import and eternal significance of what was revealed, according to Elder McConkie. Hence, "the Lord wanted independent witnesses who could bear record that the thing had happened."[25]

Some have questioned why this revelation came when it did. Some critics of the Church suggest that it came in response to pressures upon the Church. External pressures on Church leaders regarding the blacks and the priesthood immediately before the revelation were minor compared to the 1960s, when the issue of civil rights was a major issue. As to why the revelation came when it did, Elder McConkie stated that it "was a matter of faith and righteousness and seeking on one hand, and it was a matter of the divine timetable on the other hand."[26] President Kimball further stated: "There are members of the Church who had brought to President David O. McKay their reasons why it should be changed. Others had gone to Joseph Fielding Smith and Harold B. Lee and to all the former presidents and it had not been accepted because the time had not come for it."[27]

AFTER THE REVELATION ON THE PRIESTHOOD

Could there be any news revealed since the Restoration that has caused so many of His children to immediately respond with such exquisite gladness and gratitude as did this marvelous revelation? I will never forget the overwhelming feelings I experienced after hearing of the revelation. Although we did not have any black male members of the Church in southern Africa at that time—until 1978 the Church had little involvement with blacks—it was powerfully evident that the revelation had a great and immediate effect upon that continent and its people. After June 1978, blacks began contacting us about the Church, although they knew nothing about the revelation. I will cite two examples.

First, I received a letter, dated June 8, 1979, from a non-LDS black man in Zimbabwe. He asked if he could translate the Book of Mormon into the Shona and Ndebele languages, the two African dialects of Zimbabwe. He said he had been called of God to take the gospel message to his people. He ended his letter with: "I wish you [to] confirm this with the prophets."[28]

Second, about the same time, I received a packet of materials from the Church missionary department. It contained a letter from a group of Africans in an isolated part of South Africa who had founded their own church and called it "The Church of Jesus Christ of Latter-day Saints." Missionary work soon commenced among them.

I will also share three experiences that brought tears of gratitude to some faithful brethren in Africa. Soon after I arrived in South

Africa as a mission president in 1976, I met a black African by the name of Moses Mahlangu. As he shook my hand he said, "So you are the new mission president." I told him I was and asked if he had known any others. He named each mission president who had served during the previous twelve years. When I asked him how he knew them, he told me his conversion story.

While serving as a lay minister in a Protestant church, Moses found a copy of the Book of Mormon in their church library. He began to read it. He soon knew it was true. He searched until he found the Church and met with the mission president. The mission president was so impressed with Moses' knowledge and testimony of the gospel and his sincerity and honesty that he wrote to the First Presidency asking permission to baptize Moses. Because of the strict apartheid laws at that time, it was illegal for Moses to attend any religious meeting with a white congregation. That would prevent him from receiving the sacrament. The mission president advised Moses that he would have to wait for baptism. And so Moses waited—for fourteen years. During that time he came by the mission office every few months and got a supply of pamphlets and copies of the Book of Mormon, which he distributed as he preached among his people. He held meetings in his home regularly and taught his people about the Book of Mormon and the Restoration of the gospel. He was fluent in nine languages and a most articulate gospel teacher.

Soon after the revelation of 1978, I was privileged to conduct a baptismal interview for Moses. It was one of my most sacred and humbling experiences. To every question I asked, I received the same answer: "I have been keeping that commandment for fourteen years." For fourteen long years, this great soul had been faithfully living the gospel and sharing it with his family and friends.

Another experience involved Joseph W. B. Johnson of Cape Coast, Ghana. In 1964 he was given a copy of the Book of Mormon, which he prayerfully read. He received a witness of its truth and a vision directing him to preach the message of the Restoration to his people. Brother Johnson wrote often to Church headquarters requesting literature and missionaries to teach and baptize them. Church literature was sent, but he was told, "The time is not yet; you must wait." For fourteen years he devoted his time and energies to teaching the gospel, gathering believers, and organizing and strengthening twelve

Church congregations in Ghana. Brother Johnson was sustained by frequent spiritual experiences, but he and his people became discouraged when their pleadings and prayers to be sent missionaries were not answered. Then, on the night of June 9, 1978, because of despair and discouragement, he could not sleep. He felt impressed to listen to the BBC shortwave news broadcast, which he had not done for several years. After struggling with the old radio for more than an hour, he finally tuned in to the BBC at midnight. He related: "I heard the message of President Kimball's prophecy concerning the priesthood, that all worthy males in all of the world could receive the priesthood. I burst into tears of joy, because I knew the priesthood would come to Africa, and if we did the right things, we would all receive the priesthood."[29]

A third experience involved a faithful member of the Church in South Africa. He was a convert of twelve years and a counselor in a branch presidency. About six months before the revelation, this good brother shared a deep concern with me. His wife was not a member of the Church and was not supportive of his involvement in the Church. That put a strain on their marriage, but he tried his best to work things out. They had two sons, whom he had raised in the Church. One boy was nine years of age and the other almost twelve. Although it was not apparent, his wife came from a black lineage. His sons were not aware that they could not hold the priesthood. Deacons were needed in their branch and the boys were wondering why the oldest one had not already been ordained. Both were talking about serving missions. He did not know what to do or how to approach this matter. He was afraid his sons might either resent their mother or resent the Church.

I told him that he would need to speak to them and urged him to fast, pray, and study the scriptures in preparation. He said he would. Four months later he had not yet talked with his sons about the matter, but he assured me that he would soon.

As soon as I heard about the revelation on the priesthood, I thought of this good man and his sons. Not having his phone number, I called his branch president and asked him to go immediately to his counselor's home and inform him of the revelation. Upon hearing the news, this great soul collapsed into a chair, put his head in his hands, and began to sob uncontrollably. Over and over he said,

"Thank God! Thank God!" He had been fasting for two days in preparation for the difficult task. He was planning to speak to his sons within minutes. An enormous burden had been removed. I was grateful for the infinite wisdom and goodness of a loving Heavenly Father who considers the welfare of the Church but also the heavy burden of one faithful father.

I was inspired by the way members of the Church generally responded to this revelation. The key to accepting revelation faithfully is found in the following statement by President George Q. Cannon: "The Latter-day Saint who lives near to God, and has the Spirit of God constantly resting upon him or her, never has any doubts about any principle that God has revealed. When the gathering was taught they were prepared for it; when the payment of tithing was taught they were prepared for it; . . . when celestial marriage was taught they were prepared for it. . . . There was no doubt in their minds, because the same Spirit that taught them that this was the truth in the beginning, and that God had spoken from the heavens, taught them also that all these things were true. But when you have doubts respecting counsel given by the servants of God, then be assured, my brethren and sisters, there is room for repentance."[30]

After the announcement of the revelation of 1978, I inquired of priesthood leaders in Africa as to how the Saints were responding to the revelation, which would affect Africa more than any other part of the world. There was generally great surprise and joy throughout Southern Africa. I heard of only one negative response, and it came from a brother who often complained about home teaching or other things he was asked to do.

One of our most important challenges may be to see things as our Heavenly Father does. That is especially true when it comes to His revelations and His children. When a revelation of such magnitude comes, surely the Lord requires us to respond so that His purposes can be fulfilled, especially by showing pure love for His children.

Elder McConkie warned us: "We talk about the scriptures being unfolded—read again the parable of the laborers in the vineyard (Matthew 20) and remind yourselves that those who labor through the heat of the day for twelve hours are going to be rewarded the same as those who came in at the third and sixth and the eleventh hours. Well, it's the eleventh hour; it's the Saturday night of time. In this eleventh hour the Lord has given the blessings of the gospel to the last group of laborers in the vineyard. . . . All are alike unto God, black and white, bond and free, male and female."[31]

For many of us, first hearing the news of this revelation is a memory frozen in time, because of the deep feelings of joy and gratitude which it brought. President Gordon B. Hinckley observed: "I need not tell you of the electric effect that was felt both within the Church and without. There was much weeping, with tears of gratitude not only on the part of those who previously had been denied the priesthood and who became the immediate beneficiaries of this announcement, but also by men and women of the Church across the world who had felt as we had felt concerning this matter."[32]

Because of the tremendous significance of this revelation, it would be well for us to record our feelings and experiences for our posterity. Future generations may search our journals for our impressions of this marvelous revelation that occurred in our lifetime. It is important that we leave for our posterity a legacy of faith through our testimony of the Lord's prophets in our day.

It is my witness that the revelation on the priesthood came directly from God to His prophets and that this is one of the most significant revelations of this dispensation. I also testify that with this marvelous revelation came the responsibility to see and feel as the Lord does. It is required of each of us to have pure love towards all of our Father's children regardless of their country, culture, or color— for "all are alike unto God" (2 Nephi 26:33).

NOTES

1. Bruce R. McConkie, "The New Revelation on Priesthood," in *Priesthood* (Salt Lake City: Deseret Book, 1981), 134–35.
2. McConkie, "New Revelation on Priesthood," 131.
3. Spencer W. Kimball, "When the World Will Be Converted," *Ensign,* October 1974, 4–5.
4. McConkie, "New Revelation on Priesthood," 130.
5. See statement of the First Presidency of The Church of Jesus Christ of Latter-day Saints, August 17, 1949, Archives, The Church of Jesus Christ of Latter-day Saints, Salt Lake City.
6. Spencer W. Kimball, "Revelation: The Word of the Lord to His Prophets," *Ensign,* May 1977, 78.

7. Spencer W. Kimball, *The Teachings of Spencer W. Kimball,* ed. Edward L. Kimball (Salt Lake City: Bookcraft, 1982), 448–49.

8. Kimball, *Teachings,* 448–49.

9. Kimball, *Teachings,* 448–49.

10. See Martin Berkeley Hickman, *David Matthew Kennedy: Banker, Statesman, Churchman* (Salt Lake City: Deseret Book and David M. Kennedy Center for International Studies, 1987), 343–44. See also address by David M. Kennedy to Religious Education faculty, Brigham Young University, Provo, Utah, October 2, 1992.

11. McConkie, "New Revelation on Priesthood," 130.

12. McConkie, "New Revelation on Priesthood," 131–32.

13. In *Calgary Herald,* January 12, 1985.

14. In *Daily Herald,* Provo, Utah, January 30, 1987.

15. Loren C. Dunn, monthly letter to mission presidents and regional representatives in the Northern Plains Area; copy in possession of author.

16. In *Church News,* January 6, 1979, 15.

17. Kimball, *Teachings,* 451.

18. McConkie, "New Revelation on Priesthood," 127; Lucile C. Tate, *David B. Haight: The Life Story of a Disciple* (Salt Lake City: Bookcraft, 1987), 279.

19. Tate, *David B. Haight,* 279–80.

20. McConkie, "New Revelation on Priesthood," 128, 133–34.

21. McConkie, "New Revelation on Priesthood," 135.

22. Gordon B. Hinckley, "Priesthood Restoration," *Ensign,* October 1988, 70.

23. Tate, *David B. Haight,* 280.

24. McConkie, "New Revelation on Priesthood," 128.

25. McConkie, "New Revelation on Priesthood," 134.

26. McConkie, "New Revelation on Priesthood," 132–33.

27. In *Church News,* January 6, 1979, 15.

28. Pete Solomon letter, June 8, 1979, sent to the Church; copy in possession of author.

29. E. Dale LeBaron, ed., *"All Are Alike unto God"* (Salt Lake City: Bookcraft, 1990), 21.

30. George Q. Cannon, in *Journal of Discourses* (London: Latter day Saints' Book Depot, 1854–86), 13:375.

31. McConkie, "New Revelation on Priesthood," 137; see also 2 Nephi 26:33.

32. Hinckley, "Priesthood Restoration," 70.

Scripture Index

PEARL OF GREAT PRICE

INDEX

testimony of, Bruce R. McConkie
on, 116; translations of, into
African languages, 341
Booth, Ezra, 179–80
Boynton, John, 287
Brother of Jared, vision of, 189–90
Bunyan, John, 27–28
Burning, literal, at Second Coming,
209

Calling and election, 227–28,
231–32; Bruce R. McConkie on,
227; Marion G. Romney on, 227,
232; Joseph Smith on, 227–28
Callings, magnifying, 222–23
Cannon, George Q.: on marriage
and family, 310–11; on
preparedness of Saints for
revelation, 344
Carthage Conspiracy, spiritual
warning of error in, 18–19
Celestial kingdom: vision of, 99,
326; qualifications for, 196–97
Celestial marriage, 81–82
Certificate of incorporation, for The
Church of Jesus Christ of Latter-
day Saints, 51, 107
Children, as stewardship, 303
Children of God, 133
Cholera, 262; George A. Smith on,
258; Joseph Bates Noble on, 258;
in Zion's Camp, 258–59; Joseph
Smith on, 265–66
Christensen, Richard, 51
Chronological approach, to
understanding the Doctrine and
Covenants and the Joseph Smith
Translation of the Bible, 144–45
Church of Jesus Christ of Latter-day
Saints, The: David Whitmer on
organization of, 48–49, 54; New
York statutes for organization of,
49, 50; certificate of
incorporation for, 51, 107;
Manchester, New York,
mistakenly identified as place of
organization of, 51–54;

establishment of administrative
structure of, 60–61; westward
movement of, 63–64;
government of, 135–36
Clark, J. Reuben, on common
consent, 134, 139
Comfort, as purpose of revelation,
12
Commandment, first, 30, 31–32
Common consent: understanding
and meaning of, 134–35,
140–41; historical perspective
on, 136–38; Orson F. Whitney
on, 137; practice and procedure
of, 138–40
Confessions of faith, articles and
covenants as, 114
Confirmation: as purpose of
revelation, 15–17; spiritual, 43
Consecration, law of:
misunderstanding of, 155;
revealed, 155–58;
implementation of, 158–61,
173–74
Conversion, Harold B. Lee on, 197
Corrill, John, 171
Counselor, who worried over
talking with sons about
priesthood, 343–44
Covenant, new and everlasting,
80–81
Cowdery, Oliver, 289; writings of,
on articles and covenants,
104–5; writes articles and
covenants, 105–6; contests
addition to articles and
covenants, 115–16; and Literary
Firm, 162

Daily, Bill, 103
Daily, Brenda, 103
Daily, William D., 103
Daniel, on restoration, 69–70
Dante, 27
Dead, redemption for, 97–98
Degrees of glory: vision of, 152;

"record of John" in section 93, 74

Joseph Smith, prophetic position of, 38–39

Joseph Smith Translation of the Bible: contributions of, 62–63; importance of, 142–43; relationship of, to Doctrine and Covenants, 142–43, 145, 153–54; as forerunner, 152–53

Journey motif, 27–28

Justice, and mercy, 185–86

Kennedy, David M., and map of Africa, 335–36

Kimball, Heber C., 255, 281; on Zion's Camp, 259

Kimball, Spencer W.: on revelation on priesthood, 3, 4–5; on idolatry, 31; presides over sesquicentennial celebration, 52; on forgiveness, 187; on universal preaching of the gospel, 334–36; and map of Africa, 335–36; prays about revelation on priesthood, 339

Kimball, Vilate, 286

Kingdom of God, 70, 84–86

Kingdoms, order of, in section 76, 194

Kingdoms of glory: comparison of, 199–200; progression in, 200

Kirtland, Ohio, problems of Thomas B. Marsh in, 280–88

Knowledge, revelation of, during Millennium, 44

Lake, Dennis, 253

Land, eternal inheritance of, 79

Lee, Harold B., 235; on revelation, 11; emphasizes section 20 during administration, 107, 115; on democracy and theocracy, 135–36; on conversion, 197; on questionable publications, 216–17; on priesthood work in the home, 222; on Church of the Firstborn, 226

Licenses, 106–7, 115

Life, sanctity of, taught in Zion's Camp, 262–65

Light: as aspect of glory, 236–38; and process of salvation, 238–39; and truth, relationship of, 239–41; and truth, reception of, 241–42; and truth, Jesus Christ as source of, 242–43

Light of Christ, Bruce R. McConkie on, 230

Literary Firm, organization of, 161–62

Lucifer: fall of, 193–94; influence of understanding, on marriage and family, 301–3

Lund, Anthon H., on vision of the redemption of the dead, 321

Mahlangu, Moses, conversion and faithfulness of, 341–42

Malachi, Moroni quotes, to Joseph Smith, 92

Manchester, New York, mistakenly identified as place of Church's organization, 51–54

Marriage: celestial, 81–82; eternal, influence of understanding, on marriage and family, 299–300

Marriage and family: importance of understanding eternal nature of, 296–97; practical implications of, 305–9

Marriage relationship, of Emma Smith, 121–22

Marsh, Thomas B.: repentance of, 276, 293; warnings to, 276–77; problems of, in Kirtland, 280–88; letter of, to Parley P. Pratt, 281–82; problems of, in Missouri, 288–91

Matthews, Robert J., and Explanatory Introduction, 57

Maxwell, Neal A., on purpose of Zion's Camp, 270

Visions: of earth's inhabitants, 194;
order of, in section 76, 194

Walker, Lucy, 126
War, prophecy on, 7
Watters, Virginia, 104
Watters, Wayne E., 103, 104
Wentworth letter, as scripture,
39–40
Whitmer, David, 289; on
organization of Church, 48–49,
54
Whitmer, John: on confusion over
law of consecration, 156; and
Literary Firm, 162
Whitmer, Peter, Jr., 164
Whitmer, Peter, Sr., Church
organized in home of, 48, 50
Whitney, Elizabeth Ann, 124, 126
Whitney, Newel K., 164, 166, 182,
235
Whitney, Orson F.: on common
consent, 137; on vision of the
redemption of the dead, 324
Widtsoe, John A., on D&C 1 as
preface, 23–24
Wife, who supported husband in
Zion's Camp, 254
Wilcox, Elbur, 259
Williams, Frederick G., 165, 181,
235–36
Witnesses, to Book of Mormon,
109–10
Women: sacred experiences of,
118–19, 130–31; patriarchal
blessings of, 124
Woodruff, Wilford: on Doctrine and
Covenants, 6; on protection of
Zion's Camp, 256; on purpose of
Zion's Camp, 272

Word: definition of, 35; location of,
39–42; and Doctrine and
Covenants, 42–43; truth of,
known by revelation, 43;
reaffirmation of, 44–46
Words of eternal life, diligence in
following, 230–31
World, wickedness of, 30–32
Worlds, other, 192–93

Young, Brigham: on scriptures, 6;
on debts of Joseph Smith, 169;
on surplus property, 170–71; on
"snubbing" of Apostles, 280;
leads Quorum of Twelve in
Nauvoo, 291–93; on our
relationship with Heavenly
Father, 298; on spirituality in old
age, 319–20

Zion: scriptures on, 147–49;
revelations concerning, 147–50;
redemption of, postponed,
167–69
Zion's Camp: historical background
of, 248–52; contributions of,
252–59; B. H. Roberts on, 253;
wife who supported husband in,
254; Joseph Smith instructs,
254–55; protection of, 256–57;
cholera in, 258–59; Heber C.
Kimball on, 259; Joseph Smith
prophesies scourge on, 259;
missionary labors of, 259–62;
sanctity of life taught in, 262–65;
successes of, 269–72; purpose of,
Neal A. Maxwell on, 270;
purpose of, Brigham Young on,
271; purpose of, Wilford
Woodruff on, 272